MW01088451

GATHERING CROWDS

GATHERING CROWDS

Catching Baseball Fever in the New Era of Free Agency

Paul Hensler

ROWMAN & LITTLEFIELD
Lanham • Boulder • New York • London

Published by Rowman & Littlefield
An imprint of The Rowman & Littlefield Publishing Group, Inc.
4501 Forbes Boulevard, Suite 200, Lanham, Maryland 20706
www.rowman.com

6 Tinworth Street, London SE11 5AL, United Kingdom

British Library Cataloguing in Publication Information Available

Library of Congress Cataloging-in-Publication Data

Names: Hensler, Paul, 1956– author.
Title: Gathering crowds : catching baseball fever in the new era of free agency / Paul Hensler.
Description: Lanham, Maryland : Rowman & Littlefield, 2021. | Includes bibliographical references and index. | Summary: "This book captures the state of baseball after the demise of the reserve clause gave birth to free agency and fueled the national pastime's surge in popularity. It examines how baseball grew and evolved in the 1980s and the controversies that followed, including drug scandals, gambling, and issues involving race, women, and sexual orientation."—Provided by publisher.
Identifiers: LCCN 2020042186 (print) | LCCN 2020042187 (ebook) | ISBN 9781538132005 (cloth) | ISBN 9781538132012 (epub)
Subjects: LCSH: Baseball—Economic aspects—United States. | Baseball players—Salaries, etc.—United States. | Free agents (Sports)—United States.
Classification: LCC GV880 .H46 2021 (print) | LCC GV880 (ebook) | DDC 331.2/817963570973—dc23
LC record available at https://lccn.loc.gov/2020042186
LC ebook record available at https://lccn.loc.gov/2020042187

™ The paper used in this publication meets the minimum requirements of American National Standard for Information Sciences Permanence of Paper for Printed Library Materials, ANSI/NISO Z39.48-1992.

For Cassidy, Claudette, Jim, Freddy, John, Matt, and Tim, and for all those who have helped and continue to help baseball historians, researchers, and writers.

CONTENTS

PREFACE

"Spring Training Arrives in This Issue!" blared the banner on the cover of the March 5, 1977, *Sporting News*, and cleverly framed in photographer Frank Worth's picture immediately below the publication's bold header were three prizes that California Angels owner Gene Autry had landed in the inaugural free-agent sweepstakes. Thirsting for a chance to field a lineup chock-full of high-caliber talent, Autry placed himself in the vanguard of club moguls who would become accused of playing "checkbook baseball," a practice that involved the expenditure of funds for free agents rather than patiently waiting for players to arrive from the organization's farm system.

The trio of Autry's new charges—all smiling for the camera and cheekily posed reaching into saddlebags emblematic of the place where the Angels magnate kept his money—were outfielders Joe Rudi and Don Baylor, and infielder Bobby Grich, the first in what would be a lengthy series of such personnel signings by the Singing Cowboy in the ensuing years. The résumés of Rudi and Grich included multiple All-Star selections and the Gold Gloves they won, and while Baylor came less credentialed, his physique spoke to the base-stealing speed and power-hitting potential that made him a threat on the bases and at the plate. The insertion of these three players into the Angels lineup was an instant fix forecasted to propel California to the top of the American League West.

Not wanting to be left by the wayside, other teams sought to bolster their chances for a run at a divisional pennant—or better—by the quick addition of prime free agents. The San Diego Padres took on relief ace

Rollie Fingers and catcher Gene Tenace, both of whom, like Rudi and Baylor, were alumni of the Oakland Athletics. In Arlington, Texas, the Rangers spent for another former Athletic, shortstop Bert Campaneris, and Campy's past teammate, Sal Bando, cast his lot with the Milwaukee Brewers. Pitcher Wayne Garland departed Baltimore for Cleveland, and reliever Bill Campbell left the Twin Cities for Fenway Park, but the plum that would prove to pay the biggest dividend was outfielder Reggie Jackson, the Yankees acquisition who, like Garland, was also late of Baltimore.

Jackson's brief, stormy tenure under manager Earl Weaver was reminiscent of the years he had spent in Oakland battling Athletics owner Charlie Finley, and it also served as a precursor to the wrangling in which he would partake with his new field manager in the Bronx, Billy Martin. Jackson was joined in New York by former Reds hurler Don Gullett, and the pair graced the cover of *Sporting News* on the eve of Opening Day 1977. In total, 24 free agents found new homes or, as was the case of Willie McCovey, returned to his major-league roots in San Francisco.

The windfall enjoyed by this select group of ballplayers was the result of what is commonly referred to as the Messersmith decision, which was the outcome of the legal battle waged by Marvin Miller on behalf of the Major League Baseball Players Association to strip the game of its longstanding reserve clause. When arbitrator Peter Seitz handed down his verdict in December 1975, he decreed that the careful wording of the clause that had been a fixture of the uniform player's contract covered only a single renewal of said contract, not a series of repetitive and inferred renewals by the player's club, which in essence forever bound that player to his team until it decided his services were no longer wanted.

Players with six years of major-league service who chose to play one final year with their team thus fulfilled their obligatory "option year" and became eligible for free agency. The fallout of the Messersmith case was carefully shepherded by Miller: If *all* players had been deemed eligible for free agency, then the flooding of the market with so much labor would have lessened the value of the available players. By using a threshold of six years of major-league service as the standard for admitting a player to the free-agent market, Miller kept the labor supply in check while allowing the demand portion of the economic equation to work as he envisioned, escalating the salaries offered to the free agents, especially the most attractive ones. Although money was not necessarily the final word in a player's negotiations with a prospective new club, it was certainly a major factor in determining that player's ultimate choice of employer. In Jackson's case, he desired the bright lights of New York and to have a better chance to get back into the World Series than to go to a team like San Diego, which was in a rebuilding process.

As the two dozen freshly minted free agents donned the uniforms of their new clubs, they faced a pressure heretofore not experienced by players, namely, living up to the terms of their new and luxuriant contracts. Generations of their predecessors relied on the generosity of the teams that employed them to furnish a financial incentive deemed to be fair to both player and team owner, although in reality the owner always held the upper hand in contract negotiations. With the tables now turned and players able to make demands of any prospective new team, players had the option of finding the deal most favorable to them.

However, with free agents now being paid amounts far in excess of those that they would have been making according to the old reserve system, there was the creation of an implied expectation that the player would perform at least as well as—if not better than—he did prior to gaining free agency. Big monetary rewards broadly assumed a commensurate amount of offensive production for position players and quality innings and/or appearances for pitchers, although as history would show, this was not always the case.

Major League Baseball in 1977 reached a turning point that was dramatic in its own way, as it was in 1969, when expansion forced the creation of divisions in each league and rule changes were instituted to boost offensive production. As true free agency began to wield its influence on the business climate affecting the national pastime, 1977 was the "year of the economic revolution," yet it was punctuated by other events inherent in baseball's progress and movement into a more modern era.[1]

***

As the creation of this book transitioned from ideas wandering in my head, to an outline, and, finally, to a manuscript, one of the early decisions to be made related to the time frame of the work. The beginning point, as described earlier, sets the opening boundary, while the ending point is almost as definitive. The year 1989 has its own convenient constraints: By the calendar, it clearly delineates the end of the 1980s, but it also marks the end of the short tenure of commissioner A. Bartlett Giamatti. As imperfect as these limits may be, they nevertheless furnished valuable guidelines to follow, and within these years there is certainly a trove of baseball history worth exploring.

That said, there are occasions where stepping back farther or looking ahead a bit more were needed to round out the narrative of a particular topic. For example, the chapter on ballparks looks at the Metrodome and SkyDome, both of which opened in the 1980s, but it was reasonable to devote attention to Oriole Park at Camden Yards, which opened in 1992. Its inclusion is somewhat by necessity: The design of this facility began late in the 1980s, making it a topic of interest, and its construction was a watershed event because of the huge impact it had on the design of so many ballparks built thereafter. If Marvin Miller could be elected to the Hall of Fame in his role as the king of baseball's economic revolution, then the same honor is due for Janet Marie Smith, the queen of baseball's architectural revolution who fronted the effort to construct Camden Yards. She would later take her discerning eye to other cities and apply a deft hand in construction and remodeling endeavors.

This book's narrative covers a wide swath of territory, beginning with labor and economic issues, then reviewing the terms of the commissioners of the age. Next, as the problem of drugs seeped into the game, it presented a challenge to the integrity of the national pastime, this coming before steroid use became fully understood in the 1990s. There was a reduced number of newer ballparks coming on line, and this was shown to be the sunsetting of the multipurpose stadiums whose scourge was not fully understood at the time their blueprints were first drawn up a generation earlier. While changes in the ownership of major-league clubs were inevitable, there were more rumors about expansion than concrete action taken. When true free agency took hold, the frequent postseason appearances of the Yankees in the late 1970s and early 1980s seemed to validate the initial fear that spending vast amounts of money on free agents was upsetting baseball's competitive balance. But the work of several respected general managers assuaged the trepidation felt in some small-market cities when their less well-monied franchises were built into winning clubs. Much space is granted to these topics as they underpin the business side of the national pastime.

Certainly related to economics but with a focus on appealing directly to fans, marketing the game to the general public soared in the 1980s, and it is a topic worthy of much attention. In my previous work, *The New*

Boys of Summer: Baseball's Radical Transformation in the Late Sixties, the chapter on the game vis-à-vis American society turned out to be the book's longest—and for good reason. This new volume provides an updated version of those important general themes: Racial issues, the role of women in the game, changing attitudes among players, sexuality, and handicapped awareness feature prominently, as the country's cultural landscape continued to evolve.

The period from 1977 to 1989 was a formative time for this author as well. Reading much about baseball's history deepened my appreciation of the national pastime throughout the years, but more recently I have been able to look back at events of 30 to 40 years ago with a fresh perspective. In this regard, *all* fans have the opportunity to reflect on how the game has adapted to the times and endured despite one calamity or another. My hope is that the narrative in these pages will provide context to a time frame in which baseball grew, matured, and prospered.

ACKNOWLEDGMENTS

This book grew from a simple idea I had mere days after Christmas 2018, and when I proposed it to my editor at Rowman & Littlefield, Christen Karniski, her enthusiastic reception was most encouraging. My notion seemed to move at lightning speed from proposal to annotated table of contents to Christen's presentation to her editorial board, and within just a few weeks, we had a deal for the book you are now reading. The pace of research and writing was, for me, a controlled frenzy, or to put it in more positive wording, a time during which much was accomplished without the project going off the rails. The date for submission of the manuscript package was on a somewhat tight deadline, but given the hours I was devoting to the effort, there was a good chance that I would be able to come in just under the wire.

Fast-forward to early March 2020, at which time six chapters were fully complete, with two others whose drafts were about 98 percent finished and pending review comments from trusted friends. Just as the coronavirus pandemic was declared by the World Health Organization, I was trying to gather more material to finish the last two chapters, an obviously parlous time when so much of what we consider normal life began grinding to a halt. Thanks to some crucial assistance by the staff at the A. Bartlett Giamatti Research Center at the National Baseball Hall of Fame and Museum in Cooperstown, New York, provision of said material came through at a time when I thought such acquisition would be delayed for weeks, if not months. I appreciated requests for the status on my progress from Rowman & Littlefield's Julie Kirsch and Erinn Slanina, who assisted Christen by trying to keep the lines of communication open during the pandemic shutdown. Thanks also to Lara Hahn for handling the final production phase of the book.

During the journey of creating this book, I have been fortunate to draw on the expertise of people who are far more knowledgeable about various aspects of baseball than I could ever hope to be. Their academic and real-life experience served as invaluable input to helping my narrative, and for this I thank Bill Nowlin of the Society for American Baseball Research (SABR) and former major-league pitcher Mike Trombley.

In the course of more than 12 years of baseball writing, I have been privileged to meet some wonderful people who have inspired my work and contributed directly to this volume due to their willingness to critique chapters and passages of the narrative related to their respective areas of interest and knowledge. Ed Edmonds, Dave Bohmer, and Patricia Bryan have become friends through our attendance at the Cooperstown Symposium on Baseball and American Culture, as well as Curt Smith from the NINE Spring Training Conference. By an astounding coincidence, and just at the time I was writing about baseball's drug problems, I was connected with Dr. Allan Lans, former New York Mets team psychiatrist who is a close friend of Marc and Sherrie Kingsley, the owners of the Inn at Cooperstown and whose comfortable accommodations I enjoy when visiting the Hall of Fame.

Although he has retired from his position as senior vice president of the Baseball Hall of Fame, former Detroit Tigers executive Bill Haase is a gentleman whom I always seemed to be running into while in Cooperstown. Also among the SABR crowd are Andy McCue, an award-winning author who has been kind in his praise for my work, and Bob Wirz, a fellow member of the Connecticut SABR chapter who spent many years serving as the public relations director for both Bowie Kuhn and Peter Ueberroth. Leslie Heaphy directed me to Larry Lester for an obscure detail I sought, and I appreciate his being able to fill in the blank for me. I also thank Leslie for reviewing one of this book's largest chapters, and Mitch Nathanson, who offered suggestions to smooth out some bumps as the narrative crossed the finish line.

As has been the case in writing my earlier baseball books, my research appointments at the Giamatti Center have always been handled professionally and with courtesy. Librarian Jim Gates and his staff are the keepers of the resource flame that underpins so much of the material that ultimately found its way into the pages of the book you are now reading. Aid rendered by library assistant Emily Wilson was much appreciated and also that of manuscript archivist Claudette Scrafford, who has cheerfully reviewed vast swaths of this book to ensure that information drawn from the Hall of Fame's special collections has been properly handled and accounted for. And last but certainly not least, the diligence and efficiency exercised by research manager Cassidy Lent will make any writer feel welcome. Whether booking my appointments or tending to the last-minute additions to my resource request list, she is unfailingly patient and pleasant, thereby making my work there all the more enjoyable. As the pandemic of 2020 took a firm grip throughout the world, Cassidy did everything possible to deliver requested material at a time when society was shutting down and making impossible those accustomed trips to Cooperstown. Also hampered by the pandemic but still coming through with pictures for this book was John Horne, the photograph archivist at the Hall of Fame.

No small amount of morale-boosting helps any author, and this book project has been bolstered by other friends I've made along the way, notably Symposium confrères Jean and Dan Ardell, Charles DeMotte, Frank Houdek, Lee Lowenfish, Willie Steele, Tim Wiles, and Tom Wolf. When in Cooperstown, sustenance in the form of delicious food and liquid refreshment can be found at the Doubleday Café, a most welcome oasis where the crew takes splendid care of those unwinding after a long day at the Giamatti Center and the Hall of Fame.

And, not surprisingly, the biggest thanks go out to my wife Donna, my biggest fan whose love and support make everything I do worth the effort.

I

THE FIGHT OVER LABOR

The new age of free agency has spawned its own corpus of literature and field of study, in no small part because the dynamics of baseball's economic structure changed radically after the demise of the reserve clause in 1975, and the opening of the game's labor market at the conclusion of the 1976 season. When players were able to test the market and move on to new teams, the return on investment was not always favorable. Bobby Grich and teammate Joe Rudi were sidelined with significant injuries in 1977, and thwarted California's immediate pennant hopes, but along with Don Baylor, who would become the American League (AL) Most Valuable Player (MVP) in 1979, they eventually delivered the goods for owner Gene Autry. Other teams and players, however, were not so lucky.

As the Cleveland Indians sought to strengthen a promising roster that featured young talent in the form of Duane Kuiper, Rick Manning, and Dennis Eckersley, the Tribe signed a free-agent pitcher whose star seemed on the rise. Wayne Garland, a 26-year-old product of the Baltimore farm system, won 20 games for the Orioles in 1976, and seemed to be the latest example of the fine pitchers who had emerged while in the care of that franchise. But when overworked in his new home in Cleveland—he pitched more than 280 innings in 1977, on his way to losing 19 games—Garland quickly broke down and never approached the stardom once predicted for him.

Mixed results could be found in San Diego, where the money spent on Gene Tenace and Rollie Fingers yielded 93 losses and a fifth-place finish for the Padres in the National League (NL) West. The 35 saves Fingers recorded—best in the majors—were a vindication but did little to improve the Padres' lot, and his relief counterpart in the AL, former Twins closer Bill Campbell, moved on to Boston, where he led that circuit with 31 saves. But as *Sporting News* editorialized while the 1977 campaign unfolded, caveat emptor remained the overarching principle. Noting that some teams like the White Sox and Twins were "compet[ing] with the champagne drinkers [while] on a beer budget," *Sporting News* cautioned that attempting to buy a pennant through expenditures on free agents may not be the best business practice.[1]

One club that did succeed in this endeavor was the New York Yankees, who landed the biggest of the high-profile free agents but also wisely augmented that transaction by acquiring two other key players via the trade route. Shortstop had been an intractable position for the Yankees, but Bucky Dent arrived in the Bronx when the White Sox shipped him to New York for Oscar Gamble, pitching prospect LaMarr Hoyt, a minor leaguer, and $200,000. Dent, along with an earlier and brilliant trade acquisition, Willie Randolph, solidified the Yankees middle infield, but the kingpin who drew the most attention during the initial free-agent sweepstakes in the fall of 1976 also propelled his new team to the heights of the baseball world.

Former AL MVP Reggie Jackson, whose résumé also included six All-Star Team selections and a penchant for slugging ability, had been wooed by a number of clubs after he played out his option year in Baltimore. The allure of helping the Yankees, who had been dispatched by the Cincinnati Reds in the 1976 World Series, reach baseball's pinnacle was further buttressed by owner George Steinbrenner's offer of a five-year, $2.9 million contract. Although Jackson received significant—and in some cases higher—offers from several franchises, including San Diego, Los Angeles, and Montreal, he chose the Yankees in part because being in New York helped connect him to some of his nonbaseball business interests that were based there. Knowing that the lights burned brightest in the Big Apple, Jackson took his place with the Yankees in a press event that the *New York Times* described as "more a coronation than an unveiling."[2] What followed for the Yankees was a tumultuous season, but when they captured the World Series, the Game 6 finale highlighted by Jackson's trio of home runs, fans of the Bronx Bombers reveled in the team's return to the Promised Land.

One of the aforementioned "beer budget" owners fully understood the value, in the strict business sense, of what a player of Reggie Jackson's stature meant. "Joe Rudi is a great player, but when one of our pitchers strikes out Joe Rudi, you hear only polite applause," White Sox owner Bill Veeck said. "When one of our pitchers strikes out Reggie Jackson, it brings down the house."[3] The type of contract that put Jackson in pinstripes was beyond the reach of a commoner like Veeck or the Twins' Calvin Griffith, but it did not diminish his appreciation for the value that a player with Jackson's reputation brought to the box office.

Nonetheless, Veeck was shrewd enough to understand that a player entering his option year wanted to produce in the best way possible so that when he filed for free agency, he would be armed with an impressive array of recent statistics and thereby positioned to negotiate the best terms possible with the team who would ultimately become his new employer. Thus, noted Veeck's biographer Paul Dickson, he "conceived a scheme he dubbed 'rent-a-player,' by which he traded for other clubs' stars in their option years."[4] This maneuvering allowed Veeck to craft a team in 1977 that surprised both on the field and at the gate, with the roster at Comiskey Park now stocked with an abundance of long-ball threats, for instance, Oscar Gamble (31 home runs) and Richie Zisk (30 homers), who formed the nucleus of the "South Side Hit Men."

Gamble and Zisk predictably took their talents elsewhere in 1978, but the ChiSox captured lightning in a bottle for one special year and increased their 1977 home attendance by 80 percent (from 914,945 in 1976 to 1,657,135). As much fun as it was to see a game at Comiskey, Veeck's methodology could only support a short-term strategy, and with the passing of successive seasons, the forces prevailing over the labor market grew "increasingly hostile to owners operating on a shoestring."[5] These were the conditions that put small-market clubs like Oakland, Minnesota, and Pittsburgh at a disadvantage, but it must be noted that Athletics owner Charlie Finley had alienated so many of his star players for so long that their flight from his clutches was a fait accompli when the 1976 season concluded.

From the players' perspective, the financial windfalls they reaped were not only a reward for past performance, but also, especially in the case of those who signed new multiyear contracts, a provision of security for the future. But the new market produced a curious mix of competing interests. Players discovered that teams willing to spend extravagantly were pushing their salaries to levels almost unimagined when the reserve clause was struck down. Yet, this in turn created an unpleasant greed factor. When the plum of the second class of free agents, Lyman Bostock of the Twins, reached the open market following the 1977 season, his agent declared with more than a whiff of smugness as the bidding began, "We just plan to sit back, rub our hands, and wait for the money to fall into them."[6] Gene Autry paid $450,000 for Bostock's only season in a California uniform before the player's untimely death, and the salary portion of his pay—$400,000—already equaled that of his new teammate and fellow free agent Joe Rudi, and far exceeded that of teammates Grich and Baylor. Lacking the credentials accumulated by Autry's famed 1977 trio, Bostock had no postseason experience, nor had he ever made an All-Star Team, but nevertheless he and his salary leaped into the stratosphere of the day based solely on his .318 batting average during three seasons in Minnesota.

The financial melee at the close of the 1970s was joined by other luminaries, some players who exercised their right to change addresses, and others who stayed put yet still were able to leverage the salaries of their brethren to best advantage. In the Bronx, relief ace Rich "Goose" Gossage and starter Tommy John joined the Yankees after playing out their options, while Jim Rice of the Red Sox and Pittsburgh's Dave Parker remained with their respective clubs for renewed, greatly enriched contracts. Rod Carew, coming off a 1977 season in which he challenged the coveted .400 batting mark, had one year remaining with the Twins, and the expiration of his three-year contract fueled rumors of his departure to either the Yankees or the Angels.

Having seen the prior departures of Larry Hisle, Bill Campbell, and Lyman Bostock, Minnesota owner Calvin Griffith evinced no stomach for losing one of the top players in Twins history, but neither did he display any inclination to pay Carew a competitive market rate as now dictated by the wealthier clubs. When the Twins first baseman sat down with Griffith in late March 1978, in the hopes of brokering a new contract, the mogul fulminated, "All these f---ing owners don't realize they're ruinin' the f---ing game by giving out all that f---ing money. . . . I'm not going to ruin my f---ing organization like that."[7] In October, Griffith tried to apologize for racially insensitive remarks he made at a Lions Club meeting in a town south of Minneapolis, admitting that he was under the influence of a "couple of drinks, and, in answering questions from the group, I was trying to be funny."[8] Deeply offended, a host of Twins vowed to never again play for Griffith or to otherwise escape from the organization, including Carew, who was now entering his own option year. Realizing that an impasse had been reached, Griffith's only way out of this conundrum was to trade Carew rather than watch another player leave via free agency with no compensation coming to the Twins in return.

After months of speculation about where Carew might be traded, a deal was finally consummated in early February 1979. To ensure that Carew would be guaranteed to avoid the free-agent market, the California Angels signed him to a five-year, $4 million contract, which put him in an echelon with former Cincinnati Red Pete Rose, who headed east to Philadelphia for a four-year deal worth $3.225 million. The momentum of salary escalation for the top level of talent headed to the free-agent market appeared unabated, and while Marvin Miller and the members of the Major League Baseball Players Association (MLBPA) were gleeful of the financial gains, there was nothing but angst emanating from the executive offices of other owners—besides Griffith's—and the suite of Commissioner Bowie Kuhn.

***

Free agency, per se, was only one factor contributing to baseball's escalating payrolls. The other issue was a process used to settle a contract dispute between a player and his employer concerning what that player should be paid for the upcoming season. Salary arbitration involved submission of proposed salary amounts by the player and team management, as well as the presentation of supporting arguments before an impartial arbitrator, who, after hearing the player—accompanied by his agent—and a club representative state their respective cases, would decide which salary figure was appropriate. Because the arbitrator was not at liberty to offer an alternative salary—that is, by splitting the difference between the two proposed amounts—his was a winner-take-all decision. The club and player could come to an agreement at any time, but once in motion, the proceedings could become a denigrating and humiliating experience for the player.

In the course of stating their cases, the player sought to maximize the positive aspects of his performance and also compare himself favorably with other players with similar statistics who were earning as much, if not more, money than he himself was requesting. Seeking to economize and spend the least money possible, the club in turn would take the opportunity to stress the player's negative exploits in an effort to justify the lower salary that the team preferred to pay. The club's portrayal of a player in the harshest terms was often traumatic for him and could lead to much ill will, but such was the nature of arbitration.

While the reserve clause was in effect, teams could reduce a player's salary, at times inflicting a 20 percent cut; however, once arbitration was instituted in 1973, it served as a mechanism whereby the club was almost obligated to offer even a token raise to a player whose previous year's performance may have been less than expected. With pay cuts now virtually a thing of the past, the burgeoning tide of both salary arbitration *and* access to an open labor market conflated to lift the dollar figures of all contracts. Of the dozen cases in 1979 that went to an arbitrator, eight were decided in the player's favor—five of whom played for Finley's Athletics—and the other four in favor of the team.

Any team's decision to remain on the sidelines rather than participate in acquiring an expensive free agent was not immune to the forces of the realities of the new market. With salaries of free agents now far beyond any previously awarded and the pay of arbitration-eligible players also rising in various degrees, the conditions impacted clubs like Griffith's penurious Twins, whose own players would benefit from going to arbitration. Although initially viewed as a "harmless mechanism" when it was instituted, salary arbitration allowed "players to link their demands . . . to what free agents commanded in the open market," and in the wake of the Messersmith verdict, "[owners] hadn't foreseen . . . how free-agent riches would rain onto other players."[9] The case of Montreal Expos infielder Rodney Scott presents an interesting example.

The speedy Scott was valuable as a basestealer who could also leg out triples when batting, and his manager, Dick Williams, viewed him as the team's MVP. Yet, since facts and figures can be twisted to serve virtually any purpose, Scott, at bottom, was awarded $225,000 based on a batting average of a measly .224, and if it were possible for *him* to draw such a salary, what was to prevent other weak hitters from requesting a similar contract? Thus were the unintended consequences of arbitration.

Indeed, the group of club magnates had backed themselves into a corner: With arbitration part of the collective bargaining agreement and rich owners driving up salaries because they could not resist the temptation to add a top-tier free agent by simply opening their coffers, there was much hand-wringing in the front offices of many teams. The wealthier clubs knew they had the financial resources available to dole out high-paying contracts, but the Finleys and Griffiths lacked the kind of revenue stream—be it from gate attendance, concessions, parking, or the sale of broadcast rights—that was present in the large markets of New York or Los Angeles.

***

While the battles of labor played out in the immediate post-Messersmith era, they did so under the cover of the 1976 Basic Agreement, which was due to expire on December 31, 1979. During the intervening period, there was barely a gathering of club executives that was not accompanied by the ominous rumbling that foretold of baseball's imminent financial doom. Adding strong voices to this dour refrain were Commissioner Bowie Kuhn and Ray Grebey, head of the owners' Player Relations Committee (PRC), who was responsible for directly negotiating with Marvin Miller, head of the MLBPA.

The strategy in Miller's camp was clear: full speed ahead in continuing the course that was enriching the union's membership. But the message from the coalition of owners, the PRC, and the commissioner was conflicted in spite of their ostensibly united front. The constant refrain from that group would have one believing that baseball was at the precipice of a disaster. At the winter meetings in December 1978, Kuhn delivered his state-of-the-game address and pointed out an alarming trend: Fifty-three percent of the players comprising the first two groups of free agents were signed by only five teams (out of 26), demonstrating a "clear tendency for some of the star players to seek only contending teams."[10] One of those contenders, the Yankees, had just captured its second consecutive World Series and had already signed free-agent pitchers Tommy John and Luis Tiant just weeks earlier, swelling their payroll all the more; therefore, a paradox existed between the commissioner's cry of peril and the willingness of some owners to spend liberally.

Division within the ranks of ownership regarding the philosophy of salary expenditure was palpable. Griffith, a small-market man who agreed with Kuhn's comments, inveighed against the millions the rich clubs were dispensing. Yet, for a team like the Yankees, blessed with a well-fortified revenue stream, it was not only desirable, but also almost obligatory to do everything in their power to put the best team possible on the field. "Whoever heard of anybody trying to be second best?" demanded New York general manager Al Rosen. "Finishing first is the American dream," Rosen argued, and then he noted with a political flourish, "The United States Constitution guarantees every American citizen freedom of contact, and we have been exercising that privilege."[11] Even Kuhn himself confessed that the perceived offending parties among the owners were conducting business in a forthright manner and that their actions did not in any way violate the terms of the collective bargaining agreement with the players' union. But how to resolve the impasse between those teams who could afford to spend and those who could not?

The commissioner offered the suggestion of compensation, whereby a team losing a free agent would receive a player—or players, or perhaps cash—from the organization that signed him. That is, when Joe Rudi signed with the Angels, California would then have been obligated to provide the Athletics—Rudi's prior club—with a player from within their system. The reasoning was that some recompense was owed to the free agent's originating team because they paid to sign the player originally—as an amateur—and then had to bear the expense of bringing him through their farm system. Royals owner Ewing Kauffman stated that his franchise had disbursed $2.8 million in 1980 alone for his farm system and argued, "I don't see how we can continue to spend that much when we can't get something back because of free agency."[12]

Predictably, the proposal of compensation drew the wrath of Marvin Miller, who argued that, in his view, competitive balance improved in the two years that free agents could exercise their rights. Neither did Miller see any clubs about to file for bankruptcy, basing his opinion on data that indicated nearly $279 million in total team revenues but only roughly $69 million in salary expenditures. Even adding in the $8.3 million that owners directed to the players' pension fund, Miller wanted to know "what happened to the other $200 million?"[13] The PRC maintained that Miller was skewing expenses by focusing only on salaries paid to the players rather than taking into account money paid to support the farm system, administrative personnel, and the costs of operating stadiums within a franchise's purview; however, the owners' unwillingness to share specific accounting information enabled Miller to use this intransigence to the union's advantage: If the owners are crying poverty, then why not prove the point by revealing all the numbers?

While the riches continued to accrue to the free agents, there was still a bit of concern on the part of some players, for example, Baltimore pitcher Jim Palmer. The Orioles ace expressed worry about the future dynamics of the game if free agents gravitated toward wealthier teams or those located in more comfortable climates. Yet, in an ironic twist, George Steinbrenner, who was perhaps the most generous spender, locked horns with Miller by claiming that the union head "took, took, took" whatever he could on behalf of the players, and the Yankees mogul was thirsting for the chance to fix a system now seemingly broken by the voiding of the reserve clause.[14]

Although one year remained before the expiration of baseball's collective bargaining agreement at the end of 1979, both sides of the labor struggle saw the formation of dark clouds on the horizon. Entrenching for the bitter fight they foresaw, the players began to contribute to a fund from which they could draw money should a predicted work stoppage come to fruition in 1980. But in August 1978, Major League Baseball (MLB) had endured a one-day strike by umpires, who then argued at the winter meetings for better pay and benefits, notably reimbursement for hotel bills, which umpires had to pay out of their own pocket at a cost of several thousand dollars each season. The dispute concerning benefits for a few dozen men would take center stage well in advance of the anticipated brawl between players and owners.

***

The walkout by major-league umpires on August 15, 1978, was squelched by a federal judge who instructed the arbiters to live up to the terms of their own collective bargaining agreement with the NL and AL, which was in force until the end of 1980. An attorney from Philadelphia, Richie Phillips, was counsel for the Major League Umpires Association, as well as referees for the National Basketball Association, and while not seeking pay raises for the umpires as exorbitant as those of the players, he understood very well the disparity between the earnings of basketball officials—10-year veterans received at least $45,000 for an 82-game season—and their counterparts on the diamond, a $32,500 minimum for nearly twice the number of games. This is to say nothing about the vast differences in physical working conditions: Basketball referees could enjoy a respite and bathroom break at halftime; games were always played in the relative comfort of indoor arenas; and although much running was involved, there was a lack of danger from being injured by a thrown or struck object like a baseball. Little wonder then that baseball umpires wanted to improve their lot.

Negotiations between Phillips and NL president Chub Feeney and AL prexy Lee MacPhail during the winter took place, but to no avail, and as spring training of 1979 drew near with no settlement in sight, the umpires withheld their services and forced amateur and semiprofessional umpires to fill the void for exhibition games. A tactic that Phillips tried was to have the umpires deal individually with the leagues, and he pointed out that the umpires' collective bargaining agreement determined the minimum salaries but did not preclude any "individual to negotiate beyond the offer the league has extended" because "our umpires have individual contracts" with their respective leagues.[15]

When the leagues sought an injunction to force the umpires back to work, they were rebuffed when a judge in Philadelphia informed them that with the umpires' individual contracts having all expired, they were no longer technically employed by either league. How can an employee be forced back to work when no legal contract existed? As the impasse continued through March, Feeney and MacPhail were confident that if no accord could be reached, the substitute umpires used during the preseason would be up to the task. The leagues also tried to call up umpires from the trio of Triple-A circuits, but this met with limited success because even though minor-league umps were not unionized, they were reluctant to take the place of a striker with whom they might one day be working at baseball's highest level.

Striking umpires staged picket lines at major-league ballparks as the regular season commenced, and sympathetic unionized workers from other vocations refused to cross those lines, in some cases causing a steep decline in attendance at a number of games. As the strike stretched from April into May, it became evident that the replacement umpires were ill-equipped to handle some difficulties on the field or even manage the consistency of their strike zone. The nadir came in an April 24 contest at Shea Stadium between the Mets and San Francisco Giants, the game recap in *Sporting News* informing readers of that evening's travesty:

> Youngblood knocked in three runs with homer to spark Mets to 10–3 triumph over Giants in game protested by both teams after game delay of 28 minutes in arguments over controversial call. With Met runners on first and third, and none out in the first inning, Mazzilli lined shot to

> deep right-center that Clark caught as Taveras tagged and scored from third. Clark, however, dropped ball, and his throw to second caught Hebner, who had not tagged up from first, thinking the ball had been dropped. Umpires ruled Clark had caught ball but returned Hebner to first in compromise situation since Hebner saw one umpire signal that the ball had been dropped. Montanez walked when play resumed, and Youngblood hit a three-run homer.[16]

There can be no wonder that Giants pitcher Vida Blue would have lost his edge from standing idle for nearly a half-hour as the dispute dragged on. Speaking in broad terms about the effects of the substitutes, at least one writer complained that with baseball lacking the professionalism demonstrated by the diligence of the major-league arbiters, "the game under any other conditions is 'bush.'"[17]

In the meantime, away from public view were the negotiations taking place between Phillips and baseball's Executive Council, a contingent of select club owners from both leagues. But even within the ranks of the council there was an internal issue. George Steinbrenner of the Yankees had been recently added to the group, in part because of an open position that needed to be filled, and in part as a way of getting the volatile Yankees owner to curb his mercurial temper by letting him assume a position of responsibility in the highest offices of the game. As the presidents of the AL and NL were furnishing updates to the Executive Council regarding the negotiations with the umpires, Kuhn claimed, "It came to our attention from a reliable source that these reports were being leaked by George to Richie Phillips, the union head," an action Kuhn suspected as an "antidote for [Steinbrenner's] constant criticism of the umpires."[18] Once presented with the allegation, the Yankees magnate dismissed it but soon thereafter resigned his post on the council.

As the ugliness of numerous incidents continued to blemish the game, pressure mounted on the leagues to end the strike and return the regular umpires to the field. At last, three weeks after the debacle at Shea Stadium, a resolution was finalized in the form of an agreement that covered the remainder of 1979 and each of the next two seasons. Umpires were granted salary raises that averaged about $7,500 per man and included paid time off during the season, a new benefit that also paid the umpires for travel expenses to and from home.

Always seeming to be in a no-win situation because there was the certainty that someone would be dissatisfied due to a call they made, the regular umpires were nonetheless warmly greeted by fans when they took the field in Boston and Chicago on May 19.

***

The roiling over the umpires' strike finally was resolved, but this imbroglio would prove to be a mere warm-up act for the main event when the owners and the players squared off at the conclusion of their basic agreement at the end of 1979. There was a pause in the rebirth of the Yankees dynasty that year, the Baltimore Orioles claiming first place in the AL East and then beating the Angels in the American League Championship Series (ALCS) before falling in the World Series to a spirited Pittsburgh Pirates team led by manager Chuck Tanner and slugger Willie Stargell. The lack of a big-market team in the Fall Classic seemed not to detract from the excitement generated by the Bucs' adopted "We Are Family" theme. In fact, this enthusiasm was a continuation of the previous season's "Baseball Fever" that gripped an increasing number of fans.

Giddiness aside, Bowie Kuhn had in the summer of 1979 convened a meeting of the Executive Council, at which he told a select group of owners and closest associates, "For the year 1978, there were in excess of $252 million in long-term contract guarantees to players compared with the industry's gross revenues for that year of $278 million."[19] He also suggested several ways to address what he viewed as a situation that could cripple the financial outlook of many teams that had already indulged in spending on free agents: requirements for insurance coverage on long-term contracts, a cap on any given team's total commitment to long-term contracts and/or its total payroll, and prohibitions on multiyear or guaranteed contracts.

In the two short years during which free agents were allowed to find new teams, an impressive track record of spending—and debt accumulation—had led Kuhn to this point. While the dollar figures he quoted may have been accurate, the amounts guaranteed were not entirely payable up front, but rather during a span of years into the future. For him to compare this amount to only one year's worth of industry revenue—while ignoring any projected income stream during the length of those same contracts—created a skewed perspective.

Nonetheless, this rationale served as the basis for the claxon call of imminent fiscal calamity. One member of the Executive Council, Detroit Tigers owner John Fetzer, wrote to Kuhn and expressed his deep concern about the program of "wild spending" to which several teams had committed. In his missive, Fetzer quoted one of his fellow magnates, saying, "There are probably opportunities available for the development of creative and significant restraints which the commissioner can and should impose upon all clubs *in order to protect us from ourselves*."[20] The paradox, invoked here by Fetzer as an entreaty to Kuhn for help, was unmistakable. Ray Grebey, director of the PRC, would accurately describe this as a condition in which the "actions of one club directly effect [*sic*] the ability of all other clubs to negotiate satisfactory individual player contracts."[21]

Baseball's annual winter meetings featured the commissioner's address punctuated by the accustomed drumbeat of financial peril swirling about the major leagues. Noting that more than half the teams lost money, with eight sustaining losses of at least $2 million each, Kuhn stated that since 1975, the average player salary had risen from $46,000 to $121,000, a figure that had been inflated appreciably by the onslaught of multiyear, multimillion-dollar contracts since late 1976.

Delighting in their new prosperity, the players were not likely to make any concessions during the coming round of talks for the next version of a collective bargaining agreement with the team owners, and if the players saw fit to begin contributions to a strike fund in anticipation of a potential work stoppage in 1980, so too were the club magnates determined not to be caught short either. In advance of their talks with Marvin Miller, the teams purchased $50 million of strike insurance, created a $7 million "mutual-assistance fund," and, not wishing to have a reprise of Steinbrenner's recent suspected cozying up to the enemy, established a penalty of a half-million dollars for any owner found acting in any way detrimental to the negotiating process. Kuhn later wrote of the owners, "Quite obviously, they were gearing up for an unprecedented effort to unify the management position as Miller had so successfully unified the players."[22]

The negotiations between the players and the PRC started shortly after the World Series and lasted through the winter months, but as if to echo the conditions of the Cold War between the United States and the Soviet Union, there was a great degree of suspicion and mistrust between baseball's opposing factions. Miller and Kuhn sat down for a social chat over cocktails before the winter meetings, but the tête-à-tête quickly floundered when the commissioner—perhaps with the words of Fetzer's memo still in mind—confided to the union leader, "Marvin, the owners need a victory," which Miller immediately interpreted as a request to abrogate his duties to the players for the sake of letting the club moguls correct their course.[23] Only one thought could possibly have been running through Miller's head: *A victory? For the owners? They held the upper hand for more than a century thanks to the reserve clause, and now you say they need a victory?*

That Kuhn tried to serve as a back-channel to the union may have spoken well to his intentions to facilitate the bargaining process, but to do so by pleading on behalf of the magnates with desperate overtones to a man whose resolve had delivered the players to a most financially rewarding promised land was an embarrassment. Miller had worked diligently to craft the business of the players' union to the best advantage of his constituents, and he would never retreat from the hard-earned gains won for his side.

In an effort to rein in that for which they themselves were largely responsible due to their lavish spending on free agents, the owners desired to implement a compensatory system whereby a club losing a free agent would be able to select a major-league-quality player from the team that signed the free agent, after the signing team protected 15 players from such selection. Regarding players with less than six years of service, the PRC sought to cap their salaries and limit their contracts to a single year.

During the ensuing months, management removed its demand for capping salaries, thought by some to be the biggest impediment to securing a new agreement. But owners were unbending on the compensation issue, and negotiations with the union muddled through the remainder of spring training in 1980. The players took a dramatic step by cancelling the final week of exhibition games, with plans to end their refusal to play in time for the opening of the regular season, but they voted almost unanimously to strike on May 23. This strategic date was selected because it was the beginning of Memorial Day weekend, a time when owners could count on a healthy infusion of revenue thanks to traditionally heavy attendance at the ballparks.

Miller believed that the club magnates "seemed intent on provoking a strike," as they insisted on "an end to salary arbitration and individual player contract negotiations, the substitution of a fixed salary schedule, and compensation to a club losing a free agent," all of which he viewed to be "really extreme" demands.[24] As Opening Day approached, the owners explored the possibility of implementing a public relations ploy to bolster their position with the fans, as evinced in the title of a memo discussed at a meeting of the Executive Council. "IF THERE IS A PLAYERS' STRIKE, SHOULD OWNERS PLACE A NEWSPAPER ADVERTISEMENT?" was the heading of a proposed broadside that would have explained the issues at stake from the viewpoint of management. While the "purpose and content of ad are positive" with "no distortion of facts," by its very nature it could not help being provocative and against the players' union. Kuhn's marginalia beneath the pros and cons summarized on the first page—"polarizes"—spoke volumes in a single word.[25]

Scheduled to run in several major newspapers, the advertisement stated the owners' case for compensation for a free agent lost to another team, but the primary theme was greed on the part of players. Although the council noted that the "expense of the ad shows that the owners have plenty of money," the ad's banner asked rhetorically, "If you were making $140,000 a year [the approximate average major-league salary], would you strike?" The text continued by injecting more information that showed how well-off the players already were—"The average major leaguer is in the top one percent of all the wage earners in the country. . . . He works seven months a year. . . . He is given $30 a day for meal money alone!"—before repeating the $140,000 question. After stating its position on the importance of compensation to the clubs, the ad closed by putting the ball in the players' court: "We wish we could promise you that we could immediately put this nonsense behind us and play ball. But as of this moment, we can't promise anything. A lot depends on that fellow with the $140,000 salary."

Kuhn's position had a natural inclination toward the side of management, despite the ill will that some owners held against him, but to parrot the line for which he became famous, Kuhn wanted to ensure that the "best interests of baseball" were being served, however he may have been able to discharge this duty. Yet, this never provided any relief to Miller, who increasingly and sardonically viewed Kuhn as nothing more than a dupe for the owners.

As Memorial Day weekend approached, a player walkout appeared to be a certainty, but the facade of a solidly united front by the players was not what it may have seemed. Columnist Dick Young claimed that Mariners first baseman Bruce Bochte was of the opinion that a "secret ballot [to vote on a strike] . . . would have produced a ratio closer to 5–3," a view similar to that of Boston shortstop Rick Burleson, who said, "Some players now say that if there were a vote today [May 19], 13 of our 25 players would vote against a strike."[26]

But a flurry of activity between Miller and the PRC resulted in a new four-year basic agreement and amendments to the players' pension, the deal brokered by 4:00 a.m. on the morning of May 23, with the help of Ken Moffett, a federal mediator who was enlisted as a facilitator. The players claimed victory through maintenance of the owners' 33 percent contribution of national broadcast revenue to the pension fund, as well as increased benefits for eligible retirees, a reduction from three years of service time to two years for a player to qualify for salary arbitration, the minimum pay for players was increased from $21,000 to $35,000 during the four years of the deal, and several other minor concessions were gained by the union. The player compensation demand was submitted to an ad hoc panel—the members were players Sal Bando and Bob Boone, and general managers Frank Cashen and Harry Dalton—for further evaluation during the ensuing year.

"Out of the Strike Zone," *Sporting News* joyously proclaimed on the cover of its next issue. Ray Grebey and Marvin Miller smiled for the cameras when the accord was announced, and there was no reason to run the owners' inciteful newspaper ad. But the subheading of the accompanying article beheld ominous overtones: "Strike Threat Delayed to '81," and indeed that would be exactly the case.[27] There would be pressure on Bando et al. to come up with a plan that would placate both sides, and if they were able to do so, then it would in turn be grafted onto the newly reached pact. "If, however, the two sides cannot agree on compensation, the owners may, between February 15 and 20, 1981, *unilaterally put into effect* the compensation (a major or minor leaguer for a 'premier' free agent) they had proposed during the six months of negotiations."[28]

Given the frayed nerves of the various parties at the bargaining table as the witching hour drew near, the postponement of a player walkout may have been the right course of action, buying time to allow calmer heads to prevail, while at once removing any possibility of a lack of baseball at the close of May. Still, the main sticking point between players and owners had not been fully resolved, and the procrastination only forestalled the inevitable.

***

In the run-up to the 1981 season, the New York Yankees again secured the services of the top free agent to test the market, Dave Winfield. Formerly a member of the San Diego Padres, Winfield played out his option in 1980, in less-than-favorable circumstances. The lanky outfielder was expecting to receive a 10-year deal worth about $13 million, but Padres club president Ballard Smith was so reluctant to meet the demand that he revealed a look at his team's financial statement to prove that the club was already operating at a loss.

The previous signing of free agents Rollie Fingers and Gene Tenace, followed by the arrival of Rick Wise and John Curtis, failed to enable the Padres to reach .500, and the possible departure of Winfield stood to dim the team's chances even further. For 1979, Smith claimed that the team lost more than $400,000, basing this figure on expenses of $8.5 million and revenue of only $8.1 million.[29] The San Diego president blanched at the thought of committing to a long-term contract to retain the services of his best player. For his part, Winfield felt slighted by the organization, which, he believed, was "downgrading his performance" in an effort to make him a less-attractive free agent.[30]

Before entering the draft by which teams claimed negotiating rights for any given free agent, Winfield had advised 17 clubs not to waste their selection on him because he had no desire to play for them. Only nine teams were up to the standard Winfield deemed worthy of consideration, and when George Steinbrenner opened his coffers, the ex-Padre reaped a 10-year contract estimated to be valued between $15 and $23 million depending on the calculation of cost-of-living increases.[31] Spurred on by his new wealth, Winfield determined to continue the work of his Winfield Foundation, a charitable organization whose mission was to aid children in need.

The argument that the rich teams were gaining at the expense of their less well-off brethren still held currency, and even a journeyman like Claudell Washington—at the age of 25, the one-time All-Star (in 1975) had already played for four teams and distinguished himself by batting over .300 just once, .279 overall)—was signed by Atlanta to a five-year contract worth nearly $5 million. Braves owner Ted Turner was the media mogul who also trained his sights on Winfield and free-agent hurler Don Sutton, which was understandable given their track records of proven talent, which eventually landed them in the Hall of Fame.

But Turner's interest in the enigmatic Washington—noted by one major-league scout as a player who "can come up with the unbelievable throw but sometimes falls asleep in the outfield"—and his rush in signing him the day after the 1980 free-agent reentry draft prompted many executives to roll their eyes in disbelief.[32] This scout's observation also hinted at a form of complacency that affected some corners of the game, namely the perception of a lack of hustle as demonstrated by players. During the 1980 season, reporters in Los Angeles found that Mickey Hatcher—still trying to gain a footing in the big leagues at the time—was alone among the Dodgers who gave maximum effort, while a member of the Cubs replied, "Next team, please," when asked about which of his teammates was the most enthusiastic player.[33]

Bake McBride of the Phillies, who played most of his career on Astroturf fields and suffered from knee problems, nevertheless drew the ire of fans who did not appreciate his reluctance to exert himself more than he seemed to be. "My feeling is why should I try to please the fans with a special effort when I know in my heart I'm pleasing myself," McBride offered in self-defense.[34] While McBride may have had a legitimate desire to pace himself so as to ease his discomfort, his comment came across as solipsistic and would add fuel to the growing debate about whether ballplayers were overpaid and lackadaisical.

After three years of free-agent signings, the overall attitude of players was disappointing to not only the owners, who were right to expect an appreciable return on their investments, but also others associated with them. "I can't believe it. I really can't. It's sad," said one player's agent, "I watched them three straight games, and (they looked as if) they could've cared less whether they won or lost," and while this indifference was taking root, trips to the disabled list in this period were skyrocketing. "The increase is stunning," noted one executive, who added, "It is difficult to think that long-term contracts have not played a role in this."[35]

Thus, the signing of players like Claudell Washington was the kind of transaction that agitated the internal ranks of club owners, many of whom wondered what the logic was in overpaying to obtain a mediocre talent, while it was also the type of deal that Marvin Miller relished as another feather in his cap, as well as that of the MLBPA. Such contracts caused Miller to scoff at the statements from team magnates and the commissioner claiming that the game was in a constant state of fiscal danger and then contradicting themselves by spending wildly on free agents virtually irrespective of the player's achievements.

As the calendar turned to 1981, the four-man panel created to investigate the owners' compensation issue still had not come to any conclusions, and by the opening of spring training camps in mid-February, the owners decided to initiate the compensation plan in accordance with the terms of the 1980 agreement with the players. Viewing the move by club management with disdain, Miller interpreted the compensation system envisioned for top-flight free agents as being truly applicable to only a handful of players like Winfield. "Do you mean to tell me they're ready to shut down the industry just because they want compensation for three or four players?" he asked in disbelief. "Come on! How can anybody believe that?"[36] The players fired their own salvo by marking May 29—the Friday *after* Memorial Day this time around—as the date on which they would strike.

Owners devised a rating system whereby a free agent would be classed as a "ranking player" if during the previous season he was in the top 50 percent of his league's players in plate appearances or pitching appearances, and if he were selected by at least eight teams in the free-agent reentry draft. Both criteria were meant to categorize the free-agent player (or pitcher) as a regular performer rather than a substitute, and the demand for his services would be demonstrated by the fact that eight or more clubs sought him in the draft. "The signing club would protect only 15 players on its roster if the free agent ranked in the top 33 percent, and protect 18 in the case of any other 'ranking player.'"[37]

Ken Moffett, the head of the Federal Mediation and Conciliation Service, was again called in mid-April to intervene as both sides dug in for what promised to be a messy brawl. As the impasse dragged on, in early May the players upped the stakes when Miller filed an unfair labor practice charge with the National Labor Relations Board (NLRB) regarding the issue of the owners' failure to furnish proof that the "free-agent sweepstakes were bankrupting any clubs."[38] Demanding to see club data from 1978 through 1980, Miller drew criticism for waiting so long in the negotiations to make this request, which the magnates were not going to fulfill anyway.

The players and Miller seemed as united as could possibly be, but the owners, already committed to an internal code of silence to keep any uncomfortable dissension at bay, were rumored to be showing signs of breakage. The strike date loomed ever closer, but on May 27, the NLRB filed for a temporary restraining order, putting the job action on hold while players and owners agreed to endeavor for another week to obtain an agreement. The NLRB petition was trying to delay the compensation discussion for yet another year.

On June 3, Miller, PRC leader Ray Grebey, and Bowie Kuhn testified at the court hearing of the NLRB petition, during which Kuhn's financial laments were raised, but Grebey noted significantly, "At no time in my dealings with the owners have any expressed the inability to pay salaries."[39] Indeed, as *Sporting News* reported, "If the owners claimed financial hardship at the bargaining table, they would have to show the players their books," and the attorney representing the NL, Louis Hoynes, offered the opinion that among owners, "There might be an *unwillingness* to pay, to refuse to be silly—and there are indications of that. But an inability to pay? It's inconceivable."[40] The counsel for the NLRB thought that owners should reveal details of their financial records to substantiate the claims of distress, but the owners refused to provide such evidence and said that they were implementing the compensation system brokered the previous year.

Laid bare at the hearing was acknowledgment of the existence of two groups of owners and their respective philosophies of dealing with free agents: There was a contingent who would not spend on free agents—those who did not act "silly" by offering exorbitant contracts—and another faction who chose to pay the high salaries they themselves were doling out because they could afford to; otherwise they would be foolish to spend money they did not have. George Steinbrenner suffered from no financial problems and obviously had the means to pay the Jacksons and Winfields that he coveted, and as much as Calvin Griffith abhorred the manner in which Steinbrenner and his ilk ran their teams, choosing to abstain from pursuing free agents was his personal preference.

Days after the hearing and while all parties awaited a ruling from the court, Miller offered the creation of a compensational pool of players—drawn from the 40-man rosters of every team—from which a club losing a Type-A free agent could select a replacement, but the PRC demurred. On June 10, Judge Henry Werker denied the injunction sought by the NLRB that would have forced owners to disclose their financial information, ruling that Miller had been aware "for several years" of the owners' alleged losses and had adequate time to request this substantiating data from them rather than wait until February 27 to do so. Werker interpreted Miller's maneuver "not a sincere effort to obtain access to clubs' financial records, but rather a bargaining tactic by the association to prevent implementation of the PRC's proposal."[41] With Miller's charge of unfair labor practices now a moot point, the hope for a resolution of the dispute now reverted back to the strident process of collective bargaining between the two sides.

Bowie Kuhn later wrote, "If the injunction were granted, the effect would have been to postpone the strike and the clubs' implementation of compensation for a year," this comment speaking to the complexity of how intertwined the issue of compensation and the affordability of free-agent salaries had become.[42] The day after Werker's ruling, a marathon meeting between the PRC and the players featured revisions related to compensation, but no agreement could be reached. Games of June 11, were completed as scheduled, and there followed another futile effort in New York by a handful of NL players to breathe life into a possible settlement, but there was no hope.

"It's not compensation they want," said Ed Farmer of the Chicago White Sox, referring to the root desire of the owners. "All they want to do is hold down salaries."[43] Players were now left to shift for themselves in finding a way home as baseball commenced its first in-season strike.

***

In his autobiography, Marvin Miller stated unequivocally, "The 1981 strike was the most principled I've ever been associated with," and he quoted relief pitcher Sparky Lyle, who captured the spirit of what the players—given access to an open labor market—had been trying to accomplish since the striking down of the reserve clause that dated to the early 1880s: "We have a hundred years of catching up to do."[44] A painful price would be paid by every party concerned: Striking players were forfeiting their paychecks; ownership was losing its revenue stream from a variety of sources, including ticket sales, concessions, and parking; ballpark personnel such as ushers and vendors were now unemployed; and, of course, the fans who bought those tickets and concessions and patronized the very stadiums now rendered inaccessible were now deprived of an integral part of their leisure activities and entertainment.

Who were the villains in this unfortunate episode? Were they the greedy and ostensibly overpaid players, or were they the owners, who in some cases were unfathomably wealthy from their corporate ties and business affairs? The fans could easily direct their wrath at either faction—or both—and be correct. Letters written to the editor of *Sporting News* expressed indignation at both parties as the strike lengthened.

> Marvin Miller should go to Russia where he belongs.
> An owner who isn't willing enough to keep a player doesn't deserve compensation when the player goes elsewhere.
> It's time to take a stand on outrageous player salaries.
> Dave Winfield deserves his money partly because his case will encourage other great multitalented athletes to choose a career in baseball over some other sport.[45]

Shortly after the strike began, the baseball commissioner was feeling the heat of his perceived lack of involvement to develop a resolution. Kuhn defended his role, which for the most part was away from public view. "I don't know how I can be more active than I am, contrary to those who are going around beating their breasts and saying, 'Why isn't he doing something?'" Kuhn complained to columnist Milton Richman. "I can assure them I am not just sitting around my office doing nothing."[46]

In late June, the editors of *Sporting News* asked fans to send their opinions on the strike directly to the publication, which in turn would forward them to the commissioner's office and the warring sides in the dispute. Upon compiling all the letters sent in, the weekly thanked those who wrote, "even though the response came close to overwhelming us."[47]

Taking a bit of the sting out of the owners' suffering was a partial payment of strike insurance that they began to collect on June 24. One of scores of insurance companies among whom the risk had been spread, Lloyd's of London had underwritten 20 percent of the $50 million benefit, and this initial remittance of more than $440,000 was delivered ahead of schedule. The magnates had, for the previous two years, also contributed an estimated $10 to 15 million to a "mutual assistance fund . . . created by assessing each club 2 percent of gate receipts."[48] When the strike lasted one full month, speculation was rife that perhaps the season would be lost as the impasse continued unabated.

The owners' proposed newspaper advertisement that never ran in 1980 was now recast as a booklet in response to "quite a number of provocative questions [that] have been asked by a great number of interviewers from all areas of the media."[49] Drawn up in a format of frequently asked questions and lacking the snarky overtones of the ad, the pamphlet clearly enumerated the position of ownership and contained only a few financial figures regarding the players' pension plan, as well as a mention of the average major-league salary, now higher than $150,000, an increase of $10,000 from 1980. Despite the more polished prose of ownership's most recent release, Miller undoubtedly would have found its contents just as propagandistic as that of the original advertisement.

The month of July saw the annual All-Star Game as the strike's latest victim, and Eddie Chiles, owner of the Texas Rangers, "had given up on any more games being played this season."[50] A select few players were still being paid because they were either on the disabled list or their contracts stipulated that their paychecks would continue regardless of any interruption of work. The Rangers beat reporter noted that the number of players staying in the Arlington area to work out on their own began to dwindle as the strike wore on. In some cases, players went back home to find work—and a paycheck, *any* paycheck—while others drifted away as their interest in keeping in shape faded.

In one respect, the strike failed miserably: The Hall of Fame induction ceremony in Cooperstown took place on August 2, as planned. Welcomed to baseball's shrine were St. Louis Cardinals ace Bob Gibson, one of the game's most intense competitors whose exploits in 1968 epitomized the "Year of the Pitcher"; Rube Foster, dubbed the "Father of Black Baseball"; and slugger Johnny Mize, the "Big Cat" who beat up NL pitching from 1936 to 1949, with the Cardinals and Giants, before finishing his career with the Yankees. Roundly booed by the crowd of 7,500 people was the baseball commissioner, who felt that he had not done enough to bring a halt to the strike.

Through late July, the PRC and the players held 17 bargaining sessions, to no avail, and the free-agent compensation issue had evolved into a "philosophical difference" concerning whether the compensatory pick would come from a pool of players (favored by the union) or directly from the team signing the free agent.[51] The U.S. secretary of labor, Raymond Donovan, was pressed into service in the hope of expediting a resolution, but as the Cabinet member "became acquainted with the personalities and issues involved in the strike, he grew increasingly frustrated," according to Marvin Miller.[52]

Donovan developed a habit of muttering to the press about the difficulties of the negotiations, so a news blackout was implemented, a move that may have squelched some negative imagery getting into press, but it prevented the striking players, who by now were scattered throughout the country, from receiving the latest news about the bargaining sessions. The few generic status reports that did reach the media prompted a handful of players to speak out in frustration and thereby give the impression that the union was losing its unity, which Miller found abhorrent. The union head made the decision to personally hold regional meetings and explain face-to-face what was happening in the negotiations, and attempt to allay the angst felt by some of his charges.

In late July, a compelling deadline was on the horizon, namely the expiration of the owners' strike insurance on August 8. This looming event coupled with another development that had an ameliorative effect on the stalemate. There were whisperings that Ray Grebey of the PRC was on the way to being replaced, and Miller was privately contacted by Lee MacPhail, president of the AL, who soon supplanted Grebey as the primary negotiator. When Miller and MacPhail spoke, the former reiterated his favored compensation-via-pool proposal but stressed that the union membership had not officially approved the concept; however, Miller told MacPhail that if the owners accepted the pool, which Miller viewed as inviolable, and abandoned direct compensation, he would strive to convince the players that the pool was the lynchpin to settlement of the strike.

Executives of the players' union were adamant in their refusal to brook direct compensation, but the pool proposal, which had been advanced by Miller prior to the strike, was now deemed viable—for the most part—by the PRC. At the beginning of week 8 of the strike, Miller, MacPhail, and their associates met, but the PRC attempted to tweak the pool proposal. Miller was having none of it, basing his refusal on the fact that if he had to return to the union's executives for approval for yet further owners' changes, even more time would be lost in this latest round of haggling.

One final, significant hurdle remained, lurking out of view while the fight over compensation was most visible. Off the job for more than seven weeks, players nonetheless expected to receive credit for major-league service time despite their absence from work, and this ostensible secondary issue presented another stumbling block. Again standing firm, Miller also won this battle, and a Memorandum of Agreement was drawn up between players and owners.

The final accord included the compensatory pool system, in which clubs signing Type-A free agents could protect 24 players throughout its franchise (26 for nonsigning teams), with all other players eligible to be in the pool. A team losing a "pool player" was exempted from another such loss for two years or until it signed a Type-A free agent of its own, and the team would also receive $150,000 from a separate compensation fund. Type-A free agents were to be classed using a formulation that determined if he was in the top 20 percent of his peers at his position, Type B in the top 30 percent.

A host of other terms were agreed to, including a new minimum salary of $40,000 beginning in 1984, and the players' paychecks would resume as of August 1, while they spent a week quickly reacclimating themselves to playing baseball once more. To forestall a recurrence of the ugliness that was just ended, players and owners agreed to extend the collective bargaining agreement, as well as the pension agreement, for an extra year. The extant collective bargaining agreement was due to expire on December 31, 1983, and with the strike settled but still obviously fresh in everyone's mind, neither side had any appetite to even think about that next round of potential strife. Better to build a degree of procrastination into the current deal than to revisit the harsh reality of bargaining unpleasantries seemingly so soon again.

When both sides reviewed the memorandum, they overwhelmingly approved its terms, the owners assenting 21–2—with three teams abstaining—while the players polled 627 for it and only 37 against. Peace was officially at hand, and now it was time to return to the fields of play.

***

The strike's creation of a two-month lull in the middle of the season prompted the next debate: how best to resume action, which fans of all stripes missed? The decision was made to reopen the season with the All-Star Game in Cleveland, an occasion that served as an extravaganza to reignite interest in the national pastime. "It was just like old times," chirped *Sporting News*, and the record crowd of 72,086 fans who packed Municipal Stadium for the delayed Midsummer Classic on August 9, was emblematic of the trend in recent years that showed a steady increase in annual attendance.[53] The NL squad prevailed over the AL, 5–4, and all seemed well for at least one evening, and the real business of the regular season resumed apace.

The revival of the regular season called for each team to pick up where the calendar indicated, all games between June 12 and August 9 now permanently erased. Topping the gate on August 10, was the crowd of more than 60,000 who filed into Philadelphia's Veterans Stadium to see Pete Rose eclipse Stan Musial for the all-time record for base hits in the NL, at 3,631. Fans in the City of Brotherly Love relished the chance to see history being made, but in other cities, there was less urgency to head to the ballpark. The novelty of the All-Star Game having worn off, only 4,773 fans returned to Municipal Stadium to see the Indians lose to Milwaukee.

It was a foregone conclusion that 1981's attendance would be anomalous because about one-third of the schedule had been cancelled. But an artificial stimulant was built into the resumption of play: The two divisional leaders in each league as of June 12, were awarded a "first half" pennant, and the post–All-Star records of all teams were reset to no wins and no losses, allowing teams to vie for a "second half" pennant, with the winners of each half to square off for the actual division pennant. The league championship series and World Series would be played in their accustomed fashion. While this methodology worked well in the AL, the same could not be said in the NL.

The first-half AL East winners, the Yankees, faced the Brewers, who won the second half, and New York won an exciting best-of-five series to advance to the ALCS against Oakland, the first-half AL West champs, who then swept the second-half winners from Kansas City. The Athletics were in turn swept by the Yankees, who went on to the World Series.

In the Senior Circuit, unfortunate circumstances prevented the two divisional teams with the best composite records for both halves from participating in the postseason. St. Louis and Cincinnati performed well enough to place second in both halves, and for the entire season, the Cardinals' winning percentage of .587 was ahead of Montreal's .556, but because St. Louis failed to capture the NL East in either half, they lost out in their bid to move on. In like fashion, the Reds compiled the best overall percentage (.611) in the NL West but did not surpass Los Angeles in the first half or Houston in the second half.

In the NL divisional series, the Expos beat the Phillies and the Dodgers bested the Astros, both matchups going the full five games before the Dodgers outlasted the Expos to take the NL crown in yet another five-contest thriller. Lastly, the Dodgers overcame a two-game deficit against the Yankees and won four straight to capture the World Series and close out a tumultuous year.

***

The offseason of 1981 was a time for all sides to regroup in the aftermath of the biggest calamity to that point in baseball's history. But just as the peace of the American Civil War bred its own brand of discontent and resentments, so too did the settlement of the national pastime's labor dispute. As the players continued to reap virtually unbridled financial gains through ever-increasing contracts—in terms of not only dollars, but also the number of years of those contracts—they can be viewed as the unqualified victors, at that time and in the following decades. Yet, the major domos of the respective camps paid an uneven price for the havoc that had been wrought.

Ray Grebey, head of the PRC, was a "loser in the sense that his job in baseball became untenable as a result of the strike."[54] Now permanently out, he was replaced by Lee MacPhail, whose application of an even hand in negotiations won him much favor. Even though Marvin Miller led the union through its biggest battle, he soon thereafter assumed a diminished role with the MLBPA. This, however, should not be interpreted as a lessening of the influence he wielded on behalf of the players, and this imprint would impact Miller's successor, Don Fehr, who had served as counsel for the union. But the man who became a punching bag for players, owners, and fans for his apparent aloofness during the fracas received the biggest flogging.

Commissioner Bowie Kuhn was roundly criticized for being missing in action as the strike persisted, but in his memoirs, he insisted that he kept track of activities of the players and owners, the latter group being the men who ultimately determined who could and would serve as commissioner. The position of commissioner implied—especially to fans—that the occupant of the office possessed a sort of omnipotence to bring the strike to an end, but such was not the case. He could act as a mediator of sorts, but the ultimate responsibility for establishing the labor rules governing the game rested with the two sides locked in the impasse.

Whether his means of communication were in-person meetings or by telephone, Kuhn spent almost all of his time dealing with the owners and the PRC. Kuhn's fate as commissioner was determined by the owners, who hired him and set the term of his employment or dismissal, and thus existed a counterintuitive system in which the man who was supposed to be the boss of the owners could in reality be fired by them. The strike eroded their confidence in Kuhn, and it led to a rebellion by a cabal who sought his ouster. Even a small group of owners had the ability to block the reelection of Kuhn as baseball's top executive, and the petulance of such magnates as Eddie Chiles of the Texas Rangers and Oakland's Charlie Finley, who had little stomach for Kuhn, could have a harsh impact on the chances of Kuhn continuing in his role. Despite the levity of a successful World Series, a witching hour was drawing near that would determine Kuhn's fate when baseball's winter meetings convened in December. The postmortem of the strike included unflattering portraits that Kuhn and Miller painted of one another, as if the slinging of a last handful of mud would allow the hurler to have the final say.

In the ensuing decades, player salaries skyrocketed, and baseball franchises grew to be worth hundreds of millions of dollars, even billions in most cases. Despite the surfeit of wealth enjoyed by owners and players, who had formed the most successful union in the history of labor, journalist John Helyar wrote, "That didn't mitigate the players' mistrust or anger, which carried over in negotiations [with the owners] for years to come."[55] To a large degree, this miasma will always be present.

For many aficionados who welcomed the settlement of this latest episode of the labor conflict, the All-Star Game in Cleveland signaled a new beginning of summer, but the disgust vented by one fan may have best summed up the situation of those whose discontent would not be easily assuaged: "So the overpriced prima donnas (players) and the feudal barons (owners) have finally reached agreement. It's now time for the suckers (fans) in this circus of unmitigated greed to blow the dust off an old baseball cliché and give it new meaning: 'Wait 'til next year.'"[56]

***

The remainder of the 1980s was pockmarked by tussles that briefly interfered with the game on the field but not to the extent of the upheaval of 1981. The spring of 1982 saw record attendance at the training camps, and the enthusiasm demonstrated by fans carried into the regular season and the years that followed, indicating a large degree of forgiveness by those who purchased tickets. Changes were also in store on both the union front and in the commissioner's executive suite.

Marvin Miller ceded his position as director of the MLBPA and was replaced by Ken Moffett, who was the former federal mediator. Moffett had amiably engaged two of the leading members of the union, Mark Belanger and Doug DeCinces, and he curried much favor with the players and seemed to be a natural fit to assume Miller's place after the 1982 season. But Moffett, who "advanced himself as a candidate" and was enthusiastically received by the union's search committee, quickly drew suspicion as to his commitment to the organization.[57] Miller intended to step aside and serve only in the role of a consultant, and help Moffett's transition into the directorship, but he admitted that after seeing the manner in which Moffett was conducting his affairs, "one incident after another revealed [Moffett's] approach to the job."[58]

Early departures from meetings and unreturned telephone calls did not endear Moffett to those who had entrusted him with union duties, but particularly alarming was Moffett's poor comprehension regarding the recent television contract, the extension of the league championship series, and the impact that these items had on the players. Miller took the initiative to alert the players of Moffett's shortcomings, and less than one year into his three-year contract, Moffett had done little to gain the confidence of the players. Moffett chose not to stay for an important grievance hearing that involved the union's dispute regarding the owners' ratio of 60 percent to 40 percent of assets to liabilities as a standard to determine the financial stability of each ballclub, a case that could have required owners to open their books to prove that some teams were indeed in financial trouble. It was this kind of lackluster attitude that had union representatives believing that Moffett might project the image of a "weak link in negotiations for a new labor agreement" at the expiration of the current contract, so the MLBPA removed Moffett in late November 1983.[59]

Moffett was embittered by his treatment by the union, and when Miller was implored to come out of retirement—he agreed only to do so on an interim basis until a new replacement could be found—he was blasted by Moffett for returning for the sake of protecting the "monument" he had built.[60] This was a rare display of public discord by the MLBPA, and the group took action to right its ship: It agreed to settle a lawsuit brought by Moffett to collect the two years' worth of salary he stood to lose, and Don Fehr, who had been counsel to Miller for a number of years, was named as the new director of the MLBPA. More intimately familiar with the union's policies and mission, Fehr was the logical choice in the wake of the Moffett contretemps, and Miller again retained a consultant's role. Choosing not to be as actively involved with the union as he had been previously—after all, he was supposed to be retired—Miller felt that the players collectively had lost some of their cohesion as bargaining for a new pact with the owners ensued, and he hoped that Fehr would evince a united front for the players heading into the next round of negotiations with the owners.

If the track record for the previous twelve years provided any clues, the expiration of the extant agreement on December 31, 1984, created an aura of dreaded expectation. Taken in its entirety, the brief strike of 1972, the lockout of 1976, an "almost strike" of 1980, and the major disruption of 1981, pointed to more acrimony. Before the issue with the players could be addressed, however, the new commissioner, Peter Ueberroth, was immediately confronted with a problem upon taking office on October 1, 1984.

The umpires wanted concessions before working the upcoming league championship series, and Ueberroth initially deferred to AL president Bobby Brown and his NL counterpart, Chub Feeney, for their ruling on how the matter should be handled. In the meantime, postseason play commenced with replacement arbiters employed until October 7, at which time umpire union chief Richie Phillips agreed to binding arbitration to settle the dispute. Assuming the role of arbitrator was Ueberroth himself, who, on October 15, generously ruled in favor of the umpires, and the "decision reportedly stunned the club owners and league presidents."[61] The old payout of $225,000 for working the All-Star Game and all postseason contests was increased to more than $1 million for 1984 through 1986, and umpires could pool their funds to be distributed to all umpires, not just those selected for the highest-profile games.

With the calendar turning to 1985, players and owners embarked on another painful negotiating process. Unlike his predecessor, Ueberroth strove to put himself more in the public eye during the bargaining, but this tactic led to allegations that he was "grandstanding" and "appeared more interested in playing to the gallery than in accomplishing things."[62] He even met with Marvin Miller and Don Fehr to confess that the owners were maintaining dual accounting ledgers, employing one set as evidence that "at least 18 of the 26 clubs were losing money."[63]

The 1985 season opened as planned, but arduous bargaining between the two sides yielded no accord, and the players, not buying into the owners' proposal of a salary cap, announced a strike date of August 6. In the run-up to the appointed day, once again fans were venting their frustration about the likelihood of yet another breach in an otherwise enjoyable baseball season. *Sporting News* editorialized, "The intention here is not to condemn the players, although it would not be a difficult case to make. The intention is to alert them to what their ultimate employers—the fans in the stands—think of their attitude toward the game."[64] To many fans, the issue could be distilled to a single word—greed—so it came as little surprise that when no settlement was brokered, the players again walked off the job as they had in 1972 and 1981.

This time around, a more expedient agreement was achieved, and the strike was quickly curtailed after a two-day stoppage. This new accord extended until the end of the 1989 season and included monetary gains for the players in the form of a higher minimum salary ($60,000, up from $40,000), a better percentage from World Series ticket revenue, and a significant increase in the owners' contribution to the player pension fund (a total of $196 million during a six-year period ending in 1989), as well as higher pension benefits (a maximum annual payout of $91,000 instead of $57,000). The $196 million figure was a direct result of the latest television contract that the owners had brokered with NBC and ABC.

A pivotal compromise was obtained between Fehr and Barry Rona, attorney for the PRC, who spoke for committee leader Lee MacPhail, namely, owners abandoning their demand for a salary cap on arbitration awards and the players acceding to an increase in the number of years of service—from two years to three—for a player to be eligible for salary arbitration beginning in 1987. Perhaps most noteworthy was the elimination of free-agent player compensation, the major issue of the 1980–1981 discord. In conjunction with this, the reentry draft of free agents was discontinued, and any player who fulfilled his option year was now free to negotiate with any club, with the stipulation that his former team could retain rights to him by offering salary arbitration.[65]

Each party breathed a sigh of relief knowing that another bullet had been dodged and the remainder of the decade would benefit from a lack of labor unrest. The games that were cancelled by the two-day strike were rescheduled, and play resumed with hardly a ripple. Fans may have been happy with the brisk resumption of play, and the major figures who brokered the deal had their chance to shake hands and smile for the cameras, not least of whom was the commissioner. Ueberroth was intent to barge in on a private meeting between Fehr and Rona—held at MacPhail's apartment—in an effort to force a resolution to the strike, but when he arrived, he discovered that the heads of the union and the PRC had already come to terms. As the final paperwork was compiled, the commissioner, who had been on the job for less than one year, held a press conference to announce the deal, and he was hailed as a hero by some of the New York press, despite the fact that Fehr and the tandem of Rona and MacPhail had performed the heavy lifting.

But the man who orchestrated so many of the advances made by the MLBPA was disappointed. Miller understood the finer points of negotiating methods and strategies, one of which was never to meet alone with an adversary. The lack of a witness in this most recent case did smooth the bargaining between Fehr and Rona, but the concession of the players to give back one year in arbitration eligibility had to have been a loss in Miller's view. And although the pension fund received a tremendous increase, from $15.5 million annually to an average of $32.7 million for the duration of the latest national television contract, this was far less than the union's original demand for $60 million, which would have maintained the approximate one-third share the fund received from similar deals.[66]

"For the first time in its almost 20 years of existence," Miller lamented, "the Players Association took backward steps," also observing that the pension fund had lost some of its importance to many of the current players because they were now making substantially more than their predecessors, thereby enabling the nouveau riche to set aside their own funds for retirement, whereas the less-monied veterans of yesteryear were more dependent on a viable pension.[67] Indeed, this disparity would become even more pronounced as contracts for the superstars beyond the late twentieth century climbed into the hundreds of millions of dollars.

***

The appointment of Peter Ueberroth as commissioner brought a savvy businessman to the game's highest office, and in the course of imparting his wisdom to the group of owners—most of whom were business moguls themselves—he managed to convince them that they were their own worst enemies concerning salary expenditures for free-agent talent. During the early stages of Ueberroth's tenure, he lectured the owners about exercising greater fiscal restraint, and the consequence of his homilies was a less-than-subtle movement away from the earlier frenzied bidding for the best free agents on the market. "Even the top players failed to attract offers from anybody except their old teams," noted *Sporting News*, which further explained, "Many clubs, burned by past free-agent mistakes, ascribed the absence of bidding to a shift in strategy—grow your own talent."[68]

This rather sudden adoption of fiscal sanity in the mid-1980s raised the eyebrows of many observers who were incredulous that such stars as Kirk Gibson and Carlton Fisk would have difficulty peddling their talent to a new team and also ended up signing for less money than a high-quality player might have expected to command on the open market. Long-term contracts were now limited to a maximum duration of three years, with some teams, for instance, the Kansas City Royals, offering deals for just one season due to their unfortunate experience with players involved with illegal drugs. Owners cut corners even more by limiting active-roster sizes to 24 players, one less than the maximum allowed. That by 1986 so many teams had chosen to manage their affairs in this manner put more than a hint of collusion in the air.

The unapologetic culprit behind this policy shift was the commissioner, who ran meetings with the owners by calling them out for their financial indiscretions. At one gathering in October 1985, during which he was making a point by taking a straw poll to see who among them was going to sign free agents—all declined, under duress or desire to avoid embarrassment—he instructed the trio of major-league counselors also present, "Stop this discussion if at any point it smacks of collusion."[69] With no interruptions forthcoming, Ueberroth berated the magnates for their foolish behavior in spending lavishly on free agents, especially those who grew comfortable with a well-compensated existence on the disabled list. This latter clutch of players was raking in about $50 million at the time.

In the ensuing years, Lance Parrish, Andre Dawson, Jack Morris, and Brett Butler found the market to be a cold place to seek the same financial riches as had been bestowed on the Wayne Garlands and Bruce Kisons of the baseball world. If a free agent declined to submit to arbitration by January 8, and had not contractually committed to his old team, he was ineligible to sign until May 1, by which time virtually every team had already had its roster set for the regular season. Also complicating a player's dilemma was the fact that he could become a free agent only every five years, although teams were free to waive this stipulation.

The MLBPA filed charges of collusion against the owners in early 1986, and in September 1987, an arbitrator ruled that the owners had in fact acted in a collusive manner. Tom Roberts found that the "owners violated the provision of the Basic Agreement forbidding either clubs or players from acting in concert," the latter party included as a corrective to prevent a recurrence of the joint holdout staged by Dodgers aces Sandy Koufax and Don Drysdale in 1966.[70] Roberts allowed Gibson and six other players to become free agents a second time to test a more equitable market. Signing with the Dodgers, Gibson won 1988 MVP honors in the NL and provided a signal moment in World Series history with his dramatic pinch-hit home run to win Game 1 and fuel his team's eventual upset of the Oakland Athletics.

Owners in turn sought to ease the pain of being caught by creating an entity known as an Information Bank, into which a team's bidding price for a free agent could be placed and other clubs could request data on how much money had been offered to said player. This window dressing only masked the underlying purpose of holding contract offers down by letting an opening bid serve as a threshold not to be crossed, or exceeded only marginally. Another collusion grievance was filed by the MLBPA in February 1987, and the case in front of arbitrator George Nicolau produced the same judgment, with a ruling against the owners. In these two collusion cases, a total of 21 players were granted second-chance free agency, and a third group of another 16 players from 1988 was accorded the same privilege.

The collusion episodes were part of baseball's ugly side of the business, and it was only through the dint of a man who understood profits and losses that owners were finally able to rein in salary expenditures. Yet, these supposed savings were but a temporary salve because baseball had hoisted its own petard: A final judgment of $280 million was handed down against MLB in December 1990, by which time the ringmaster who had shamed the owners into their action was gone. Peter Ueberroth's only term as commissioner ended on March 31, 1989, while the award of more than a quarter of a billion dollars eventually ended up in the pockets of more than 650 players.[71]

***

The unbridled gains made by the players were accompanied by a parallel track: The value of the teams also escalated in like fashion, the starkest example of this being the New York Yankees of George Steinbrenner, who purchased the club in 1973, for $10 million, and had he lived would have seen it ascend to an estimated value of $4 billion by 2018. But more pertinent to the dawn of the 1990s, the wrangling between players and owners featured a lockout in 1990, and then reached a nadir when a strike beginning on August 12, 1994, forced the cancellation of the remainder of the regular season and further resulted in the loss of all postseason play.

Prior to that debacle, ways to address the growing gap between "have" and "have-not" teams—which is to say large-market franchises like the Yankees and Dodgers versus such small-market clubs as the Twins and Pirates—were being discussed. Concepts of revenue sharing had been bandied about among owners in the 1980s, and as the coffers of teams swelled—some more than others—due to the sale of broadcast rights, the pot of gold continued to grow for both sides. The televising of games, while nothing new, had been bolstered by pay-TV in the 1960s, augmented with the advent of cable television and further broadened by burgeoning satellite communications in the 1970s and 1980s, which gave rise to what came to be known as superstations.

Besides ticket and concession sales, the other major source of the money flowing to major-league clubs derived from broadcasting rights sold to media outlets, which in turn charged their corporate customers for the privilege of advertising and also billed their subscribers who watched the games from the comfort of their homes, bars, or eateries. The revenue garnered by each of the 26 teams was unequal, and when the spending habits of some clubs led to wide disparities in payrolls—also complicated by a fear of competitive imbalance—there was genuine concern about the future of the game being financially redefined strictly in Darwinian terms.

Was there was a modicum of truth about the cries of poverty by some owners, after all?

2

MONEY, MONEY, MONEY

Baseball is a corporate business, and any such enterprise exists for the purpose of making money, or at least enough of a profit to sustain its operations or otherwise satisfy its ownership. In the century since it became a professional sport, Major League Baseball (MLB) expenses and revenues grew with the times, and as technology introduced new means by which the game could be delivered to consumers, so too were new streams of income created. The embryonic days of radio broadcasting of the 1920s were soon followed by the age of television, and the sale of broadcasting rights in each case produced revenue for the clubs. Allowing the broadcast of games in either medium involved a difficult decision on the part of the owner, who was most likely to fear that the provision of live play-by-play would give fans more reason to stay home and listen on the radio or watch a game on TV rather than travel to the ballpark and pay admission.

As these fears were allayed when attendance failed to decline precipitously and both radio and television gained acceptance by all parties, new wrinkles were introduced as existing technology improved to allow the creation of radio and television networks capable of broadcasting games throughout the country. Thus, baseball contests could be delivered beyond the range of the territory belonging to the home team, possibly infringing on the regions claimed by other teams for *their* own broadcasts.

By the mid-1970s, particularly as the end of the reserve-clause era drew near in 1976, satellite communication and cable television offered increasingly extended means of proliferating the telecasts of many sports into the homes of paying subscribers, whose numbers also were on the rise as an untold number of miles of cable was strung across the country and into the homes of millions of people willing to pay for clear reception of television signals that furnished a greatly expanded variety of programming.

If the beer barons beginning in the late nineteenth century saw value through the intertwining of breweries whose products could be sold to a captive audience attending baseball games, there was also a similar connection decades later that linked the broadcasting of baseball games to pay-TV and cable subscribers. Team owners in the modern age were just as willing to avail themselves of a capitalistic opportunity as were their predecessors. The magnates' sale of rights to carry the telecasts of their games became the bedrock of their financial foundation.

While these new ventures were all well and good, prima facie, there was nonetheless an inherent factor of inequity present. Since not all major-league markets were of similar size, the revenue generated by local broadcasting and advertising would subsequently never be equal, and as the time went on, the disparity between large- and small-market clubs worsened. By 1988, for example, the New York Yankees had signed a 12-year contract with Madison Square Garden Network for $486 million, and "their local broadcast revenue was estimated to be . . . almost 20 times greater than the Montreal Expos'," and the team's coffers were stocked further by another 10-year deal with apparel manufacturer Adidas for $95 million.[1]

The various segments of revenue that collectively formed the income for any team were countered by the expenses that determined whether a club made or lost money, and the never-ending battle of the bottom line caused issues not only within the front offices of each team as they tried to control expenditures, but also among the teams themselves as they tried to compete by putting the best team on the field.

The key—and by far largest—expense was the club's payroll, and with the reserve clause serving as a shackle that kept a player bound to his team, owners had the option of making take-it-or-leave-it salary offers during contract negotiations. This unilateral ploy worked until the Major League Baseball Players Association (MLBPA) was able to put salary arbitration at the disposal of veterans with three years of service, but once the reserve clause was struck down—thereby creating an open labor market for those players who were eligible to shop their services to other teams—the rich clubs unleashed a deluge of dollars to attract top-flight talent, and the escalation of payrolls began apace. Rising player salaries, a trend that the union wanted to see perpetuated, clashed more stridently with the burgeoning revenues flowing to the club treasuries, which owners sought to maximize for *their* benefit. This tug-of-war between profits and losses manifested itself in the conundrum between exercising financial restraint in spending for salaries—and possibly risking fielding a less competitive team—and taking the decision to spend on a pricey free agent that could fill a void in the lineup heretofore preventing a team from reaching the playoffs.

The balance sheets of the industry of MLB as provided to the game's Executive Council showed a contrast to what Bowie Kuhn was promulgating in his state-of-the-game speeches to the owners. Granted some teams showed better profits than others, yet the aggregate fiscal experience of the major leagues was hardly at the precipice of a calamity.

***

Without question, any business enterprise can be sustained so long as there is a revenue stream capable of allowing that entity to make at least a marginal profit. Baseball's lifeblood of money came primarily from tickets purchased by fans and the sale of broadcasting rights to media outlets, and in the wake of the Messersmith decision, overall attendance began a steady climb that lasted through the 1980s.[2]

Despite the severe drop at the gate in 1981, due to the lengthy strike by players, the trend beginning in 1977, the first year of free agency, was unmistakable. Only a handful of minor shortfalls interrupted the continuing rise, such that during the span of years shown in figure 2.1, game attendance climbed from 31.3 million to 55.1 million, a 76 percent increase. Also to be taken into consideration, besides ticket sales, was the increase in concession sales: More fans going to games meant that more food, beverages, and souvenirs were being sold.

There was an underlying imbalance at work, however. While the composite numbers indicated a sanguine financial picture, a breakdown by individual clubs gave a different perspective. In 1977, the Los Angeles Dodgers topped the majors with attendance of 2.95 million, trailed by Philadelphia (2.7 million) and Cincinnati (2.5 million), but in the Bay Area, less than 1.2 million fans *combined* went to the Oakland Coliseum

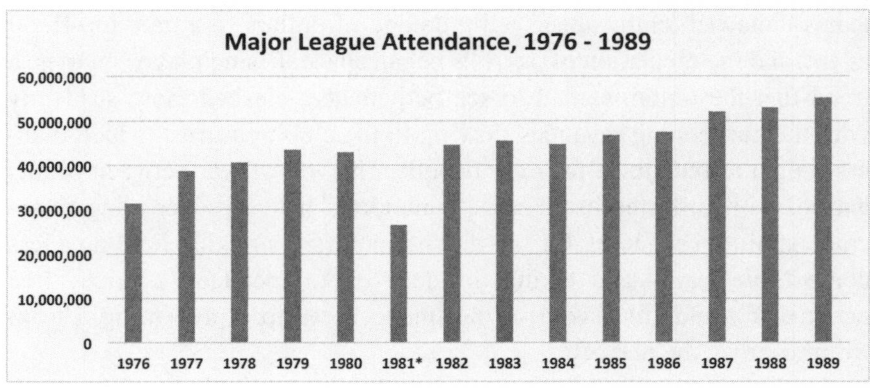

Figure 2.1. Major-league attendance, 1976–1989. (*1981 was a strike year.) Baseball-reference.com

(495,599) and Candlestick Park (700,056). There would be an ebb and flow to these figures as the fortunes of teams changed, whether through the implementation of revised business strategies by new ownership, improvements that facilitated a more productive minor-league system, or a conscious effort to spend more on free agents. But the dilemma of big-market teams versus those in smaller markets was not going to disappear in the foreseeable future, if ever, and a way to distribute more equitably the expanding stream of money coming into baseball via media contracts on levels both nationally and locally had to be found.

As the popularity of the national pastime rose, fan interest was not limited to people actually going to the ballpark. MLB's Executive Council was informed by Tom Villante, Bowie Kuhn's director of marketing and broadcasting, that "two highly important technological changes were presenting substantial new marketing opportunities for baseball: satellite delivery of television signals to distant points and proliferation of delivery means to the home TV viewer."[3] Revenue from the sale of radio broadcasts had been a staple for decades, but it paid far less than television, and a synergy developed whereby live attendance combined with TV viewing to stoke more enthusiasm for the sport, and club owners began taking notice with greater scrutiny.

The "distant points" referred to by Villante were being reached by cable television and satellite dishes installed at residences, and the creation of new networks catered to niche markets and dedicated interests.

Ever since late 1976, when future Atlanta Braves owner Ted Turner took UHF channel 17 and began to transition it into WTBS, the first television superstation, satellite signals took on increasing importance.

With the programming of WTBS beamed into living rooms throughout the country, Turner leveraged his ownership of the Braves to add his team's games to the broadcast fare and employed the catchphrase "America's Team" to describe his baseball offering, although the poor performance of the Braves in the late 1970s though 1981 provided little incentive to tune in. The media mogul later claimed that the "distant signal revenues" of WTBS amounted to $3.5 million in 1981, "whereas the Braves lost approximately the same amount of money." Yet, Kuhn was aware that this same type of revenue for 1982 was projected to fetch about $20 million for Turner.[4]

While the Braves' fortunes at that moment were of little threat to markets beyond their competition outside Atlanta—how many people really wanted to watch a lousy baseball team?—a potential, greater evil was lurking just below the surface. The introduction of superstations had "broken the monopoly that each major- and minor-league team held over its local market, flooding an area with daily broadcasts of one or more rival teams. Owners feared that cable broadcasting would undercut their home attendance."[5] The Chicago Cubs, New York Mets, and San Francisco Giants soon followed the example set by the Braves, while the Los Angeles Dodgers, Baltimore Orioles, and Boston Red Sox also explored joining this latest broadcasting trend.

By the early 1980s, the emergence of WTBS was accompanied by other similar ventures initiated by other like-minded entrepreneurs, some of these focusing exclusively on full-time news coverage (Turner's CNN), politics (C-SPAN), and sports (ESPN). The USA Network had assumed a role in the late 1970s of carrying MLB on Thursday evenings, and in the years that followed, ESPN grew from its humble roots in 1979, of carrying sports that drew little interest—Australian rules football, dirt-track auto racing, swim meets, and such seldom-watched collegiate sports as lacrosse—and became a powerhouse in the sports media industry under corporate ownership by the Walt Disney Company.

***

"It's 1985," began a futuristic memo presented at a gathering of baseball's Executive Council in late 1980.

> The telecommunications explosion is in full force, and baseball is about to harvest the seeds sown in the early 1980s. Back then . . . baseball recognized the importance of some form of revenue sharing to the financial health of baseball. Back then, baseball had the foresight to design a master plan which had the potential to generate greater revenues for all clubs by accommodating both local and national telecommunications properties.[6]

The vision of tens of millions of dollars to be raised annually was compelling: A national game—"free" and "over-the-air"—on Monday evening that would preempt all local television broadcasts was expected to reap $20 million, and a Friday night contest "reserved for [a] national pay-TV network on an exclusive basis" also would preclude all local TV and deliver $41 million per year. Far lesser amounts—between $2 million and $11.7 million—were believed to be attainable for broadcasts that would cover other nighttime telecasts during the week, Saturday afternoon and evening, in addition to 10 late-season Sunday afternoon games to take advantage of whatever pennant races were likely to be of the greatest interest.[7]

In all, the "1985 estimated rights" for regular-season action would run to $241.2 million for local television (free and subscription), national TV (free, subscription, and basic cable), and twice-weekly "games of the week." When the "jewels" of the All-Star Game and the entirety of post-season contests were included for $60.1 million, the grand total would come to a little more than $300 million per year. (In actuality, by late 1982, there was "fierce competition among three networks" for baseball's showcase events, and to keep these major outlets from losing interest, a scheme was developed to rotate the All-Star Game, the league championship series, and World Series among them. An internal memo, likely written by Villante, observed that it was "essential to keep all three Networks *interested and competing*," the better to convert that enthusiasm into hard cash for MLB's coffers.[8] Braves owner Ted Turner refused to stand idle, making what he felt was a bona fide offer as a fourth network, but he was rebuffed.)

A series of options were offered for how best to divide the regular-season pot—national and local—among the 26 teams. One was a simple, even split, which would yield $11 million per club, while another proposal would enable teams such as the Yankees, with their larger local contract, to receive a pro-rated payout.[9]

The dollars involved were noteworthy, and Bill Giles, executive vice president of the Phillies, sought to take television proliferation even further by suggesting to Bowie Kuhn, "We should create our own 'Baseball Television Network,'" thereby envisioning a forerunner to the twenty-first century's MLB Network. Putting his marketing mindset to good use in early 1981, Giles's proposal included a "Game of the Day" that would satisfy the demand he perceived across a broad spectrum of baseball's fan base: "Independent TV stations are crying for good programming," he alerted the commissioner, adding, "I do not see anything wrong with every television market having at least one baseball game a day throughout the season providing there is not a conflict with a team's home game or own telecast."[10] With such a large store of regular-season games available, the concept of so many offerings was presciently called a "warehouse in the sky," presaging the twenty-first-century Cloud by several decades.[11]

Yet, as the issue of how to distribute television money among the clubs remained problematic—and continually being discussed—Giles adjusted his thought process a bit. Again writing to Kuhn, he posed some provocative questions. "Why should a visitng [*sic*] team get a share of gate receipts and not a share of concession, parking, and scorebook sales?" which would certainly benefit the away team, but then he shifted to a more self-interested business query: "Why should a home team spend 100 percent of a marketing plan and then share the benefits of the expense with the visiting club[?]"[12] Whether intended or not, this question directly addressed the recent misfortunes of the waning days of Charlie Finley's ownership of the Oakland Athletics, at which time Finley did virtually nothing to promote his team, especially after the desertion of so many of his star players to free agency after the 1976 season. The spirit of Giles's missive was to assume that all owners would make a good-faith effort to advance the cause of their respective clubs to the ultimate betterment of all.

By the early 1980s, differences in revenues had been examined for some time. A special committee of owners, led by Milwaukee's Bud Selig, studied the problem and, in February 1982, noted a gap of $6.3 million in average revenues between the eight most profitable teams and the eight least profitable clubs for the 1978 season, and not surprisingly, for 1979, the least profitable teams were those whose expenses were highest. And confirming the unavoidable aspect of physical market size,

Selig said, "It was probable that the Clubs in the large metropolitan areas would enjoy a more substantial rate of increase in their local broadcast revenues than would clubs in cities such as Milwaukee, and that *the disparity in revenues from this source would in the future grow even larger*."[13] The implication was obvious: The Yankees, Dodgers, and their ilk would forever be advantaged over the Brewers, Twins, and their less-fortunate brethren unless the revenue pie could be more evenly shared.

At the same time, however, the Executive Council was wary of "enormous sums of money" flowing to teams as the result of long-term contracts for the sale of local broadcast rights, in addition to "increasing ownership interests in clubs by broadcast entities," with Ted Turner being a prime example. These types of dealings portended baseball's subservience to media priorities, possibly leading to an "undesirable transferral [*sic*] of control over baseball clubs to interests motivated primarily by broadcast, rather than baseball, considerations."[14] In his own defense, Turner testified before a U.S. Senate subcommittee that current satellite communication allowed for provision of an "information alternative to the cable subscriber far superior to conventional news media," and he argued that government regulation of this expanding medium would result in the "loss of audience and the advertising revenues derived therefrom." Interference in the form of federal regulation "would destroy the Superstation and the dependant [*sic*] Cable News Networks," Turner observed, while further proving his point by noting that the recent broadcast of Braves games, which included their record-setting, season-opening 13-game winning streak in 1982, was exactly the type of sports programming to which fans should have access.[15]

Also in early 1982, several recommendations for more equitable revenue sharing were suggested. This included an increase in the percentage of gate receipts given to National League (NL) teams to put this in line with the practice in the American League (AL), which used a 25 percent share; a fee of four or five cents per subscriber for each game broadcast on cable television; and "over-the-air broadcast revenues from local television . . . grandfathered at current levels and incremental revenues thereafter . . . *shared on some equitable basis*."[16]

This nebulous "equitable basis" across all revenue streams was eventually decided, but years would pass before the development and implementation of what came to be known as a "luxury tax" was imposed on clubs that spend greatly, especially on their payroll. In the same meeting where Selig was briefing the owners, Kuhn floated a novel idea of having the "Player Relations Committee . . . arrange for . . . a cadre of negotiators to be available to the clubs for the purpose of assisting them in the negotiation of player contracts," done with the intention of trying to hold down the cost of contracts given to players with less than five years of service time. In conjunction with this effort was a proposal that "long-term guaranteed contracts be required to make provision for current funding, perhaps limited to that portion of such contracts extending beyond the third year."[17] This was a ploy to curb player payroll costs by forcing the issue of having money reserved immediately to make good on lengthy contracts rather than by relying on future earnings to cover such commitments. Even wealthier teams might be reluctant to commit to expensive deals knowing that they had to have most of that money available up front.

***

In the course of the owners wrangling over revenue sharing, the MLBPA took an increasingly closer look at the finances at stake and formulated an interesting interpretation of how their playing should be legally considered. The union attempted to make a compelling case that involved a copyright of the players' performance on the field, and the MLBPA was claiming in early 1982 that they "owned all rights to MLB games, including the right to license telecasts of them."[18] If the union could legally validate this claimed ownership, then the players stood to reap a huge windfall from the various media contracts then in effect, as well as those in the future.

The ramifications of a possible judgment in favor of the players forced the Player Relations Committee (PRC) to devote the highest level of attention to the matter, and it hired Bowie Kuhn's old law firm to investigate. In the summation of a confidential report to Ray Grebey and the PRC, Willkie Farr & Gallagher acknowledged the existence of a "line of amorphous and evolving authority explicitly recognizing performers' rights" but ultimately found that,

> Central to the clubs' position are the undisputed facts that they have expended substantial time, effort, and money in developing and producing their business, and that the players are their employees. The clubs take the full economic risk of success or failure. . . . Each game—and any reproduction of it—is the product of the clubs' efforts

> and the performance by their employees within the scope of their employment. It is the resultant product which has commercial value. That product—the baseball games—should be recognized as belonging to the Clubs.[19]

This case would play out during a span of several years, the union maintaining that the owners "could not contract with broadcasters to televise games without first acquiring express authorization from the players performing in them."[20] When Judge Jesse Eschbach issued his ruling in October 1986, he cited that the players' "performances" were executed in accordance with their employment; therefore, the owners and their teams were entitled to the copyright of the broadcasts, as was argued in the report of Willkie Farr & Gallagher.

Had the MLBPA been victorious rather than the owners, it can only be left to speculation as to how big a portion of the hundreds of millions of dollars in media contracts would then have found its way to players already averaging salaries in excess of $430,000.[21]

***

The formation of a Revenue Sharing Committee in the fall of 1980 was done with the aim of ensuring that the equitable distribution of funds would ensure that MLB would remain economically viable for the 26 clubs, possibly allowing for the expansion of one or both leagues. While the mission of revenue sharing also was to "maintain competitive balance without destroying individual incentive for imaginative, dedicated, and hard-working organizations," the committee members admitted that by the spring of 1982—and seven meetings later—they had reached no conclusion on how best to implement a sharing program and expressed the fear that following its present course would only visit economic ruin on the game.[22]

The committee stated many of the points made earlier in this chapter regarding the division of funds deriving from radio and television, and it recognized that "meaningful pennant race[s]" were "necessary for fan interest."[23] After repeating the obvious detriment of escalating player salaries, which hampered all teams, the members then enumerated the reasons why opponents of revenue sharing believed it to be unattractive. The antisharing camp decried the practice as "creeping socialism" and a "subsidy [given] to poorly run clubs," arguing that revenue sharing "eliminates the incentive to win or promote" and claiming that franchise operation was more expensive in larger markets and therefore required those teams to retain more income.[24]

The detractors did make some good points, but the best example outside of baseball serving as a guiding light for the national pastime to follow was the National Football League, whose team "owners freely admit that many football clubs could not compete except for revenue sharing," and neither did they harbor any concerns about "socialistic" aspects of the practice.[25] Baseball's Revenue Sharing Committee concluded that a solution would be difficult to forge: "As much as each of us would like to have total control over our individual operations, there must be a certain amount of interdependence among clubs. And no issue goes more to the essence of that interdependence and partnership than revenue sharing."[26]

Data available following the 1982 season highlighted the disparity of broadcasting revenues received by the 26 teams. That year was the first time each club took in at least $1 million in such monies, and although the vast majority of clubs made less than $3 million, five teams earned at least $4 million: the Expos ($8.1 million), Phillies ($6.5 million), Yankees ($6.5 million), Mets ($4.25 million), and Blue Jays ($4 million).[27] Montreal showed an increase of nearly sixfold from 1980, the Mets' amount rose by almost triple from the previous year, and the Yankees more than doubled their take in 1980. These surges certainly benefited the recipients, but the slower-paced growth—or stagnation—for the preponderance of clubs punctuated the friction concerning revenue sharing between the haves and the have-nots.

Accompanying baseball's financial angst was the announcement of a new venture proposed to begin operating in 1983. The United States Football League (USFL) launched that year, its schedule and season opening to coincide with baseball's spring training and lasting until early summer. The creation of a new league in a rival sport drew the notice of baseball's highest office, an assistant to Bowie Kuhn informing the commissioner that the USFL was "quite certain it can obtain extensive cable coverage and probably also land a national network contract."[28] This gridiron enterprise could only have caused angst among baseball owners because any new and unwelcome competition would siphon away fans from baseball stadiums and cause media outlets to recalculate their near-future expenditures, some of which would now be diverted to the purchase of rights to broadcast USFL games.

Thankfully for baseball, the nascent football league experienced growing pains common to fledgling operations, and the USFL folded after but three seasons. But the trial, if anything, proved that as the general health of the U.S. economy improved in the early 1980s, such progress served as inspiration to entrepreneurs who dared to think big and were willing to fund an undertaking with the broad scope inherent in a major sports league; however, one going concern not sharing in the emerging prosperity was the National Broadcasting Company.

In late January 1983, the *Philadelphia Inquirer* reported, "The NBC television network looks like a capsizing ship with a jolly captain, a retreating army with a smiling general, a losing football team with a coach who says he is building character."[29] Mired a distant third behind CBS and ABC in prime-time and daytime ratings, NBC and its executives drew criticism for a perceived lack of concern in the face of financial crisis. Yet, the network nevertheless positioned itself to hold fast as a mainstay of baseball telecasting through the remainder of the decade.

CBS ultimately was not a party to baseball's new broadcasting contract, but by February, NBC—financial woes notwithstanding—committed to split the "jewels" with ABC for rights to the All-Star Game, league championship series, and World Series at a cost of over $1 billion. Not completely shut out of the proceedings, the radio branch of CBS paid $3.7 million for rights to the jewels in 1983 and later agreed to a five-year contract at $32 million to run through 1989.[30]

An interesting discussion occurred the same week as the story was reported from Philadelphia, when the Executive Council met and broached the subject of interleague play, which Bowie Kuhn credited Bill Giles of the Phillies for having advanced this idea. Another major media entity, Home Box Office, created by Time, Inc., in the early 1970s to show movies on cable TV and having matured into a "monopolistic position" for that segment of the entertainment market, was enthusiastic to embrace a new variety of baseball scheduling that would "serve to distinguish their programming." Baseball executives found the potential partnering with HBO to be "most sensible to use pay television as the vehicle for the first exposure of interleague play in order to build the pay concept for the future."[31] Interleague play did not come to fruition until the 1990s, but by that time MLB had intended to have its own "pay-cable television network" operational for the distribution of games to "already existing cable systems."[32]

As spring training camps assumed their place in the spotlight in 1983, the bounty of the various media contracts enjoyed by MLB may have served to keep Kuhn in office. A cadre of owners, the group being just large enough to prevent the commissioner from retaining his position, had sealed his fate the previous November. Yet, Kuhn stood to remain on the job until early August 1983. Ted Turner was a member of the anti-Kuhn contingent, but with the latest 1984–1989 contract "mak[ing] every team healthy again financially [by] adding $6 million per team per year," he believed that the "deal might warrant reconsideration."[33]

Turner's forgiving mood was short-lived, however. A few weeks later as the details of the new contract were being finalized, the Braves owner railed that "we've been taken to the cleaners," and he was prepared to offer $1.2 billion for the same package just brokered with NBC and ABC.[34] The caveat, of course, was that WTBS—or a subsidiary of it—would be the carrier, but there was substance to Turner's boast: Citibank and Manufacturer's Hanover confirmed that his credit was good, so with two pillars of the financial industry lending credence, Turner indeed had the means to support his claim.

Notwithstanding the brinksmanship by Turner, the owners collectively agreed to the $1.125 billion pact on April 22, 1983.[35] With this large issue laid to rest, the focus later shifted to what Philadelphia's Bill Giles dubbed "MLS—Major League Sports," a proposed venture he had discussed with the New York Times Cable Company in May 1984. Firm in his belief that a "quality sports channel will be eagerly accepted by cable operators and the public," Giles was of the opinion that "sports and news would go good together and maybe save cable operators from carrying CCN [*sic*]." Aside from this swipe at Ted Turner, who Giles also claimed was "making enemies among cable operators," the Phillies executive opined that the introduction of another version of ESPN ("ESPN II") would be "very welcomed."[36]

Giles's envisioned MLS would debut in April 1986, and carry more than 90 regular-season baseball games, as well as an undetermined number of contests from the National Basketball Association, the National Hockey League, and the United States Football League. This olio would be seasonally augmented with collegiate football and basketball offerings, as well as boxing, and filled out with programming dedicated to sports news and a late-night show patterned after ABC's *Nightline*. Giles estimated that the financial benefit would be as high as $960 million, based on 30 million subscribers and a corresponding amount of advertising revenue.

It is important to remember that relative to the time—the mid-1980s—satellite technology was maturing as a viable means of communication, while also undergoing changes and improvements. That two top baseball executives, Ted Turner and Bill Giles, were in the vanguard of contributors who helped deliver more sports programming to American homes was emblematic of the direction in which baseball and sports in general were heading. When communications innovator Bill Rasmussen used a $10 million grant from Getty Oil in 1979 to found the Entertainment and Sports Programming Network (ESPN), by January 1989, ESPN had joined the ranks of baseball's TV heavyweights when it outbid several competitors—Turner among them—for the right to telecast single games on Sunday and Wednesday evenings, and doubleheaders on Tuesday and Friday evenings. This four-year package, to begin in 1990, would add another $400 million to the major-league treasury and served as a companion deal to the one brokered by CBS—finally successful in attaining rights other than for radio—for $1.1 billion.

***

The issue of revenue sharing persisted through the end of the 1980s with no discernable solution arising. Columnist Peter Gammons said of the dilemma in 1985, "One place they can start is figuring out how to balance the revenue from parking, ballpark restaurants, and luxury suites. The top eight clubs in baseball make a combined $10,774,882 from those three items. The bottom eight total $660,074. That, friends, is economic disparity."[37] Shortly thereafter he asked a rhetorical question: "Revenue sharing? Don't hold your breath waiting for clubs to start dividing up the difference between the $80 million of TV revenue requested by the players and the $32.7 million the athletes will receive. One owner, who could benefit by revenue sharing [stated], 'Talk about the potential for fratricide!'"[38] It appeared that the degree to which owners were willing to share and share alike was inversely proportional to amount of money they were taking in, and the wealthier among the magnates preferred to maintain the status quo.

Although *Sporting News* noted that some progress had been made by the end of that season by way of prorated payments to the players' pension fund "based on attendance and TV market size," there still existed in

1989 such yawning gaps as those between the Yankees and Twins for radio and TV revenue, $50 million and $4 million, respectively.[39] During an interview in February 1990, commissioner Fay Vincent was asked about the possibility of a proposal to use revenue sharing as part of the package to be offered to the players in the current round of bargaining for a new Basic Agreement, but, doing an imitation of Bowie Kuhn, he declined to comment so as not to "become a part of the negotiations."[40]

At the close of the 1980s, much in-fighting remained between the big-market teams and those in small markets with regard to how revenue was to be divided—if at all. Yet, there was a shift in the cries of financial angst. In the not-too-distant past, the tone of Bowie Kuhn's state-of-the-game address had been infused with economic gloom—for instance, his remarks before a Congressional House Judiciary Committee's Subcommittee on Monopolies and Commercial Law, in which the commissioner claimed, "The 18 clubs that lost money in 1980 lost considerable sums: a combined total of approximately $41 million."[41] But as the decade proceeded, the division between the rich and less well-off clubs became more pronounced and led to a plea for the equitable distribution of media funds. "The current system (of escalation of players' salaries and lack of revenue sharing) is a prescription for disaster," said the deputy commissioner, Steve Greenberg, and a term abhorrent to players and their union—salary cap—was also being floated as a mechanism to control labor costs.[42]

Was this hand-wringing in vain? Yes, it was, not only from the standpoint of how baseball's fiscal picture developed in the ensuing decades—stretching well into the twenty-first century—but also at the time of an in-depth study published by *Sporting News* in late 1990. "For the time being, it's impossible for the owners to plead poverty, try as they may," was the verdict.[43] It would take until 1996 before definitive steps were enacted to impose a competitive balance—or "luxury"—tax. Yet, even future variations of this concept failed to stem the tide of salaries bestowed on the best free agents.

***

There is no small degree of difficulty in accurately assessing the economic state of the game or any major-league team. Addressing the enduring paucity of fiscal baseball data despite the wide assortment of revelations ranging from the Pentagon Papers to Watergate's "Deep Throat" to Wikileaks, University of Wisconsin-La Crosse professors Kenneth Winter and Michael J. Haupert wrote in 2011, "Until recently, the primary financial information of contemporary Major League Baseball (MLB) teams seemed the only secret left intact."[44] A research topic of Winter and Haupert was necessarily focused on only three years of data (2007–2009) of six clubs, the only information they were able to acquire for their project. And for the purposes of the narrative in the pages of this book, the task is no less difficult.

The reluctance of club owners to share data was manifest in their lack of enthusiasm to reveal it even for internal use within baseball's executive hierarchy. In February 1980, Bowie Kuhn directed that queries be sent to the 26 major-league teams, but during a March meeting of the Executive Council, he "noted that returns of the completed financial questionnaires . . . had been slow coming in. . . . The council concurred in the importance of this undertaking."[45] With 20 pages of data to be entered for an assortment of schedules, the completion of a survey was an arduous process to say the least.[46]

Six months later, barely half of the teams had complied with the request, leading to fears that "even on the basis of such partial returns, it

Table 2.1. Financial Information Questionnaire, 1980

Schedule	*Category*
A	Balance Sheet
B	Statement of Changes in Financial Position
I	Summary of Operations and Changes in Owners' Equity
II	Operating Revenues
III	Spring Training Expenses
IV	Major-League Team Operating Expenses
V	League Championship Series and World Series Expenses
VI	Player Development Expenses
VII	Stadium Operations Expenses
VIII	Ticket Department and Publicity and Promotion Expenses
IX	General and Administrative Expenses
X	Certain Statistical Information

Source: Papers of Bowie K. Kuhn, National Baseball Hall of Fame Library, National Baseball Hall of Fame, Cooperstown, New York.

was quite apparent that serious difficulties confronted the industry. . . . Only one of the 14 responding clubs was budgeting a surplus in future years, and . . . the remaining Clubs were all projecting red figures of varying sizes."[47]

The Executive Council's minutes of their September meeting include a most compelling passage from the discussion of baseball's financial issues:

> [Kuhn] then discussed with the council discussions which he had been conducting with Mr. Robert Walker of the Los Angeles firm of Paul, Hastings & Janofsky regarding the feasibility of various initiatives which might be undertaken to improve the situation and described the advice which had been rendered by Mr. Walker with regard to these proposals. At the conclusion of his explanation, the commissioner emphasized that *certain of the suggested initiatives obviously presented an unacceptable level of legal risk, and expressed the view that neither he as commissioner nor baseball as an industry should embark on any program either overtly or surreptitiously which involved such risk.* It was his conclusion, therefore, that efforts in this area should be limited to the area of persuasion and "jawboning" as to which there appeared to be no substantial risk of adverse legal consequence.[48]

It is telling that while Kuhn's old law firm, Willkie Farr & Gallagher, continued to handle various affairs for MLB, here an outside office was retained for counsel regarding proposed activity that possibly might place the game in legal jeopardy. Much can be read between the lines of the aforementioned wording, but this reading could very well have been the planting of seeds that a few years hence became the collusion among owners to withhold bidding on free agents. The omission of wording that would further explain what constituted these "initiatives" and "proposals," to say nothing of the "unacceptable level of legal risk" involved, presents itself as damning circumstantial evidence and easily leads to the conclusion that something nefarious was at play. Only when Peter Ueberroth became commissioner a few years hence and inculcated the magnates with his business philosophy did collusion begin to blossom.

While collusion was being hinted at, baseball's hierarchy adopted a policy to determine club solvency, highlighted by the desire for each team to maintain a minimum 60/40 ratio of assets to liabilities as proof of its viability. Yet, even this approach was viewed as flawed by Yankees owner George Steinbrenner, who observed,

> The 60/40 split . . . concerning capitalization of the various teams would not fly because there are too many ways that capitalization and net worth of a corporation can be bandied about and made to come up about any way you would care to have it come up. Corporate ownerships present a real threat in this area because they have the wherewithal to put money in and take it out at will.[49]

Imperfect as this arrangement may have been, the 60/40 standard remained in effect for years beyond Steinbrenner's warning. Continuing to fret about all manner of unchecked expenses, baseball's Finance Committee, in the summer of 1982, not only insisted that 60/40 be adhered to, but also implemented a recommendation provided by the accounting firm of Ernst & Whinney. Teams were instructed to use a baseline of $20 million as the minimum amount that any club should post to their questionnaire for the value of all noncurrent baseball assets. The accountants explained,

> This establishes a nearly uniform value for the baseball assets of each club, eliminating the differences caused by stadium ownership or lease and the differences in franchise and player contract values between Clubs which have been recently acquired and those which have been held for some time.[50]

When this bit of sleight of hand was retroactively applied to data from 1980, indeed, five teams previously failing the 60/40 test could now be deemed out of danger, with five others coming within five points of also passing.[51] Conversely, of the six clubs whose ratios were adversely impacted by the revision, only one fell below the acceptable ratio, while five remained above 60/40. It is inconclusive whether use of this trick continued in future computations, but if nothing else, it proved Steinbrenner's point—in a different application—about what can happen when numbers are "bandied about."

In 1983, with Kuhn once more spearheading a query for financial information that was to include forecasts of assets-to-liabilities for 1983 through 1985, Ernst & Whinney was charged with compiling the responses. The gravity of the situation prompted Kuhn to issue a warning for the "imposition of sanctions for failure to submit financial data in a timely fashion," and he implored "all clubs [to] act as necessary to see that the requirements of the disclosure resolution are met."[52] As Kuhn was about to hand over the keys to his office to Peter Ueberroth late in the summer of 1984, 10 teams were below 60/40, and 6 more at 64/36 were deemed to be at risk. Yet, at almost this same time Ernst & Whinney completed its survey of 1983 data.

In its report to the commissioner, the firm's cover letter—as if to validate George Steinbrenner, again—provided the following caveats:

> Although certain reclassifications and combinations have been made to various expense categories as submitted by the individual clubs, other inconsistencies in account classifications may still exist. Accordingly, the reader or user of the accompanying financial summaries should consider these matters in interpreting the data shown herein. We have not audited or reviewed the accompanying summaries, related schedules. or data, other than the income and expenses of the Major Leagues Central Fund [the repository for money received mostly from broadcast contracts], and, accordingly, we are unable to and do not express an opinion or any other form of assurance on them.[53]

The annual balance sheets for this period may not provide the last word on the financial state of the game, but they show how much MLB was reaping and how much it was paying out.

***

The finances of MLB beginning in the mid-1970s present a definitive upward trend in expenses and income. Distilled to its essence—and from the owners' perspective—as long as their revenue could outpace their largest expenditure—namely, player salaries—then they were likely to be content in shouldering this burden as part of the exigencies of doing business. Obviously, maximizing profits was the key to the magnates' happiness, but the players, especially once unmoored from the reserve clause, watched with alacrity as their salaries ascended to unparalleled heights. Information culled from several years' worth of statements given to baseball's Finance Committee, most of them labeled "Consolidated Condensed Income Statement," contain unaudited data presented here as examples of the overall profit and loss status of MLB.

Three primary components were listed: operating revenues, other income, and operating expenses. Revenues included receipts from radio and television broadcast rights, ticket sales, and income from investments and interest earned. The expenses were comprised of those for spring training, player development, team replacement (bonuses for high school and college player draftees, plus scouting costs), stadium operations, ticket department and promotion, general and administrative expenditures, and costs related to the commissioner's office and PRC, but the overarching number was blithely labeled "Team," even though this segment was the highest expense.[54] For example, "Team" indicates the following categories and amounts for all clubs in 1983 (see table 2.2).[55]

Of the previously mentioned items, the salaries of the players far outstripped any other expense. Paired against revenue, also on the rise since the mid-1970s, the breaking point appeared to occur during 1979 and 1980, more likely the latter year, although no data other than estimates was available to substantiate this until actual figures became available again in 1981.[56]

Table 2.2. Team Expenses for All Clubs in 1983

Player salaries	$214,644,631
Salaries of managers, coaches, trainers, clubhouse staff, and others	$11,778,893
Workmen's compensation and payroll taxes	$1,437,200
Players' Benefit Trust	$15,500,000
Hotels and meals	$6,732,286
Transportation and road trip expenses	$14,452,628
Uniforms and playing equipment	$1,225,146
Clubhouse expenses	$870,307
Bats	$327,599
Baseballs	$1,232,867
Medical expenses (team physician, supplies, hospital costs, etc.)	$1,133,465
Players' moving allowances and expenses	$465,336
Insurance (life, accident, team travel, disaster, etc.)	$5,475,882
Other	$2,019,504
TOTAL	$277,295,744

Source: Papers of Bowie K. Kuhn, National Baseball Hall of Fame Library, National Baseball Hall of Fame, Cooperstown, New York.

Table 2.3. **Combined Summary of Operations, 1975–1983**

	11975	1976	1977	1978	1979*	1980*	1981	1982	1983
Operating Revenue	162,589,094	182,035,149	233,285,111	265,308,026	302,242,000	339,000,000	279,148,414	442,642,488	521,656,909
Operating Expenses	166,312,851	186,704,462	236,155,850	265,303,440	302,416,000	352,000,000	384,533,669	534,737,436	588,260,780
Income (Loss)	–3,723,757	–4,669,313	–2,870,739	3,586	–174,000	–13,000,000	–105,385,255	–92,094,948	66,603,871
Strike Insurance Proceeds	N/A	N/A	N/A	N/A	N/A	N/A	46,800,000	N/A	N/A
Other Income**	–1,264,736	–384,298	–1,819,396	–1,439,509	109,000	N/A	–1,968,977	–12,172,831	–16,235,741
Loss before Income Taxes	–4,988,493	–5,053,611	–4,690,135	–1,434,923	–65,000	N/A	–60,554,232	–104,267,779	–82,839,612

*Estimate

**Includes losses from interest expense

Source: Papers of Bowie K. Kuhn, National Baseball Hall of Fame Library, National Baseball Hall of Fame, Cooperstown, New York.

Annual losses from 1975 through 1979 were approximately $5 million or less, and 1979 was basically a break-even year, with a loss of a mere $65,000. Considering the broad scope of MLB's enterprise, these negative balances appear to be acceptable; however, after a spike in operating expenses in 1977, due in large part to the signings of the first free-agent class, there was a tremendous increase—even if the estimates are treated as valid—between 1978 and 1981, where both years are supported by real data. The jump in operating expenses from more than $265 million (1978) to more than $384 million (1981) represents a nearly 45 percent increase, with greater inflation in the immediate years ahead. The "Team" costs as a percent of operating expenses also rose in accordance with salary increases.[57]

The operating expenses for 1981 are even more compelling when taking into account the fact that this was the year when almost two months of the season were lost due to the in-season strike, a time when virtually no major-league salaries were paid.

Nevertheless, the escalation of player salaries through free agent contracts and arbitration awards had a direct impact on the "Team" costs shown here. Thus, by late 1980, Bowie Kuhn, aware that Ernst & Whinney had documented ballooning losses soon to approach tens of millions of dollars, began sounding the alarm. "I have access to the financial

Table 2.4. Rising Team Costs

	Expense (in $)	*Percent of Team Costs*
1975	52,317,866	31.5
1976	60,563,162	32.4
1977	82,743,446	35.0
1978	97,705,914	36.8
1979*	118,692,000	39.3
1980*	147,000,000	41.7
1981	157,665,669	41.0
1982	241,014,082	45.1
1983	277,295,744	47.1

*Estimate

Source: Papers of Bowie K. Kuhn, National Baseball Hall of Fame Library, National Baseball Hall of Fame, Cooperstown, New York.

figures of the clubs, which I am not at liberty to discuss," the commissioner intoned, "but they are not good."[58]

With Nolan Ryan having already become the first player to garner a $1 million-per-year contract when he signed with the Astros following the 1979 season, baseball's fiscal condition was appropriately summarized by *Sporting News*:

> Players who opted for free agency weren't the only ones cashing in handsomely. Most clubs, though not all, were yielding to contract demands that a few years earlier would have been considered outlandish. It was now a case of offering star players long-term, multimillion-dollar pacts or seeing them become free agents.[59]

Indeed, some teams adjusted their business strategy by proactively conceding high salaries in the form of contract extensions to retain their better players rather than lose them as free agents, perhaps for an even higher salary that another team might be willing to pay.

It was exactly this mindset on the part of team moguls that spawned a spending frenzy and gave birth to the deficits described in the tables in this chapter. One unapologetic outfielder, Dusty Baker, bluntly stated, "I don't think any of us [players] is worth the money we're getting, but the owners have created this situation, and we'd be fools not to take advantage of it."[60]

There were instances in which some owners did not complain about baseball inflation and took advantage of the economic climate pervading the sport. A curious tide was at work: one that lifted the boats of players—in the form of growing salaries—and magnates, who now profited increasingly when putting their club up for sale. As attendance climbed in the aftermath of the Messersmith decision and the size of media contracts swelled in tandem, further accompanied by increasing values of the teams employing the players to whom ever-larger salaries were being paid, it can be argued that baseball finances *were* out of control. Yet, the paradox was evident as fans continued to stream through the turnstiles at the same time that club values and player salaries soared: No franchises filed for bankruptcy, nor did any go out of business or otherwise cease to exist. As revenue was ultimately redistributed to those less-fortunate teams in the mid-1990s, the perils of doing business in smaller markets was assuaged to benefit not only the recipient clubs but also the game as a whole.

***

When the New York Mets were founded with an investment of $1.8 million at the beginning of the 1960s, the well-heeled Payson family—sporting aficionado Joan Whitney Payson, in particular—who fronted the money to bring NL baseball back to New York, executed this transaction for the love of the game rather than with the expectation of a huge return on their investment. Barely two decades later, the franchise was sold for $21.1 million, an elevenfold increase.

Not that the heirs and successors to Mrs. Payson would have been destitute had the price of the sale been less, but with 26 major-league teams feeding at the trough of efflorescent media revenue and increased popularity manifest in tickets sold to an adoring public, there is no doubt that wealth was a sustainable aspect of the sport. In 1981, *Sporting News* opined with regard to the recent sale of a handful of teams, "Although some owners were crying the financial blues, the prices fetched by the five clubs that were sold hardly supported claims that baseball was in trouble."[61]

This was not to say that the playing field would always be level. Competitive balance was of genuine concern because rich teams like the Yankees were capable of using their financial power to entice the best free agents to play in the Bronx, but the empirical evidence shows that lavish expenditures did not necessarily translate to pennants. To be sure, New York was dominant in the AL from 1977 through 1981, and remained in contention in 1985 and 1986, but their large-market counterparts in Anaheim, under the aegis of the free-spending Gene Autry, could do no better than a trio of AL West titles (1979, 1982, and 1986) despite heavily investing in free agents.

Small-market teams in the Junior Circuit more than held their own throughout the 1980s, as demonstrated by Kansas City (three division titles, an AL pennant, and a World Series title, plus three other years of bona fide contention), Baltimore (still a force in the early 1980s and winner of the 1983 World Series), Detroit (who dominated in 1984, won another division title, and also was in the race two other years), Minnesota (contenders in 1984, and then surprise World Series champions in 1987), Oakland (an emerging dynasty in the late 1980s), and Toronto (like Oakland, also poised to enter the 1990s as an AL power).

In the NL, the Dodgers were the premier large-market club. Yet, rather than dolling out for expensive free agents, Los Angeles depended mainly on a farm system that continued to stock its roster with talent. In New York, the Mets emerged as contenders in 1984, and remained consistently so through the end of the decade, while St. Louis (one World Series and two other NL pennants) enjoyed success in the mid-1980s. A hodgepodge of teams from throughout the rest of the Senior Circuit (Atlanta, Montreal, Cincinnati, San Francisco, and Philadelphia) kept prognosticators guessing about pennant winners at various times, but the broader point is that while some teams tried to buy their way to a pennant, no club in either league was successful in this endeavor. The reliance on a productive minor-league system and player acquisition through heady trading proved more profitable than recklessly expending on free agents.

When ultimately implemented, revenue sharing provided baseball with greater economic stability and eased the way for continuing viability that was further instrumental to expansion efforts, which had been discussed at the 1983 winter meetings and finally came to fruition in the 1990s. This was the age before "Moneyball" captured the fancy of front offices and begat the current version of baseball's business model. As if money had not already been rooted in baseball, the degree to which it had by the end of the 1980s showed that the national pastime was on a continuum of unparalleled riches for players and club owners.

3

A TALE OF THREE COMMISSIONERS

The organization chart of most businesses reflects a structure in which the highest-ranking officer occupies the top position, clearly indicative of the responsibility entrusted to that person in the overall functioning of the enterprise, as well as the power wielded by him or her. In general terms, the chief executive needs to exert control over the operation—hopefully in a legal and tactful manner—to ensure its viability and stability while at once serving the best interests of all parties.

An argument can be advanced that *anyone* named as a successor to the inept William Eckert, the fourth commissioner of baseball, would have been an improvement. As interest in professional football grew throughout the 1960s, a development that threatened baseball's status as America's favorite sport, Eckert was ill-equipped to face the mounting challenge emanating from the gridiron. Thankfully for him, he at least had Lee MacPhail and Joseph Reichler as top-flight assistants to guide him through the baseball business that had to be conducted, but the propping-up of such a weak character could last only so long, and by December 1968, the club owners ousted the former U.S. Air Force general from the commissioner's office.

Named as Eckert's interim replacement, Bowie Kuhn brought a knowing demeanor to his new position. Working as an attorney for the National League (NL) for more than a decade, Kuhn was intimately familiar with the inner workings of the game, to say nothing of being a genuine fan. Whether they realized it or not at the time, when the owners, in early 1969, chose Kuhn to be commissioner, little did they know that they were handing the reins to a man who would soon lead baseball into what would become a 15-year period of burgeoning prosperity. As demonstrated in the previous chapters of this book, there undoubtedly were growing pains associated with this progress, but such was the price to be paid for the achievements garnered by players and owners, and the swelling number of fans who visited stadiums throughout the country through the 1980s were proof that baseball had succeeded in thwarting any threat posed to its popularity.

For his part in this prosperity, Kuhn received his just rewards, and a perusal of the paper trail he left in the trove of his documents available in Cooperstown speaks highly to the diligence he brought to his commissionership as the national pastime crossed from the stodginess of the old 10-team leagues into a new modern era of the 1970s and beyond. Kuhn, however, also received his just desserts.

The baseball commissioner does not answer to the millions of fans who follow the game, nor does he report to the hundreds of players who comprise the major-league rosters. Rather, he serves at the pleasure of men—as well as the occasional woman—who hold the key to his fate as to whether he will serve as the commissioner. When Bowie Kuhn came to office, 24—and then, beginning in 1977, 26—team owners sat in judgment of him, for these were the individuals who determined the occupant of baseball's highest-ranking office. The election of the commissioner required a minimum three-quarters majority in each league, and of these 26 club owners—14 in the American League and 12 in the National League—four nays among magnates in either league spelled doom for the commissioner's tenure. Thus, the power possessed by the commissioner was not held in an absolute sense, and the days of Judge Kenesaw Mountain Landis and his virtually unchallenged brand of autocracy would never be seen again. An inability to please all of the owners all of the time was an inherent pitfall for any commissioner, so keeping the number of dissidents to a minimum was the lynchpin to job retention.

As fair-minded as Bowie Kuhn tried to be, he curried little favor with owners who questioned his judgment on certain issues or were on the wrong side of rulings Kuhn was forced to make at various times. George Steinbrenner was suspended due to his corporate campaign contributions to Richard Nixon, and the commissioner also incurred the wrath of Ted Turner concerning the issue of superstations. Charlie Finley was riled when Kuhn invalidated Finley's June 1976 sale of Joe Rudi and Rollie

Fingers to the Boston Red Sox, as well as another cash transaction to ship Vida Blue to the New York Yankees, thereby creating an irrevocable breach between the Athletics owner and the commissioner. Kuhn fined Padres owner Ray Kroc in 1979, for openly stating that he would pursue free agents Graig Nettles and Joe Morgan; the sticking point was that both players were still under contract with other teams at the time Kroc made his comment, which was viewed as tampering by the commissioner. The Orioles' Jerrold Hoffberger was cited for allowing the governor of Maryland to throw out the first pitch at a World Series game without Kuhn's consent, a violation of baseball's desired separation of sport and politics for such events.

But the final turning point for Kuhn's tenure proved to be the players' strike of 1981, when his perceived inaction was interpreted as detrimental to a swift resolution of the dispute. Handcuffed to a great extent because the commissioner "[doesn't] make labor policy or labor decisions," Kuhn was the target of a cabal of owners at that year's winter meetings held in Hollywood, Florida.[1] The grousing over Kuhn had been in motion for some time, and Jerome Holtzman of the *Chicago Tribune*, who shed no tears over the commissioner's fate, opined that Kuhn could retain his job if he was willing to become a "ceremonial commissioner . . . whose principal functions would be limited to Opening Day appearances, and as a watchdog for the so-called 'integrity of the game.'"[2] In other words, the owners were willing to retain Kuhn as long as he applied himself as a baseball-smart figurehead who stayed out of their way and, in essence, maintained a low profile in the manner of Eckert.

The plotters against him affixed their signatures to a letter stating "their intent not to vote for the renewal of Commissioner Kuhn's employment contract," and the number of signatories confirmed that Kuhn would be stymied in any bid to retain his job.[3] Four American League (AL) club owners—George Argyros (Seattle), Eddie Chiles (Texas), George Steinbrenner (New York), and Edward Bennett Williams (Baltimore)—who favored the deposing of Kuhn comprised a bloc that in itself would have been adequate to the purpose of nonretention, but 5 of the 12 NL magnates found the commissioner no longer suited to the task. Gussie Busch (St. Louis), Nelson Doubleday (New York), John McMullen (Houston), Ballard Smith (San Diego), and William Williams (Cincinnati) joined the anti-Kuhn camp, which held the belief that "the time has come . . . for a new, dynamic, and creative leadership for baseball, unencumbered with

Figure 3.1. The longer Bowie Kuhn remained as commissioner of baseball, the more he fell out of favor with a block of team owners who were crucial to his chances for keeping his job. National Baseball Hall of Fame and Museum

the burdens, scars, and prejudices of the past." Praised for his "great integrity" and "fine characteristics," the 55-year-old Kuhn had, in the view of these nine, at least, acquired a kind of sclerosis in his almost 13 years in the post.[4] The solution, according to this clique of magnates, was new blood in the commissioner's office, and although the missive was ceremonially shredded during a meeting of NL owners on December 10, 1981, the act was a disingenuous attempt to prove to Kuhn that no harm was intended; however, Kuhn knew better: "All that was shredded was paper," he wrote later. "The spirit of that letter was intact."[5]

Now a lame duck until the expiration of his term on August 12, 1983, Kuhn demonstrated exactly the same great integrity that his detractors had unctuously attributed to him. He could have stepped aside and left a void—as would happen a decade hence when the administration of a different commissioner was forcibly concluded—but his concern for the well-being of the game, its "best interests," as he often cited, trumped any thoughts he may have had to abandon his job. For Kuhn there would be no winning this power struggle, and the czar of Major League Baseball (MLB), whose position was theoretically situated at the head of the game's hierarchy, was subject to the same conditions as his predecessor had been in December 1968, when Eckert was hustled off the stage. Rather than accept the fate to which he was now consigned, Kuhn admired the allegiance of the owners who were in his court and felt an obligation to return the "trust and confidence" they had shown in him. Regarding the nine conspirators, Kuhn found them to be "arrogant men who were scheming to control baseball for their own selfish purposes."[6]

For their part, the owners of both leagues sought to restructure baseball's administrative framework, a task that was guaranteed to be fraught with conflict between those wishing to see the commissioner—*any* commissioner—hold sufficient power to execute his duties and others who envisioned a reduction of his influence on how the highest levels of baseball's business would be conducted. Ironically, Houston's John McMullen preferred keeping Kuhn on the job rather than have restructuring dilute the powers of the commissioner, but the Astros director stopped short of fully endorsing him. By the spring of 1982, Ballard Smith and Edward Bennett Williams had removed themselves from the anti-Kuhn forces, but there still remained sufficient negative votes in the NL to thwart Kuhn's reelection, and the unpredictability of Ted Turner was always a concern. Eddie Chiles of Texas was adamant in his opposition, and he went so far as to write to his fellow owners accusing Kuhn of offering underhanded financial incentives to keep their favor, a charge that was rebutted by Gene Autry of the Angels.

Kuhn was the loser in a vote at a November 1982 owners meeting in which five NL clubs rejected a proposal for a three-year renewal of his term. In the meantime, the list of candidates for commissioner swelled. It included such baseball-connected luminaries as Stan Musial, Hank Aaron, Willie Mays, Lee MacPhail, Fred Wilpon, John McHale, Bob Howsam, and Tal Smith (who was the choice of *Sporting News* in 1981); at least two corporate moguls, Frank Borman of Eastern Airlines and Jack Valenti of the Motion Picture Association of America; several figures from the world of politics and government, for example, Henry Kissinger and former presidents Richard Nixon and Gerald Ford; and, tellingly, A. Bartlett Giamatti, president of Yale University. Resorting to a bit of gallows humor, Buzzie Bavasi of the California Angels wrote to Milwaukee owner Bud Selig in the wake of the 1982 winter meetings and proposed "two names that come to mind that could fit the bill." Referring to a higher power, as well as the man currently on the job, Bavasi revealed his choices: "One was crucified 2,000 years ago," he said, "and the other is being crucified by our own membership."[7] The Angels were, in fact, one of Kuhn's staunchest allies.

In June 1983, exactly two months before Kuhn's official end date, Lee MacPhail made known his willingness to accept the directorship of the Player Relations Committee (PRC) but on one condition: Specifically, he requested that every major-league club approve of his appointment. This curious caveat ran counter to the three-fourths majority of each league's owners necessary to elect the commissioner, but MacPhail believed that unanimity of the magnates was paramount to allowing him to use "whatever bargaining strategy baseball finally . . . adopted" in future negotiations with the players' union.[8] If the commissioner could not receive unanimous backing for his election, MacPhail wanted to benefit from such support so that he could at least claim that all the owners were behind him in his role as head of the PRC. Thus, rather than retiring as president of the AL at the end of that year, MacPhail had his request granted and moved into the directorship, replacing Ray Grebey.

The eight major-league owners who formed the search committee to replace Kuhn had pared its list of prospective candidates to 10 names, but there was no small degree of angst regarding whether the new commissioner should be baseball-oriented, easing his transition, or come from outside the game, which would give baseball a new leader with an untainted perspective. Bud Selig, owner of the Milwaukee Brewers, who headed the search committee, declined the opportunity, and William Simon, the current president of the United States Olympic Committee, bowed out of the running, citing his commitment to the 1984 Summer Games in Los Angeles. Another executive connected to the Summer Olympics, however, was a person of interest, one who had met with Bowie Kuhn during spring training of 1983.

Peter Ueberroth, a native of Evanston, Illinois, became the operations manager for a small airline dedicated to shuttling passengers between California and Hawaii, and later created a network of offices that handled telephone reservations for smaller hotels and air carriers. By 1978, this venture had blossomed into a travel company second only to American Express as the country's premier travel enterprise. That year also was occasioned by his recruitment to organize and run the upcoming 1984 Summer Olympics scheduled for Los Angeles.

Selling his travel firm and devoting all his energy to the Olympic cause, Ueberroth employed his shrewd business insight to bring sponsors on board at prices previously thought unattainable. Serving in an unpaid capacity, he helped bid up the offer for television rights to the Summer Games—ABC was the winner at $225 million ($150 million was believed to be the maximum any broadcaster would pay)—and expected that people who volunteered to work for the cause would do so uncomplainingly or with no regard for any compensation they might be drawing. Ueberroth was hands-on in every phase of setting up a touchstone event, and he deftly responded to the anticipated boycott of the Summer Games by the Soviet Union, which made good on its threat to stay home and also persuaded 13 other countries to follow their lead and shun the event.

In March 1983, the discussion during the meeting between Ueberroth and Bowie Kuhn centered around the possibility of baseball becoming an official Olympic sport, but other than Ueberroth indicating to the commissioner that he was aware of Kuhn's plight, there appears to have been no lobbying effort by him to seek baseball's highest executive position. Despite Ueberroth's name being bandied about, there was little serious thought to his gaining favor with the search committee because baseball needed a replacement for the commissioner well before the end of the Summer Olympics.

***

As the calendar turned to May and with no replacement for Kuhn in sight, the commissioner met with Fred Kuhlmann of the St. Louis Cardinals, a man whom Kuhn held in high regard. The Cardinals executive told Kuhn that convincing team owner Gussie Busch and Mets owner Nelson Doubleday, the latter especially averse to revenue sharing, to lend Kuhn support might well be the key to his survival. The close relationship enjoyed by Busch and Doubleday led Kuhlmann to believe that swaying either owner into the Kuhn camp would likely mean that the other would follow. Also, nearly every major-league club vended Anheuser-Busch products at their stadiums—Milwaukee, Montreal, and Toronto being the only exceptions—and it was believed that some team owners might sever their business ties with Busch unless he softened his stance against Kuhn. A breakfast meeting with Kuhlmann, Kuhn, and Doubleday was arranged, but the gathering quickly turned sour when the confrontational Met mogul voiced his resentment of the commissioner and further demanded his resignation.

A restructuring of the upper level of MLB was also in the works at this time. The commissioner's job would be recast as the chief executive officer of the game, while a deputy commissioner or chief operating officer was to be placed second in command. Kuhn also would allow for his removal based on a simple majority of owners' votes instead of 25 percent in each league. Doubleday was adamant that Kuhn should not be given the reins of CEO, which was a condition Kuhn refused to concede, and there appeared little chance to broker any rapprochement. Running to the press to find a sympathetic ear, Doubleday told *Newsday* that with Kuhn still in office, a "World War III" of sorts would engulf the game.[9]

The witching hour of Kuhn's mid-August departure loomed ever larger, and the list of candidates was now down to three: Kuhn, as a holdover; James Baker, a politico from the Reagan White House; and Peter Ueberroth, who was still bound to his Olympic duties for at least another 13 months. If the forces opposed to Kuhn would not allow their minds to be changed, perhaps an interim solution that they could tolerate would leave Kuhn in office for a while longer, although the conditions practically dictated that Kuhn had to remain by default. Peter O'Malley of the Dodgers was a firm Kuhn ally, and the commissioner often counseled his opinion in the approach to the anticipated imbroglio about serving beyond his term's expiration. There were rumblings that the anti-Kuhn owners might go so far as to seek a court injunction to preclude his retention. A key gathering of owners and executives took place in Boston on August 2, at which Kuhn announced that he was giving up any furtherance to remain in any capacity as commissioner, but he agreed to stay in office until a replacement was found, in large part because he "wanted a hand in determining who my successor would be and in shaping his powers."[10]

Kuhn's temporary term was one issue on which the owners could miraculously and unanimously concur. In fact, the commissioner's first reprieve lasted until the winter meetings in December, where owners again renewed him until March 1984, and then for a third and final time when Kuhn was extended until September 30, thereby permitting the officially elected Peter Ueberroth to at last assume his duties as Kuhn's successor beginning the next day. "Clearly a transitory bridge needs to be built at all times, and having Bowie there . . . will be very helpful in a smooth and effective running of the commissioner's office," stated Bud Selig of the search committee.[11]

This "bridge" was important to baseball's continuity given that the sport's business needed attention in the face of various issues and controversies: possible expansion, as well as television contracts, in the case of the former, and a drug scandal chief among the latter. But the naming of Ueberroth was not warmly received by some baseball writers. One beat reporter, Bill Conlin, had been bemused by the consideration of Ueberroth for the commissioner's job and was further insulted—fatuously so—that the Olympic head would put baseball on the back burner until the Summer Games were over. "I hate to rain on Ueberroth's parade," Conlin carped, "but big-league baseball is more important to the psychic well-being of this country than almost any Olympic sport he can name."[12]

Taking note of the new appointee's penchant for profits, Dick Young envisioned baseball devolving into a commercial dystopia should Ueberroth find a way to put the Budweiser logo on home plate, and Young "fear[ed] for the baseball fan under the upcoming reign of Ueberroth if the bottom line always has to come first."[13] Young was also rankled by the number of curtain calls Ueberroth took even after the Games concluded, while the many volunteers who worked for and supported the event rapidly faded from public view.

***

Bowie Kuhn departed a beaten man who could not overcome the handicap of having just enough detractors to block his reelection. Yet, he held his head high as the press retold Buzzie Bavasi's "crucified" comment and jokes were made about the number of farewell addresses Kuhn delivered throughout the course of the multiple extensions he had received. In early July, and as his tenure was genuinely coming to a close, Kuhn was feted at a brunch in San Francisco—with Ueberroth in attendance—and a reporter noted that although Kuhn was "regularly castigated as a stuffed shirt by the players and charged with lacking business acumen by the owners . . . it was these same detractors who gave him a standing ovation."[14]

Ueberroth was the ultimate winner in the protracted search process, and his arrival as not only the new commissioner but also the man to be "formally recognized as the chief executive officer" came with some major concessions made by team owners.[15] He credited his predecessor with affecting the structural updates to the top level of baseball, which meant that Ueberroth would benefit from an organization whereby all of the game's various entities now reported directly to him in his capacity as the chief executive officer. Kuhn admitted that while the commissioner's job was "not impossible, it's very, very difficult." Yet, he believed that the new man on the spot would have greater opportunity for success "because the powers of the office have been enhanced."[16] Those powers included his direct oversight of both league presidents for baseball administration matters and the ability to fine teams as much as $250,000, replacing the old maximum of a paltry $5,000. A change in voting for the commissioner now held that only a simple majority of *all* club owners was necessary, one caveat being a minimum of five favorable votes in either league. Chicago White Sox board chairman Jerry Reinsdorf said, "Ueberroth knew how badly baseball wanted him, and he would have been dumb if he hadn't demanded the right to dictate the terms under which he would accept the job."[17]

Baseball's premier publication found much to like in the new commissioner and praised the fortifying of his power. "When opposition to Kuhn surfaced in 1982, the talk was of slicing up the commissioner's job among several specialists, plus boards, commissions, and councils to oversee the specialists," editorialized *Sporting News*. "Ueberroth's demand for more power, not less, must have changed some minds. There was no way the owners could emasculate the post while trying to bring in a quality man to fill it."[18]

The attention Ueberroth gave to fiscal stability was manifest in his pre-Olympic enterprises and further enhanced in the wake of the Summer Games, those bounties the result of the control he was able to wield over those ventures. With his sights now trained on MLB, Ueberroth indicated that he would not abandon certain principles that had worked so well for him. He told Howard Cosell in an interview for ABC Television's *Sportsbeat* program, "I think the danger that the commissioner has to look at is to be sure that nobody wrecks their organization, the financial underpinnings of a ballclub. . . . So you have to be sure the structure of the organization stays financially sound."[19] In this, Ueberroth would also succeed, but it would come at a cost.

***

The official passing of the torch from Bowie Kuhn to Peter Ueberroth began on October 1, 1984, but just three weeks after the closing ceremonies of the Summer Games, the soon-to-be new commissioner received from Kuhn a detailed memorandum highlighting various agendas pertaining to meetings Ueberroth would be attending during a span of several days in early September. Ueberroth may have sensed a touch of familiarity to the high-level categories—legal, secretary/treasurer, and chief of staff—to be discussed, but the individual items related to arbitration, disciplinary proceedings, gambling and tampering memoranda, baseball legislation and rules, the umpire development program, and the administration of baseball's Central Fund, as well as its pension and insurance programs, may have impressed as a bit alien.[20]

Yet, heaped on an already crowded list were other items noted by Kuhn's staff: the need for another attorney to work in the commissioner's office; baseball functions at which Ueberroth's attendance was expected in discharging his duties; a memorandum enumerating 18 areas of administrative responsibilities, ranging from every aspect of amateur baseball to drafts to such special interests as the Jackie Robinson Foundation; a third memo dedicated exclusively to a dozen broadcasting issues; four areas of concern put forth by the commissioner's director of information that he believed to be hampering his department's efficiency; 10 points that the chief of security brought to the table for discussion, not least of which was baseball's drug problem; and, finally, licensing and promotional efforts that would put the game—and team names and logos—in a wider public view.[21]

The subjects here stress the importance of why a businessman—and, in particular, a very successful businessman—was seen as crucial to serving baseball in both a corporate and marketing sense. Ueberroth's youth, dynamism, and recent Olympic deeds, not least of which was an estimated $150 million profit for the Summer Games, foretold a man well-suited to moving the game forward as the 1980s progressed.[22] Although Ueberroth was now casting his allegiance with the national pastime, he was also named to the board of Irvine Co., a California-based real estate company, just two weeks before assuming the commissionership.

Once on the job—literally and immediately—Ueberroth had no benefit of a honeymoon period, as he was swept up in a controversy that involved his quick immersion into the sometimes-frenetic realm of baseball when he was confronted with a dispute primarily regarding umpire compensation for postseason play. "Just because you took a financially draining venture such as the Olympics Games [*sic*] and turned them into a smashing success doesn't mean you can reason with an umpire," cautioned a columnist for *USA Today*.[23] The issue had been festering for three months, as the counselor for the umpires' union, Richie Phillips, failed to reach an accord with AL president Dr. Bobby Brown and NL president Chub Feeney. As the league championship series were about to commence, the lack of a resolution forced substitute umpires into action when the regular arbiters walked out, and after initially deferring to the league presidents to let them deal with the problem, Ueberroth agreed to act as the mediator when the case moved to binding arbitration. On October 15, and with the regular umpires having called the just-concluded World Series, Ueberroth ruled in favor of the umpires, much to the dismay of the club owners.

A minor drama unfolded on October 5, when the new commissioner informed the press that the starting time for Game 5 of the American League Championship Series would be moved from a night game to an afternoon contest to accommodate a scheduled presidential debate between Ronald Reagan and Walter Mondale. This became a moot point when Detroit swept Kansas City in three games, but the occasion showed Ueberroth's willingness to place baseball in proper context vis-à-vis the 1984 election, but another incident occurred at the onset of the National League Championship Series in Chicago when reporter Claire Smith was

Figure 3.2. After fulfilling his obligations to the 1984 Summer Olympic Games, Peter Ueberroth replaced Bowie Kuhn as commissioner. Successful in the world of travel business and as organizer of the Summer Games, Ueberroth never lost sight of the importance of a healthy bottom line regardless of the enterprise. National Baseball Hall of Fame and Museum

denied access to the San Diego Padres clubhouse at Wrigley Field. When the matter concerning female media members was expediently settled, Smith soon thereafter met Ueberroth on the eve of the World Series, and the commissioner viewed her misfortune as a nonissue. "It won't happen again," he pledged. "Let me know if does."[24]

The man who supposedly thrived on solving problems was getting his share of them to deal with, and Ueberroth exhibited his enlightened side in Smith's case. Sensitive to the image of the Olympics, Ueberroth carried this mindset to his new job and was willing to face down any chauvinists who were preventing an evolving press corps from doing their job. Other traditionalists, for instance, the club magnates, would find Ueberroth rankling in other ways. Shortly before his term as commissioner began, Ueberroth was asked if would be leading baseball into the twenty-first century, thereby implying that his tenure would last nearly as long as Bowie Kuhn's. "First, the good Lord would have to agree to that—then the owners," he replied with a smile.[25]

However, even before Ueberroth assumed the commissionership, he said that he would follow Kuhn's lead and distance himself from any frays with the Major League Baseball Players Association (MLBPA), but several sage observations by columnist Leonard Koppett shed light on the difficult road still ahead for him. In his Olympic post, Ueberroth had "dictatorial powers" over all manner of the Summer Games, and the success and profitability of the event spoke very well of his performance.[26] But even with the embellishments he gained as the conditions to his employment as commissioner, he now had to countenance a group of baseball team owners whose agendas tended to focus on their own interests rather than the collective good of the game. Lording over an army of low-wage workers and unpaid volunteers was one thing—Los Angeles mayor Tom Bradley said, "Peter sees himself as [General George] Patton, he's Hannibal crossing the Alps on a white elephant"—but trying that same approach with more than two dozen businessmen who lorded over *their* own businesses was not likely to sit well with them.[27]

And while the national pastime was evolving into a television sport—the superstations were proving this more and more—a baseball season was an annual seven-month marathon performed daily in front of live audiences whose numbers were in the tens of millions. The Olympics, on the other hand, necessitated a years-long period of organization in preparation for a sprint lasting less than three short weeks, and television coverage was of paramount importance for delivering the event to a worldwide audience. "Does Ueberroth have any understanding of these differences and what they mean to his behavior as commissioner?" Koppett asked.[28]

Early in his administration, Ueberroth acknowledged that "baseball has had too much of a local mentality" and needed to expand not only in terms of adding new clubs to cities in North America, but also in the sense of broadening its international appeal.[29] Baseball was a demonstration sport at the 1984 Summer Games, with the U.S. team featuring future big league stars Will Clark and Mark McGwire, so the opportunity to reach out to foreign markets was in the early stages of gaining greater significance.

At his first winter meetings as commissioner, in Houston, Ueberroth addressed the superstation dilemma of clubs transmitting games into territories outside their home area, receiving only a single dissenting vote on a resolution intended to force payment by teams with outsized broadcasting ranges that infringed on other clubs. Suggesting that teams "pool the money and split it up equally or else cut back the number of games on the air," Ueberroth offered this simple answer to the problem, but coaxing owners to accept his "business solution" was another matter.[30] As mentioned previously, an equitable judgment on handling this dilemma would not be rendered until well into the 1990s.

***

Peter Ueberroth liked to think of himself as "fair" rather than "tough" when it came to running a business or dealing with people, even though White Sox owner Jerry Reinsdorf preferred the latter description. "Every time someone said, 'He's a tough guy. He's autocratic, he wants things his way,' I loved it."[31] The financial windfall of the Olympics Ueberroth ran became a cornerstone of the reputation he brought to his new job as baseball commissioner, but this aura was not without its faults. "Ueberroth could be imperious with those whose dedication did not seem adequate to him," reported *Time* magazine in its 1984 "Man of the Year" profile. "One day in the [Olympic office] cafeteria, he stopped to talk to some women having lunch. The chat was pleasant until one of the ladies asked about possible salary increases. Ueberroth, [who himself was an] unpaid volunteer, turned cold and snapped, 'You shouldn't be working here if you don't understand what we're trying to do.'"[32] Setting an example of monetary fasting for others to follow, Ueberroth forfeited one year of his $104,000 Olympic salary in an effort to encourage the recruitment of volunteers, which was a magnanimous gesture. Yet, his rebuke of the underling, who quite likely was at the lower end of the paid-worker range, was revealing.

Also named "Man of the Year" by *Sporting News*—but only for his Olympic work, not with baseball—Ueberroth, during his first full year on the job, received high marks for tackling a number of issues, big and small. "I think he's the best thing to come along since chocolate ice cream," crowed George Steinbrenner in the spring of 1985, adding that the commissioner was a "tremendous talent."[33] How long Ueberroth actually remained in baseball was a subject of debate: As a Republican from California, he was persistently rumored to be stepping into the political arena by seeking the nomination for a U.S. Senate seat in the 1986 election, but he was steadfast in his declaration that he would honor his full five-year term as Kuhn's successor.

The power Ueberroth exercised in the 1984 umpire dispute and his stepping in to resolve the August 1985 players' work stoppage—however debatable his actual influence may have been—impressed at least one reporter as acting in a manner that past baseball commissioner Kenesaw Mountain Landis "would have loved." There was no disputing the contrast between Ueberroth and the "stodgy and painfully legalistic" Kuhn, and although the thorny issue of drug abuse was one area that the former Olympic chieftain wanted to address head-on, Ueberroth would meet resistance by the players' union.[34] In trying to smother baseball's drug dilemma by exerting dictatorial influence, Ueberroth discovered that he had no direct say in the matter and would have to find common ground with the players to forge a resolution.

The problem of cocaine use infected a small minority of players. Yet, the sanctity of the game, as well as a favorable public image, rested on its integrity, which stood to suffer substantially should the general community of players be perceived as users of illegal substances. Thus, the commissioner "with a social conscience" found the battle against drugs to be his cause célèbre, just as First Lady Nancy Reagan would make her antidrug "Just Say No" campaign a touchstone of her husband's administration.[35] By 1986, Ueberroth's proposal to randomly test players for drug usage was scotched, but he meted out various punishments to the players involved in the case of Curtis Strong, a Philadelphia caterer who had supplied drugs to numerous clients, including those players in the clubhouses at Veterans Stadium.

***

Marketing talent that Ueberroth exercised in his travel business and his work for the Olympics also informed his commissionership. This endeavor did not always necessarily meet with the glowing approval of some past corporate sponsors who found themselves outbid by new endorsers, but Ueberroth understood that his allegiance was with baseball first and foremost. His predecessor, Bowie Kuhn, also noted that he had a "superior sense of public relations," which he employed to great advantage.[36] In 1987, five sponsorships carrying a price tag of at least $5 million each were renewed, and the revenue raised was in turn distributed on a prorated basis to the 26 clubs, with $250,000 the minimum payout. Arby's, Chevrolet, Equitable Life Assurance Society, Fuji Film, and IBM expressed satisfaction with the return they received on their investment and association with MLB. The entering of Fuji and IBM into baseball's fold was no coincidence, each having been sponsors of the 1984 Summer Games and thus no stranger to the commissioner, and the beneficiary of this, of course, was baseball's bottom line.

Nor was Ueberroth shy about making demands for higher sponsorship fees from corporations when he believed them to be warranted. He brought this pricing philosophy—some might have viewed this as extortion—with him from his time running the Olympics, his mantra being, "Sponsors should pay a premium price for associating with a premium event."[37] Ueberroth proved his point by deciding that Gillette's long-running $250,000 sponsorship of the fan balloting for the All-Star Game was inadequate to the occasion. Executives of the shaving-product entity were appalled at the commissioner's suggestion to quadruple its payment and refused to comply, but after enduring a year with no sponsor, Ueberroth landed a million-dollar deal with *USA Today*. This was yet another instance where the commissioner employed his shrewdness and upheld his reputation for maximization of profits.

Deftness of salesmanship for Ueberroth did not always translate into favorable public countenance, as in the case of his appearance at the annual New York baseball writers' gathering in January 1987. Sensitive to the approaching 40th anniversary of Jackie Robinson's seminal breaking of the color barrier, the commissioner had stated at the recent winter meetings that he wanted to see minorities make greater strides in gaining access to front-office jobs, which was a sage observation on his part. Ueberroth told the writers that he believed the upcoming season should be dedicated to Robinson's memory, also a "noble and worthy gesture," as Phil Pepe wrote after the event, "but isn't it gauche to repeatedly remind us of it?"[38] What especially riled Pepe was Ueberroth's "turning the Hall of Fame election into a racial issue" when he lectured the writers that had African American Billy Williams not been chosen in the most recent balloting, "there would have been a lot of questions and a lot of people wondering why." Pepe noted that those who voted did so unbiasedly and could stand on their record with no regrets.

The topic of race became the epicenter of a firestorm in April 1987, when Los Angeles Dodgers vice president Al Campanis said in a television interview that blacks were not qualified to hold positions in baseball management. The ensuing controversy prompted Ueberroth to pledge that he would resign from office unless tangible progress was made in minority hiring. After meeting with the commissioner, civil rights activist Reverend Jesse Jackson challenged baseball magnates to revise their "minority hiring policies that they know are 'immoral and unjust.'"[39]

More than two years into his tenure, Ueberroth nonetheless felt that the game was changing for the better, in part to what he viewed as a modified organizational structure "where the major-league hierarchy is in shape, where the chain of command is clearly defined," thanks partly to his desire to let the two league presidents "have a more visible role in baseball."[40] Bans against Mickey Mantle and Willie Mays for their public relations duties with casinos, instituted by Kuhn to avoid any hint of baseball being associated with gambling, were lifted by Ueberroth, who noted that the number of club owners with ties to horse racing tracks was also diminishing on his watch. The betterment of the national pastime was appearing in the turnstile figures at major-league ballparks throughout the country almost every year, the 50-million mark in attendance about to be surpassed for the first time in 1987.

In somewhat mocking fashion, writer Joe Gergen reported, "The image-conscious Ueberroth is determined to make baseball squeaky clean," and there was no mistaking that he was following his own business directives and moral compass in the service of the game.[41] Ueberroth's mindset reflected the fact that he governed knowing his place at the top of baseball's organizational chart with the team moguls beneath him, both on paper and in reality. By turning the power structure in an unconventional way, Ueberroth correctly sensed that a portion of owners who had welcomed him to office in the wake of the Olympics were, by the end of 1987, anxious to see him move on. His informal head count told him that he did not have enough "yeas" to carry a successful bid for another term.

The owners—Ueberroth's underlings—were discomfited in another unconventional way, that being the manner in which the commissioner conducted business meetings with them. Increasing the number of gatherings each year from two to four, the commissioner also selected venues that were different from the "usual spots" and thus enabled him to "wield greater power if the owners were on unfamiliar ground."[42] While at the meetings, moguls were subjected to logistics carefully crafted to strip away the clubiness they had come to know previously at such assemblies, with Ueberroth acting as a "stern schoolmaster," devising seating arrangements that prevented owners from sitting too close to one another, berating speakers who he felt talked more than their share, and generally "treat[ing] them like retarded children."[43] And the content of the message he consistently delivered—with no small degree of condescension—was, *you should think less about winning games and more about making money because that is your business*.

Ueberroth's boldness in putting forth his agenda won him little popularity with the men who were once so anxious to bring him on board. Yet, the résumé Ueberroth built contained valuable achievements aside from the continued rise in attendance. A reversal in the number of teams losing money spoke to the improvement of the game's accounting ledger: Only 20 percent of teams made money as he entered office, but now 75 percent broke even or were in the black. Gains made with minority hiring brought more creditability to the sport, and after three full years of Ueberroth's tenure, the number of known drug users remained nearly static (28 in 1985, 30 in both 1986 and 1987), while the number of people tested rose from 275 to 1,000. And charitable contributions by MLB went from zero in 1985 to $2.5 million.[44]

By the time of the winter meetings in December 1987, and with his welcome worn out long ago, Ueberroth announced that despite the disturbances he had created, he would not resign prior to the expiration of his term as commissioner in late 1989. But by the late spring of 1988, he realized that even by the election standards he imposed as part of his conditions of baseball employment, he knew he would not be able to gain the necessary simple-majority votes to continue. On June 7, Ueberroth gave owners the requisite 18-month notice in advance of a possible extension and announced that he would decline another five-year term, but as was the case with his predecessor, "He will remain through a transition period to assure the dignity and the continuity of the institution."[45] His December 1989 departure date was subsequently moved up to the early spring of 1989, because, in his words, "On April 1, I will have spent exactly 10 years serving in the sports world, and that's enough."[46]

Intending to leave office in good order, as well as according to his terms, Ueberroth wanted a voice in determining who the next commissioner would be, "and [Ueberroth and his replacement] will play active roles in the negotiations of the next television and labor agreements, and in expansion plans."[47] The announcement drew praise from some owners—Carl Pohlad of the Twins enthused that, "Ueberroth's support for a new term was unanimous"—but the commissioner himself admitted, "I never like to participate in a popularity contest because I'm never going to win one of them."[48] Two weeks later, whether to lure him back into the fold or simply reward him for his past work, the magnates increased Ueberroth's salary to $450,000, but the effort had no impact to the decision already taken.

Glowing—in some cases, grudging—admiration for the job Ueberroth did, however, was not manifest among all observers. One scribe at the 1988 winter meetings in Atlanta noted that the commissioner's biggest legacy might well be the collusion cases recently adjudicated against the owners and blamed Ueberroth for his role in perpetrating the scheme against the top free agents. "The commissioner convinced the clubs they could get away clean," wrote a reporter from Southern California. "When the big bill arrives in their mailboxes, Ueberroth will be miles away from their anger."[49] At the time of the settlement in December 1990, by which time Fay Vincent was in the commissioner's office, the original damage total ran to $280 million, but numerous "appeals and arbitration decisions," which took 13 more years to process—until May 2004—pushed the ultimate payout to the astronomical sum of $434 million, received by more than 650 players.[50]

Having moved his office from Manhattan to El Toro, California, outside Los Angeles, his preferred base of operations, Ueberroth was derided as the "FedEx commissioner" because he was often not present in New York and so much paperwork was sent to his home in Newport Beach.[51]

Citing the commissioner's continuing association with a stock brokerage, the *New York Post* lambasted him as the "no-show commish" for the amount of time he spent with E. F. Hutton while reaping the substantial monetary benefits derived from this and other endeavors outside of baseball.[52]

Once Ueberroth negotiated the $1 billion TV package set to begin in 1990, the *Post* again reviled him for selling out so many formerly free over-the-air games in favor of telecasting them on ESPN and thus available only to cable subscribers. To the dismay of many, the traditional "Game of the Week" was to become extinct after its decades-long run, but historical hindsight shows that baseball was repositioning itself to take advantage of new television technology that was offering a vastly increasing number of channels that could not possibly be handled by old VHF and UHF means. Baseball was confronting a future from which it could not turn away, and the business-oriented Ueberroth positioned the national pastime to face the reality of the day while making sure that it would be well-compensated for its trouble.

In the waning days of his tenure, Ueberroth appeared ready to resume his career in the travel industry by assuming the role of point man for a group negotiating to purchase Eastern Airlines for $464 million. Although the deal collapsed less than two weeks after he left office, he was successful in mid-August when he partnered with his brother to purchase Hawaiian Airlines, which became a homecoming of sorts for the former commissioner.

***

Peter Ueberroth's premature departure left at least one owner wondering why he was in such a hurry. George Steinbrenner chafed at the commissioner's decision to exit early, complaining, "He rode off into the sunset and left the tough stuff. He had six or seven months left on his contract, but his P.R. people advised him to get out because the things he had left to face were no-win situations."[53] This predicament had more than a whiff of cowardice, and the man who prided himself on tackling difficult problems was now passing the buck to a brand new commissioner possessed of just a few years' experience in baseball. One columnist for *Sporting News* asked, "Did Ueberroth Pass a Torch or a Live Grenade?"[54]

The explosive components handed over included some delicate issues: the Pete Rose gambling imbroglio was unfolding, and the billion-dollar television contract Ueberroth inked had the MLBPA thirsting for a bigger share of the revenue. The TV windfall for the owners now foretold of another likely labor battle, naturally, concerning money.

Now seated in the commissioner's office was A. Bartlett Giamatti, former president of Yale University and a man of letters capable of viewing the game of baseball in its most romanticized and literary terms. Giamatti would have been a perfect fit to present at any of several annual symposiums dealing with baseball and American culture, and the zeal coursing through his veins was analogous to the team he "learned to love as a small boy in the 1940s [who] were in the early stages of living out the consequences . . . of 'The Curse of the Bambino.'"[55]

Giamatti's gaze was not fixed solely on the Red Sox, however. Born to well-educated parents, it was inevitable that Giamatti would take their lead to get the best education possible. Prepping at the renowned Phillips Academy in central Massachusetts, he had matriculated in 1956, at Yale, where he eventually received his Ph.D. in Renaissance literature. After a brief teaching stint at Princeton, Giamatti was again at Yale by the fall of 1966. There he first served as an assistant professor and began his climb up the school's academic and administrative ladder. It was during his time at Phillips that he availed himself of what became a fatal habit, having been granted permission by his parents to "smoke moderately" where permitted on school grounds.[56]

Giamatti's ascent occurred during the turbulent late 1960s, during which time New Haven saw its share of racial violence and antiwar protests. Yet, he used his wit and charming personality to connect with students throughout his tenure. When the president of Yale resigned in 1977 to become the U.S. ambassador to Great Britain, Giamatti was rumored to be among the candidates in line to replace Kingman Brewster, even though he lacked management experience. When apprised of the possibility of heading his alma mater, Giamatti famously retorted, "It's news to me. The only thing I ever wanted to be president of was the American League."[57] The departing AL president at the time, Lee MacPhail, supposedly offered to exchange jobs with him, but Giamatti politely refused, and former Yankees infielder Dr. Bobby Brown was appointed instead.

Despite the ostensibly humorous baseball reference, Giamatti had actually hoped to be nominated, and upon engaging in a successful interview with Yale's search committee, he was chosen to be the next president beginning July 1978. As his biographer observed, the "deep emotional commitment" he had to the school was practically in his genes: "Yale had been his home for more than 20 years. It was his father's school. It was his life."[58]

What the new 40-year-old president also stepped into was an often-volatile administrative arena in which unionized maintenance and custodial workers at the school had fought bitterly for benefits, and, in 1983, attempts by white-collar workers to form a union succeeded by a margin of just 39 votes. While Yale's labor strife simmered, Giamatti had been interviewed twice for the job of baseball commissioner by the time of that year's winter meetings, but "some of his views, during secondary rounds of interviews, irked a few Search Committee members."[59] Lacking an offer from MLB, there would be no retreat from Yale for its president.

By the 1984 fall semester, when the newly formed union local struck for better wages, Giamatti found himself on the receiving end of shouts by protesters who also waved signs at passing motorists reading, "Beep! Beep! Yale's Cheap!"[60] Giamatti was normally possessed of a pleasant gregariousness. Yet, as a man who valued his privacy and had the belief that he could befriend anyone, he took the strikers' attacks personally.

Although the issue was ultimately resolved after a cooling-off period during the 1984 Christmas holiday season, the embattled president said in the spring of 1985 that he would resign his office one year hence. "The inevitable adjustment of the low wage levels of white-collar workers had now to be made more quickly than Yale wished," and although the dispute was not a financial disaster for the university, it cast Giamatti in an unfavorable light for being "stubborn" and "emotional" in dealing with the union.[61]

Now a lame-duck executive, Giamatti cast about for a new job with a better salary than what he was drawing from Yale, and now favoring a position in the corporate world, he encountered Fay Vincent, a graduate of Yale Law School, late of Columbia Pictures, who was then serving as an executive vice president with Coca-Cola.

Interviews with a number of companies that had been personally arranged by Vincent failed to produce new employment for Giamatti, leaving both men bewildered at the lack of interest in the Yale president, whose personality could easily enable him to serve as an "executive in charge of public issues, the corporate ambassador to the outside world."[62] Giamatti's plight came to the attention of Brewers owner Bud Selig, who remembered the Yale president's earlier interviews for baseball commissioner. With NL president Chub Feeney choosing to retire, several NL team executives—Dodgers owner Peter O'Malley chief among them—nominated Giamatti to be the new head of the Senior Circuit. In June 1986, he was approved unanimously by NL owners, his term of office to begin in December.

Giamatti's love of baseball was manifest in his devotion to the Boston Red Sox, as well as his keen ability to express that affection with the written word. Seeming to be a hopeless romantic, he penned *Take Time for Paradise*, a small book published posthumously, but his most noted piece was an essay titled "The Green Fields of the Mind," a thoughtful paean to the national pastime. Such work undoubtedly places Giamatti above any previous commissioner for literary ability, but he also was imbued with a clear sense of right and wrong as it pertained to baseball. In the foreword he wrote for a 1987 baseball anthology, the NL president tellingly stated, "[Baseball] fits so well because it embodies interplay of individual and group that we so love, and because *it conserves our longing for the rule of law while licensing our resentment of lawgivers*."[63]

The "rule of law" Giamatti referred to was in the context of the playing rules of baseball. Yet, he was consistent in his belief of probity as it applied to every aspect of the game. Although, as he settled into the NL president's chair, he expressed "mixed feelings" about mandatory drug testing for players—"[I]t seems like voluntary testing is to be desired," he told *USA Today*—and he was soon to be on a collision course with one of the game's most visible stars in an effort to uphold baseball's sanctity.[64]

***

Giamatti still enjoyed his connections to academia, but these did not deter him from performing his duties, nor should they have. On April 30, 1988, the Cincinnati Reds hosted the New York Mets, and with the contest tied, 5–5, in the ninth inning, umpire Dave Pallone called Mookie Wilson safe on a close play at first that enabled the Mets to score what proved to be the winning run. Reds manager Pete Rose immediately argued the call, and the ensuing dustup became physical when Rose shoved Pallone, who supposedly cut or scratched Rose on the cheek. Pallone was removed from the game for his own safety as irate fans showered the field with debris.

When Giamatti meted out punishment for Rose's misdeed, the 30-day suspension was viewed by many observers as excessive in the extreme. "A point would have been made if Rose had been given a 10-day suspension," wrote Peter Pascarelli in *Sporting News*. "It would have upheld the sanctity of an umpire's physical safety and sent a warning that bumping incidents would not be tolerated."[65] The beat writer also believed that by overreaching with his edict, which also included a $10,000 fine for Rose and a tongue-lashing administered to Reds broadcasters Marty Brennaman and Joe Nuxhall for live comments about the incident deemed by Giamatti to be inciteful, the NL president was grandstanding for the press rather than handling the issue in a more forthright manner.

In the wake of the unsuccessful appeal of his suspension, Rose made a revealing comment that presaged an even larger confrontation he would have with Giamatti. Indicating a preference to pay a steeper fine than miss 30 games, as well as his fondness for gambling, Rose said, "Ten thousand dollars? That's a lot of money—5,000 daily doubles."[66] With that, Rose did his penance and marched ahead toward a controversy that continues to stain his record.

Almost two years into his five-year stint as president of the NL, Giamatti was rumored to be the odds-on successor to Peter Ueberroth. An informal tally of owners indicated unanimous support in the NL and a solid majority of AL magnates in favor of Giamatti advancing to baseball's highest office. On September 8, 1988, he received unanimous support to become baseball's seventh commissioner.

In April 1989, the torch of the commissionership was passed to a man whose love of the game would be an antidote to the business-oriented focus that drove Ueberroth. Although Giamatti lacked the business sense and legal insight of his two immediate predecessors, he was instilled with an "abiding interest in the integrity of baseball and unblinking decisiveness," qualities he ably demonstrated during his brief time as NL president.[67]

The game was financially healthy, but the unending and thorny issue of a new Basic Agreement with the players, as well as the sidebars of free agency and arbitration, were sure to be on the new commissioner's agenda in the days ahead, to say nothing of keeping an eye out for the general well-being of the game. To soothe his craving for literature, Giamatti continued to write on his own time, as the *New York Times* reminded readers when it printed an excerpt from his upcoming book. Suffused with profundity and replete with a variety of literary figures, he meditated on the meaning of "home" as it pertains to baseball.[68] Whereas Peter Ueberroth was named one of 1985's "best dressed men" by the Fashion Foundation of America while Giamatti was still embroiled in disputes at Yale, the past commissioner could not charm with words or appeal to one's aesthetic sensibilities the way that his replacement could.

***

In the nearly three years that Bart Giamatti served as NL president and commissioner, he was a witness to several touchstone events. His replacement as head of the NL, Bill White, became the first African American to hold such a high administrative office, and this appointment came two years after the notorious remarks made by Al Campanis. An eight-time NL All-Star and winner of seven Gold Gloves during his playing days, White had served for 18 years in the Yankees broadcast booth. Giamatti also welcomed another minority player, former Dodgers pitcher Joe Black, to his staff in the capacity of a part-time consultant to a committee formed to assist players fighting personal problems.

As groundbreaking as White's new position was, another blow against stereotypes was struck in favor of women when Pam Postema, a female umpire with more than a decade of experience in minor-league work, was invited to spring training in 1988. Although she was not picked to fill one of two vacancies among NL arbiters, her selection for camp was nonetheless emblematic of the continuing evolvement of the game.

The salient episode of Giamatti's time as NL president was the Pete Rose–Dave Pallone tussle, but this proved to be merely a foreshadowing of the controversy of Rose's gambling affair. As rumors of his betting activity began to burgeon as spring training 1989 was winding down, Rose became the focus of ever-intensifying scrutiny. Attorney John M. Dowd was employed by the commissioner's office to determine whether Rose had violated MLB Rule 21, which prohibits uniformed personnel from wagering on baseball games. By mid-August, Dowd concluded his investigation and reported to Giamatti that Rose had indeed broken this most sacred rule and was now subject to "permanent ineligibility."[69]

In making his ruling, which was consistent with those handed out nearly seven decades earlier by Judge Kenesaw Mountain Landis in the infamous Black Sox Scandal, Giamatti handed Rose a permanent suspension. The punishment shocked and disappointed many that one of the preeminent players of the latter part of the twentieth century, and one who had recently set a new record for most base hits, was now found to be on the wrong side of baseball's most integrity-related law. The ruling was announced in New York on August 24, to a horde of assembled media, and it marked a sad occasion in the game's history.

With the traditional Labor Day holiday now approaching, Giamatti chose to steal away to his vacation home on Martha's Vineyard to recuperate from the heightened anxiety of the previous week. Departing New York via private charter on September 1, Giamatti arrived on the Massachusetts island and went to his residence, only to be felled by a massive heart attack that afternoon. The Associated Press reported that his wife and one of his sons were with him at the time, but the "'all out' efforts to revive him failed," his death coming just two weeks after "Giamatti dismissed the suggestion that he had been overly stressed by the Rose matter."[70]

Whether the burden of the climactic conclusion of the Rose investigation or the fact that he was a terrible chain-smoker played the greater role in Giamatti's demise will never be known, but his reign as commissioner came to a most unfortunate and abrupt ending just five months into his term. The sports world was stunned by his passing, and the tributes paid in his memory spoke to the unapologetic adoration he showed for the national pastime. "Because he loved the game and understood its place in America, he did not insult real fans with clichés. How could he? He was one of them," wrote one longtime scribe who appreciated Giamatti's genuine feelings and respect for a sport, which ran counter to the "hairspray world of hucksters, where what they love to call 'the bottom line' is the Bible."[71]

Thanks to the intriguing timing of the creation of a new bureaucratic niche—deputy commissioner—it was Fay Vincent who immediately stepped in to fill the tragic void in the commissioner's office. Now approved by an executive council comprised of eight club executives and the two league presidents to serve as the acting commissioner, Vincent in turn would report to that same council as the sport recovered from its latest body blow. The new commissioner was also quickly tested by an event beyond his control, steering the World Series to its completion when it was interrupted just before the first pitch of Game 3 at Candlestick Park by the Loma Prieta earthquake.

Giamatti and Vincent had become not only close friends, but also allied business associates in the realm of baseball, and the *Washington Post* noted, "Watching the two play off each other was like watching old friends share as many inside jokes as common values."[72] Vincent's arrival from the corporate world spelled the end of the ephemeral rein of baseball's most literary-minded commissioner, and it also meant a resumption of owner usurpation of baseball's power structure.

***

A common thread links Bowie Kuhn, Peter Ueberroth, and Bart Giamatti, that being the warm and enthusiastic welcome they received upon their selection by the owners as the newest commissioner of baseball. The figurative breath of fresh air with which each initiated his term is analogous to a team's changing its manager: A "player's manager" whose club does not produce is viewed as weak, forcing the hiring of a disciplinarian skipper to instill a purposeful focus. When the disciplinarian fails in *his* mission, the cause is often attributed to his ways and means being too strict and/or otherwise contributing to a tense atmosphere in the clubhouse, thereby necessitating the hiring of a new manager who lets his players operate under less stifling authority. When a team is winning, whatever method the manager is using almost always seems to be the right way, and the peccadilloes he commits in the course of doing business are often ignored or excused. Rarely does a single player or a small group of players threaten the power structure of the manager, coaching staff, and the rest of the uniformed personnel.

The case of a baseball commissioner presents a different paradigm. Bowie Kuhn's replacing the incompetent William Eckert came at a crucial juncture for baseball in the late 1960s, and the acumen Kuhn brought to his post, as well as his own love of the game, pulled the national pastime away from the abyss that it was close to falling into. But as one baseball historian observed, Kuhn may have fared better had he been more aware of the rising power of Marvin Miller and the MLBPA, dating even to the early 1970s before the reserve clause was struck down in 1975. Kuhn's failure to recognize this development blinded him to any attempt on his part to possibly broker a compromise on the reserve clause and imminent free agency. "Further, his dislike of [Charlie] Finley, shared by most owners, also struck them as too arbitrary in blocking the sale of players."[73]

Peter Ueberroth, a true businessman possessed of little emotional attachment to the game, was thought to be best qualified to lead the game in a time of changing economic realities. Having manipulated the owners to save themselves from a fiscal calamity—although those same magnates generally resented the way in which he wielded his power over them—Ueberroth facilitated his own quick exit and ceded the commissionership to baseball's ultimate romantic.

Bart Giamatti's brief tenure will always be defined in terms of the Pete Rose betting scandal, and although the former NL president inherited the framework of the 1990 television contract, the next round of labor talks with the players on a new Basic Agreement was on the horizon, and this issue may not have ended well for him. Whether there would have been a replay of his situation at Yale can only be left to speculation, but it can be stated confidently that the clout exercised by Local 34 in New Haven paled in comparison to that wielded by the MLBPA, whose power to this day remains virtually unchallenged. Marvin Miller was "convinced that had [Giamatti] lived longer, he would have seen the same fate as Kuhn and Ueberroth" because of the likelihood of a clash with the players' union and subsequent loss of support among the owners.[74]

Bowie Kuhn was subjected to a type of "rule by minority" because of the 75 percent job-approval threshold in both leagues that was necessary for him to keep his position. While this criterion changed when Ueberroth replaced him, it was nonetheless imperative to hold the number of naysayers to a minimum. Recognizing by 1988 that the votes were not there, Ueberroth left rather than lose face by waiting for the owners' balloting to indicate that he was no longer wanted. Only five months in office, Giamatti was enjoying a honeymoon period, but it was only through the fate of premature death that he was spared the indignity of being chased from office by the same group of owners who wholeheartedly welcomed any commissioner to his post. As was the case with his three predecessors, Giamatti, had he lived, would have almost certainly left office with less favor among club ownership than when he arrived, just as Fay Vincent—like Ueberroth, another successor with a business background—would discover in the 1990s. Such is the realm of the baseball commissioner.

Part of that realm also is the economic disparity that exists among any group of owners, past or present. The degree of difference between big- and small-market clubs is immutable, but the common trait among the owners is the copious wealth that allowed them entrée to the circle of moguls in the first place, and these men—mostly—are used to getting their way in the world of business. Seldom do they need to counsel what the common good is for a greater community of people, and this myopia can have harmful consequences, as demonstrated by the issue of revenue sharing. Once Bowie Kuhn began to lose his grip and a sufficient number of negative votes imperiled his job, the likelihood of his being able to reverse the feelings of those against him was slim. The cabal of magnates who conspired to depose him was vivid proof of the fragility of the commissionership and indicative of where the true power really lies. For his own part, Peter Ueberroth was guided by his informal count of dissidents and chose not to undergo a political fight to retain his seat, a move that also spared him the embarrassment of appearing to be fired.

The changing of the guard in baseball's highest rank remains part of the game's life cycle, and perhaps any commissioner can be destined to ultimately fail in the eyes of those who hold the true power of the executive hierarchy. Commissioners who died in office, Kenesaw Mountain Landis and Bart Giamatti, obviously do not apply here, while the tenures of Ford Frick and Bud Selig, "arguably two of the most effective commissioners" in the view of historian David Bohmer, concluded "on their own volition."[75] Yet, there is a trust to be upheld by that primary officeholder to protect baseball's integrity and serve—again, borrowing from Kuhn—its best interests. The triumvirate of Bowie Kuhn, Peter Ueberroth, and Bart Giamatti steered baseball through its heyday, for better and for ill, in the post–free agency era running through the end of the 1980s.

Although Kuhn used the proper pronoun "we" in the context of the many different people he encountered during his journey as commissioner, the closing he wrote in his memoirs is worth noting when also applying "we" in terms of this chapter's three commissioners. "Whatever the problems, whatever the errors of commission or omission," he wrote, "we had wrestled with a lofty challenge and found the way."[76]

If the continuing popularity of the game stood for anything, this surely was true.

4

THE PERVASION OF DRUGS

The abuse of alcohol and drugs in the United States of the 1980s was nothing new. Such vices had been on the scene for decades and were a reflection of the forces impacting the country's society and culture. For centuries, drinking was found to be socially acceptable even in the face of temperance movements and the enactment of Prohibition in the 1920s, although consumption of illicit substances would not become mainstream until the second half of the twentieth century. It was inevitable that the world of sports would ultimately reflect what was happening in everyday American life. Drinking, the most prominent bugbear, had been a constant companion of the national pastime from its very beginning, and the ready availability of all forms of alcoholic beverages to those of majority age—and illegally to minors—even during the days of Prohibition meant that anyone possessed of a thirst for spirits would be able to satisfy their craving.

While the great jazz artist Louis Armstrong proclaimed a daily consumption of cannabis in his adult life as a beneficial alternative to alcohol, little evidence exists of similar use by ballplayers in the early aftermath of World War II. The earliest reference to marijuana came in 1948, when *Sporting News* reported that a minor-league player for San Antonio was injured during a confrontation with a disturbed individual whose action, police believed, "was another in a series of similar attacks attributed to a craze brought on by marijuana smoking."[1] A columnist for the *Chicago Herald-American* joked about the Chicago White Sox being unfazed by the perceived threat of stunted growth supposedly brought on by the use of pot, and in spring training of 1955, as players were being tested in positions other than their accustomed place in the field, one reporter described it as the "most improbable infield lineup even a marijuana addict could have dreamed up."[2]

In the post–World War II era, increasing permissiveness began its spread throughout the land, and the breaking down of cultural mores—especially by the late 1960s—signaled a major upheaval in a country formerly imbued with a conservative mindset. The ever-present rebellious side of youth manifested itself more overtly in reaction to the Vietnam War, and this movement was punctuated by a greater acceptance of drug use among the Baby Boomer generation of Americans. Alcohol was now accompanied by marijuana as a substance of choice, with hallucinogenic and harder drugs like heroin and cocaine lagging behind in overall use but nonetheless posing a threat to public health. Also not to be ignored was the consumption of amphetamines, barbiturates, and tobacco products, the carcinogenic effects of the latest not fully understood until the second half of the twentieth century.

The laying bare of vices enjoyed by ballplayers came through the 1970 publication of Jim Bouton's *Ball Four*, his commentary fully invested in the revelation of players' sexual escapades and their use of alcohol and pep pills. Prior to cocaine gaining unwelcome currency in the late 1970s, "cocaine," in the winter of 1946–1947, pertained only to the name of a Cuban pitcher, Cocaine Garcia from Havana. Yet, dealers of the drug were known to exist and held in contempt for their attempts to prey on youth in their quest to create new customers, but in some medicinal circles, cocaine was thought to be used for its pain-killing qualities. Detroit pitcher Hal Newhouser admitted to receiving an injection of Novocain during the 1945 World Series, but his attending physician denied administering cocaine because of its addictive properties.

As the 1960s progressed and the antiwar movement and counterculture arena grew, drug use gained in prevalence, with LSD, as championed by Timothy Leary, now serving as a vehicle for those following Leary's mantra of "Turn on, tune in, drop out." A new publication, *Avant Garde*, arrived in late 1967, promising readers and monthly subscribers a "feast of gourmet food-for-thought" that would be the "quintessence of intellectual sophistication."[3] That this magazine's advertisement in *Sporting News*—highlighting articles soon to be published, for example, the "coming of synthetic (and therefore legal) marijuana," "prison poems of Ho

Chi Minh," and "pornographic film festivals at Lincoln Center by 1970"—could get past the sober editors of the "Bible of baseball" is nothing short of intriguing.

The toll of illicit drugs had an indirect connection to baseball when Jackie Robinson Jr. was arrested in early 1968, for possession of marijuana, heroin, and a .22-caliber pistol, but by this time drug use was becoming endemic among young Americans. By the turn of the decade, even hockey star Derek Sanderson admitted that he knew a lot of pot smokers, and Detroit hurler Denny McLain, who was about to see his career unravel completely, said that marijuana had been offered to him during his days growing up in Chicago. "We don't have a greater problem than the drug problem," Jackie Robinson Sr. told the Maryland House of Delegates in early 1970, his plea coming at a time when his son was undergoing rehabilitation.[4] The elder Robinson further viewed pot as a gateway substance that would lead its users to move on, as his son had, to more virulent drugs.

The release of *Ball Four* shortly after Robinson's testimony put yet a different spin on the drug issue. Dextroamphetamine sulfate, a drug developed in the 1930s but later given to World War II soldiers to enable them to stay awake—and hopefully alert—for extended lengths of time, became an often-used remedy for hangovers suffered by ballplayers who imbibed too much liquor. This practice employed one drug to solve the problem caused by another, and in pill form this chemical was known as a "greenie," which became the subject of hushed conversations in clubhouses. Not openly acknowledged until Bouton deflowered the veil of silence about greenies, revelation of the pills caused no small amount of angst among baseball management, particularly the image-sensitive office of the commissioner. "Some of the guys have to take one just to get their hearts to start beating," wrote the Seattle Pilots pitcher.[5] If team officials, including trainers, denied the availability of greenies, there still seemed to be a way for players to procure them through teammates, players on other clubs, or possibly the same team medical staff that claimed not to dispense them.

By early March 1971, Commissioner Bowie Kuhn had worked with doctors from Johns Hopkins University and the Greater Baltimore Medical Center to formulate an antidrug program to deal with the scourge. An entity called the Baseball Physicians' Association was created at the time to partner with Kuhn's Drug Education and Prevention Program, the goal of which was the elimination of drugs throughout the sport. Yet, not only was alcohol missing from the list of substances, but also the target audience for the venture was the baseball-playing youth of America, *not* major leaguers. "It was at first feared that widespread involvement of big-league players with barbiturates, amphetamines, and androgenic anabolic steroids . . . had touched off the campaign," readers of *Sporting News* were informed, which further explained that the Major League Baseball Players Association (MLBPA) representative for the Yankees was relieved to learn that schooling the union membership was not the objective of the program.[6] Kuhn later wrote that information sessions were conducted with players and team personnel, and a "Baseball vs. Drugs" brochure was distributed to players, as well as public schools and libraries.

Despite this good-faith effort, however, it appeared to be just a façade to cover an underlying issue that not only refused to be tamed in the realm of baseball, but also had precedents in other sports that were international in scope. Paul Gardner, a British pharmaceutical expert, noted that through the 1960s, the Italian Soccer Federation and bicycling races in Italy, as well as volleyball, boxing, and weightlifting events in Europe and Cuba, were experiencing drug problems with various competitors who were caught consuming pep pills. While Gardner praised the "Baseball vs. Drugs" initiative, he also believed that it was "designed to reassure the public [rather] than solve the problem."[7]

"I felt our drug program and the vigilance of our security personnel had alleviated the drug problem in baseball during the 1970s," Kuhn recalled.[8] This observation may have had some validity as it pertained to the major-league level, but there was a false sense of security nonetheless about how deeply rooted the problem actually was. Worse still, in the ranks of baseball's farm system—encompassing at least three teams per major-league franchise—the small budgets of those clubs did not allow for elaborate measures to keep drugs in check.

The true cause of the problem for many players may have had little to do with exposure to drugs when they became professional ballplayers even at the lowest ranks of the minor leagues. Indeed, as drugs seeped into high schools throughout the country with each passing year, scholastic athletes of every stripe—including underage drinkers—could find substances in their hometowns, opening an unwelcome door into the world of abuse. With teens still living at home, at least parents could exercise some degree of control to stem the tide of drug use, a case that Bob Oliver of the California Angels witnessed in his offseason work as a juvenile police officer in Santa Ana, California. He was nevertheless dismayed by the number of children barely in their teens who were already trying or using drugs at such an early age.

News from the world of sports could also jolt the senses. In late 1970, boxer Sonny Liston was found dead in his home, the cause of his demise determined to be a heroin overdose. Liston joined a cavalcade of famous personalities who succumbed to the drug decades before the overwhelming heroin crisis of the 2010s. Few, if any, heroin addicts were among baseball players, but one columnist presciently observed a sad truth mere weeks after Liston died. Bob Addie wrote, "The major leagues (baseball) have been apprehensive about rumors that some players are using marijuana, but nothing has been proved. Some say that when the true facts come out, as they did in Vietnam, the drug story will be shocking."[9]

Walt Williams, an outfielder with the White Sox, helped to spread awareness by counseling young people on the evils of drugs by pointing out that hard-drug addicts he knew had started with marijuana and moved on to more dangerous substances. And pot became a worrisome focal point, with such famous athletes as the National Football League's (NFL) Duane Thomas and basketball star Kareem Abdul-Jabbar finding their names in the newspaper for arrests related to possession or being the subjects of rumors of usage.

As valiant as attempts to thwart substance abuse on various levels may have been, resistance not to drugs but to prevention programs began to arise, not only in baseball, but also in other sports. Football players' union chief Ed Garvey claimed that the NFL's crackdown had the unsavory taint of "McCarthyism," and indeed a conundrum began to manifest itself as increasing numbers of players made headlines for their drug-related arrests and trips to rehabilitation.[10] Players' union would soon make an argument that testing programs like urinalysis, when forced upon the entirety of their membership, were tantamount to deeming *all* players guilty and thus putting them in the uncomfortable position of having to prove their innocence. Players in both the NFL and Major League Baseball (MLB) especially would resist the imposition of such tactics.

Meanwhile, baseball's list of offenders and suspects continued to grow. Ron LeFlore of the Detroit Tigers, who confessed to being a heroin user at the age of 15, was caught after a robbery that was perpetrated to finance a later drug purchase; Bobby Bonds, recently traded from the Giants to the Yankees, was denying rumored drug use; and Reggie Jackson, whose first autobiography was soon to be released in 1975, caused a stir when some passages in the galley pages of the book—mentioning his use of greenies—found their way into a story printed in the *Oakland Tribune*. And a horticultural predicament arose as a result of outdoor concerts being staged at several major-league stadiums: Groundskeepers in Oakland and Anaheim reported large numbers of marijuana plants sprouting in their respective outfields due to pot seeds left behind by rock fans—and obvious pot smokers—to germinate in the turf.

A notorious case involving a future Hall of Famer developed shortly after the publication of the Jackson book. Former National League (NL) Most Valuable Player (MVP) Orlando Cepeda was arrested for possession of 165 pounds of marijuana, and following his conviction he was given a five-year prison sentence, later reduced to 10 months. Years passed before Cepeda righted his reputation and developed reliable work habits that put him back in baseball's good graces, but the episode was another example of a high-profile star coming undone by the temptation of drugs.

The late 1970s became a time during which baseball at long last recognized alcohol as an issue, due in large part to the work of former Brooklyn Dodgers pitcher Don Newcombe, who as an alcoholic knew firsthand the ravages of strong drink. Newcombe was at the forefront of an educational program instituted through the commissioner's office in 1978, and that same year he saw the famous World Series confrontation between the Yankees' Reggie Jackson and Dodgers hurler Bob Welch, a battle in which Welch claimed victory by fanning the slugger to close out Game 2. But Welch had been nursing an alcohol habit since his high school days, and following the 1979 season, he spent five weeks at a rehabilitation facility. "It marked one of the first times an active professional athlete openly discussed a drinking problem," and the treatment Welch received undoubtedly enabled him to achieve the level of success he enjoyed in the 1980s.[11]

Welch shared his story at a gathering near Santa Barbara, California, hosted by San Diego Padres owner Ray Kroc and his wife, Joan, in November 1980. The Kroc's initiative—dubbed Operation CORK, or "Kroc" spelled backward—was created to confront alcoholism in baseball, and the baseball executives in attendance were encouraged to see to it that an employee assistance program (EAP) was created for every club.

Duly impressed by the presentation, Bowie Kuhn "indicated his intention to establish such a program for all of baseball's administrative offices in New York City," to ensure that the bureaucratic side of the business would not be forgotten.[12] A vital aspect of the EAPs was providing the means for a player (or team employee) to voluntarily come forward to seek treatment for a drug or alcohol problem without fear of disciplinary measures being imposed. With alcoholism gaining greater public awareness, the comic images of Foster Brooks and Otis, the "town drunk" of *The Andy Griffith Show*, were in the process of being supplanted by the work of advocacy organizations like Mothers Against Drunk Driving—founded coincidentally just months before the Operation CORK meeting—as well as new and stiffer penalties for operating motor vehicles and watercraft while under the influence.

***

Whether it was called blow, nose candy, or toot, cocaine provided a quick blast of euphoric feeling that had its user craving the next delivery. The socioeconomic circumstances surrounding cocaine was not the sole domain of rich athletes: Caught attempting to smuggle cocaine into the United States in early 1976, was the daughter of Yankees manager Billy Martin, who had two bags of the drug secured to her legs while passing through an airport in Colombia; however, "the culprit for the cocaine craze was money. . . . Cocaine had become the recreational drug of choice for the affluent."[13] Young professional athletes of all stripes, not just baseball players, fell into a netherworld when their first sampling led to increased use funded by a paycheck an average person could only dream of making.

Once having found a new market underpinned by athletes whose discretionary income was rising significantly, cocaine evolved into a status symbol in which the wealthy could afford to indulge, while also being comfortable in the knowledge that the traces of its usage did not linger in the body, allowing coke users to escape detection more easily than those who smoked marijuana. Henry Fitzgibbon had a twofold concern in his capacity as MLB's security director. In a memo to his boss in preparation for a meeting of major-league general managers in the fall of 1979, Fitzgibbon informed Bowie Kuhn that there was an ever-present danger from the "association of players with the criminal element, primarily gambling figures."[14] Although Fitzgibbon's immediate focus here was "prevent[ion of] embarrassment to the player, club, and professional baseball," implied in this message was an inherent threat of gamblers also having ties to drug dealers, with whom there was the potential to create an odious consort of players throwing games to placate gambling interests while also facilitating their supply of cocaine as a reward. The second item in Fitzgibbon's note was self-congratulatory: "Our Drug Education and Prevention Program is in it's [*sic*] ninth year, and professional baseball remains largely free of drug abuse problems," but at least he acknowledged that "cocaine is the 'in' drug" and implored GMs to report any instances of known or suspected drug issues.[15]

The cocaine problem, especially, had escalated the drug conundrum beyond the alleged marijuana found in Reggie Jackson's suitcase when he traveled to Montreal in late 1976, as he shopped his services as a free agent, or pitcher Bill Lee's admitted use of pot, which he consumed with pancakes. Some young women on the Ladies Professional Golf Association (LPGA) tour were known to be "smoking marijuana just like they were sipping tea," as the LPGA commissioner, Ray Volpe, observed.[16]

An object lesson in the evils of escalating abuse was vividly described in the memoir of Darrell Porter, a first-round draft choice of the Milwaukee Brewers in 1970. Fresh out of high school, the catching prospect ascended the franchise's minor-league ladder and debuted with the Brewers the following year at the tender age of 19. Porter reached the major leagues on a full-time basis in 1973, but along the way he had experienced culture shock by partaking in the consumption of beer, then marijuana, and eventually cocaine. *Snap Me Perfect! The Darrell Porter Story* was the 1984 account of his life and career—with a few years yet to be played in the major leagues—in which he details the missteps he took after leaving home to apprentice as a baseball professional.

Young, naive, and growing up in Oklahoma City under the thumb of an unkind father, Porter excelled in scholastic football and baseball, his selection of the latter sport becoming the career path that saw him become a four-time All-Star. Upon discovering beer in the low minors, Porter's trek became accompanied by pot, and, in 1973, he was introduced to cocaine, which he described as the "Cadillac of narcotics, the drug of choice of the jet set."[17] A trade that sent him to the Kansas City

Royals in 1977, did little to curb his appetite for drugs, nor did several brushes with law enforcement that he narrowly escaped.

By early January 1980, he purposely shunned people who saw him while out and about, and there was an unsavory routine driving his life: "Get up about noon, drink coffee, do a Quaalude, sniff cocaine, and drink beer."[18] When spring training ensued weeks later, Porter had recognized the death-spiral he was spinning into and resolved to straighten out his life when he heard former Brooklyn pitching star Don Newcombe speak to the Royals. A reformed alcoholic himself, Newcombe had players privately answer a 15-question survey about their use of alcohol, and when Porter answered almost every one positively—even a mere three "yeses" indicated a problem—he quickly sought out Newcombe. When Porter admitted to an eight-year involvement with substances, the most recent four of which were "real heavy," Newcombe lambasted him for being a "disgrace to baseball."[19]

Gruff as Newcombe's reaction was, it rapidly forced Porter to face Royals general manager Joe Burke and reveal the condition into which he had fallen. By telephone and without delay, Burke counseled Newcombe, who arranged for Porter to check into the Meadows, a rehabilitation center in Arizona. Before embarking on his journey to the clinic, Porter purchased a Bible to supplement his coming treatment, and with religion, as well as professional help, guiding his recovery, he pulled himself back from the edge of the abyss. Marrying for a second time and signing a five-year contract with St. Louis, he seemed to have become a model for recovering addicts to follow, his capstone being his stint as the Cardinals' top catcher when they won the World Series in 1982.

As virtuous as Porter was in serving as an antidrug speaker after his retirement from the game, his later demise revealed the extreme difficulty of an addict completely ridding himself of the possibility of a relapse. In early August 2002, by which time his weight had ballooned to an unhealthy 300 pounds, Porter, aged 50, drove his car off a road and somehow entangled with a tree stump. Trying to dislodge the disabled vehicle in scorching heat, he collapsed and died. The medical examiner discovered "cocaine in his system," which he believed contributed to a state of "excited delirium," which in turn led to "behavior that is agitated, bizarre, and potentially violent," thus Porter's ill-fated attempt to free the car.[20]

***

As drug abuse began to take its toll on Darrell Porter beginning in the 1970s, his descent was accompanied by the similar woes of other athletes. Vitas Gerulaitis (tennis), Leon Spinks (boxing), Don Murdoch (hockey), Ronnie Franklin (horse racing), and Bob Hayes (football) were charged with possession of marijuana and/or cocaine, or otherwise admitted to using either substance. Rumors swirled about Boston Red Sox pitcher Roger Moret, whose fall into a catatonic state in the spring of 1978, was thought to have been induced by drugs. Hurler Don Gullett claimed no knowledge of pot growing on his farm in Kentucky in the summer of 1977, a time at which Bill North of the Oakland Athletics was arrested for possession of cocaine. Two Miami Dolphins linemen were charged with selling a pound of cocaine to undercover agents, and by the early 1980s, college athletes—primarily men, but not exclusively—were being kicked off their respective teams for various drug violations. The scourge of substance abuse had no bounds and appeared to be taking root more deeply in society and sports.

Shortly after Darrell Porter's return to the Royals in the summer of 1980, a scandal erupted over pep pills supposedly used by some Philadelphia Phillies players. Yet, by early August, the controversy had "faded away into virtually nothing," providing an exoneration of sorts for suspected users like Mike Schmidt, Pete Rose, Larry Bowa, and Greg Luzinski.[21] "LITTLE MISUSE OF DRUGS SEEN," blared a headline in *Sporting News*, the related article indicating that a number of major-league medical staffs had rid their training rooms of greenies. Such action was merely a palliative measure because the "medical men acknowledged, however, that amphetamines are readily obtained through other sources," and San Diego Padres president Ballard Smith stated that despite the focus on drugs, alcohol abuse remained a constant source of trouble plaguing the game.[22] More evidence contrary to baseball's naive outlook was manifest on other pages of *Sporting News*: So bad was the problem in the NFL that Howard Balzer's weekly NFL column began featuring a section labeled "The Drug Scene," later amended to "The Court Report," which recapped player arrests, rehabilitation stints, and the like.[23] Neither was the National Basketball Association (NBA) immune from the drug infestation: "Coke is rampant in the league. I mean, 75 percent [of players] use it," claimed one cager who departed the NBA in 1979.[24]

When Ferguson Jenkins of the Texas Rangers was arrested in Toronto during a late-season 1980 road trip for having a small assortment of drugs in his luggage, the incident touched off a tempest that naturally drew the interest of the commissioner's office, as well as the MLBPA. When Canadian law enforcement reduced the charge to possession, equivalent to a misdemeanor, Bowie Kuhn, sensitive to the damage done to baseball's image, was having none of it, and he suspended Jenkins. Upon appeal, however, an arbitrator restored Jenkins to active duty, much to the chagrin of Kuhn, as the union "dashed any hope I might have harbored that the Players Association would take a supportive view of my efforts to deal with the drug problem."[25]

As if to validate the appeal by the MLBPA, a Canadian judge found Jenkins, a native of Canada, guilty, but then he vacated his verdict when the pitcher's attorney gave an "emotional plea for leniency."[26] The plea worked, and Jenkins walked away with a clear record, much to the consternation of Kuhn, who felt that efforts to punish wrongdoing would be thwarted by the union, as well as an arbitrator ruling on an associated grievance filed by the offending player. The commissioner felt that the outcome "knocked the last latches off the floodgates," which he believed would soon allow baseball players carte blanche in possessing or using drugs with no attendant consequences.[27]

As an alternative use of cocaine—freebasing—became alarmingly fashionable, baseball's ignorance of it in the summer of 1980, infused with the blithe illusion that the elimination of drugs from the trainer's room had solved the problem, was, by the end of 1981, slowly giving way to the reality and gravity of the situation. To better describe the scope of substances for which a patient could be treated, the term "chemical dependency" came into vogue, and the Meadows facility in Arizona was expanding its operation to other parts of the country to handle the increase in people needing help. On average, patients could expect a tab of $6,000 or more for a stay of five to six weeks.[28]

Yet, the death of former White Sox pitcher Francisco Barrios in April 1982, did little to dissuade other ballplayers, who along with the population at large were being implored by First Lady Nancy Reagan's "Just Say No" antidrug campaign. She was featured along with Bowie Kuhn in a public service announcement—"Sports stars are greatly respected by youngsters, and they are capable of helping our young people 'kick the habit,'" went her script—but the message seemed lost on those who were supposedly being idolized.[29]

As players like San Diego's Alan Wiggins (arrest for possession, followed by treatment) and Juan Bonilla (voluntary submission to rehabilitation) added to the growing list of known users in the summer of 1982, one medical director of a California drug facility claimed in a televised interview that "90 percent of the [major-league] players admitted to some use of cocaine."[30] Reacting to this allegation with predictable outrage concerning blanket criticism directed at his union's members, Marvin Miller, in his memoir, nonetheless unleashed his bile—two full pages worth—regarding Bowie Kuhn's treatment of Ferguson Jenkins but remained virtually mum about other drug cases that had left an unpleasant stain on the game. Corrective action, especially that initiated by Peter Ueberroth, was derided by Miller as "all for the camera," but the fact is that some players, including several of All-Star caliber, paid a dear price, not least of which included the squandering of potential Hall of Fame careers, as well as time served in prison.[31]

In the midst of the 1983 season, Billy Sample of the Texas Rangers tried to put the drug problem "in perspective with the rest of society," but the more he spoke about it, the deeper the hole he dug for himself. "So many people, and I don't know why, think that to be an athlete you can't partake in the same activities other people do," said the outfielder. "*You can have successful athletes who drink, smoke, take amphetamines and on down the line.* But I guess when parents bring their children to the ballpark, to keep their children from going astray, they want us to be role models. But I didn't sign any guarantees saying I'll be what the social role says we should be."[32] Some of those "successful athletes" included Babe Ruth and Mickey Mantle, but the overriding effort to link a sober lifestyle with helping to achieve positive results on the field of play were skewered by Sample's unfortunate observation. Athletes, by their mere appearance in public, are de facto role models whether they choose to be or not.

All the while, stories continued to make their way into the press pertaining to drug use by players. Tim Raines admitted to carrying vials of cocaine in the back pocket of his uniform pants—and sliding headfirst into bases so as not to break the containers holding the drug. Los Angeles Dodgers reliever Steve Howe was in the early stages of chronic abuse of both alcohol and cocaine, and Ron LeFlore of the White Sox, already on manager Tony La Russa's bench for several violations of team policy, was charged with possession of controlled substances and unregistered firearms.

One notable name, who confessed to once being a brutal alcoholic, was doing his best to counter the bleak news emanating from the baseball world. Former Cleveland ace Sam McDowell had turned his life around in dramatic fashion and became a certified addiction counselor, but he stated that despite the commissioner's office decree that teams set up assistance programs, few clubs had been able to do this effectively, and the uneven manner of implementation was hampering potential treatment for those in need. "One general manager was telling me about how his team had a chemical abuse program just because it was affiliated with a rehabilitation center," said the former strikeout artist. "I pointed out to him that mere affiliation didn't mean he had a program in place."[33]

***

The bolstering of assistance programs would become a crucial issue as the 1980s progressed, with the ominous floodgates prophesied by Bowie Kuhn soon to let go a torrent of players caught up with drugs. Perhaps the saddest case of abuse concerned Los Angeles reliever Steve Howe, one of a succession of notable young players joining the Dodgers at that time. Howe's addiction became a worst-case scenario that demonstrated the stranglehold that cocaine can have on an abuser.

As teams were preparing to embark on spring training in early 1983, the Dodgers revealed that Howe and his teammate, Ken Landreaux, had been treated the previous year for substance abuse. While Howe was miffed that word of his problem had surfaced in the press, his manager, Tommy Lasorda, expressed paternal-like disappointment, saying, "I can't understand how someone—not just a ballplayer, anyone—can get involved like that. . . . It's illegal, it's immoral, it's unhealthy. It can ruin a guy's career."[34] For his part, rather than exhibit any remorse for his action, Howe instead was "peeved" that his addiction and treatment came to light, but he was also hopeful that his "new lease on life" would help him move forward.[35]

The too-familiar tandem of alcohol and cocaine had seeped into Howe's world, with use of the drug ruling his daily routine by September 1982. Feeling confident and clean as his fourth big-league season commenced, by mid-May Howe had already logged half as many saves as he had the entire previous year, but before the month was out, Howe was back in rehab and fined $54,000 as a second-time drug offender. In a notice sent to all major-league teams, their respective executives, and drug counselors, Bowie Kuhn insisted, "Discipline was imposed on Howe because of his admitted failure to follow his drug treatment program and his renewed use of drugs after undertaking rehabilitation treatment at the Meadows in Wickenburg, Arizona, last winter."[36]

When Howe filed a grievance about the penalty, John Candelaria of the Pirates declared that the commissioner's office "should have thrown him out of baseball, at least for a year, at least for a year with no pay" so that a strong message would be sent to the players' community at large.[37] At the same time that one of Howe's teammates, Dave Stewart, was claiming he was unaware of Howe's taking drugs again, he confessed on the eve of the opening of the 1984 season that he shielded Howe from view in the Dodgers bullpen so that he could snort cocaine.

A virulent cycle took form for the troubled pitcher, in which a series of stints in recovery were followed by relapses. Eventually Howe would be suspended seven times, his career path wandering from the Dodgers to three other teams willing to gamble that he had freed himself of the grip of substance abuse. The coda of his drug-infested life came in 2006, when he died in a one-vehicle accident, and an autopsy found methamphetamine in his system.

In the summer of 1983, Kuhn addressed all players in a drug policy memorandum he hoped would remove any doubt from baseball's approach to dealing with the problem. Kuhn emphasized the available education and treatment program, and reiterated that those voluntarily seeking help would not be disciplined for a first-time offense. But the commissioner was adamant in repeating, "As stated in posted club rules, the possession or use of illegal drugs of any sort (including illegally obtained prescription drugs) is strictly prohibited."[38] The Dodgers enlisted the help of a Los Angeles–area doctor to recommend a course of action to head off potential problems. But an assistant to the commissioner noted two distinct flaws in Dr. Forest Tennant Jr.'s findings. "I would be curious to know how [team officials] would propose to react to a player's decision *not* to 'volunteer' for testing . . . a voluntary program in my opinion is likely to be haphazard [unless] an effort [is made] toward encouraging all players to volunteer in their own self-interest," Ed Durso, the commissioner's legal assistant, told Kuhn.

Durso also faulted Tennant's suggested testing protocol of "announced time and place of collection" of samples, especially for admitted users, as "totally inappropriate."[39] The commissioner, fully vested in the importance of testing, believed that "random spot testing of [the] team" was the best measure, with a player penalized by a suspension without pay should he refuse to cooperate, but he knew full well that the players' union would see such a tactic as presumption of guilt rather than innocence.[40]

At about the time that the Tennant report was being delivered to the Dodgers, several current and recently released members of the Kansas City Royals were being scrutinized by the FBI for various degrees of involvement with cocaine. Although suspicion of U. L. Washington's possible participation had been dropped, the same was not true for Vida Blue, Jerry Martin, Willie Wilson, and Willie Aikens, all of whom, by mid-October, had pled guilty to federal misdemeanor charges of possession. Beyond the immediate disciplinarian reach of the commissioner's office, the group that would become known as the "Kansas City Four" first had to face sentencing in the Kansas City, Kansas, U.S. District Court.

Aikens, Martin, and Wilson were given three-month jail sentences set to begin and end on differing dates, but Kuhn also added a one-year suspension for each of them. An arbitrator hearing grievances for the three commuted the suspensions to end on May 15, 1984, allowing them to return to work. The commissioner was miffed because of the message the ruling sent, implying that as long as drug violations were put through the grievance process, the end result would carry less severe consequences; however, Kuhn admitted satisfaction that the arbitrator upheld the probation and drug-testing caveats the commissioner ordered. Yet, beat reporter Peter Gammons observed that the jail sentences were adequate and that Aikens, Martin, and Wilson had already been made examples of. "What could be worse for their rehabilitation than to take away their avenue back into the mainstream of society?" he asked.[41] Aikens signed with Toronto, for whom he played 93 games in 1984; Martin joined the Mets (51 games); and Wilson returned to Kansas City (128 games in 1984, with another decade in a major-league uniform still ahead).

The case of the last of the Kansas City Four was complex and generated no small amount of controversy. While Aikens, Martin, and Wilson were caught up with cocaine to a lesser degree and had tested negative to prove that they no longer had drug issues, Vida Blue had been released by the Royals in early August 1983, after failing to win a single game. Gammons took to his column to excoriate Blue for "car[ing] only about being off on his own cloud" while laughing all the way to the bank full in the knowledge of the guaranteed money he was owed by the Royals (more than $2.5 million through 1988).[42] Blue was contrite and expressed remorse at his sentencing in front of a U.S. magistrate—Kuhn said that Blue was "eloquent" when he spoke—but because the depth of his involvement with cocaine was far greater than that of his trio of Royal teammates, Blue had set himself up for a greater fall.[43]

Rather than dabbling in drugs or placing a telephone call to a dealer in an attempt to purchase cocaine for someone other than himself, as was the case with Aikens, Martin, and Wilson, Blue was at a level far above that of a casual user. The pitcher had made the acquaintance of Mark Liebl, labeled as a "super fan" who evolved into the "centerpiece of a league-wide cocaine network and had connected players all around the majors to the drug."[44] The basement of Liebl's home was a den where he hosted drug parties and burnished a sordid reputation for being a supplier to big-league players, one of whom was Blue. In October 1983, Blue pleaded guilty to possessing three grams of cocaine and received the same three-month sentence as Aikens and colleagues. Upon his release from prison, Blue was ignored by major-league teams for several months, but, in June 1984, he attracted the attention of the San Francisco Giants, one of his former teams.

During a prison interview with Bowie Kuhn, Liebl, who was by then serving a sentence at Fort Leavenworth, informed him that Blue himself served as a dealer to other players. Not only was Blue an active user, but also his role as a distributor cast his situation in a more unseemly light, and Blue had grown financially in debt to Liebl as he dealt and used more cocaine. As Kuhn's office continued to investigate, he informed the Giants that they could negotiate with the unemployed pitcher but only sign him with Kuhn's consent.

After his release from prison, Blue, who was saddled with a one-year suspension by the commissioner, revealed the extent of his involvement—cocaine use during 1982 and 1983, visits to Liebl's home and the purchase of cocaine from him, and more—and "while Mr. Blue denied that he ever distributed cocaine to another player, he admitted in this

Figure 4.1. After taking the baseball world by storm in his early years with the Oakland Athletics, Vida Blue fell into an abyss of drug use and distribution of cocaine. He was among a number of notable players swept up in the drug scandal of the early 1980s. National Baseball Hall of Fame and Museum

interview to having introduced Mr. Liebl to four Kansas City teammates."[45] But Blue generally refused to cooperate with Kuhn's probe, forcing the commissioner to keep his sanction in effect.

The MLBPA came to Blue's defense whenever Kuhn tried to impose one form of punishment or another, but their most recent grievance in the midst of the season-long suspension was denied. Arbitrator Richard Bloch weighed the arguments for and against Blue, and found that the "commissioner has satisfied his burden of proving just cause. The evidence firmly supports each of the [five] charges" of which Blue was accused.[46] Forfeiting the remainder of the 1984 season, Blue later signed with the Giants for the 1985 and 1986 seasons, achieving a modicum of success by going 18–18 in a total of 61 starts.

The misdeeds of the Kansas City Four struck particularly hard with the owner of the Royals. The crimes perpetrated, and the attendant convictions of the players left Ewing Kauffman "stunned." Feeling a "twinge of betrayal" because he labored "so hard to build a winning team in a sport that he considered wholesome, all-American, family entertainment," Kauffman believed that athletes had an implicit duty to the fans who supported them and were bound by a rule, written or otherwise, holding them to a higher standard of conduct despite the inherent frailties of life and the human condition to which they were also subject.[47]

***

The Blue saga played out against a backdrop of a reform movement by baseball to control the ostensible drug epidemic. On the day that the commissioner's office announced the upholding of Blue's suspension, the press release ended by stating, "Blue's case is not covered by the newly adopted joint player/management drug program since it involves a conviction on a drug possession charge."[48] That new program had been forged in the course of several preceding months, beginning with a memo from Ed Durso, the counsel of Kuhn's office, outlining a series of items comprising the plan.[49]

Training of management personnel to properly select the people to be given responsibility to administer the program.

Education of players and nonmanagement personnel through provision of information about baseball's drug policy.

The multistep initiative of treatment, rehabilitation, and aftercare for those needing help.

Disciplinary measures, featuring amnesty for those voluntarily admitting a problem and punishment for nonamnesty cases.

It was obvious that baseball could not eliminate the drug problem, but trying to head off the issue through education of the players to better recognize the peril of drugs and assist those affected was a rational approach; however, the list of cocaine users—suspected and confirmed—was growing. Lonnie Smith of the St. Louis Cardinals voluntarily stepped forward in June 1983, but two of his teammates were rumored to be afflicted. One of them, Keith Hernandez, was just a few years removed from being a NL co-MVP, and the first baseman drew unsparing ire from his manager, Whitey Herzog.

When Herzog noticed a reduction in Hernandez's offensive hustle, he confessed,

> I can't say that I knew Keith had been doing drugs. . . . Unless you spot a guy snorting coke or smoking marijuana, or unless some reliable witness comes to you or it blows up in the press, you never know for sure. At the same time, a manager has to be either stupid or looking the other way when a player's work habits change as much as Hernandez's did.[50]

With Hernandez's contract soon to expire and his right to veto any trade about to take effect, Herzog decided it was better to trade him rather than risk being stuck with a player possessed of a "horseshit attitude."[51]

Hernandez was shipped to the Mets—"addition by subtraction," said Herzog about ridding him from the Cardinals—and in early 1984, the player angrily denied insinuations by the former head of the players' union, Ken Moffett, that some players, including Hernandez, had been recently traded because of suspected drug involvement.[52] Exhibiting outrage and threatening to sue over a breach regarding a "confidential conversation" he had while in his role as the St. Louis player representative, Hernandez would change his tune a year later when he was compelled to testify in a federal drug trial.[53]

Some members of the press were crying out for baseball to clean itself up, notably syndicated columnist Milton Richman. "Protective of the players as he is in his role as executive director of their association, can [Marvin] Miller possibly make any kind of reasonable argument in defense of drug use that will be accepted by the fans?" he openly asked, and then answered his own question by concluding, "I doubt it."[54]

In the spring of 1984, baseball's Executive Council was responding to a memorandum it had received from Morgan, Lewis & Bockius, a law firm the commissioner's office had retained to seek its opinion about a joint drug program hoped to be favorable to both the MLBPA and the owners' Player Relations Committee (PRC). While acknowledging that the enforcement approach taken by professional basketball "merely provide[d] [a player] greater incentive to deny and conceal" his drug problem, baseball's perspective held that,

> There appears to be some evidence that the threat and imposition of discipline has not resulted in abatement of the problem. To the contrary, it appears to be increasing and, therefore, raises a legitimate question as to whether different experimental approaches should be tried. The philosophy of the Joint Drug Program is founded on the premise that unless we can begin to bring the Players Association into a joint and cooperative effort, the likelihood of success in handling the drug problem is extremely small. This program is an attempt to take the first step toward building bridges with the association and hopefully working jointly to erode the distrust and adversarial nature of the relationship. If this program works, it will be because the association has enough incentive to work with the clubs cooperatively to discover the drug problems and assist the clubs in getting rehabilitative help for the players.[55]

Further discomfort was evident in the development of a way to test players for drug usage, if any way could be implemented at all. Al Rosen, president of the Houston Astros, at once supported random testing and scoffed at those claiming such a methodology would impinge on the civil rights of the players. "Everyone agrees we're talking about an illness, but drugs, unlike cancer, are an illness of choice," Rosen told *Sporting News*. "And baseball owners should have a right to protect themselves against a loss from players who choose to become ill."[56]

In a private note to the head of the PRC, Gussie Busch and Fred Kuhlmann criticized a proposed joint agreement and told Lee MacPhail that such a proposal "falls far short of being 'a determined drug enforcement program,'" and "[it] will let the MLBPA 'off the hook.'"[57] The pair of Cardinals executives had already seen the havoc wrought on their team, so it was with little wonder that they were extremely sensitive to any shortcomings of the joint program.

When four months of bargaining between the PRC and the union ended in late May, and the issue went to a ballot by the union, the players overwhelmingly approved the measure, in large part because it was toothless in the eyes of ownership—there was no stipulation for mandatory testing, and detection of amphetamines and marijuana was absent. Dr. Donald Ottenberg, a consultant working with the special committee formed to conclude a joint plan who "had earned the respect and confidence of [representatives of owners and the union]," observed that the program did indeed lack definitive substance in some areas, but he said of one key point of contention, "universal mandatory testing entailed a number of different medical problems and thus could not be regarded as a panacea."[58]

Kuhn took a swipe at the union when he speculated "whether cooperation can realistically be expected from the Players Association," his remarks coming in the wake of an arbitrator's overturning of the commissioner's suspension of pitcher Pascual Perez, whose arrest for cocaine possession in his native Dominican Republic came under a cloud of suspicion when he recanted his confession to police.[59] A frustrated Gene Autry, owner of the California Angels and a renowned free-spender, vented in a letter to Texas Ranger mogul Eddie Chiles:

> I am not in favor of baseball having to pay a player to stay sober or to stay off drugs in order to play the game. He is supposed to be in condition and remain in condition from the time the season opens until the World Series is over. I can understand helping a first-time offender, but after that I cannot see paying these fabulous salaries to someone who is not able to perform and won't help himself. This is not a one-way road.[60]

After delaying their own vote on the measure and debating what they viewed as shortcomings of the plan, the owners, on June 21, 1984, finally convened and consented to the program. Kuhn's office released a statement in which Roy Eisenhardt, Oakland Athletics president and a member of the owners' committee that addressed the issue, stated that the plan as ratified was "not a panacea, but a good constructive first step shaped in the fashion recommended to us by professionals in the field."[61] A follow-up missive outlined the nine rules that codified measures for amnesty and discipline, including lifetime suspensions in egregious cases.

The joint plan was on a short leash given that either side had the option to terminate it at the end of the season, the timing also coinciding with the departure of Bowie Kuhn and the commencement of Peter Ueberroth's term as his replacement. The new commissioner found the MLBPA adamant about plans for mandatory testing. Yet, he also understood the need to uphold the integrity of the game. In the spring of 1985, Donald Fehr, now the acting director of the MLBPA, continued to adhere to the union's policy that maintained a player's innocence of drug involvement—in any way—until proven guilty. But by this point, the players were isolated in their resistance to any sort of drug testing program.

Ueberroth was later decried by Marvin Miller for his grandstanding posture and concern for the image of the national pastime, while Fehr held fast to the idea of testing as being "inappropriate." When Ueberroth revealed a program to test virtually all baseball personnel—owners, administrative staffs, scouts, as well as several thousand minor leaguers, everyone *except* major league players—Fehr was miffed about "the hasty way in which Ueberroth announced the plan" with little prior notification to the MLBPA.[62] But as the roll of names of drug users continued to expand—Daryl Sconiers, Mike Norris, and Alan Wiggins (again) heading for rehab—the head of the umpires union stated a plain truth: "No one cares if the ticket manager of a NL team is doing cocaine," said Richie Phillips. "The concern is with the players."[63]

The commissioner held out an olive branch of sorts, explaining that no penalty would be issued for first-time offenders caught in the random testing procedure, to be conducted three times per year. "There are laws in society to punish people. I don't see my main role as commissioner to punish people," said Ueberroth.[64] But as the year progressed and the players dug in their heels, there was one agency from whom they could not escape, ignore, or protest their right to privacy. The air around the game and the drug affairs were turning very sordid, and hand-wringing began in earnest in late May, when indictments by a federal grand jury in Pittsburgh produced an event from which the players were unable to hide.

***

After hearing the testimony of more than a dozen baseball players since the beginning of 1985, the U.S. attorney for western Pennsylvania indicted seven men whose normal vocations were nothing out of the ordinary: photographer, heating and air conditioning workers, bartender, charity administrator, caterer. They were to be brought to trial for establishing three networks of drug distribution whose clients included unnamed major leaguers. One of the alleged dealers sold cocaine to players to cultivate friendships with them "but found the business so lucrative he made it his full-time job and flew to Florida every two weeks to purchase a pound of cocaine, which has a market value of $44,800."[65]

Slowly being pulled back was the curtain behind which drug-using players were hiding. Shielded from mandatory testing but not federal indictments, ballplaying customers of drug dealers were now in the uncomfortable process of having to face the klieg lights of television cameras and the tape recorders of journalists seeking their side of a story, not soon to go away.

In an extensive study that detailed a carefully constructed scheme for servicing cocaine users, the *New York Times* discovered that

> 165 counts covered in the indictments [show] that the dates of 133 counts match days on which the Pittsburgh Pirates were home during the seasons from 1980 through 1984. In the case of [accused dealer] Dale Shiffman, who was indicted on 111 counts, 87 counts with dates in 1983 match every single one of the 87 days the Pirates were in Pittsburgh during that season, either with games scheduled or days off.

When asked for his comment on this curious coincidence, the U.S. attorney, J. Alan Johnson, was mum, but another law enforcement official paid the newspaper a compliment by saying, "You've certainly done your homework."[66] A lawyer from Philadelphia whose client, caterer Curtis Strong, briefly provided food service for the Phillies, had knowledge of the date matchings and observed, "Without question this whole thing involves the ballplayers."[67]

After the seven alleged dealers entered pleas of not guilty and awaited trial, the *Times* authored another lengthy report in which a dismaying number of players—and, in some instances, specific names—involved with cocaine were disclosed.[68] The startling revelations included this: "One owner, who requested anonymity, said an agent had told him [in 1984] that he could field an all-star team in each league with players using cocaine," as well as an admission by some club executives that the drug problem was growing rather than abating. Ueberroth concurred that there was no lessening of the issue and believed it to be the biggest concern facing the game, which he also feared might lead to further trouble if the influence of gamblers began to work in concert with drug dealers.

One month before the trial was to occur in Pittsburgh, disappointing news spilled from the *Times* story:

> Players representing almost all the 26 major-league teams have been named in connection with cocaine use.
> Two players—Dale Berra of the Yankees and Dave Parker of the Cincinnati Reds—were among the players named as cocaine purchasers.
> A former member of the San Francisco Giants cited the names of four players on the 1985 team as frequent cocaine users.
> The officials said those likely to be called to testify in [Strong's] trial, scheduled for next month, include [Keith] Hernandez, [Dale] Berra, [Dave] Parker, Lee Lacy of Baltimore, Lonnie Smith of Kansas City, Al Holland of California, Jeff Leonard of San Francisco, and Enos Cabell of Los Angeles.

Neither did the city of Pittsburgh have a monopoly on drugs: A former ice-cream salesman in Milwaukee was sentenced to 22 years for running an illicit distribution enterprise that hauled in $17 million annually, and at least 10 players from the Brewers, White Sox, and Indians were identified in a probe by the FBI and the Internal Revenue Service, the latter organization having reviewed bank transactions among suspects. Dick Davis, Paul Molitor, and Claudell Washington confirmed purchasing from the salesman-turned-dealer.

As was the case with the NBA and the NFL, MLB could no longer claim, as it did in August 1980, that there was "little misuse of drugs" and that "use of illegal drugs in baseball is no more prevalent than in any other sector of society, *in fact, perhaps less*."[69] The volume of easily recognizable names—with more to follow—indicated that players with star power were caught up in what was turning into a crisis. Ken Moffett, jettisoned as head of the MLBPA, whose comments more than inferred a drug problem among the union membership, had to have felt a rueful sense of vindication.

Players called to the witness stand during the September 1985 trial of Curtis Strong in Pittsburgh were granted immunity from prosecution, including Keith Hernandez. The stellar first baseman shed his earlier outrage at being an accused cocaine user and admitted to consuming "'massive amounts of cocaine' during the second half of 1980." He added, "I played a game under the influence of the drug."[70] Now with the

Figure 4.2. At first vehemently denying any use of drugs, a contrite Keith Hernandez regained his footing following a trade from the St. Louis Cardinals to the New York Mets. He became an integral part of the turnaround in the Mets' fortunes during the mid-1980s. National Baseball Hall of Fame and Museum

Mets, Hernandez claimed that 40 percent of players at that time were users but believed that the recent prison sentences for the Kansas City Four had served as a wakeup call to discourage others from further such drug use. In the aftermath of his June 1983 trade from St. Louis to the Big Apple—about the time he said he had quit cocaine—Hernandez chose to reside in Connecticut rather than the immediate environs of Manhattan, the better to avoid possibly being drawn back to the temptation of drugs. Through the good graces of teammate Rusty Staub, who was also a noted restaurateur, Hernandez was coaxed into Midtown to partake in Staub's ritual of using his eatery's delivery van to chauffeur several Mets around the city to show them the positive aspects of so many cultural opportunities on offer there. "As a result, he began to like the city. Then he *really* liked the city," Staub later commented of Hernandez, who by this time had not only turned his life around and relocated from Connecticut, but also assumed an important leadership role with the Mets.[71]

When the trial ended on September 20, Strong was found guilty on 11 counts of distribution of cocaine. The following week, another trial commenced in a series of courtroom dramas that would eventually result in guilty pleas, conviction, and prison time for the seven dealers with Pittsburgh connections. "Who Deserves Apology?" asked a headline in *Sporting News*, which in a posttrial editorial noted that Keith Hernandez offered contrite remarks to Mets fans but ignored the man to whom much of his bile had previously been directed. "If Hernandez was looking for worthy recipients of his apologies, how could he pass up Ken Moffett?" Recall that Moffett claimed having "encountered bitter opposition within the union to any sanctions against drug users" and demonstrated a willingness to employ testing as a means to rid the sport of its dangerous problem.[72]

Flush with the verdicts that proved the miscreants' guilt, Ueberroth determined to mete out suitable punishments and implement the long-sought testing plan. The penalties came in three classes: one-year suspensions for the seven players deemed "facilitators" for both using cocaine and having a role in its distribution (Joaquin Andujar, Dale Berra, Enos Cabell, Keith Hernandez, Jeffrey Leonard, Dave Parker, and Lonnie Smith); 60-day suspensions for four other users (Al Holland, Lee Lacy, Lary Sorensen, Claudell Washington); and no suspensions for 10 players named during the trials (Dusty Baker, Vida Blue, Gary Matthews, Dickie Noles, Tim Raines, Manny Sarmiento, Daryl Sconiers, Rod Scurry, Derrel Thomas, Alan Wiggins). Those suspended for one year had the option of revoking their suspensions by donating 10 percent of their base salary to a drug rehabilitation program and performing 100 hours of community service for two years or more, and the 60-day group could be reinstated with a 5 percent donation and 50 hours of community service. All of the above would be subjected to mandatory random testing as a condition of reinstatement. Setting up a mandatory testing program, however, would prove far more difficult for Ueberroth than it was for him to impose his edicts of suspension.

***

No small amount of controversy attended the debate about random testing. Matters of privacy, civil rights, and presumption of innocence abounded, and were staples in the major-league players' quest to avoid submitting to testing. Minor leaguers, beyond the reach of any protective benefit of the Players Association, were slated for testing, and as vocal as the union was about upholding the rights of their big-league membership, no one rushed to the defense of their colleagues in the lower ranks.

Marvin Miller, serving as consultant to union head Donald Fehr, criticized those punished by Ueberroth for lacking the fortitude to challenge the penalties they had been dealt, telling the *Los Angeles Times*, "We apparently don't have one man—and I use that term advisedly—who has the courage to stand up for his rights." Snidely looking at Ueberroth as a crusader reveling in his position to rule on drug-using players, Miller asked, "I mean, is Ueberroth the law? Do you sit back and accept that?"[73] Miller believed that the punished players had nothing to lose by appealing their cases, and he further worried that the reaction to the trial verdicts, which prompted some players to act on their own volition and freely submit to testing to prove their drug-free condition, would undermine the unity of the association in its desire to have no players tested.

For their part, team owners had begun to dig in, inserting testing clauses in contracts to make sure a player had incentive to stay clean, with more than 450 players so affected for 1986. But in other levels of management, concerns arose about the suspected inaccuracies and false-positive results that hampered the credibility of several current testing procedures. General manager Dal Maxvill of the Cardinals, while agreeing that the scourge of drugs had no place in the game, also fully understood the stance of the union because unreliable test results were pernicious in their own way. In the meantime, a significant grievance was making its way to a hearing that would allow MLBPA to claim victory in the contentious issue.

In seeking to come to terms with the San Francisco Giants prior to the 1986 season, Joel Youngblood balked at the inclusion of a testing provision in his nonguaranteed contract but then relented. When the Giants thereafter withdrew their offer, a grievance was initiated, and arbitrator Tom Roberts compelled the Giants to sign Youngblood. A final resolution was handed down by Roberts in late July in which he ruled, "The drug-testing clauses in nonguaranteed contracts were in violation of the 1985 Basic Agreement, thus upholding the union's position. . . . The ruling applied to all except the 44 with guaranteed contracts and to those players disciplined by Ueberroth."[74] Pleased with the decision, Donald Fehr commented, "It reaffirms an important principle in this industry. Management cannot bypass the [players] association and use *individual negotiations* to change the players' term and conditions of employment."[75]

Peter Ueberroth sought to keep the elimination of drugs as the centerpiece of his administration, testifying in front of a Select Committee on Narcotics Abuse and Control shortly before the Roberts decision. He spoke in glowing terms of the sport's advances since he took office.

> I am here today because I am angry, because I am scared, and because I am committed to helping this country declare war on cocaine, marijuana, and heroin, and to help win that war. I will tell you that baseball is defeating the problem. Frankly, the battle is over. There will be a flare-up or two that you may hear or read about, but the institution of baseball has returned proper dignity to itself and would hope to become an example for other institutions . . . and also, baseball players can again become role models for the millions of youngsters that are out there.[76]

The commissioner defended the accuracy of testing, citing "thousands of Olympic and amateur athletes" and "hundreds and hundreds of professional baseball players who are in the minor leagues" who did not question the findings of a test, and, he stressed, "The system guarantees absolute confidentiality for any of the minor-league players tested." Ueberroth went on to inform the committee that during World War II he felt that some of his basic civil rights were violated because of wartime blackout restrictions. "I was inside the sanctity of my own home, but I couldn't turn on a light because it was against the law. I'm against that kind of law, but it was a law of an emergency nature that helped us face a problem, which was a war. We have to declare war on drugs, and drug testing is one of many, many partial solutions."

Ueberroth later addressed the goal of ridding baseball of a legal substance—chewing tobacco—which did eventually occur beginning in the minor leagues in 1993, but not before returning to the theme of his crusade: "We are stopping drugs in baseball. . . . It is over. You are not going to hear of any more baseball scandals from these days forward." This upbeat attitude, however, would not square with the reality of the circumstances.

Drugs were not eliminated from baseball any more than they were from society, and the national pastime was not spared from further embarrassment in the near future nor in the decade ahead. More top-ranking players would succumb to the temptation of drugs—LaMarr Hoyt, Dwight Gooden, and Darryl Strawberry come to mind—which aborted or derailed promising careers. A harsh reminder of the peril of these substances came just weeks after Ueberroth's testimony when a promising basketball player recently drafted by the Boston Celtics, Len Bias, died from an overdose of cocaine.

By the summer of 1987, Lonnie Smith, one of the players swept up in the Pittsburgh affair, told the *New York Post* about a lack of oversight by the commissioner's office in ensuring that his punishment was being properly administered. The article—with typical *Post* cheek, it was titled "Drug En-farcement"—told readers that fines to be paid and the hours of community service to be performed, which were conditions applying to a player's reinstatement, were not being properly accounted for or monitored. There were inconsistencies in handling drug offenders, Smith claimed. "It's not fair," he said of a recent incident that put the lie to Ueberroth's boast of an end to drugs in baseball. "Look at [Dwight] Gooden. He doesn't have to pay nothing. Where's the justice? Is it okay because he's a Cy Young winner?"[77] For his part, the commissioner was dismissive of Smith's complaint, telling ABC-TV's *Good Morning America* program, "If you penalize someone, they're never pleased."[78]

Cocaine would not completely vanish from baseball-related headlines, but it did fade to a large degree; however, its place would soon be taken by another substance that would drag the national pastime into another unpalatable episode and subject it to more scrutiny stretching into the twenty-first century. Steroids and performance-enhancing drugs (PEDs) gained currency and seemed to pick up where cocaine was leaving off.

***

In the last few years of the 1980s, a new malaise crept into the landscape of the national pastime. Although the true impact of steroids on baseball would not be felt for another decade, the introduction of these performance-enhancing substances into the world of sports had already been occurring for a number of years. A former physician for the U.S. Olympic team, Dr. Max M. Novich, said in 1972, that the use of steroids could stimulate one's appetite and enable those ingesting them to gain weight and strength, while a U.S. gold medalist in the 1956 Summer Olympics stated in testimony in front of a U.S. Senate committee in 1973, "The overwhelming majority of athletes I know would do anything, and take anything, short of killing themselves to improve athletic performance."[79]

The procedure that came to be known as doping gained currency at various times dating to the late 1800s, when European bicyclists consumed ether-laced sugar tablets, sizable quantities of caffeine, or concoctions of brandy, heroin, cocaine, and strychnine. Some early twentieth-century boxers even drank strychnine in combination with alcoholic beverages during their matches. But the use of such bizarre methods was believed to be isolated to the realm of individual sports rather than team competition. With steroid use growing more prevalent during the 1960s, the International Olympic Committee sought to ferret out athletes and disqualify those found to have used any of the more than 100 different substances that were difficult to detect once subjected to the metabolic process of the human body.

As new substances were introduced—their having been created with the purpose of avoiding detection—a cat-and-mouse scenario developed in which the athletes and their facilitators tried to keep ahead of sports officials intent on determining which athletes were in violation of drug prohibitions. But even relatively common over-the-counter medicines had the capability of felling an Olympian: At the time of the 1976 Olympics, the number of banned substances had reached 300, and an "athlete could lose a medal because he swallowed a cough drop."[80]

More disturbing than the ostensibly harmless act of taking a throat lozenge or nose drops to relieve sinus congestion was the increased use of steroids, especially among football players wishing to bulk up with the muscle mass necessary on the gridiron to outperform their rivals. In a 1992 deathbed confession at the age of 43, lineman Lyle Alzado admitted to taking large amounts of human-growth hormones and steroids to enhance his strength and performance, a risk he believed worth taking to become a three-time All-Pro player. Controversy ensued regarding the extent to which Alzado's brain cancer had been impacted by steroids, but his demise was nevertheless alarming.

A practical benefit can be derived from a controlled application of a steroid, as was administered to George Brett of the Kansas City Royals in 1979, in an attempt to remedy a thumb injury, and in 1985, for San Francisco outfielder Jeffrey Leonard's wrist. Cortisone, which also is a steroid, had been widely used for treating inflammation of joints, and baseball players, notably pitchers, found much relief through its use.

However, the legitimate uses of steroids to address injuries ran counter to their nefarious employment for purposes of performance enhancement. In 1983, the Pan Am Games in Caracas, Venezuela, were defamed by the disqualification of 15 athletes—most of them weightlifters—as well as a "suspiciously large number of track and field athletes [who] either were scratched from their events or withdrew with sudden 'injuries,' presumably to avoid . . . being tested."[81] Medical professionals also began to express worry about the long-term effects of steroid use and openly questioned how beneficial the supposed rewards were in contrast to the dangers involved.

Away from the weightlifting and track and field arenas, at least one athlete, basketball player Jim Rowinski of Purdue University, seemed to have legitimately turned his physique into a hulking form through weight training. Yet, he could not shake the nickname "Steroid," which his teammates had bestowed on him. And one baseball player, Brian Downing of the California Angels, turned heads earlier in 1978, when he displayed bulked-up muscles credited to lifting weights, although he was later unfairly associated with being a forerunner in baseball's slide into the steroid era.

Burgeoning rumors of steroid use in the mid-1980s fueled speculation that collegiate athletes were so infected. Bob Goldman, a high-ranking official with the Amateur Athletic Union, claimed that with muscle-building a priority for young athletes, steroids had become a centerpiece for that effort, and he observed, "College coaches don't want to hear about drug tests," as they would hamper their work in building competitive teams. At the same time the issue was gaining attention, the NCAA "tabled a proposal to ban so-called performance-enhancing drugs," but at least three schools—Penn State, Pittsburgh, and West Virginia—announced in 1984, that their football programs would test players for drugs *and* steroids.[82]

In the realm of football especially, the rare player of the 1960s who weighed in above the 300-pound mark had long been supplanted by linemen almost expected to be near or above that weight a generation later. Even six deaths linked to steroid abuse in 1984 and early 1985 failed to discourage athletes from involvement with these substances. Drug smuggling, long associated with marijuana, cocaine, and heroin, now included illegal steroids when a British weightlifter was arrested on this offense.

Steroids appeared to have a more logical fit with football players than baseball players, in part because muscle-bound performers on the diamond were believed to be hampered by excess body mass, rendering them less effective in throwing a ball and swinging a bat. That thinking began to change in 1986, when an outfielder with the Oakland Athletics won Rookie of the Year honors and blazed a trail indicating his certain election to the Baseball Hall of Fame.

***

Born in a suburb of Havana, Cuba, and emigrating to the United States in 1965, Jose Canseco graduated from a South Florida high school where he played baseball well enough to attract the attention of the Athletics, who drafted him in the 15th round of the 1982 amateur draft. The early death of his mother came in 1984, when Canseco was in his first full year of Class A ball, and prompted him to pledge to make himself a superior player. He then embarked on his first experience with steroids, introduced to him by a former high school friend. The results were impressive, to say the least.

Along the way in his formative years in the minors, Canseco continued to use steroids to bulk up his formerly rawboned frame. Sporting a physique that was the envy of any bodybuilder, he took the American League (AL) by storm in 1986, by capturing that circuit's Rookie of the Year Award, batting a modest .240, but dazzling with his 33 homers and 117 RBIs. Canseco's production the following year was similar (.257, 31 home runs, 113 RBIs), but then he added speed to his repertoire in 1988, and stole 40 bases, led the majors in homers (42) and RBIs (124), and was selected the AL MVP in leading Oakland to the first of three consecutive pennants. Now firmly established, this uber-talent became the inaugural member of the "40–40 Club" and was "hailed as the prototype of the next generation of superstar players."[83]

Augmenting Canseco's performance was that of his new teammate, slugging first baseman Mark McGwire, who would follow Canseco in winning laurels as the top AL rookie in 1987. The pair teamed up for a ploy in which they were marketed as the "Bash Brothers," trading on the likes of the former "Blues Brothers" comic team of John Belushi and Dan Aykroyd. But coursing beneath the slick publicity was the role of Canseco in becoming the self-styled "godfather of steroids in baseball."[84] McGwire also fell under the muscle-building regimen used by Canseco, and as he fortified himself with steroids and joined the ranks of the top home-run hitters, the Oakland teammates often marked their slugging feats by bumping raised forearms in celebration.

As other major leaguers of the late 1980s quietly took note of the benefit reaped by the two Oakland stars and began their own steroid use, the NFL was taking steps in an attempt to curb this latest substance issue by announcing a plan to educate personnel about the hazards associated with steroids. In 1987, officials at the NFL combine found that almost 10 percent of 330 players had tested positive for drugs, alcohol, or steroids. For his part, Canseco was merely the subject of a well-publicized rumor that surfaced on the eve of the 1988 American League Championship Series.

Speculation about Canseco's alleged link to steroids commenced upon a statement made by *Washington Post* columnist Thomas Boswell on a late-night talk show. When Boswell stunned viewers by claiming that the slugger was the "most conspicuous example of a [baseball] player who made himself great with steroids," damage control suddenly leapt to the forefront of the business of baseball even though Boswell's own editor at the *Post* refused to allow the comments into print.[85] Immediately assuming a defensive posture, Canseco naturally denied any involvement with steroids, instead attributing his muscular build to physical exercises and weight training. In the playoff's opening game, Boston fans treated him to a chorus of "Ste-roids! Ste-roids!" during each of his plate appearances.[86]

Just weeks after Canseco was taunted at Fenway Park, Congress passed the Anti-Drug Abuse Act of 1988, which, among its directives, "amends the Federal Food, Drug, and Cosmetic Act to make it a criminal offense to distribute or to possess with the intent to distribute any anabolic steroid *other than in accordance with a physician's order for the purpose of treating disease.* [It] authorizes the imposition of longer prison terms if distribution or intent is directed to an individual under age 18."[87] Two years later, another measure, the Anabolic Steroids Control Act, classified steroids as a substance commensurate with amphetamines, opioids, and morphine, and in late spring of 1991, steroids were included with baseball's banned substances per commissioner Fay Vincent's edict.

Despite the legislation enactments and the good intentions of baseball's eighth commissioner, the lurid episode of what came to be labeled the Steroid Era was still years away from fully running its course and thus beyond the time frame of this book. Nonetheless, the crippling players' strike of 1994 found redemption in several notable events subsequent to the labor action: the attention devoted to Cal Ripken Jr. in his quest to break Lou Gehrig's consecutive games-played record and the chase by a number of sluggers to break the single-season home-run record. As fans packed stadiums in the late 1990s to watch dueling power-hitters vie for the most long balls struck, the pumped-up players at the forefront—chiefly, Mark McGwire, Sammy Sosa, and Barry Bonds—were lauded for their efforts. And the publicity—to say nothing of the boost in revenue—for the clubs and their owners signaled that baseball had shed the ills of the ugly strike and put the national pastime back atop America's sporting realm.

As the '90s progressed, baseball's façade of wholesomeness withered as before-and-after photographs of players suspected of using steroids drew scrutiny. Players exhibiting lean figures early in their careers had now ballooned in size—Bonds and pitcher Roger Clemens, for example—and not until the beginning of the twenty-first century would concrete steps be taken to finally put into practice an effective all-encompassing drug-testing policy. In 2005, Mark McGwire pleaded Fifth Amendment privilege in front of a U.S. House committee when questioned about his alleged steroid usage, but his former Bash Brother was less reticent. Jose Canseco published a tawdry memoir revealing the truth of his involvement—steroids for personal use and his role as an enabler for other teammates' use—and putting the lie to the denials he first issued in the wake of the Boswell accusation.

On the heels of Canseco's entry into the 40–40 Club and subsequent heckling by Boston Red Sox fans, there was another rupture at the Summer Olympic Games in Seoul, South Korea. Ben Johnson, a Canadian sprinter, won the 100-meter dash but was then stripped of his gold medal after testing positive for an anabolic steroid, Stanozolol. Commenting in *Sporting News*, columnist Art Spander wrote, "We're sorry. Sorry for Ben Johnson. Sorry for a society that puts so much emphasis on success that an athlete will try anything to find an edge."[88]

A new wrinkle, inchoate but nevertheless emerging, had been introduced to the national pastime, where cheating with scuffed baseballs, corked bats, spitballs, sign-stealing, and subtle landscape tailoring of the infield grass or foul lines had been part of the game for generations. Rather than tampering with equipment, the playing field, or one's hands through the application of foreign substances, performers on the field were now turning inward—in the most literal sense—in an attempt to obtain that edge.

***

The insidious problem of drugs in the United States persists to the present day, and during the years covered by this book, it is clear that every sport was impacted by the issue. Athletes faced temptations on two fronts: Performance-enhancing substances could improve their chances for success on the field of play, while recreational drugs offered a means of psychological escape. Baseball players were exposed to both, and as we have seen, more than a few of them fell victim to the allure of these substances.

With regard to PEDs, academics Elliott J. Gorn and Warren Goldstein point out a crucial distinction between athletes seeking fame and those with less ambitious goals. Amateurs and weekend warriors find little need for the benefits of steroids, "but if an Olympic medal can be glimpsed in the distance, or a four-year scholarship to a private college, or a television commercial, the calculation changes." At the professional level of most sports, the financial stakes have grown too high to ignore any chance to land a contract or an endorsement earned through athletic achievement. Gorn and Goldstein conclude, "The use of drugs—recreational drugs to alter moods, performance-enhancing drugs to increase strength and endurance, analgesics to enable pain to be endured—grows out of the larger assumption that our bodies can be objectified in the most extreme ways in order to attain the desired end, victory over an opponent."[89]

Ordinary people are not subject to the same win-at-all-costs mentality as athletes, but the problem of recreational drugs casts a wider net across the whole of society. Marijuana users or those addicted to cocaine are found in every walk of life, with the only differences between the citizen and the ballplayer being the chosen walk of life and the size of the paycheck. As virtuous as the war on drugs may have been, its failure to eradicate them leaves the conundrum intact among the general public. The segment of baseball history covered in these pages is only a portion of the continuum in which the national pastime and the less attractive aspects of our culture coexist.

5

TAKE ME OUT TO THE (NEWER) BALLPARK

In the general time frame covered by the pages of this book, several brand-new stadiums were opened to varying degrees of acclaim, but by the end of the 1980s, the makings of a dramatic shift were in the process of being rendered on paper and in blueprints. New stadiums constructed from the mid-1950s onward—or extant facilities that were expanded to accommodate Major League Baseball (MLB)—served their intended purpose of providing fields for their hometown teams. With historical hindsight, it can be easy in the current day to criticize the uneven manner in which these endeavors were handled at the time Dodger Stadium, Shea Stadium, and a host of other facilities were built. Whether these ballparks were poorly situated (Candlestick Park), were less than ideal due to alterations forced by the addition of new decks and sections (Metropolitan Stadium in Bloomington, Minnesota), or became prime examples of what came to be pejoratively called "concrete donuts" or "cookie-cutters" because of their formulaic shape and seemingly indistinguishable features (Veterans Stadium in Philadelphia, among others), the so-called modern stadiums of the generation leading into the mid-1970s had begun to mature and, in many cases, revealed themselves to be ill-suited to fan-friendly environs for the configurations of both baseball diamonds and football gridirons.

The purpose of hosting dual sports in one stadium was to allow a more favorable return on a municipality's investment in footing the bill for constructing said facility, but it became quickly evident—especially for baseball fans—that new stadiums, with so many seats located far from the playing field, had stripped away any sense of intimacy that had long been inherent with places like Shibe Park, Ebbets Field, or the Polo Grounds. Adding to an ambience shot through with plastic and artifice was the proliferation of Astroturf, installed by necessity at indoor facilities because, as had been proven at the Astrodome, real grass was unable to grow in enclosed spaces. Yet, the "carpet," as it were, also found favor at outdoor stadiums because of its durability and low maintenance. That players found running on artificial surfaces tough on their legs and knees—Astroturf, Tartan Turf, and their ilk were laid over what in essence was a large tract of asphalt—and field-level temperatures in the summer could be stifling, at more than 100 degrees, there were discoveries made in the wake of the increased use of artificial surfaces and given less consideration than the supposed savings vis-à-vis the upkeep of natural grass fields. Such shortsightedness yielded to better qualities of man-made surfaces but not until years later.

These assets and liabilities were part of the growing pains and learning curve endured by stadium planners and architects who designed these facilities, as well as the players who used this newest generation of stadiums. Not until the late 1980s did an updated version of the old, classic ballparks begin to take form, and then only on paper. From 1977 until the later years of the following decade, revised takes on the concrete donuts of the 1960s era continued to sprout, for better or worse.

***

The first American League (AL) indoor stadium, home to the major-league Mariners, as well as the Seahawks of the National Football League (NFL) and the National Basketball Association's (NBA) Supersonics, was the Kingdome of Seattle. Designed in the aftermath of the dispute in which the 1969 expansion Seattle Pilots moved to Milwaukee to become recast as the Brewers in 1970, the officially named King County Multipurpose Domed Stadium drew inspiration from the Houston Astrodome and the New Orleans Superdome, and it was intended to hold the typically rainy weather of the Pacific Northwest at bay, eliminating rain delays and game postponements.

Ground for the stadium was broken by local Seattle officials in November 1972, an event significant in that baseball had no plans to add new teams at that time. Yet, the city remained confident that a new weather-resistant facility would draw the attention of baseball executives who might consider expansion or the transfer of an existing franchise in the near future. The building of the Kingdome was hampered by construction delays, cost overruns, a labor dispute involving some of the building contractors, the incompetence of the primary firm in charge of the project, and problems with buttresses used to support the concrete roof. Finally completed in the spring of 1976, the Kingdome still had no baseball tenant but was poised to accept one. The birth of the Mariners just two months prior to the completion of the Kingdome occurred when the AL approved Seattle and Toronto as new franchises.

The Kingdome featured an audio system with speakers that were suspended from the ceiling 110 feet above the playing field—raised to 133½ feet in 1981—and batted balls that struck them were considered in play. "Batted ball hitting any suspended object, such as speakers, wires, streamers, etc., in *fair* territory shall be judged fair or foul in relation to where it lands or is touched by a fielder. If caught by a fielder, the batter is out and the base runners advance at their own risk," explained a note in a Mariners game program.[1] While such feats were rare, a foul ball becoming stuck in a speaker was ruled a strike, but those in fair territory became ground-rule doubles; however, the general milieu of the Kingdome was conducive to batted balls becoming home runs: From 1977 to 1989, only Tiger Stadium outpaced the Mariners' venue for homers allowed in the AL, 2,215 to 2,159.

With their home park fully enclosed, the Mariners succeeded in warding off inclement weather, but the Kingdome also earned the dubious nickname of "the Tomb" because of the vast amount of concrete used in its construction. In an age when municipally funded multipurpose stadiums were built to maximize the return on investment to the local government, the ballclub cheerily observed, "As of January 1981, property taxes were no longer collected to finance the Kingdome, and the taxpayers of King County ended up paying only $11½ million for their $67 million stadium."[2] This may have been welcoming news at the time, but it became a specious statement in the mid-1990s when, according to the *Seattle Times*, repairs of cracks in the roof and falling ceiling tiles ran to $51 million.[3]

As virtuous as the Kingdome tried to be in hosting MLB, the stadium came to grief by the end of the twentieth century and was razed to make way for another facility. Meanwhile, running concurrent to the era of the

Kingdome and several time zones to the east—and in another country, no less—a National League (NL) franchise was in the throes of dealing with its own unwieldy version of a state-of-the-art stadium that was meant to be able to tame the elements but became wracked with its own miseries.

***

As a major accommodation for the upcoming 1976 Summer Olympic Games scheduled for Montreal, Canada, a new stadium to be used for a variety of track and field events had to be constructed as one part of the complex that would serve as the host site. The city's energetic mayor, Jean Drapeau, had succeeded in overseeing Expo 67, the World's Fair of 1967, which popularized his charming metropolis and became a signal event in the country's history. Drapeau fronted several efforts in the 1960s to secure the opportunity for Montreal to be the site of the 1972 Olympics, but undaunted by those failures, he succeeded in securing the Summer Games for 1976. Montreal now had the chance to capitalize on a "building boom" that would improve its municipal infrastructure and allow it to expand for purposes of economic development.[4]

When the city was awarded a NL expansion franchise to begin play in 1969, Jarry Park, a small public recreation area, was hastily upgraded into a stadium that was intended to only temporarily serve as the Expos' home field.[5] Few would have imagined that eight full seasons would pass until a new stadium became the permanent replacement for quaint Jarry Park, which had a seating capacity of a little more than 28,000.

With Jarry Park having become a viable enterprise by mid-1969, thoughts of catering to the future Summer Olympic Games assumed the highest priority in the minds of Drapeau and city planners, despite the fact that the city had obtained its NL franchise on the condition that a replacement for Jarry Park be put in place by 1972. The new facility would not only need to accommodate various Olympic events, but also, in its post-1976 life, it had to be conducive to football—in the North American sense—and baseball. Whether a dome would cover the new stadium was an unsettled issue, but inclusion of such a structure was favored.

Political and bureaucratic maneuvering caused problems in the design phase; cronyism manifest in the country's Liberal Party underpinned the selection of the general contractor; and the requisite bidding process for contracting out work was ignored, supposedly in the interest of saving time and expenses. Ground had finally been broken in April 1973, but cost overruns for materials and delays in the building process caused by lingering winter weather generated much anxiety concerning whether the stadium could be completed by the summer of 1976. A tower looming 540 feet high and canted at a 45-degree angle over the stadium was built to operate a folding, retractable roof made of Kevlar, and although in theory this feature held the attraction of opening the stadium to natural light, it proved to be so troublesome that during the lifespan of the stadium it was engaged less than 100 times.

The stadium was nicknamed "the Big O" as a play on its shape and the fact that it was officially called Olympic Stadium—or Stade Olympique by the French Canadians. Yet, this catchy phrase was morphed into the snide homonym of "the Big Owe" because the amount of money poured into it left little doubt of its status as a financial boondoggle. All told, the bill ran to $770 million (Canadian dollars).

Upon the grand opening of the stadium in mid-July 1976, for the Summer Games, there was a field of natural grass on its floor, but this was replaced with ubiquitous Astroturf the following year. The Expos officially moved in as a primary tenant in mid-April of the following year, after the resolution of a dispute between team owner Charles Bronfman and the Olympic Installations Board. Accusations by a newly elected Quebec government regarding "us[ing] public funds to help private business" caused a stir, and Claude Charron, the PQ's minister of sport, also contemptuously dismissed Bronfman's desire for a stadium club that would cater to "les gros legumes (fat cats)."[6] The impasse was resolved during spring training in March 1977, when the Quebec Provincial government and the team agreed on how revenue would be split for advertising and concession revenues, as well as a percentage of gate receipts.

Olympic Stadium hosted baseball as scheduled, and although uncomfortably cool temperatures and wind pervaded an early homestand—one reporter labeled the place a "larger Candlestick Park"—a Montreal beat writer predicted that if the new home team played to its potential, "they will be wildly accepted and this concrete cavern could become one of baseball's great stadiums."[7]

Fans flocked see the Expos in their new venue, as attendance more than doubled from 646,704 during the last year at Jarry Park to more than 1.4 million in 1977, and as the team's exciting lineup matured in the coming years—future Hall of Famers Andre Dawson, Tim Raines, and

Gary Carter, as well as manager Dick Williams, leading the charge—Montreal found itself among the contenders in the NL East. A 1980 Expos team magazine envisioned the possibility of 2.5 million fans coming to Olympic Stadium, given the synergy of a solid ballclub attracting fans who could easily use the expanded Metro system to reach the stadium.[8]

Yet, the aforementioned prognostication holding that Olympic Stadium would be a great ballpark did not come true. Instead, it joined a lineup of current facilities that were already found in Pittsburgh, Cincinnati, Philadelphia, and Seattle, each of those stadiums infused with the unattractive banalities of concrete, plastic seats, artificial turf, and symmetric outfield dimensions. Had its roof system been less cumbersome and enabled the originally installed natural grass field to remain a viable asset, the Big O might have retained more charm than being consigned to its existence as yet another blasé, modern stadium.

Following the completion of Olympic Stadium, the next ballpark to be constructed was baseball's first stadium with an air-supported roof, another facility that had a large degree of artificiality, as did its contemporary brethren.

***

When Calvin Griffith vacated the nation's capital following the 1960 season, his former Washington Senators were rechristened as the Minnesota Twins. The home field for the relocated franchise would be Metropolitan Stadium—also labeled Metropolitan Sports Area Stadium, as an early Twins souvenir placard put it—in Bloomington, Minnesota, a ballpark that for several years served the Minneapolis Millers, the top minor-league affiliate of the New York Giants. Construction of "the Met" came at a time in the early 1950s when such major-league teams as the St. Louis Browns and Boston Braves were actively seeking other cities in which to play.

Interests in the Twin Cities wanted to move quickly in raising a new stadium with the hope of attracting a major-league team to the area, perhaps the Giants themselves. After roughly seven years of haggling with local officials about the need for a new ballpark, as well as picking a site for it—an old cornfield was ultimately selected—the Met opened in April 1956, less than one year after the groundbreaking ceremony.

Originally having a modest seating capacity of roughly 20,000 contained in a three-tiered, cantilever configuration, this design had a specific eye toward easy expandability, which is what took place when the Senators arrived, and an accommodation was made for another 10,000 seats. Subsequent additions eventually pushed the total capacity to 50,000, but the rambling way in which the new sections were grafted onto the existing structure was less than ideal for the purposes of baseball.

The Minnesota Vikings of the NFL were cotenants at the Met, and while some of the later grandstands were added to hold football crowds of increasing size, the general sightlines still favored viewing of baseball games. As the NFL team grew more competitive by the end of the 1960s, "the Vikings, not the Twins, were the hot ticket."[9] With barely 15 years of service time to its credit, the Met became the object of discussions by Minnesota state legislators and Twin Cities leaders as to whether a new facility in downtown Minneapolis should be built. Options included remodeling the Met to suit the Twins while at once building a new stadium on adjoining land solely for purposes of football, this latter alternative also intending to include the University of Minnesota's grid team.

In 1977, state lawmakers approved a bill that created a commission whose duty it was to explore the construction of a new stadium closer to Minneapolis to augment an initiative for economic development near Industry Square. The decision to employ an air-supported roof would mimic that of the Pontiac Silverdome near Detroit, which served as the new home of the NFL's Lions.

As 1979 drew to a close with winter about to set in, work began at the site and lasted for more than 18 months to form the basic bowl structure of the stadium, and by June 1981, formation of the roof, which "consisted of two layers of woven fibercloth glass, each 1/32-inch thick," was underway.[10] The entire roof—loudspeakers and lighting systems were also suspended from it—was inflated by a score of 90-horsepower blowers to a height of 186 feet. Although the number of fans in operation varied at any given time, they nevertheless were in constant use to keep the roof from sagging or collapsing.

Thoughtfully included in the stadium's design was an allowance for air-conditioning if deemed necessary for installation in the future. When the Hubert H. Humphrey Metrodome opened in April 1982, the following summer made it abundantly clear that the heat of the Upper Plains could not be tolerated in such a facility without some means to cool the indoor air. Quickly earning the dubious nickname of "the Sweat Box," the Metrodome received its much-needed air-conditioning system in time for the beginning of the Twins' longest homestand of the 1983 season.

The Metrodome's playing field, located 47 feet below street level, was covered in artificial Super-Turf, and like the turf at Seattle's Kingdome, this surface was also "fast" and "not kind to us pitchers," recalled one former Twins hurler.[11] And another feature of the stadium's baseball configuration was the lower section of the right-field grandstand, which contained a series of rows holding 7,600 seats. This seating arrangement was extended for football games, but for baseball games the rows were retracted, making for an outfield wall that was 23 feet in height, the upper 16-foot portion covered with a plastic sheathing that was dubbed the "Baggie," sometimes the "Hefty Bag." With advertising that sometimes adorned it, the Baggie evoked memories of signage at Ebbets Field.

As can be the case with any enclosed arena, the inability of sound to escape created an audial atmosphere that can only be described as deafening. When fans were roused to cheer as loudly as possible for the home team—be it the Twins, Vikings, or Golden Gophers—noise could reach unhealthy levels of nearly 120 decibels, roughly the equivalent of a jet plane. Such a frenzy served the Twins well, especially during their drive to World Series titles in 1987 and 1991, when the home-field advantage played a crucial role in their success.

The air-supported roof and Baggie gave the Metrodome its own cachet, as did the slightly asymmetrical distances to the outfield fence. Yet, in many respects, the structural fare at what was also called the "Homer Dome" differed little from its modernistic contemporaries. Like the Astrodome and Kingdome, baseball was being played indoors on artificial turf with no chance to see natural light or breathe fresh air. But the Metrodome would endure through the 2009 season, at which time the Twins would move to a new ballpark that was following the latest trend of the retro-park movement.

***

"FROM THE EX TO SKYDOME" was the bold-lettered subheading of a Toronto Blue Jays *Scorebook* magazine sold at Exhibition Stadium in the first half of the 1989 season. "The Ex" referred to Exhibition Stadium, the home of the AL's Canadian expansion franchise created in 1977, and SkyDome was the new state-of-the-art stadium to be opened when the

Blue Jays began their homestand on June 5, 1989. When the Blue Jays finished with a record of 89–73 in 1983 and 1984, they were on the verge of breaking through as legitimate contenders in the tough AL East, and the talent assembled on their roster boded well for the future. Attendance at home games had nearly doubled from 1982 to 1985, and despite its modest seating capacity of 44,649 for baseball games, Exhibition Stadium still boasted attendance well in excess of 2 million each year from 1984 to 1988, the last full season in which the Blue Jays played there.

Yet, the Ex was lacking in several key respects. The jury-rigged way in which the baseball field was set up made for some seats to be inordinately far from home plate, and the harsh weather of the early spring came with its own consequences: Speaking of the Blue Jays' inaugural season, former manager Roy Hartsfield recalled, "That Opening Day was the most amazing thing in all my years in baseball. The snow was so thick, we couldn't see the white lines."[12] And there was the occasion in late April 1984, when a game was called off after only five pitches had been thrown because the wind was so fierce. "It would have been a travesty to play," said home plate umpire Don Denkinger, adding, "When the wind blows like this, there's not much resemblance to the game of baseball."[13] Locals also poked fun at the stadium by relabeling it "Prohibition Stadium" because beer was not allowed to be sold there until late July 1982.

By the early 1980s, movement was afoot to build a new stadium that would shut out inclement weather such as occurred in November 1982, when the Canadian Football League's Grey Cup championship was played in a deluge of rain. A domed stadium with a retractable roof was deemed imperative, but its design had to be kept functionally basic to avoid a repeat of the misfortune inherent in the roof at Montreal's Olympic Stadium.

Selection of the new ballpark's site was of great importance to maximize the benefit to not only the stadium but also greater downtown Toronto. "Its designers tried to contribute to the traditions of baseball stadiums as both venues of entertainment and places of urban connection," noted architectural critic Paul Goldberger, and thus the site selected for SkyDome was at the base of the massive CN Tower.[14] With exactly this in mind, the facility, also in close proximity to the transportation hub of Union Station, would come to include a hotel built directly into the stadium, with some rooms having a view of the playing field. Numerous restaurants, a health club, a small movie theater, and a miniature golf course augmented the stadium complex, catering to not only the sensibilities of baseball fans, but also people in search of a unique leisure-time experience.

A seven-week strike by laborers thwarted plans to open SkyDome in April 1989, but the facility was finally ready by early June. At a cost of $425 million (Canadian), the new SkyDome's salient feature was a 31-story roof with three moving panels, and its simplicity of operation allowed it to be closed in 20 minutes. Naysayers were concerned that the retractable roof—7½ acres in size and weighing more than 18 tons—would be problematic during the roughly 200 times that it would be opened and closed each year. This mechanism did have its share of fits and starts, but in general the roof accomplished its purpose.

Crowds of more than 52,000 people would fill the club seats, luxury boxes, and grandstands, and now available was a new on-site television facility that eliminated the need for out-of-town broadcasters to employ their own production trucks. Season-ticket sales were envisioned to be 45,000 (of 54,000 seats total) in early 1989, although this was scaled back to 26,000, and an attendance number of 3 million was being forecasted during the course of a full season.

On June 5, 1989, SkyDome opened for major-league business after Canadian songstress Anne Murray reprised the performance of her country's national anthem and "The Star-Spangled Banner," just as she had sung them at the Blue Jays' first home game 12 years earlier. The maiden voyage of this new stadium was not to be taken lightly. SkyDome was so magnificent that Bobby Cox, the former Blue Jays manager who delivered Toronto its first division title in 1985, observed, "For the next few seasons, the Jays could finish 100 games out of first and still draw 3½ million people a year."[15] Coach Wayne Terwilliger of the Minnesota Twins took one look and said, "There's just so much inside here. It's like a shopping center."[16] SkyDome evoked the sensation of immensity even before its hotel opened shortly after the baseball season concluded. Lodging came at a hefty tariff by 1989 standards, at $175 for a regular room, and there were dozens of suites facing the playing field that cost $850 per night when events were scheduled, only half that amount for open nights.

The Blue Jays ended the season with 37 consecutive sellouts, and many observers of what was on offer at this newest wunderkind of stadiums thought they had glimpsed the future. Kim Lockhart, the editor of the team's scorecard-magazine, put readers on high alert to the grandeur that visitors to this architectural marvel could expect to behold. "Warning to newcomers: The first sight of SkyDome tends to snatch the breath away. . . . Beyond center field, the stadium rises in decks like the side of an ocean liner, only larger," and the italicized adjective "*awesome*" was used more than once to describe sensory aspects of the place. Capping his rave review, Lockhart commended his colleagues at *Sports Illustrated* for having "saluted SkyDome as avant-garde, the first stadium of the 1990s."[17]

The effusive praise for SkyDome was not universal, however. As history would prove, Toronto's addition to the trove of modern sports facilities would be the last multipurpose stadium built in North America. As other older ballparks reached maturity—in some cases, exceeded maturity—their modern-day replacements would not be modeled after SkyDome, but instead draw architectural inspiration from stadiums of yesteryear. In Chicago, a city whose two ballparks each had been in service for more than seven decades, planning was underway to construct a new version of Comiskey Park on the South Side. When the White Sox disclosed the model of their proposed replacement, Illinois governor James Thompson snidely pointed out how much better his constituents' new facility would be when compared to the modernistic SkyDome. "Our stadium will look like a real baseball park," the politician quipped, and Comiskey II would be lacking a roof, artificial turf, and hotel accommodations as if to evince pride in its relative spartan qualities.[18] If SkyDome was to be Toronto's gourmet feast, Chicago would pride itself with a new Comiskey Park that catered to those with less ambitious appetites.

***

At a time when the creation of SkyDome was migrating from blueprints to the reality of concrete and steel, Chicago was putting in motion plans to devise a replacement for aging Comiskey Park. Built on the site of a former city dump, Comiskey's locus on Chicago's South Side was far less attractive than that of its intracity rival to the north, and the surrounding neighborhood at times was fraught with its own brand of urban peril. But the place that was also known as White Sox Park from 1962 to 1975 had hosted the AL club since 1910 and gained its share of fame and notoriety in the ensuing decades, especially during the years in which Bill Veeck owned the team.

Comiskey Park's service life was drawing to a close due in no small part to old age, and the thrill of commemorating the ballpark's 75th anniversary in 1985 was dimmed by the sad truth that, by the estimate of Sox chairman Jerry Reinsdorf, at least $15 million would be needed to upgrade the venerable stadium. Comiskey having reached the dreaded condition of "outdated" now forced team officials to begin the process of planning for the future by building anew rather than through refurbishing.[19]

Late in the winter of 1986, team ownership was in the process of political wrangling with municipal officials, and a pawn in the form of a threat to move to a new city was used as a bargaining chip to force the construction of a new stadium. "The upkeep and taxes are so high that Reinsdorf and [White Sox vice chairman Eddie] Einhorn want the city to buy Comiskey Park and maintain it with little or no rent, or else they'd like to have a new stadium built. Then, Reinsdorf could tear down the old park and develop the land," Peter Gammons told readers of *Sporting News*, but also at work was a ploy by the Sox to leverage a threat to move to the nearby town of Addison if the club failed to secure a satisfactory deal for improved accommodations in Chicago.[20]

Labeled "two hustlers" by an irate Chicagoan, Reinsdorf and Einhorn were winning little favor in what was increasingly being viewed as an extortionist scheme to force the construction of a new stadium.[21] Voters in Addison narrowly defeated a referendum in November 1986 that would have sanctioned a new stadium there, this setback coming at the same time those going to the polls in Sarasota, Florida, agreed to replace aged Payne Park, the White Sox spring training facility. Also that year, the cities of Phoenix, Denver, and Washington, as well as interests in northern Indiana, were enticing the Sox to consider their offers to relocate.

The controversy concerning the White Sox staying or moving was resolved in December during a special session of the Illinois state legislature, when both chambers passed a measure to build a stadium on the parking lot immediately south of the old Comiskey Park. The tab was forecast to be in excess of $100 million for the new facility, and a joint commission of city and state officials was created to oversee the project. The bill was actually voted down in the Illinois House but then approved on a second ballot, and a state representative from Skokie explained his enthusiasm for the bill by indicating that he was "not prepared to play sudden death with a $120 million impact on my community."[22] The state Senate gave its blessing on a 30–24 vote—not exactly an overwhelming endorsement—and one of its members, echoing the "hustler" label given to the Sox moguls, called for the removal of Reinsdorf and Einhorn from team ownership in exchange for the deal with the state.

This quid pro quo was dashed, and the bill's passage heralded good news: It prevented the loss of a storied franchise to another city and sanctioned the construction of a single-purpose stadium with a natural-grass field, a thankful departure from the concrete donuts that had been in vogue for a generation. A dome that was part of the original design was no longer included, and Governor Thompson was correct in his assessment that the new stadium would indeed evince the traits of a traditional ballpark.

This pivot away from the Big O's and Veterans Stadiums dotting North America was for the better. Yet, an opportunity was ultimately missed that would have created a better urban milieu into which the new Comiskey Park could have settled. Philip H. Bess, an architect who was passionate about his interest in baseball, addressed the Chicago Architectural Foundation in the spring of 1985, shortly after Comiskey Park was embarking on its special anniversary season. "One hopes that new stadiums can be built once again on tight urban sites," he told the gathering, "but if this proves impossible then perhaps the formal idiosyncrasies once mandated by the urban context must now be *provided* by the architect."[23] Two years hence, Bess advanced his argument for the creation of the exact setting he had described in his speech.

Alas, Bess's rendition of a proposed Armour Field, a symmetrical stadium yet patterned roughly on a design of the old Polo Grounds with accompanying retail and residential space, was viewed as too radical and never gained traction with developers and city officials, and his prescient vision became a lost opportunity. In 1989, construction began on the new Comiskey Park, and it debuted on April 18, 1991. Upon its opening, the new Comiskey Park delighted fans with its broad concourses, unobstructed views, and clever amenities (for example, a pet check to entice dog owners and a coat/briefcase check to lure businessmen to a game). Sensitive to the traits that made the original Comiskey so special, the White Sox ensured that the "scoreboard still explodes after a White Sox player homers, and is decorated with similar bright pinwheels. The picnic area from the old left-field corner was moved to an expanded area in right. Organist Nancy Faust is still at fan-level and still plays 'Nah Nah Hey Hey Goodbye.'"[24]

Naturally, the point can also easily be made that any new facility would have been an improvement on the cramped, old Comiskey. The new stadium—now carrying the updated, self-aggrandizing moniker "Great Baseball Palace II"—was not, however, the most important ballpark built in the late twentieth century, but its significance lies in the fact that it broke the trend that demanded the construction of multipurpose stadiums. The Kansas City–based architectural firm that designed the new Comiskey Park was, at this time, on the verge of introducing another new ballpark that was destined to reshape the design of baseball stadiums from the 1990s into the twenty-first century. The plans developed by the sports division of Hellmuth, Obata & Kassabaum enabled the firm to set a new standard that would become an influential template for both major-league and minor-league ballparks throughout the country.

***

As the concrete donuts of the 1960s and 1970s sprouted in major metropolitan regions to take the place of older stadiums, the Baltimore Orioles continued to labor at staid Memorial Stadium, which welcomed the former St. Louis Browns when that team moved east at the end of the 1953 season. Shaped in a wishbone footprint configuration and with a second deck added in time for the maiden voyage of the AL Orioles the following year, Memorial Stadium was located in a residential neighborhood on 33rd Street and had hosted some memorable baseball and football teams in the succeeding decades.

But the new, fresh look of the stadiums coming into use as the 1970s progressed was casting a shadow over venerable Memorial Stadium and making the place seem passé. While attendance at baseball games was fair to middling into the following decade despite some exciting teams that were perennial contenders led by manager Earl Weaver, Colts fans were voting with their feet in expressing their dismay about the wretched performance of a once-proud football team. Season-ticket sales that had once reached 49,000 in the early 1970s dropped to 25,000 a decade later, and the manner in which owner Robert Irsay conducted the team's business created resentment among many fans.

When Irsay was unable to get the city of Baltimore to commit to performing renovations on Memorial Stadium—including the addition of revenue-generating skyboxes—he resumed exploring a transfer of the Colts to another location, ultimately settling on Indianapolis in March 1984, when the infamous late-night caravan of moving vans packed up the team's possessions and headed for its new home. After vowing not to build a new stadium just two months earlier, William Donald Schaefer, the mayor of Baltimore, was stunned at the departure of the NFL team and quickly reset his priorities to make sure that the Orioles would not follow suit. Claiming ownership of the Colts via eminent domain, the city of Baltimore filed suit but lost this bid to retake the football team in December 1984, and those municipal officials at last "accepted the idea that cities had to meet the demands of [professional sports] leagues and franchises," and thus had to contemplate replacing Memorial Stadium.[25] As a gubernatorial candidate in 1986, Schaefer, already enthusiastic for a new baseball stadium, was also favoring a second facility for football in the hope of attracting another NFL team.

Schaefer's preference of the Camden Yards area as the venue for at least one new stadium was no accident. "That site had the virtue of downtown location and proximity to the increasingly important Washington, D.C., market," a point that made business sense, not least of which were the area's connection to several major highways, but a second reason may have been motivated by a bit of cronyism: "It also abutted a warehouse recently bought by a group of investors that included Schaefer's leading [political] fundraiser."[26]

The other leading actor in this drama was Orioles owner Edward Bennett Williams, a prominent Washington-based attorney who, almost since his purchase of the team in 1979, had instilled fear among many locals that he would move the club to the nation's capital. Williams, in his role as team president of the NFL's Washington Redskins since 1965, was no stranger to the business of sports, and the flight of the Colts provided the lawyer-owner with tremendous leverage in brokering a deal with Baltimore lest the city lose its baseball team.

When the Maryland Stadium Authority was created by the state legislature in 1986, its purpose was to "*build*, manage, and maintain quality facilities to retain Major League Baseball, and return NFL football to Maryland," and the "extensive powers" vested in this body "liberated it from the inconvenience of arguing with local interests," especially those in opposition to various aspects of a proposed new stadium.[27] As more than implied by the word "Authority," this agency could wield its power without the irritation of taking input from outsiders, namely members of the public who may not have agreed with its mission.

Working solidly to the benefit of the project was the indisputable fact that Camden Yards would be an extension of work that had already been accomplished at Baltimore's Inner Harbor, just a few blocks to the east, and a new convention center also anchored the land diagonally opposite the proposed stadium's site. Williams affirmed commitment to a long-term lease at the new stadium, and by the autumn of 1987, bureaucratic hurdles had been cleared. Ground was broken in January 1990, on land that once included a tavern operated by the father of native son Babe Ruth.[28]

In eager anticipation of this new ballpark, the cover of the Orioles' late-season 1989 game program had been adorned with an artist's rendering of Oriole Park, and the team's 1991 media guide was ebullient about what was in store once the facility was completed for its debut the next season. Fans would enjoy easy access via mass transit in the form of many bus lines and a new stop on a light-rail system; a "state-of-the-art drainage system" was to be installed to hasten wet-weather issues; all 46,500 seats had unobstructed views of an asymmetrical field of natural grass, the growth of which was to be done per groundskeeper Pat Santarone's specifications; and the architecture of the stadium "will take its image from baseball parks built in the early twentieth century, featuring steel (not concrete) trusses, an arched brick façade, a sunroof over the gentle slope of the upper deck."[29] More spacious legroom and seat widths meant a more comfortable experience for fans, who could enjoy the ambience of the great looming presence beyond right and center field: The outsized former Baltimore & Ohio Railroad warehouse, which was once the largest such building in the country, was to be repurposed as club offices and space for restaurants, shops, and banquet facilities.

When the ballpark finally opened in 1992, the Orioles paid homage to the site's past, noting, "The earliest event of historical interest in the Camden Yards area dates back to 1781–82, when the great French General Comte de Rochambeau and his forces camped there on the way to and from Yorktown, [Virginia]," during the Revolutionary War.[30] The body of slain president Abraham Lincoln also passed through on the way to Springfield, Illinois, for interment in 1865.

Architect Janet Marie Smith partnered with Orioles president Larry Lucchino to give Oriole Park at Camden Yards a sense of practicality that was cleverly cloaked in nostalgia. Lucchino had Smith "study the older parks," and he added, "and we did our best to quantify what gave them character and authenticity, and to figure out how to translate that without seeming kitschy in the approach."[31] She further credited the Orioles' manager at the time, Frank Robinson, for sharing his thoughts about his days playing in the very ballparks that Smith and company were trying to replicate. His recollections of time spent at Crosley Field, Connie Mack Stadium, and elsewhere helped Smith formulate the template that would be used to create Oriole Park. David Ashton, who designed, among other things, the scoreboard clock and oriole weathervanes for the new stadium, insisted that baseball was foremost in the thinking of the planners when he declared, "The idea wasn't to turn this into a theme park."[32] Brickwork enhanced the eye appeal for what was evolving as the new standard by which future ballparks would be built.

A historic look back enabled Smith to highlight the significance of what long-term impact Camden Yards and what came to be known as the retro-park movement had on not only the national pastime, but also the national urban scene. "The most important beneficiaries of this trend are the American cities that are now proud hosts to Major League Baseball," she said, and she cited Cleveland, Denver, Pittsburgh, San Diego, and San Francisco as prime examples of "baseball [having] been used to redefine downtown and take advantage of existing infrastructure."[33] Smith's talent and overwhelming success in Baltimore led her to follow Lucchino to Boston, where Fenway Park had been the subject of a similar "renovate or replace" debate by the early 1990s.

Despite the richly deserved kudos garnered by Smith and her followers in the retro-park movement, a degree of innocence was lost in two respects as the Camden Yards–inspired movement, rooted in the late 1980s, took flight. First, the financing of newly built stadiums via public funding created much resentment among the taxpaying public, who saw monies that could have been spent on education, housing, or infrastructure like bridges and highways now diverted to building stadiums occupied by professional sports teams—the values of which were ever increasing—whose players average salaries, also soaring, were light-years ahead of that of the common fan. One sociology professor wrote that the "profound hegemonic hold baseball continues to have over the hearts and minds of the American public" has led "Major League Baseball . . . to pursue to a practice of legalized extortion" to further its interests to the detriment of public services now sacrificed for the sake of sport organizations.[34]

Second, the success of Camden Yards rightly encouraged other municipalities to follow Baltimore's lead, and those cities reaped the fruits of their labor. But unlike Baltimore, where the primary focus remained on the game of baseball, a version of one-upmanship held that each succeeding ballpark had to offer more amenities than its predecessor. Extending into the twenty-first century, this trend has teams building ballparks to be centerpieces of entire areas that the clubs control themselves, the Battery at Trust Park (formerly SunTrust Park) in Atlanta being a prime example.

As ambitious as these projects are, production of such manufactured environments—in which the clubs have exclusivity of commercial and residential properties contained therein—comes at a cost. Paul Goldberger noted that such ersatz cityscapes upset the "harmonic balance" between "the rural and the urban, the natural and the man-made" that can be found in a true city environment, becoming a "simulacrum" devoid of urban authenticity and the key asset of diversification.[35]

Moreover, humble ballpark concourses of the past, with hot dog stands and other simplistic concessions, "have been transformed into shopping malls with restaurants, food courts, museums, theaters, children's playgrounds, video arcades, and swimming pools," many of these frills "tailored towards attracting spending from corporate entertainment budgets [and] drawing in wealthy consumers" seeking "premium experiences for their exclusive enjoyment."[36] The Hall of Fame plaque of Chicago White Sox owner Bill Veeck notes that he was a "champion of the little guy." Yet, the passage of time and the explosion of money in sports in the decades since he was a baseball mogul have recast the little guy—meaning those possessed of a limited budget—as a quotidian relic.

***

The time frame of baseball history dealt with in these pages encompasses the major turning point at which the physical plant of the national pastime underwent a crucial transformation as the millennium approached. The evolution of wood-structure ballparks in the late nineteenth and early twentieth centuries yielded such classic stadiums as the Polo Grounds, Connie Mack Stadium, and Ebbets Field, the new crop now thought of as state-of-the-art since they were vast improvements on their predecessors. As the service life of many of those ballparks waned in the 1950s, new demands came to the fore: Larger stadiums to also accommodate pro football games conflated with not only a desire to use a single facility to host both baseball and football games, but also the impulse to cater to municipalities' economic and budgetary considerations. While home MLB events numbered about 80 per season, those for pro football—including a few exhibition games—came to about 10. Certainly, so the thinking went, a common ground could be reached where both sports could peacefully coexist at the same venue.

But the degree of satisfaction obtained in that shotgun marriage could not be known until multipurpose stadiums—Shea Stadium, Three Rivers Stadium, and their ilk—were actually built and taken for a road test, as it were, beginning in the 1960s. And once tens of millions of dollars were expended on those facilities, states and cities—to say nothing of the sports teams themselves—were forced to endure the consequences of their investments, for better or worse. The renovation of Anaheim Stadium in the late 1970s to furnish a home for the NFL's Los Angeles Rams was a valiant effort, but it, too, became a square peg unable to fit into a round hole. In some cases, the bonds used to construct a concrete donut—Veterans Stadium in Philadelphia comes to mind—had not been paid off at the time said donut was razed when the team moved on to another new stadium, much to the chagrin of local government finance officials.

Planning by the White Sox in the late 1980s created a revised Comiskey Park, a serviceable, single-use stadium that remained true to how a baseball park should be configured, but the development of Oriole Park at Camden Yards, roughly at the same time, carried that idea a step further. Signaling the dawn of a new era dictating how stadiums would be grafted to an urban setting, the construction of Camden Yards was the seminal event that proved the viability of this concept and allowed Baltimore to take center stage as the pioneer in modern ballpark design. Paul Goldberger observed that while Oriole Park was not intended to be replicated in every detail in other cities, the stadiums in "Cleveland and Arlington [both opening in 1994] were the first two children of Camden Yards, but they developed from a different part of their parent's DNA."[37]

The epoch of the concrete donuts came to a thankful end in Chicago. Yet, the ensuing retro-park movement, born in Baltimore, proved that what was old was again new—and improved. By tailoring the next generation of ballparks with a sensitivity to their respective siting, aesthetics, and local history, the benefit to players on the field and fans in the seats would make for a pleasurable experience that bid farewell to the plastic, concrete, steel, and symmetry characteristic of the multipurpose age.

6

EXPANSION, RUMORS OF EXPANSION, AND OWNERSHIP CHANGES

From 1977 through the end of the 1980s, Major League Baseball (MLB) added only two teams, and to the casual observer the expansion in other professional sports appeared to have left baseball in the dust. During the decade prior to 1977, the National Hockey League (NHL) not only added teams, but also was faced by direct competition in the form of the new World Hockey Association. The American Football League merged with its more established rival, the National Football League (NFL), and the revised NFL was also staring down another gridiron circuit, the World Football League. In the meantime, the American Basketball Association was making its own inroads against the National Basketball Association (NBA), eventually brokering a deal to add four teams to the NBA.

A nationwide economic recession in 1975, and the inability of newer leagues to gain stability in a saturated sports market dimmed the enthusiasm for creating more sports franchises by the mid-1970s. As concerning baseball, the immediate quandary befalling the Seattle Pilots in 1969, and that of the San Diego Padres a few years later, was proof of the peril awaiting prospective entrepreneurs who may have believed that the allure of baseball in and of itself would guarantee success.

A draft of baseball's expansion criteria, authored by the Planning Committee and dating to 1967, would carry forward into the following decade as a blueprint for organizing new franchises.[1] The major components comprising any attempt to create a club from scratch constituted a daunting task list: The host city, stadium plans, ownership, timing of when to initiate expansion, preliminary preparation in the form of setting up a minor-league system, franchise cost, and marketing capabilities all had roles in determining how a new club would be awarded.

Stadium plans alone were vexing, as was amply demonstrated in the failure of the Seattle Pilots and their home at dilapidated Sicks Stadium. Yet, the plight of the San Diego Padres proved one instance in which a virtually brand-new stadium did little to help an expansion team. Use of an existing facility, the need to build a new stadium, leasing provisions, costs of maintenance, parking issues, and revenue from concessions and advertising were items to be weighed by cost–benefit analyses. Local ownership was preferable to absentee ownership, but this factor placed a distant second to the main priority of "financial responsibility."[2]

Setting the cost of the franchise was another complicated calculus: The entrepreneurs buying into the venture through the league's entry fee still needed capital to spend on the framework and infrastructure of the organization's front office, minor-league operation, and player payroll, while retaining some reserves to execute a marketing strategy. This delicate financial situation runs into the harsh reality of the difficulty of a new team to gain traction to quickly become competitive. "New organizations literally sell their souls to get a franchise, and the financial commitment necessary to land a big-league team can often hinder their ability to put a winning product on the field."[3]

Upon embarking on expansion in the mid-1970s, the American League (AL) had fresh memories of the Pilots' quick transfer to Milwaukee and the calamity of the Padres' near-move to Washington. To forestall any ill-fated, repeat performances, AL president Lee MacPhail spoke on behalf of the American League Expansion Committee when he implored AL general managers on the eve of the 1976 expansion draft, "It was the unanimous feeling of the committee that all 12 established clubs have a moral obligation to lend maximum assistance under the rules to the expansion clubs, in order that they may achieve economic viability and competitive parity at the earliest possible date."[4] MLB was not in a position to see another team, especially one just born, thrashing for its fiscal life.

At about that same time, baseball had several issues on the West Coast. In Northern California, franchises in both the National League (NL) and AL were failing at the box office and reinforcing the notion that the Bay Area did not have the means to support two clubs. In 1974, the

Oakland Athletics won their third consecutive World Series. Yet, they drew less than 846,000 fans, and across the Bay at Candlestick Park, attendance at Giants games was worse, at less than 520,000. A volatile combination of problems foretold a difficult path to find a solution. Oakland owner Charlie Finley continued to have a penchant for not getting along with his players, manager, and the baseball establishment in general, while the Giants found themselves at a competitive disadvantage against two superior NL West division foes, the powerhouse Cincinnati Reds and the resurgent Los Angeles Dodgers, and this was to say nothing of the Giants' tedium of having to play home games at blustery Candlestick. The plight of the San Francisco club conflated with the fallout of the relocation of the erstwhile Seattle Pilots to set in motion the events that led to baseball's first expansion since the radical addition of four teams in 1969, and the subsequent split of the AL and NL into two divisions.

***

At the close of the 1975 baseball season, the San Francisco Giants had a chance to pause and lick their wounds endured during the previous months. Strapped for cash, the financially ailing club had been staked to supplemental funding courtesy of the NL to "meet basic expenditures and salary obligations."[5] Horace Stoneham, the Giants' owner, had put the club on the market, and by that year's winter meetings in Hollywood, Florida, a group interested in purchasing the Giants emerged from the executive offices of Labatt Brewing Company in Toronto, Canada, which made the highest of several offers. The brewer had been seeking to acquire a team since July 1974, but the NL rejected its bid because it did not want the team transferred out of the country, nor did it wish to leave the Athletics with a monopoly of the Bay Area. In the case of both the Athletics and Giants, each team was still bound by the terms of the leases held with their respective municipal stadium authorities.

The possibility of allowing Toronto into the sphere of MLB was consistent with some key aspects of the Planning Committee's 1967 expansion criteria. "During the mid- to late 1970s, the GTA [Greater Toronto Area] had a large and expanding population, and an economy that experienced job growth, consisted of households with higher incomes, and contained local industries whose prosperity had significantly increased."[6] Two other major, professional sports franchises had long been domiciled in Toronto, the Argonauts of the Canadian Football League and the Maple Leafs of the NHL, and the neighboring Montreal Expos, now in existence for less than a decade, had given MLB a bit of a track record north of the U.S. border.

In January 1976, despite the NL's earlier stance against a transfer of the Giants, a deal was worked out in which Labatt would purchase the team and move it north of the border. The $13.25 million price tag included more than $5 million dedicated to "potential legal costs and indemnification payments."[7] But the city of San Francisco, through the effort of its newly elected mayor, George Moscone, was reluctant to see the Giants leave and sought a restraining order to prevent a move. Citing the economic impact of the club to the city proper, Moscone threatened a lawsuit against the team and the league, seeking damages of $3.15 billion if the sale and transfer were consummated. Moscone also claimed that several other parties were interested in purchasing the Giants—at a price at least as good as the offer by Labatt—and keeping them in town.

An interesting partnership took shape, one featuring former Washington Senators owner Bob Short and a member of the Giants' board of directors, Bob Lurie. Spurred on by Moscone, the Short–Lurie duo put together an offer to purchase the team, and in February, they took control. When NL owners insisted that Lurie be put in charge of the team rather than the freewheeling Short, Lurie was briefly left in the lurch when Short pulled out of the deal. But quickly filling the void was Arthur Herseth, a cattle-industry mogul from Arizona who seamlessly fronted the $4 million that Short would have paid for his share of the ballclub.

Lurie remained with the Giants into the 1990s, but the enduring theme of his ownership was the Giants' quest to vacate Candlestick Park, whether by a threat to move the team—with a domed stadium being constructed in the late 1980s, the city of Tampa was a candidate as a relocation site—or keep it in San Francisco, provided a new stadium could be built.

***

As the situation in San Francisco was gaining much-needed stability but not yet finalized, another factor added a complicated twist to the growing, multifranchise intrigue when the city of Seattle was offered an AL expansion franchise as part of a settlement to dismiss its lawsuit for having previously lost the Pilots to Milwaukee in 1970. Incredulously, the AL considered adding this single expansion franchise in Seattle and operating with a stilted 13-team league. Logic dictated that the AL should expand by two teams, but if only Seattle was added, then the NL would be implored to increase by one club and thereby force MLB to restructure itself as a pair of 13-team circuits operating with a new scheduling gimmick: interleague play.

The proposal to place a new AL team in Seattle was greeted with mixed reviews. One Seattle municipal official thought that the Giants' move to Toronto was foolish given that other cities in the United States might be interested in acquiring a team, another entrepreneur in the Emerald City preferred to see a NL expansion team come to town—the "Seattle people want an established club," was how *Sporting News* put it—while the mayor feared an "instant replay" of the Pilots' abandonment to another location should an expansion team be granted.[8]

The city of Seattle still had an active $32.5 million lawsuit pending against MLB in early 1976, concerning the loss of the Pilots, but the hope was that the quid pro quo of the awarding of a new franchise would persuade Seattle interests to drop their litigation. Baseball attached two other conditions to the Seattle predicament: The new team had to have a suitable leasing arrangement with the new Kingdome, and the franchise had to be backed by a local ownership group. With regard to this last stipulation, a Seattle entrepreneur named Lester Smith was in charge of the arrangements, and he was also joined by noted show-business entertainer Danny Kaye. The Smith–Kaye tandem had previously sought to purchase the White Sox with the intention of moving them from Chicago to Seattle, but they lost out to Bill Veeck, who became the Sox magnate for a second time.

On February 6, AL owners affirmed support for a new team in Seattle, officially giving the AL 13 clubs, while at once breathing a sigh of relief about not having to face litigation in the tens of millions of dollars. The Kingdome was set to play host to the NFL's expansion Seahawks in 1977, and now there would be a baseball tenant at the new stadium. With Toronto's recent quest to purchase the Giants fresh in the minds of many baseball executives, Hogtown, as Toronto was nicknamed, suddenly found itself back in the running for a team.

Drawing the rational conclusion that a league comprised of a baker's dozen of teams was an untenable arrangement, the AL, on March 26, voted 11–1—the league bylaws required a three-fourths majority—to put another club in Toronto. Factors working in favor of the interests in the

Canadian city were the recent updating of Exhibition Stadium, which could hold about 50,000 fans for baseball games, and the new franchise would logically fit in the AL's East Division as a counter to Seattle joining the AL West. The Labatt magnates, who paid $7 million for their franchise, also were free from being obligated to escrow millions of dollars for purposes of funding a legal battle in trying to wrest an established club from another city. Rather than diverting resources for a fight in the courts, the new expansion team could fully concentrate on staffing its front office and preparing for the draft, which would stock its roster with players. Obtainment of the franchise was a solid win for Labatt, which, according to one Torontonian reporter's opinion, would have benefited from "even an attempt to bring a team to [the city]" and thereby "enhance the brewery's image."[9]

***

Trying to play catch-up but falling victim to its own bureaucracy, the NL attempted to pull Toronto into its sphere with the hope of also adding a new team in Washington. Not looking good in this fray was the commissioner, Bowie Kuhn, who had suggested in 1971—as Bob Short stole away with the Washington Senators and departed for Texas—that he would insist on the nation's capital being included in any expansion plans. In September of that year, grocery store mogul Joe Danzansky attempted to purchase the team to prevent its relocation, a transaction that found favor with Baltimore Orioles owner Jerry Hoffberger at the time. But Danzansky was hobbled by shaky financial backing, and AL owners voted 10–2 to permit the Senators' transfer. Kuhn was virtually distraught at seeing the team to which he was so emotionally attached as a youth leave town.

The commissioner tried to work out a deal with Hoffberger that would have the Orioles playing select games in Washington to fill the void created by the departure of the Senators. Hoffberger, however, was tepid to the proposal, and he further wanted an assurance from Kuhn that no NL team would be placed in Washington. Yet, the commissioner was not in a position to agree to such a limitation, and in fact, "Once the [Senators'] move was made, Hoffberger was determined to defend his territory from intrusion by either league."[10] The Orioles had spent years cultivating a significant portion of its fan base from the DC area and were understandably reluctant to cede it to a new team.

In late 1973, as the San Diego Padres were about to founder financially, it appeared all but certain that they would move east to the nation's capital. Even the production staff at Topps Chewing Gum, Inc., created baseball cards of more than a dozen Padres players—decked out in San Diego's yellow and cappuccino brown uniforms—bearing the caption "WASHINGTON NAT'L LEA.," since the team name was unknown when the cards went to press for the 1974 issue. Not exactly a brand-new club, the Padres were nevertheless beginning only their sixth season of play, and Kuhn welcomed the opportunity to see baseball played again at RFK Stadium.

Joe Danzansky again emerged as a potential buyer, but his 15-day negotiating period with the NL passed without a deal as 1973 drew to a close. Several weeks later, coming to the rescue and ensuring that the team would remain in San Diego was McDonald's hamburger titan Ray Kroc, whose financial backing was superb. Kuhn lost out in his bid to restock Washington with a ballclub, but he was appreciative of Kroc's enthusiasm for team ownership. The Padres mogul also endeavored to bring winning baseball to Jack Murphy Stadium by investing in several high-priced free agents in 1977, although he passed away nine months before his team captured its first NL pennant in 1984. His widow, Joan Kroc, took control of the team, but by the end of the decade, she had grown weary of the operation and, in June 1990, sold the club to a consortium of 15 investors headed by television producer Tom Werner.

With Washington still vacant as the San Francisco–Toronto–Seattle tumult dragged on, Kuhn was being lobbied by a significant number of high-profile political elites, President Gerald Ford, former vice president Hubert Humphrey, and Speaker of the House Carl Albert, to name a few. At a time when it appeared that the Giants would move to Toronto and only Seattle would be added as a lone AL expansion team, resurrecting a team for Washington as a NL entrant would jibe only in the unlikely circumstance that interleague play would be implemented. Kuhn believed that the arrangement of two 13-team leagues was viable, but in January 1976, the NL, already enjoying "superiority at the turnstiles," demurred, at least for the moment.[11]

Several meetings of AL officials and owners took place in April, whereby Kuhn hoped for an AL deal to accommodate Toronto and Washington. Citing the Texas Rangers and Minnesota Twins as examples of franchises that had a regional fan base, the commissioner was among a group of owners who "have felt that *an area franchise* for Baltimore and Washington would be the best long-term solution," but the success of such an arrangement hinged on defining the area of interest, as well as determining a "reasonable sharing of games on an assured basis." On this latter issue, Kuhn observed, "The number of games offered by the Baltimore Club was both too limited and too uncertain to provide any chance of acceptibility [*sic*]."[12]

Resurfacing simultaneously with the AL proposal was the NL's Toronto–Washington scenario. Kuhn had been questioned about whether the NL should be given priority over any plan put forth by the AL. Contrary to its earlier demurral, the NL, on March 29, now favored its version of the Toronto–Washington endeavor by a 10–2 vote of owners, but the league provision for a unanimous ballot scuttled the proposal. Nonetheless, the NL also passed a resolution asking the commissioner to "take such action as may appear to him to be proper and in the best interests of baseball," which in essence meant to override the requirement for unanimity given the overwhelming majority. Borrowing Kuhn's favorite phrase, the NL moguls suddenly felt that *their* best interests needed to be served. The commissioner averred that the sport had "recognized that Washington should be given priority consideration in the event of expansion or franchise transfers," and he ruled that a "unanimous vote requirement should not be permitted under these special circumstances to stand in the way."[13]

Kuhn set a two-week moratorium for each league to come up with an acceptable plan, with the NL appearing to have the inside track because of its inclusion of Washington as a new—and nonsharing—site. But when the Senior Circuit reconvened on April 26, to vote again on the issue, the 7–5 majority was substantially less inspiring than the previous tally, making any attempt by Kuhn to override the unanimity aspect untenable and putting an end to NL expansion hopes. The AL remained steadfast about expanding into Toronto and Seattle, and the lack of a club-sharing option by Baltimore offered no relief for the nation's capital. The failure of baseball to honor what Kuhn believed to be a bona fide commitment to bring a team to Washington prompted him to draft a letter of resignation, but the solid support the commissioner had from most owners placed him in an awkward position of having to renege on his threat to leave.

When the AL expansion to Seattle and Toronto became fact, Kuhn suffered a blow to his prestige due to Washington being shut out of the process, and he chided the league for "taking the low road of self-interest." Congress was in no mood for baseball's ignorance and exacted its own revenge in the Tax Reform Act of 1976, which "deleted the tax shelter advantages of owning a professional sports club."[14] Baseball's wrangling with legislators and the conundrum of franchise placement did not escape the notice of a pair of irate fans who vented to *Sporting News*. "So now Congress resorts to blackmail!" charged a letter to the editor, which went on to ask, "Why should some owner be forced to take a financial bath [by putting a team in Washington] just to satisfy the whim of some of the members of Congress?" Another missive bluntly addressed the general issue of increasing the number of clubs: "Baseball does not owe a major-league team to every large city in North America."[15]

Washington was not deprived of MLB forever when Robert Short absconded with the Senators, but its return to the nation's capital would not take place until the early twenty-first century. The administrations of several commissioners would run their course before expansion occurred anywhere, finally taking place with the addition of the Colorado Rockies and Florida Marlins to the NL in early 1990s. This is not to say that no attempts were made to put baseball in other cities in the decade-long wake of the birth of the Toronto Blue Jays and Seattle Mariners.

***

In its own way, the expansion of 1977 came out as a variation of the AL's creation of new franchises for 1961, a year in advance of the NL's intention to do likewise; however, the overall economic climate of baseball in the era of free agency was putting a noticeable strain on the financial situation of mostly small-market teams, and those franchises garnered much speculation in the press about the fate that awaited them moving into the 1980s. Rather than continue a campaign of expansion likely to jeopardize the fiscal well-being of brand-new clubs trying to establish their footing, baseball fell into a lengthy pause through that decade. In the meantime, there was no shortage of teams who evaluated their sagging balance sheets and thought that a move to another venue would be in their best interests.

Occurring in tandem with threats to move were the potential sales of a number of clubs. The age of the single-proprietor business model as it applied to baseball teams was drawing to a close, and as franchises changed hands, many—but not all—new ownership groups had more diverse corporate holdings, and their ballclubs became part of the portfolio they maintained.

A notable exception to this trend was the sale of the Boston Red Sox in the aftermath of owner Tom Yawkey's death in July 1976. Yawkey had drawn up his will with the thought of easing the transition to a new owner, but when the team was put up for sale several months after he passed away, there ensued a legal donnybrook that lasted for years and took on the appearance of a bitter custody battle between rival parents. The highest bid by an outside concern—the Rawlings Sporting Goods parent company was an enterprise called A-T-O—was rejected by the team's trustees. Some former Red Sox officials failed to assemble a consortium attractive enough to pass muster with other AL owners, and ugly in-house fighting among board members, including Tom Yawkey's widow, Jean, played out in the media and came at a time when there was also fear that a lack of tax incentives might force the team to abandon aged Fenway Park and leave Boston for another area town. Ultimately, an ownership group headed by Jean Yawkey took control of the team in 1980, and she maintained her role as the club's president and primary partner until her passing in early 1992.

While some degree of Yawkey ownership remained in Boston, two other AL magnates sought to divest themselves of their clubs. The more prominent of them was Charlie Finley of the Oakland Athletics, whose team's success on the field in the first half of the 1970s always seemed to be upstaged by the antics he employed to operate the front office and meddle in the affairs of the manager and his players. Following the loss of so many prime free agents after 1976, the patchwork roster that replaced the once-dominant Athletics impressed as one of an expansion team loaded with castoffs unwanted by other clubs. Predictably, Oakland fell precipitously, and it dropped to the bottom of the AL West standings in 1977. Talk of an Oakland transfer to Washington came to naught, as did speculation of New Orleans as a new home, the latter city "frantic in its search for a principal tenant for its Superdome, a multimillion-dollar white elephant that stood empty much of the time."[16]

Arriving on the scene to deliver Finley from his plight was Marvin Davis, a fabulously wealthy oil tycoon who envisioned purchasing the Athletics and moving them to his hometown of Denver in time for the following season. The potential sale appeared to be a godsend for a number of reasons: Davis's financial standing was impeccable; the San Francisco Giants, having just endured the strife concerning their own possible move to Toronto, would now be the sole baseball interest in the Bay Area, allowing their fanbase to grow; any thoughts of placing an expansion team in Denver would now be a moot point; and, of no small significance, the baseball world would no longer have to deal with the irascible Charlie Finley. Another aspect of the proposed deal would have allowed the Giants to play roughly half of their home games at the Oakland Coliseum, enabling them to better cultivate their new, exclusive hold on the region.

All the pieces of the transaction seemed to be falling in line until the city of Oakland filed suit against Finley and Davis seeking $35 million in damages should the sale be completed. This legal action had been anticipated by the commissioner's office, which was concerned about the "availability of insurance coverage to protect against third-party claims and the Oakland club's refusal to give a general release of all present and future claims against baseball."[17]

A further complication arose when the San Francisco Board of Supervisors refused to cede half of the Giants' home games to the Coliseum, across the bay. The board was in charge of the lease at Candlestick Park, and while it was comfortable with about two dozen contests being held in Oakland, the board believed that the staging of half the season's games away from Candlestick was too great a concession. Furthermore, "San Francisco authorities also objected to a name change that would have marked the Giants as a Bay Area team," and such a rebranding with an attendant loss of identity would have been too much for city fathers to bear.[18]

With relief from Davis—or anyone else—stymied, the Athletics became a laughingstock. An Oakland furniture store merchant, Sam Bercovich, was reportedly in the market to purchase the team, and he made inroads by gaining radio rights to broadcast games in 1978, albeit on low-wattage stations. Bercovich's earnest attempt to buy the team dissolved when he was found not to have the ready cash he claimed, and the authority operating the Coliseum declined to shorten the remaining time on

Finley's lease to three years. A nadir was reached in 1979, when the Athletics lost an embarrassing total of 108 games, with little more than 300,000 fans attending home games.

The real saviors of Oakland baseball came first in the form of a new field manager, followed by a new owner with a commitment to the team's interests. When Billy Martin was tabbed to be the skipper, several players from the previous year's squad were delighted to know that Martin's all-business demeanor was certain to light a fire, and the turnaround in the club's performance was evident when the Athletics placed second in the AL West in 1980. The timing of this reversal was propitious for Finley: Instead of having to peddle the wares of his awful 1979 team to a potential buyer, Oakland was genuinely rejuvenated with more than just curb appeal.

While their attendance ranked only 12th in a 14-team league, the Athletics' turnstile count surged to more than 840,000, including a late-season game against the Yankees that drew the largest-ever regular-season crowd at the Coliseum, which contributed to the franchise's ultimate selling price of $12.7 million. The new ownership group was fronted by founding members of the family who created the clothier Levi Strauss, and the commitment pledged by new owners Roy Eisenhardt and Walter Haas took hold even though positive results may not have been always reflected in the AL West standings. By the end of the 1980s, the arrival of a trio of AL Rookie of the Year winners from 1986 to 1988—José Canseco, Mark McGwire, and Walt Weiss—conflated with the managerial talent of Tony La Russa to set Oakland on a course for three consecutive AL titles from 1988 to 1990, solidifying baseball in the East Bay.

The second notable owner who ceded control of his team was baseball's master showman, Bill Veeck. Having purchased the Chicago White Sox in 1975, for a second stint, Veeck used his accustomed flair in an attempt to breathe life into a mediocre team. The 1977 club, earning the moniker the "South Side Hitmen," overachieved on the strength of abundant power hitting that delighted fans streaming to Comiskey Park in numbers not seen since 1960. But by 1980, Veeck had barely weathered a number of unsavory storms: the ill-fated "Disco Demolition Night" of 1979; several episodes involving controversial White Sox announcer Jimmy Piersall, not least of which were his insulting comments about Veeck's wife and an incident in which he physically assaulted a sportswriter; and his failure to sign Turner Gill, the team's second-round draft

Figure 6.1. Possessed of a brilliant baseball mind but also one of the most volatile temperaments ever seen in the game, manager Billy Martin sparked a turnaround in the fortunes of the Oakland Athletics in 1980. National Baseball Hall of Fame and Museum

pick in the June 1980 amateur draft, of whom Veeck said, "He was the first draft choice I have personally visited that I was unable to sign."[19] Gill's demand for a large signing bonus put Veeck at the financial point of no return and a sad reckoning that he was unable to compete in a changed labor market to bring new talent to the White Sox. Veeck conceded that it was time to put the team up for sale.

While two offers were made, one by the financial conglomerate Merrill Lynch and a second by commercial developer Edward DeBartolo Sr., another school of thought held that Veeck's health was the primary driving force behind his decision to sell. When a summertime deal with DeBartolo was scotched due to his ownership of several horse-racing tracks and a fear of absentee ownership by the Ohioan, Veeck was hospitalized soon thereafter with breathing problems. Another possible sale to DeBartolo at that year's winter meetings fell by the wayside, this latest failure fueled by purported anti-Italian bias sourced to commissioner Bowie Kuhn, who denied the charge that DeBartolo was not the "right people."[20]

With only three AL owners voting in favor of a sale to the developer, the Chisox remained in limbo for a few more weeks until a group headed by Chicago businessmen Jerry Reinsdorf and Eddie Einhorn assembled a $20 million package comparable to that offered by DeBartolo. This bid won unanimous approval by the AL moguls in January 1981, and the Reinsdorf–Einhorn tandem would direct the White Sox into the next phase of the club's history, which featured an immediate infusion of cash—putting slugger Greg Luzinski and future Hall of Fame catcher Carlton Fisk in Sox uniforms—and the club's later move into the new Comiskey Park.

***

Aside from the departure of Finley and Veeck in the early 1980s, other team ownerships were in transition. A "palace revolt" in Houston almost cost Astros magnate John McMullen his position as lead board member when he fired president Tal Smith shortly after the club completed its most successful season in 1980, and installed Al Rosen in his place.[21] After minority owners of the Astros banded together in an attempt to buy McMullen out and were rejected in their bid, the team instituted a new corporate structure in which McMullen, who just a year earlier had partnered with Dave LeFevre to buy the club from the Ford Motor Credit

Figure 6.2. Few club owners relished running a team and connecting with fans the way Bill Veeck did, but shortly after the disaster of "Disco Demolition Night," Veeck found little to be happy about and put his beloved White Sox up for sale. National Baseball Hall of Fame and Museum

Company, remained at the head of a three-man committee that now ran the Astros. The team would sporadically contend in the NL West during the decade, capturing that division in 1980 and 1986.

The New York Mets, who had a virtual lock on the basement of the NL East from 1977 to 1983, bid farewell to a portion of their earliest roots in late January 1980, when Fred Wilpon and Nelson Doubleday Jr. fronted a group that paid $21.3 million to descendants of the Payson family, the team's original owners. Reviled since the notorious "Midnight Massacre," which saw fan favorite Tom Seaver dealt to Cincinnati in the summer of 1977, the Mets' leadership had been rudderless in operating the club, and the new ownership sought help for the front office by making former Baltimore Orioles executive Frank Cashen its choice to rehabilitate the team. The turnaround would be slow to develop, but under Cashen's direction, the Mets drafted and traded wisely to rebuild a moribund roster and revitalize fan interest. By 1984, when Davey Johnson was brought in as manager, the stage was set for the Mets to supplant the cross-town Yankees as "New York's team" and take the NL East by storm in 1986, by winning 108 games, as well as the league pennant and World Series.

Almost one year to the day that ownership of the Mets changed hands, a Southern California real estate mogul, George Argyros, took control of the Seattle Mariners, meaning that the Danny Kaye–led partnership was in charge of the Pacific Northwest's franchise for but five years. On the field, the Mariners would enjoy little success through the 1980s, finishing no better than fourth place in the AL West twice, and not until the lineup was bolstered by the teenaged Ken Griffey Jr. did Seattle make inroads in their division during the succeeding decade. By the late summer of 1989, Argyros, who purchased the club for a little more than $13 million, had divested himself of the team for $77 million, selling to Jeff Smulyan and Michael Browning, two investors with ties to radio broadcasting.

Where Marvin Davis missed out on acquiring a franchise, another oilman, Eddie Chiles, gained entry to the fraternity of owners by purchasing the Texas Rangers from Brad Corbett in early 1980. Chiles's involvement with the team dated to the previous year, when he contributed almost $1 million to the ailing franchise and subsequently led a six-man board of Rangers directors when Corbett was bought out. Chiles intended to operate the club in a more diligent manner: At the time he made his financial assistance, he upbraided Corbett for "running the baseball team like a toy."[22] The business acumen demonstrated by Chiles could be found in his efficiency-driven approach to structuring the front office and keeping the Rangers payroll in baseball's lower ranks.

Chiles's later attempt to sell his controlling share of the team in 1986 to Gaylord Broadcasting, which already owned 35 percent of the club, was denied by AL owners, who had grown leery about yet another superstation entering the ranks of ownership. When Chiles's primary enterprise, Western Company of North America, filed for Chapter 11 bankruptcy in 1988, as a result of a collapse in the domestic oil market, he denied that the unfortunate status of his oil-related supply business was impacting his baseball dealings. Yet, this had to have weighed on his mind. A reprise from Gaylord in early 1989, failed to pass once more, and finally a bid in March by a Texas combine, whose most prominent member was future U.S. president George W. Bush, alleviated Chiles of his travails at a price of approximately $46 million.

The opportunity for the sale of the Cleveland Indians went by the boards in the fall of 1980, when owner Steve O'Neill was unable to strike a deal with theater magnate James Nederlander and attorney Neil Papiano. Just a few years earlier, the Tribe, under manager Frank Robinson, appeared to be riding a wave of rejuvenation with a lineup that included the young talent of Dennis Eckersley, Rick Manning, Duane Kuiper, and Buddy Bell. Try as they might, Cleveland became mired in sixth place. Attendance at aging, oversized Municipal Stadium was poor, and with O'Neill claiming the woes of mounting debt, he sought a buyer for the team. No purchaser had been found by the time of O'Neill's death in August 1983, and when brothers Richard and David Jacobs agreed to take over the club in July 1986, losses in excess of $11 million burdened the struggling Indians. Only in the mid-1990s, upon the opening of Jacobs Field, did the effects of a new stadium combine with a contending team to revitalize Cleveland's fortunes.

The fraternity of NL owners lost a longtime member in October 1981, when the Carpenter family bowed out after controlling the Philadelphia Phillies for almost four decades. As the fiscal year was closing, lengthy negotiations by R. R. M. "Ruly" Carpenter III finally culminated in the sale of the team to a syndicate directed by the Phillies' own executive vice president, Bill Giles. Citing "philosophical differences with some of the other owners," Carpenter had grown disenchanted with "what I have seen happening in this grand old game over the last five or six years," a reference to vastly escalating team payrolls now common in the post-Messersmith era.[23] (Yet, the Phillies themselves were hardly innocent bystanders, having opened their coffers to sign free agent Pete Rose to a $3.2 million contract for four years beginning in 1979.)

No stranger to baseball front offices, Giles had previous experience with the Reds and Astros, and his tenure with Philadelphia began in 1971, as the team was moving into Veterans Stadium. His intimate knowledge of the Phillies gave him an edge in brokering the deal to buy the team. This advantage drew some criticism as being a "sweetheart deal" in which the sale price of a little more than $30 million was said to be undervalued by an estimated $2 million, but the transaction affirmed another aspect of the age: Although Giles would have full rein of the team, the biggest stakeholder in it would be Taft Broadcasting, with whom Carpenter had just months previously negotiated a contract to commence in 1984.[24] The Phillies were positioned to then let the old package with local station WPHL expire in favor of the new deal with Taft's Philadelphia-based station, WTAF, and in turn, two years later, Giles and his partnership purchased Taft's holdings.

Another media outlet conjoined with a baseball team in 1981. In Chicago, William A. Wrigley III, whose father, Philip, had purchased the Cubs in 1932, had taken control of the team upon the elder's death in 1977. Faced with issues relating to estate taxes when his mother passed away a short time later, William decided to sell the club. A $20.5 million deal was completed in June 1981, whereby the Tribune Company, owner of superstation WGN, whose original radio outlet served as the broadcaster of Cubs' games dating to 1924, now joined Taft and Turner Broadcasting as primary owners of a major-league team. Andrew McKenna became the team's board chairman, while Dallas Green, late of the 1980 World Series champion Phillies, was hired as general manager. The Cubs' contending teams of the 1980s were spurred by future Hall of Famer Ryne Sandberg, and the McKenna administration was in charge of ending decades of daytime-only baseball at Wrigley Field when lights were installed at the Friendly Confines in 1988.

***

The Minnesota Twins and Detroit Tigers, whose origins both date to the founding of the AL in 1901, also witnessed the passing of legacy ownerships in the 1980s. Calvin Griffith was emblematic of the conundrum faced by small-market clubs when free agency and resultant, expensive player contracts took hold in 1977. Having lost several front-line players, the Twins nonetheless persevered in the early 1980s thanks to a farm system that produced cornerstone infielders Kent Hrbek and Gary Gaetti, as well as, a bit later, outfielder Kirby Puckett and pitcher Frank Viola.

It was believed that when the Twins settled into the Metrodome in 1982, the new stadium would heighten interest in the team, but attendance did not keep a pace that would avoid the triggering of an escape clause Griffith included in his lease at the facility. Genuine concern arose that by drawing less than 2.4 million fans in their first three seasons at the Metrodome, the Twins would have the ability to move to another city, with Tampa Bay thought to have the best chance to lure the club away. During the 1984 season, as the turnstile estimate seemed to indicate a shortfall, a "ticket buyout" coordinated by an envelope-manufacturing entrepreneur named Harvey Mackay purchased enough tickets to thwart the lease's escape provision.[25] Early that summer, Carl Pohlad, a banking mogul rumored to be worth a half-billion dollars, bought the Twins for $32 million from Griffith and his sister, Thelma Haynes.

Pohlad committed to keeping the Twins domiciled in Minneapolis, and he, along with the team's fans, were rewarded in 1987, when the club, after winning just 85 regular-season games, prevailed in both the American League Championship Series and the World Series. The attendance clause, which Pohlad also inherited, became a moot point when the Twins drew 2 million in their title year and then played in front of 3 million in 1988. Another Series crown three years hence cemented the Twins into the early 1990s.

As vocal as Charlie Finley and Calvin Griffith were about the affairs of their respective teams—especially when the issue was salaries—the sale of the Detroit Tigers meant the departure of one of baseball's most understated owners. "John Fetzer was a sportsman owner in the noble sense," wrote columnist Dick Young in the autumn of 1983. "You rarely heard of him. He simply gave the people of Detroit good baseball, never making demands of the city."[26] At the age of 82, and with his wife ailing, Fetzer—a media magnate of the Midwest—was compelled to put his beloved team up for sale, and it fetched a cool $43 million when pizza magnate Tom Monaghan purchased the club. Monaghan was possessed of a "mild-mannered, unassuming" demeanor that closely resembled Fetzer's, but with Monaghan lacking in baseball knowledge, he was happy to have Fetzer stay on with the club as chairman of a three-man board that included Monaghan and president Jim Campbell.[27] The timing of Monaghan's purchase could not have been more propitious: One year after acquiring the team for whom he dreamt of playing shortstop in his youth, Monaghan was toasting the Tigers as World Series champions, their first crown since 1968.

Another nobleman who remained on the scene but agreed to sell a substantial interest in his club was Ewing Kauffman of the Kansas City Royals. The benevolent Kauffman had seen the Royals mature into an AL West powerhouse by the late 1970s, their appearance in the 1980 World Series capping an exciting season in which George Brett chased the elusive .400 batting mark; however, two events in 1981 gave Kauffman reason for pause: The players' strike disrupted the middle portion of the schedule—"It isn't as much fun as it used to be," he ruefully observed of the impact of business on the game—and at the age of 65, he escaped a health scare in May when a benign tumor was removed from his chest. "This brush with mortality caused him to give serious thought to the long-term future of the baseball franchise," noted his biographer.[28]

After one prospective buyer turned out to be financially unworthy in early 1983, Kauffman was buoyed by the quick emergence of Avron Fogelman, a real estate developer who had an active interest in sports as the owner of the minor-league Memphis Chicks. Fogelman bought a 49 percent share of the Royals for $11 million, a transaction that put Kauffman's mind at ease because he felt that his new partner, at the age of 43, had the energy and enthusiasm to move the Royals forward. Kauffman and his new partner agreed that building the team from within was preferable to lavish spending on free agents, and they valued the signing of the Royals' own key players, George Brett, Dan Quisenberry, and Frank White, to long-term contracts.

Fogelman had reason to be dismayed when the unseemly drug trial of 1984 became a blight upon the game and the Royals, in particular. But when Kansas City captured the World Series the next year, the achievement appeared to justify the method by which the Royals' roster had been assembled and brought them a championship. The subsequent addition of outfielder Bo Jackson to the lineup in 1987, foretold of continuing success, but by the time Fogelman purchased another 1 percent share of the team in early 1988, giving him equal ownership with Kauffman, red ink on the bottom line of the small-market Royals became a source of great concern. Also causing angst was deteriorating instability in some of Fogelman's real estate ventures and nonbaseball-related investments, and by the summer of 1989, "it appeared the Royals might become a pawn in the negotiations to resolve Fogelman's troubled affairs."[29] An alarm was further sounded concerning the fear that if Fogelman was able to gain full control of the Royals, he could sell to a party interested in moving the club to a more profitable market. That thought was abhorrent to many observers, including the head of the Major League Baseball Players Association, Donald Fehr, who could not countenance the thought of the relocation of a team with a track record of consistently drawing more than 2 million fans each season.

Ahead of the 1990 campaign, the Royals took an uncharacteristic dip into the free-agent market, signing pitchers Storm Davis and Mark Davis, partly to keep the team competitive rather than trying to rely on younger homegrown talent. This strategy clearly had an eye on forestalling a decline in attendance, which the club could not afford given its already paltry amount of broadcasting revenue it earned compared to large-market teams. Kaufman loaned Fogelman $34 million midway through the year to help him bail out of his ailing finances, a deal in which the latter put up his share of the Royals as collateral for the loan. But when Fogelman's lawyers stated that their client intended to renege on repayment, full control of the team reverted to Kauffman. But the sting of Kauffman's losing tens of millions of dollars to a partner who initially appeared to be a safe risk showed that "Fogelman had violated his trust and his friendship."[30]

Shortly before his passing in the summer of 1993, Ewing Kauffman formulated a plan whereby a directorate was entrusted with maintaining local ownership of the Royals.

***

Further changes took place in the ever-evolving world of club ownership. As the era of free agency took form in 1977, the Baltimore Orioles quickly found that their attendance was not keeping pace with baseball's overall rise at the gate. As salaries escalated in more perilous fashion—that is, from the owners' point of view—the small-market Orioles determined that raising ticket prices was their best means to generate revenue, an unfortunate option that could only further hamper attendance at Memorial Stadium. Simultaneous with this conundrum was the plight of owner

Jerry Hoffberger's interest in his beer business, National Brewery. National was also suffering loss of earnings from a decreased ability to compete with brands of beer like Budweiser and Miller, which had a broader, countrywide appeal.

In the late 1970s, the city of Baltimore was undergoing a phase in which urban renewal efforts were reshaping the municipality's infrastructure, not least of which would be the redevelopment of the Inner Harbor district. The suburban community of Columbia, with its plan for mixing private residences and supporting commercial enterprises, was integral to the long-term effort, and although the success of the Orioles and the NFL's Colts further cast the city in a positive light, support for its sports teams did not always measure up in the smaller fan base. As Hoffberger put the club up for sale, the nagging question would revolve around the effort to find a new owner who intended to keep the team in Baltimore.

In the spring of 1979, the state of Maryland tried but failed to legislate funding to help a local group buy the Orioles, but the team became a solid contender and drew more than 600,000 additional fans as it vaulted to the top of the AL East. This surge supported the decision made by well-resourced attorney Edward Bennett Williams to purchase the team in August.

Although the Orioles fell one game short of rewarding Williams with the 1979 World Series crown, they took the fall classic in 1983, a year in which they drew 2 million fans for the first time. Baltimore changed its tack on free agents and signed several in an effort to make up for the deficit of talent in the farm system, but to no avail, and in 1988, the Orioles embarrassed themselves by losing their first 21 games en route to a 107-loss season. Baltimore ended the decade with a most respectable—and redemptive—second-place finish in 1989, but Williams was not around to enjoy the occasion.

The death of Edward Bennett Williams in August 1988, forced his estate to place the Orioles on the market, and four months later a group led by Eli Jacobs purchased the club for $70 million. The Jacobs regime closed out the era of Memorial Stadium and was present at the opening of Camden Yards, which signaled the dawning of the age of new ballpark construction.

In early 1981, Cincinnati Reds principal owner and board chairman Louis Nippert sold his majority interest—$15 million was the sale price—to Vice President William J. Williams and his brother, James R.

Williams, but less than four years later the club was claiming a loss of more than $4 million. Aside from the deficit, another factor influencing the Williamses' decision to sell was the health of James, and a minority partner, who also happened to be a local car dealer, stepped in to purchase the Reds on December 21, 1984, for an estimated $11 million. Labeled as "outgoing, outspoken, [and] flamboyant," Marge Schott sought to place her stamp on the team, which ran in stark contrast to the conservative manner in which the Reds had long been handled.[31]

Seeming to always have her beloved Saint Bernard "Schottzie" by her side—the dog was fitted with a Reds ball cap at the news conference announcing the sale—Schott had a penchant for shooting from the hip and speaking her mind, to the discomfort of baseball officials, Cincinnati politicians, and many in her general realm. During her first summer as owner, Schott's general manager, Bill Bergesch, "promised me a World Series ring, and you know how women are when they don't get what they want," a compelling statement that presaged a Reds championship in the not-too-distant future.[32] But Schott's tenure as owner would be marked by a series of unpalatable events.

Pete Rose, long a fan favorite, returned to Cincinnati courtesy of a 1984 midsummer trade with the Montreal Expos, and he was installed as player-manager, serving a dual purpose of allowing him to continue his chase of Ty Cobb's all-time record for base hits while addressing the Reds' sagging spirit and low attendance at Riverfront Stadium. But Rose's altercation with umpire Dave Pallone earned him a 30-day suspension in the spring of 1988, and his permanent ban from baseball the following year in the wake of his notorious gambling scandal took much of the luster away from his eclipsing of Cobb. "By then, Schott had won a reputation as a cheapskate" who sought to dismiss the team's scouts for the simple offense of watching ballgames, and she caused no small degree of consternation when she made outfielder Eric Davis pay his own way home after being injured in a road game during the 1990 World Series.[33]

Schott caused her own brand of nuisance, notably with racially insensitive statements, homophobic comments, and remarks that put Adolf Hitler in a positive light. The Hitler tribute brought her a one-year suspension from baseball. Charitable in matters pertaining to children and animal welfare, Schott still confounded with her poor choice of words, which, as claimed by at least one sportswriter, were the result of con-

Figure 6.3. In 1984, Pete Rose returned to Cincinnati, where he received a hero's welcome and continued his pursuit of baseball's all-time hits record. National Baseball Hall of Fame and Museum

sumption of strong drink. Schott was nothing if not enduring, and she turned philanthropic toward the end of her life after selling the Reds in 1999 for almost three times the $24 million she paid for the club.

By late 1984, it appeared that the Pittsburgh Pirates were as unwanted as a team could possibly be. Warner Communications sought to unload its 48 percent stake after having bought it the previous year, and President Dan Galbreath claimed that his family's inability to purchase the Warner share left him no choice but to sell out. Although Chuck Tanner remained at the helm of the Bucs, their halcyon days of the 1979 "We Are Family" World Series championship had faded. The red ink of nearly $20 million in losses and a lease at Three Rivers Stadium that would not expire until 2010 threatened to make the team an orphan. The stain of the drug trials held in Pittsburgh offered no relief to the dilemma.

In October 1985, the Pirates changed hands after Commissioner Peter Ueberroth worked in the wings to develop a "unique experiment in community-based ownership" that placed Pittsburgh mayor Richard Caliguiri at the head of a locally based consortium now in control of the team.

While this ownership scheme was hardly unique—the Green Bay Packers of the NFL had been community-owned through publicly offered shares for decades—an infusion of cash from a $21 million bond issue helped the team regain its footing without having to relocate.[34] Along with the addition of such key players as Bobby Bonilla, Andy Van Slyke, and Barry Bonds, the Pirates enjoyed a resurgence in the early 1990s under manager Jim Leyland and captured three straight NL East pennants.

***

Throughout much of the 1980s, rumors abounded about adding another round of teams to cities that were clamoring for a major-league franchise, while some other clubs tried to leverage the threat of a move to coerce their current municipality into building them a new stadium. As this milieu evolved, Bowie Kuhn continued to play an active role in shepherding a growing list of candidate expansion locations.

By the time Kuhn entered what would be his final year in office, the commissioner remained involved with baseball's Long-Range Planning Committee and its interest in expansion. As autumn of 1983 approached, more than 20 cities spread across many time zones were listed in the commissioner's notes as potential sites for new ballclubs.[35] There were the usual domestic prospects (Buffalo, Denver, New Orleans, Phoenix, Tampa, Miami, Washington), along with a host of surprising entries (Brooklyn, New Jersey, San Antonio, Columbus, Louisville, Indianapolis, and Honolulu), but also included were some south of the border and in the Caribbean (Mexico City, Caracas, the Dominican Republic, San Juan), in Canada (Vancouver), and in the Far East (Tokyo, Osaka, Seoul, Taiwan). Kuhn also jotted down the possibility of a third major league entering the fray, as well as the formation of a club that would serve two regional cities, Miami and Tampa being a case in point.

Also at this time, the Long-Range Planning Committee engaged the services of a marketing management firm to help the national pastime peer into the future, or at least prompt it to consider the many variables that would help it develop a strategy for moving into the 1990s and beyond. Pacific Select Corp (PSC) of San Francisco delivered a report that contained several categories of issues that it believed would "provide [baseball executives with] a framework for thinking through" how various conditions would impact the game in the next decade. PSC also rhetorically asked, "How should expansion be managed?"[36]

The potential for extending MLB beyond the confines of North America was futuristic in its vision—a bit too ambitious, perhaps—but as NL president Chub Feeney informed Kuhn a few months before the commissioner left office, an overall balance sheet weighing the positives and negatives of expansion had to be considered.[37] Bringing MLB to new areas, the creation of more jobs both on and off the field, and increases in attendance and publicity for the national pastime were the elements that he believed would work in favor of expansion.

Although the marketing firm provided its input and the topic of expansion was hardly ignored, baseball was also in the process of a regime change. Shortly after Peter Ueberroth reached the commissioner's office in the fall of 1984, strong rumors suggested that Denver and Tampa were the frontrunners for new teams, and as if to belatedly vindicate the departed Kuhn, one scribe observed, "The power play being mounted by Jack Kent Cooke is going to put a National League club in Washington, either by franchise move or expansion."[38] But the never-ending issues of labor disputes, fallout related to the drug trials, four teams (Cleveland, Pittsburgh, San Francisco, and Seattle) facing serious fiscal problems, and the free-agent collusion cases preoccupied baseball executives for most of the next several years.

As spring training in 1987 began, Commissioner Ueberroth broke his silence on expansion, stating that although there need be no rush to add teams, the "game's current economic recovery" would allow for expansion to be considered once again.[39] By the time of that year's winter meetings, the roster of "prime locations" included Phoenix, Tampa, and Buffalo, while New Orleans, Indianapolis, Miami, and Washington also sought to gain entry into the select fold of the big leagues.[40] Adding six of these locales would fulfill Ueberroth's vision of 32 clubs, creating an even balance of 16 teams in each league, but the reality of how baseball business operated in conjunction with state and municipal governments, as well as the construction of stadiums, delayed the selection of new cities until 1991.

In the spring of 1988, Ueberroth believed that a regular-season schedule pared to 154 games played by a total of 30 clubs split into a trio of five-team divisions in each league was a way to tackle both expansion and realignment, which had been another situation being discussed for several years. Not until the next decade would expansion become a reality when Denver and Miami entered the NL for the 1993 season, followed five years later by Tampa in the AL and Phoenix in the NL. Conspicuous by his absence among the newer club owners was Marvin Davis, whose name appeared so frequently in the press beginning in the late 1970s that his acquisition of an existing team or expansion club seemed inevitable.

As salaries escalated in the 1980s and old-guard magnates like the Griffiths and Veecks fell by the wayside, it became apparent that team ownership had to rely on entities with stronger financial backing than had been in place for most of MLB's existence. The reality of the national pastime's updated economics is covered in an earlier chapter, and they demanded—at least in the short term—the ability of a team to withstand losses, possibly in the millions of dollars, in the hope that a reversal of fortune through improved performance on the field would translate into better attendance and increased revenue. Teams like Cleveland and San Francisco were hampered by the ballparks in which they played, so it is little wonder that new ownership or a threat to move to another city became an alternative way to conduct business.

Although many owners complained about the rising tide of red ink, it must be noted that those who sold their teams did so at a handsome profit. When the New York Mets were sold in 1980 for $21.1 million, that price was a nearly twelvefold increase above the original $1.8 million cost of the franchise 20 years earlier. The following year, the Chicago Cubs, long controlled by the Wrigley family, fetched $20.5 million, while on the South Side of town, the payment Bill Veeck made to reclaim the White Sox in late 1975, had almost doubled to a $20 million outlay five years later. Purchasing and selling prices of franchises continued to vary as the years went by, but the unmistakable trend indicated that they were on the rise.

The phrase "competitive balance" gained currency and was rightfully considered as fears persisted that the rich clubs would buy their way to a pennant, while their poorer brethren struggled to survive. Had only a handful of teams won pennants year after year thanks to mere extravagant spending on free agents, the failure of small-market clubs would likely have occurred. But in the 1980s—and before revenue sharing became adopted policy—there were pleasant surprises when Minnesota, Milwaukee, Cincinnati, and San Francisco contended at times. The inability of the New York Yankees (two AL East pennants and one AL title) and the California Angels (two AL West crowns) to dominate proved that excessive spending was done at the team's peril, and one economist indicated that the substandard performance of a club regardless of its market size might be attributed to "poor management [or] plain old bad luck," this latter factor perhaps rearing its ugly head in the form of a serious injury that sidelines a newly signed, high-priced free agent.[41]

Even a team that did not win its division title could enjoy the fruits of a season in which it contended and raised the expectations of hometown fans to the point that they were encouraged to go out to the ballpark. And when a roster like that of the Twins, Expos, and Blue Jays contained a trove of young talent percolating up from the farm system or was enhanced through some shrewd trading, the hope for a bright future could be most inspiring—and profitable.

The men in the front office who worked to assemble those rosters that became contenders were instrumental to the success that a team could enjoy on the diamond. A select few mastered their craft to such a degree that they subsequently earned their way into the Hall of Fame.

7

FRONT-OFFICE ARCHITECTS

As the complexities of operating a baseball team grew during the early part of the twentieth century, it became increasingly necessary for club owners and presidents to delegate tasks related to player personnel to a person whose primary duty would be to assemble the roster and oversee its affairs while also working with the franchise's minor-league players, farm system, and scouts. This multifaceted position in essence served as a liaison between the players and ownership. Prominent among the old guard were Connie Mack of the Philadelphia Athletics and Clark Griffith of the Washington Senators, who juggled ownership duties and various forms of player management—on and off the field—during their lengthy tenures.

But owners eventually needed someone to whom they could entrust the running of every phase of the enterprise. As the position of what came to be known as the general manager evolved, the earliest apotheosis was Branch Rickey, who created the modern farm system and served prominently in the front office of the St. Louis Cardinals and Brooklyn Dodgers. Player development and scouting were Rickey's stock in trade, but in his role as a GM, he also handled the often prickly chore of contract negotiations, as well as the execution of trades. Rickey's biographer, Lee Lowenfish, wrote of the Mahatma's philosophy of player exchanges, "You have to have the courage of your convictions in making trades, Rickey believed, knowing that the eventual outcome, especially involving young players, might not be known for years."[1]

For general managers, the painstaking process of finding the right players who will hopefully coalesce as a championship team claims more victims in the front office than it produces bona fide executives who succeed for not only one season, but also an extended period of time, perhaps even with several organizations for those having lengthy careers. Demanded of general managers is an acumen whereby they “know baseball from a business standpoint and business from a baseball standpoint,” the better to understand the interaction between the two while keeping a vigilant eye on the bottom line of his team’s accounting ledger.[2]

***

By the beginning of the post-Messersmith era, one veteran of Ohio’s major-league clubs had found his way to the front office of the New York Yankees. Previously serving as the general manager of the Cincinnati Reds and Cleveland Indians, Gabe Paul arrived in the Bronx having already provided the Yankees with an important cornerstone of its late 1970s powerhouse. Paul had traded a promising third baseman, Graig Nettles, from the Tribe to the Yankees after the 1972 season, but upon his appointment as a Yankees president when George Steinbrenner purchased the team in January 1973, Paul became the de facto GM and, in the course of the next few years, brought in Willie Randolph, Mickey Rivers, Ed Figueroa, Chris Chambliss, and Lou Piniella, all of whom were integral to the Yankees return to the top of the American League (AL) in 1976. “I am a man who likes to deal,” Paul said, crediting one of his historical predecessors: “I was brought up in the Branch Rickey School of never standing still with a winner.”[3]

When Paul left New York after the Yankees won the 1977 World Series—his next destination was a return to Cleveland—his place was taken by Cedric Tallis, late of the Kansas City Royals. Tallis had cut his teeth with several minor-league clubs in the 1950s and sought the GM position in Cincinnati when Paul resigned in 1960, to join the new National League (NL) expansion team in Houston. Tallis wound up as a front-office assistant for the Los Angeles/California Angels and was in Anaheim until Ewing Kauffman tabbed him to handle the Royals when Kansas City was awarded an expansion club for 1969. Under Tallis’s guidance, the Royals drafted wisely—the real plum was George Brett in 1973—and landed key acquisitions who formed the bedrock of Kansas City’s AL West–dominant lineup from 1976 to 1978: Amos Otis, Freddie

Patek, and Hal McRae. Tallis would not be around to see the Royals blossom because in 1974, he joined Gabe Paul in the Bronx and eventually succeeded Paul as general manager.

While the dovetailing movements of Paul and Tallis were unusual, the Baltimore Orioles had a dynamic duo in their front office in the latter part of the 1960s who would cement that club's legend before moving on to other organizations. Harry Dalton, the director of player personnel, and Frank Cashen, general manager and senior vice president, worked well together to forge the Orioles AL dynasty from 1969 to 1971. In the wake of Baltimore's Game 7 loss in the 1971 World Series, Dalton moved on to the California Angels, with whom his attempts to gain the team a pennant came up short, and in 1978, he found a new home in Milwaukee and helped to strengthen a hard-hitting Brewers squad that won the 1982 American League pennant.

Dalton's Orioles partner went to the front office of the New York Mets in 1980, after spending several years tending to Jerry Hoffberger's brewery interests and serving briefly for Commissioner Bowie Kuhn. Cashen put his mark on the Mets through a makeover of the organization's farm system and personnel, eventually producing a deep and talented lineup that new manager Davey Johnson led to the 1986 World Series title. Meanwhile, Hank Peters held forth in Baltimore and made a key trade with the New York Yankees that brought the Orioles three mainstays of their dominant late 1970s/early 1980s contenders: Tippy Martinez, Scott McGregor, and Rick Dempsey.

In Detroit, the Tigers benefited from the contributions made by general manager Jim Campbell, whose tenure of 40-plus years included World Series championships in 1968 and 1984, and another pair of AL East crowns in 1972 and 1987. Another longtime executive, Roland Hemond, served for profit with the Chicago White Sox in the 1970s, a high-water mark coming in 1977, when Hemond and Bill Veeck rebuilt the team with a series of trades that breathed new life into the South Siders.

The aforementioned general managers played important roles in the successes that their clubs had during their time in office in the post-Messersmith era. Several other eminent GMs are worthy of a closer look due to the high degree of achievement they attained, some to such an extent that they were deemed suitable for induction into the Hall of Fame. A trio of general managers, as well as a fourth who gained more renown as a field manager yet briefly served officially in both roles, came to embody the difficult task of not only building a winner—in the sense of a onetime feat—but also sustaining that degree of high accomplishment during a significant number of years, perhaps with several different teams. The following is a review of the records of Pat Gillick, John Schuerholz, Whitey Herzog, and Al Campanis, whose influence on their organizations was at once enduring and extraordinary.

***

When the Toronto Blue Jays were created in 1977, fans of the expansion team could easily have been excused for showing little enthusiasm about the chances of the club to contend against the likes of established divisional opponents. Coming at a time when the Yankees, Red Sox, and Orioles were capable of winning 100 games, the Blue Jays would have a great deal of difficulty even competing against its weaker AL East rivals in Cleveland, Detroit, and Milwaukee. In fact, not until their fourth season would Toronto break the modest barrier of 60 wins, only to be followed by the ineptness of a mere 37 victories in the strike-marred 1981 season.

Hapless for five years under managers Roy Hartsfield and Bobby Mattick, the Blue Jays cast their lot with Bobby Cox, who was given a new lease on life after his dismissal by the Atlanta Braves following the 1981 season. Cox's first year in Toronto allowed him to benefit from the fruits beginning to emerge from the farm system that had been crafted by Pat Gillick, whose prior experience with some prominent front-office executives paved the way for his journey to Canada.

Born in 1937, the native of Chico, California, became a Cub Scout and later attained distinction as an Eagle Scout. The experience of Scouting "taught me how to get along with people," Gillick said years later, and this lesson would serve him well throughout his life.[4] Gillick attended college at the University of Southern California (USC), where as a southpaw he was a member of USC's College World Series championship team in 1958. He credited famed baseball coach Rod Dedeaux with being an important influence as a young adult—"Probably the best fundamental teacher of baseball I was ever around," Gillick noted—and he pitched in the farm systems of the Baltimore Orioles and Pittsburgh Pirates before a shoulder injury curtailed his career in late 1963.[5]

Gillick fell back on the business degree he earned at USC and went to work for the Houston Colt .45s as an assistant farm director, later becoming the team's scouting director, and working closely with Tal Smith, the team's vice president and director for player personnel, whom Gillick praised for his mentoring. By 1974, Gillick found a new home with the New York Yankees, following Smith to the Bronx for a brief spell before casting his lot with the new expansion Blue Jays in 1976, as the organization's vice president of player personnel. A stint as Toronto's vice president of baseball operations eventually transitioned into his role as general manager, during which time the Blue Jays won five division pennants between 1985 and 1993.

During his induction speech at the Baseball Hall of Fame in the summer of 2011, Gillick reminisced about his tenure in Toronto that firmly established his record as a top-rank front-office executive. "For a baseball person, it was a dream come true. Imagine being able to build a team from scratch in a city where everyone was excited about finally having a major-league team," he said. While he had graduated from having to climb trees in the mid-1960s to spy on young amateur baseball players "so no other scouts would know I was interested in a prospect," Gillick developed a knack for focusing on two-sport athletes like Willie Upshaw, who excelled on the gridiron, as well as the diamond, and Danny Ainge, who eventually found the world of basketball more attractive than baseball.[6]

When Gillick was toiling in the Baltimore minor-league system, he paid attention to the manner in which the Orioles cultivated their young talent, and this experience served him well by the time he gained employment with the Blue Jays. Gillick further understood that Labatt Brewing Company, the corporate parent of the baseball team, "took a long-term approach" to assembling a competitive club and "decid[ed] not to blow our money right away" trying to field a team that perhaps stood a better chance of winning quickly.[7] Embracing a philosophy that required much patience before seeing results would not be an approach for the faint of heart, but Gillick was well-schooled by Peter Bavasi, Toronto's general manager, even though the GM "probably got more uptight about not winning games than anyone in management," according to Gillick.[8]

The sage draft choices in the early years of the Blue Jays' participation in the amateur draft soon brought the quality of player that the slow-and-steady approach was intended to deliver. Jesse Barfield and Lloyd Moseby, selected in 1977 and 1978, respectively, formed two-thirds of Toronto's vaunted outfield in the early 1980s, and they would eventually be joined by George Bell, who developed into a formidable slugger after being taken from the Philadelphia Phillies in the 1980 Rule 5 Draft. (Even 25 years later, former Phillies manager Dallas Green still had unpleasant memories of being "snookered" by Gillick when Bell was drafted.[9])

Although Gillick joked that the greatest discovery he ever made in Latin America was his future wife—Doris was a stewardess for Pan American World Airways in the late 1960s when Pat was flying to the Caribbean on scouting assignments—there was no mistaking his recognition of prospects he knew to exist in that talent-rich area. Peter Bavasi had taken a cue from his father Buzzie, who with the Dodgers well understood that "one of the pillars of the 'Dodger Way,' the organization's method for staying one step ahead of the competition, was to invest heavily" in underage players, especially those living in the Dominican Republic.[10]

The Blue Jays were keen to "focus where a huge number of players could be recruited in a hurry," and assisting Gillick in a most valuable way was Epifanio "Epy" Guerrero, a former minor-league outfielder from the Dominican who failed to make the majors but nonetheless enjoyed passing along scouting suggestions to those like Gillick who visited the island. When Gillick was still in the employ of the Astros, Guerrero unearthed a particularly tantalizing nugget in the person of Cesar Cedeño, whom Gillick was happy to bring into Houston's fold. The bond that formed between Gillick and Guerrero endured and was strengthened in the coming years.

Having earned Gillick's trust, Guerrero assumed the role of the Blue Jays' director of scouting in Latin America, and following the example set earlier by the Kansas City Royals, in 1977 he created an academy whose mission was to groom young players by providing baseball instruction in an environment that had a tangible difference from its stateside forebear: While Epy's Academy, as it came to be known, furnished attendees' room and board, it also offered classes in the English language, the better to help graduates assimilate in the United States for those who succeeded in transitioning to a professional career. Guerrero was also behind some actions that went beyond the normal recruitment of his pupils—for example, the time he financed a surgical procedure for a young and limping Tony Fernandez to have bone chips removed from his knee and subsequently signed him for profit.

However, Gillick was hardly operating in a one-dimensional manner. While it is true that "no history of the Toronto Blue Jays could be written without a nod to the Latin American players who starred for the team," the GM executed several notable trades that filled gaps in the roster or otherwise improved the club.[11] Sometimes derisively called "Stand Pat" because of a tendency to maintain the status quo with Toronto's roster, Gillick took advice from Guerrero in the matter of trading for Roberto Alomar, Victor Cruz, Juan Berenguer, Damaso Garcia, Alfredo Griffin, Juan Guzman, Fred McGriff, and others. The crafty GM also drafted reliever Tom Henke from the Texas Rangers as a compensation pick for Toronto's loss of free agent Cliff Johnson after the 1984 season.

In the late 1980s, without advice from his Latin counsel, Gillick dealt for Devon White, Al Leiter, John Candelaria, and Bud Black, and in a move that proved crucial to the success of the franchise in the early 1990s, he named Cito Gaston as the Blue Jays' interim manager in mid-May 1989. Gaston remained at the helm after Gillick was unsuccessful in handing the reins to Lou Piniella, then working in the Yankees' front office. The patience that was a Blue Jays trademark again bore fruit when Gaston brought an AL East division pennant and two World Series titles to Toronto in the early 1990s.

In the wake of his success in Toronto, Gillick moved on to Baltimore (1996), Seattle (2000), and Philadelphia (2006) for other stints, where his collective achievements earned him a spot in Cooperstown. In the course of his duties, there was a toll exacted on the famed general manager, one who took his job seriously, while also being aware that the business of baseball was infused with a degree of cruelness when matters regarding personnel had to be dealt with. There would always be elation when the victories piled up and pennants were won, but "when it came to decisions, about who would stay and who would go, about acting on the instincts that [Houston executive Paul] Richards had taught him to trust, Gillick would always make the tough call."[12]

Handling those tough calls with dignity during the breadth of his 27-year career made Pat Gillick a winner. Yet, when asked what his greatest accomplishment had been, his answer eschewed both seasons in which the Blue Jays took home the World Series championship. Pointing instead to a time that many had likely forgotten, Gillick said that when Toronto won the AL East pennant in 1985, "It felt like you go to the top of the hill." He added, "We worked so hard from '77 in the expansion draft. . . .

Figure 7.1. By tapping into Latin American talent and executing shrewd trades, Pat Gillick built the Toronto Blue Jays into a formidable contender in the competitive American League East. National Baseball Hall of Fame and Museum

I think '85 was the one where you said, 'Wow, we kind of made it to the top.'"[13]

A fellow general manager who also made his early mark with an expansion franchise would later join Gillick in the Hall of Fame, and his road to Cooperstown was inspirational in its own way.

***

As a youngster, John Schuerholz enjoyed the experience of an athletically inclined boy growing up in post–World War II Baltimore, playing baseball in the forms of wiffleball, Little League, high school and American Legion ball, and finally at the college level at what would become Towson State University. His affliction with German measles at age five, however, deprived him of hearing in his right ear. Undaunted, Schuerholz maintained "high hopes and aspirations of one day following in my dad's footsteps and playing professional baseball as he did [in the Philadelphia Athletics system]."[14]

Granted a tryout with the Orioles during his junior year at Towson in 1961, Schuerholz received a shock when, after giving what he believed to be a satisfactory performance in the first session, scout Walter Youse assigned him the task of timing batters running from home plate to first base. The not-so-subtle message to the crestfallen tryout participant was find a line of work other than playing ball. That "honest dose of scouting reality" forced Schuerholz to "redouble my focus on my teaching career," an endeavor that landed him a job at a junior high school in Baltimore but failed to satisfy his desire to be employed in some way in baseball.[15]

Now in his mid-20s and willing to forgo his future in the classroom, Schuerholz sent an unsolicited note to Orioles magnate Jerry Hoffberger as 1965 drew to a close. In his sincere missive, Schuerholz expressed his devotion to the game and his wish to be a part of it in some capacity. His last name drew the attention of Frank Cashen, a former sports reporter for the *Baltimore News American* now working as Baltimore's vice president of player personnel. Cashen relayed Schuerholz's information to general manager Harry Dalton, who in turn forwarded it to Lou Gorman, the team's director of player development. Dalton was seeking an assistant, but Gorman was screening the candidates, and with Cashen recognizing the Schuerholz name as being "good stock," the letter-writer was granted an interview and subsequently received an offer to join his hometown ballclub as Dalton's administrative lieutenant.[16]

Hired away in the middle of the school year, Schuerholz soon found himself at the Orioles' 1966 spring training camp, a propitious entrée to an organization that seven months later would become victors in the World Series. As he gained valuable experience in one of baseball's best front offices, Schuerholz was recruited by Gorman to move to Kansas City for a new opportunity to work with the expansion club that was being formed to start play in 1969. Initially resistant to abandoning the Orioles, Schuerholz was persuaded by Gorman that creating a team from its very beginning would provide both challenges and rewards. Gorman had been hired as Kansas City's minor-league director and did not hesitate to insist that Schuerholz, now a proven commodity, join him in the move to the Midwest.

The nascent Royals organization was fronted by owner Ewing Kauffman, but the infrastructure was girded by the general manager, Cedric Tallis. Gorman had been inculcated in the Baltimore system of how its teams were operated at the major- and minor-league levels, and this philosophy became the means by which Gorman handled his chores in Kansas City. By extension, it imparted further lessons for Schuerholz.

By the mid-1970s, the efforts of the Tallis–Gorman tandem had positioned the Royals to contend for the AL West title, finally succeeding in 1976, with the first of three consecutive such pennants under the guidance of manager Whitey Herzog. Tallis had been let go in June 1974, in favor of Joe Burke, but Gorman remained as scouting director until 1976, when he had the chance to move on to Seattle to lay the groundwork for yet another expansion club. That year, Schuerholz became the Royals' scouting director, later transitioning to the post of vice president for player personnel, which he held until early October 1981. In the meantime, Kansas City had broken its jinx against the Yankees, to whom they lost the three previous American League Championship Series (ALCS) tilts, and beat them for the AL pennant in 1980.

In the wake of the Royals' failure to repeat as AL champions and on the heels of a strike-shortened season in which they were swept by Oakland in the divisional playoff series, changes were in order. Kansas City had already fired manager Jim Frey, with Dick Howser taking over in the dugout, but when Burke was promoted to team president in the early fall, Schuerholz was the logical—and prompt—choice to replace him. "Immediately, two suspicions surfaced," readers of *Sporting News* were told. "One was the status of Burke's battle with cancer. The other was the report that the Chicago Cubs tried to lure Schuerholz into their den."[17] As Burke neared retirement, planning to step away in 1982, he admitted that as far back as 1978, Schuerholz was being "groomed" to assume the general manager's duties, but the Cubs were apparently only one of several teams expressing an interest in hiring the Royals' young executive.

Burke's promotion meant relief from the many day-to-day responsibilities of running the team, so now was the time to install Schuerholz as baseball's youngest general manager at the age of 41. Schuerholz also assumed the inglorious duty of negotiating contracts with the players, but what the new GM had not bargained for was the drug issue that burst on the baseball scene and wrought particular havoc with the Royals.

The 1984 season was trying, but Schuerholz persevered by reworking the roster and enabling the team to capture the AL West, albeit with a weak 84–78 record. Not least among his moves was a risky trade that brought in Steve Balboni from the Yankees, but the slugger led the Royals with 28 home runs, 77 RBIs, and a .498 slugging percentage. This proved to be a year that would also serve as a springboard for the team to reach baseball's ultimate prize.

In 1985, the team continued to maintain its competitive balance thanks to three emerging pitchers—Mark Gubicza, Danny Jackson, and Cy Young Award winner Bret Saberhagen—and Schuerholz imported former Gold Glove–winning catcher Jim Sundberg, along with outfielder Lonnie Smith, in a pair of key trades. Dick Howser, who was ingloriously jettisoned as Yankees manager after the 1980 ALCS by George Steinbrenner, had resurfaced with the Royals in 1981, and the patience demonstrated by the Royals paid a huge dividend when Howser delivered them to the World Series championship in 1985.

The Royals' World Series rings were well earned, as were the accolades that followed weeks later when Schuerholz was named "Executive of the Year" by *Sporting News*. Praised for steering the team through the rough waters of the recent past, "Schuerholz was the one who kept talking about how good things would be in the not-too-distant future," noted the publication, which added, "But there was speculation that his job was on the line [after the 1983 season]."[18]

Schuerholz also prevailed during the period of Avron Fogelman's partnership with owner Ewing Kauffman in the mid-1980s. Fogelman "had been trying to put his stamp on operations, principally by leaning on Schuerholz to act as his proxy within the front office, which led to some friction."[19] The instability generated by this awkward arrangement gave the general manager pause, and even though the Royals contended for the AL West pennant in the remaining years of the decade, by the summer of 1990, the general manager had developed a wandering eye when he heard about another opportunity. "We had fun in Kansas City winning, but it wasn't joyful," Schuerholz confessed, and during an encounter with Stan Kasten, president of the Atlanta Braves, he learned that the moribund NL club planned to move its general manager, Bobby Cox, back into the role of field manager for the 1991 season, creating the need for Cox's replacement in the front office.[20]

Slipping the bonds that had kept him in Kansas City for so long, Schuerholz, "with permission," bid the Royals farewell and immediately began to reshape the Braves by first insisting that "he wanted attitudes and thinking to change."[21] The new Atlanta general manager made several key acquisitions, not least of whom was Terry Pendleton, who became the NL Most Valuable Player (MVP) in 1991. Whereas patience had been a vital asset in cultivating an expansion team, Schuerholz's experience informed his decisions about expediently turning around a team in trouble, as he proved with the Royals in 1984.

The situation with the Braves at the dawn of 1991 can only be described as a time when all the pieces of a puzzle fell perfectly into place. Atlanta's lineup featured a balanced, run-producing offense that hit for average and power, while the pitching staff was led by four quality starters. Winning their final eight regular-season games vaulted the Braves past the Los Angeles Dodgers to begin a streak of 14 consecutive NL divisional titles, and there was no shortage of Hall of Fame talent spread throughout the organization: Pitchers Greg Maddux, John Smoltz, and Tom Glavine; infielder Chipper Jones; manager Bobby Cox; and general manager John Schuerholz all would be inducted at Cooperstown.

Enjoying more success in Atlanta than in Kansas City, Schuerholz nevertheless savored the success of division, league, and World Series championships in those cities, becoming the first general manager to win the Fall Classic in both leagues. In the spring of 1986, the Kansas City executive stated that the "one big lesson I learned from [owner Ewing] Kauffman is to make sure your organization gets strong people to do their jobs and then let them do them," and the achievements of the team were an "extension of the ownership's personality."[22]

Figure 7.2. John Schuerholz apprenticed with the Baltimore Orioles in the mid-1960s before moving on to Kansas City, where he helped deliver a World Series championship to the Royals in 1985. He later took the general manager's job in Atlanta and molded the Braves into one of baseball's finest teams of the 1990s. National Baseball Hall of Fame and Museum

A former journeyman player who, like John Schuerholz, spent a few years with the Baltimore Orioles in the 1960s and would move on to the Kansas City Royals also was later called to the Hall of Fame for his role as a successful manager. But his story is included here because of the indelible mark that he left on the St. Louis Cardinals in his role not only as a skipper, but also for his brief tenure as the general manager of that NL club.

***

Near the eve of baseball's 1982 postseason, Dorrel Norman Elvert "Whitey" Herzog told a St. Louis sports editor, "When it dawned on me that I was not going to make the Hall of Fame as a power hitter, I figured I'd better learn everything there was to know about this game so I could stay in the game I loved all my life."[23] A two-sport star in his hometown of New Athens, Illinois, "Relly," as he was called by locals, attracted the attention of the New York Yankees, with whom he signed in 1949, and thereafter beat the bushes with six different minor-league teams.

During the time Herzog spent with his first professional club in McAlester, Oklahoma, he was dubbed "Whitey" by a local sportscaster, the new nickname "referencing his bleached-out shock of hair."[24] Drafted by the U.S. Army following the 1952 season, he resumed his baseball career in 1955 with Denver of the American Association and posted numbers (.289, 21 home runs, 98 RBIs) respectable enough to get him included in a multiplayer trade to the Washington Senators. From 1956 to 1963, Herzog roamed the outfield and played a bit at first base for the Solons, Kansas City Athletics, Baltimore Orioles, and Detroit Tigers, compiling a career .257 batting average in 634 total games played. Injuries suffered in eight big-league seasons informed his decision to consider other aspects of employment in baseball.

A precursor to Herzog's future as a major-league manager came while he was in the Army, when he piloted the Fort Leonard Wood team in 1953 and 1954, winning the fifth Army championship in the latter year.[25] As his playing days waned with the Tigers in 1963, the 32-year-old Herzog segued to the Athletics' scouting staff for one year and was named the team's first-base coach in 1965, becoming part of a trend of youthful ex-players now trading their bats and gloves for coaching assignments. "The appointment of Herzog has proved to be a highly popular move here [in Kansas City] . . . his great hustle made him a favorite with fans," wrote Joe McGuff of *Sporting News*.[26]

Making him less of a favorite with a person who really mattered—Kansas City team owner Charlie Finley—Herzog became embroiled in a salary dispute by the end of the 1965 season and either resigned (Herzog's version) or was fired (Finley's version). Herzog's status as an unemployed coach lasted only about two months before he signed on with the New York Mets as their third-base coach for the 1966 campaign, and his mentoring helped convert shortstop prospect Bud Harrelson into a switch-hitter. Seemingly secure in his coaching role—his proclivity to make baserunners act aggressively had become his trademark—Herzog was suddenly out of uniform when general manager Bing Devine crafted a new front-office position specifically with Herzog in mind.

Devine sweetened the deal with a $5,000 raise to ensure that Herzog felt welcome at his new post, which included duties evaluating Mets players and scouting the minor- and major-league talent of other organizations. Proof of Herzog's keen eye was manifest in two players on the roster of his previous employer—Kansas City pitcher Chuck Dobson and his batterymate, Ken Suarez—and another who got away before the amateur draft was instituted in 1965: Future Hall of Fame hurler Don Sutton was ready to sign with the Athletics, but "our owner, Charlie Finley, who had already shelled out a lot of money for young players that year, nixed the deal. Sutton wanted $16,000."[27] One pitcher who did not elude Herzog with the Mets' first pick in the 1967 amateur draft was a virtually unhittable high schooler from West Chester, Pennsylvania, named Jon Matlack.

The Mets were casting about for a new manager after Wes Westrum resigned in mid-September and interim skipper Salty Parker was not retained. Mets management had set their sights on a former fan favorite to take the helm, but their person of interest was under contract with the Washington Senators. Gil Hodges, the former Brooklyn Dodgers star, was soon part of an unusual trade—pitcher Bill Denehy was sent, along with $100,000, to the Nats in exchange for the manager—removing any chance that Herzog would return to the field.

Instead, Herzog was shifted within the front office, assuming Bob Scheffing's job as director of player development while Scheffing took over Herzog's responsibilities. The next five years marked a crucial point in Mets history. "I learned a lot in that job in 1967," Herzog later wrote.

"It was my first taste of being involved in high-level trade talks," but in the course of the ensuing years, Herzog displayed a fair—and ultimately profitable—degree of impatience with the prospects down on the farm.[28] "I moved them along as fast as I could, and cleaned house of all the old, stagnant guys in the system," and, indeed, gone were the Eddie Bressouds, Ken Boyers, and Roy McMillans who were clogging the roster. In his time with player development, Herzog was "instrumental in sending 64 players to the parent club," and the credit he was due may have been, if anything, understated, with the more visible leadership personalities of Hodges and Yogi Berra lauded to a greater degree in the press.[29]

Herzog bristled at interference by team executives whose baseball experience was limited. Speaking of a trade between the Mets and White Sox after the 1967 season ended, he complained that the deal was ready to be finalized when club president M. Donald Grant, who was a crony of owner Joan Payson, nixed it because one of the players to be sent to Chicago was a favorite of Grant's. Irked by the kibosh, the general manager, Bing Devine, quit and was replaced by John Murphy, who allowed Herzog a free hand to continue operating in his accustomed manner, especially paring deadwood from the roster. The trade was reformulated, and ending up at Shea Stadium was the Mets' main objective, center fielder Tommie Agee, who became one of the major catalysts in the team's drive to the 1969 World Series championship.

An in-house tiff ensued when Herzog tried to persuade Hodges to move Agee to right field to make room for another prospect, Amos Otis, to play center, but Hodges won out and Agee remained in his natural position. Nonetheless, one issue on which Herzog and Hodges were in complete agreement was the value of relief pitching, and Herzog carried forward this philosophy to other teams he later worked for. Whether the reliever was Tug McGraw, Mark Littell, Bruce Sutter, or Todd Worrell, Herzog understood the burgeoning evolution of the role of the closer.

There would be no more playoff appearances for the Mets while Herzog remained with the organization through 1972. The sudden death of Gil Hodges just before the opening of that season raised Herzog's hopes that he would be given a chance to become a major-league manager. But again thwarted by the executive who proved to be a source of irritation, Herzog claimed, "For some reason, Grant always thought a former Yankee or Dodger should manage the club," and now that he was "frustrated and bored with the job," he knew it was time to move on from Shea Stadium.[30]

Herzog's next stop was Arlington, Texas, where Ted Williams had "begged out of the fifth and final year" of his managerial contract with the Rangers and recommended the erstwhile Met to replace him.[31] The 1973 Rangers were little improved over the prior season, and as the team continued falling apart during Herzog's inaugural stint as skipper, team owner Bob Short offered Herzog a chance to move upstairs to the general manager's office. Herzog did not believe himself ready to handle the chores of a GM, and in the meantime, Short became infatuated with the idea of bringing in Billy Martin, recently fired by Detroit, as manager. Soon, Herzog was out of a job and found himself in Anaheim as the third-base coach for the California Angels in 1974.

Herzog admired California general manager Harry Dalton, but the new coach claimed to have a more discerning eye than the GM—"He tends to overrate the talent he's got," opined Herzog of Dalton—when he sensed that the Angels were not likely to contend with their weak-hitting lineup.[32] Herzog filled in for four games after Bobby Winkles was fired, while Dick Williams, whose World Series experience was supposed to lead the Angels to a pennant, was brought on board as the permanent manager. Herzog returned to the coach's box, where he remained until partway through the 1975 season, when owner Gene Autry granted him permission to interview for the manager's post with the Kansas City Royals, whose well-stocked roster eased Herzog's transition. Bearing the imprint of the work of GM Joe Burke and his staff, including John Schuerholz, the Royals quickly flourished under Herzog's direction.

Inspired by the results attained with the Mets when he pruned unproductive veterans to make way for younger players, Herzog applied a modified form of this technique to the Royals by switching second baseman Cookie Rojas and outfielder Vada Pinson to the bench—rather than off the team—in favor of Frank White and Al Cowens, respectively. The same Amos Otis who was traded away from the Mets in December 1969, soon became ensconced in center field.

Beginning in 1976, the Royals embarked on a streak of three straight AL West titles, and attendance surged to more than 2.2 million in 1978, but despite assembling a team that clearly supplanted the Oakland Athletics as the class of the division, Herzog struggled to gain favor with the uppermost reaches of ownership. "I never got along with Ewing Kauffman, the owner of the club, and his wife, Muriel, hated my guts," Herzog recalled, noting that the Royals' success on the field—as well as the manager enjoying time basking in the limelight—may have played a role in creating jealousy and friction between him and the Kauffmans.[33]

The Royals stumbled in 1979, winning only 85 games and placing second in the division, three games behind the Angels. Having a contentious relationship with the Kauffmans, as well as never being a favorite of Burke, Herzog was primed to be ushered off the stage. More resigned to his fate and far less emotional than fans who were upset by his dismissal, Herzog said, "There's no disgrace in gettin' fired when you know you've done the job."[34]

Despite his unemployed status, Herzog found a measure of solace because he realized that his telephone would soon be ringing. The Philadelphia Phillies were reportedly interested, but after two firings, Herzog was circumspect about where his next destination would be, especially in matters pertaining to how a team's ownership conducted itself. The Mets, Angels, and at least two other teams also wanted Herzog in their front office, but the St. Louis Cardinals sought a manager to put the spurs to their underperforming lineup. On June 9, 1980, Herzog took the helm from Ken Boyer and tried to shake the Cardinals, languishing in the basement of the NL East 15 games below .500, from their torpor.

Reaction to Herzog's hiring was unpopular among the Cardinals players, but team owner Gussie Busch wanted a catalyst in the dugout. The new manager was blunt in his assessment of the roster, or what he called a "bunch of misfits": "Nobody would run out a ball. Nobody in the bullpen wanted the ball," and speaking of Garry Templeton, Herzog said that the talented but enigmatic shortstop was the "heart of the ballclub, which shows how bad off we were."[35] As manager, Herzog was not in a position to change personnel in a constructive manner, one that would remove troublesome personalities from the clubhouse, let alone the lineup. After gaining favor with Busch, Herzog convinced the aged patriarch of the Cardinals to install him in the general manager's post, which had been vacant since the early August firing of John Claiborne.

After less than three months as the St. Louis manager and logging a 38–35 won–lost record, Herzog was now out of the dugout, and old hand Red Schoendienst managed on an interim basis for the remainder of the season. From behind a desk in the team's front office, the new GM prepared to conduct the housecleaning that he firmly believed was neces-

Figure 7.3. Although Whitey Herzog drew more acclaim as a field manager, his work as a general manager in his early days with the St. Louis Cardinals reshaped the team's roster into one of baseball's most competitive clubs. National Baseball Hall of Fame and Museum

sary, and he enlisted Joe McDonald, formerly the general manager of the Mets, to be his executive assistant. The pair developed a knack for "working seamlessly together, with the assistant laying the groundwork over the phone and Herzog finishing the deal."[36] At the end of a dreary campaign in which St. Louis finished fourth in the NL East with a 74–88 mark and again sought a permanent manager, that position was filled by none other than . . . Whitey Herzog.

That Herzog would wear hats as GM *and* field manager—he only took one paycheck rather than two, much to ownership's delight—came as a bit of a shock since these duties in modern times had been discharged almost exclusively by two different individuals. But at a press conference announcing that the new boss was the same as an earlier boss, Herzog dispelled doubts and exuded confidence—if not hubris—in his capability to handle both jobs, declaring, "This gives me a hammer. I know there have been successful coaches in football who do it this way."[37] Even before reassuming the manager's job, Herzog had visited the Cardinals' minor-league teams before their seasons concluded and was dismayed to find rosters with a "bunch of 24 and 25-year-olds" toiling in the hope of still reaching the majors.[38] The specious records of the minor-league teams and the pennants they won did little to send bona fide prospects to the parent club, and Herzog identified but three players likely to join the Cardinals.

With McDonald at his side, Herzog set to work as the 1980 winter meetings loomed ahead on the calendar. As the pair worked the telephones with other clubs in an attempt to lay groundwork for the many trades that were long a staple of the gathering, they were having little luck until one of Herzog's former players in Kansas City, catcher Darrell Porter, declared for free agency. Herzog felt that the current St. Louis backstop, Ted Simmons, was better suited to the role of a designated hitter because his defensive skills were mediocre at best, and when Porter became available, Herzog was willing to take a chance that Porter was free of his past drug issues.

A deal was agreed upon to sign Porter, but it would not be announced until the winter meetings commenced. Herzog envisioned a lineup that included Porter catching, Simmons shifting to first base, and Keith Hernandez, normally at first, moving to left field. At first Simmons agreed to take over at first, but he reneged, telling Herzog, "You've already got the best first baseman in the league."[39] Herzog yearned for a top-flight closer, and with three catchers now on the roster—Porter, Simmons, and a young Terry Kennedy waiting in the wings for a chance to get serious playing time—he had a surplus from which he could put together a package of players to use in a trade to fill another need. When Porter's signing became public knowledge, it opened several avenues for McDonald and Herzog to explore, and suddenly Herzog seemed poised to do his best imitation of former White Sox mogul Bill Veeck, whose "Open for Business" placard at the winter meetings a few years prior drew attention to his willingness to partake in the trade market.

On December 8, 1980, Herzog bundled Kennedy and six other players with little value—in Herzog's opinion, at least—to the San Diego Padres for pitcher Bob Shirley, catcher/first baseman Gene Tenace, and the plum that the Cardinals GM coveted most, relief ace Rollie Fingers. The saves that Fingers had accumulated since signing as a free agent with San Diego were impressive: He led the majors in 1977 (35 saves) and 1978 (37), but he saved only 36 games combined in 1979 and 1980. Herzog ostensibly had his bullpen ace, but he was not finished trading.

The very next day, Herzog sent third baseman Ken Reitz and an outfield prospect, Leon Durham, to the Cubs for *their* closer, Bruce Sutter, whom Herzog knew the Cubs were willing to trade because the pitcher had beaten them in his arbitration hearing earlier that year. With Fingers and Sutter now in his stable, Herzog addressed his catching and relief-ace abundance on December 12, by shipping Fingers, Simmons, and starter Pete Vuckovich to Milwaukee for outfielders Sixto Lezcano and David Green, and pitchers Dave LaPoint and Lary Sorensen. Drawing a rebuke from some fans for trading the long-tenured Simmons, Herzog dismissed the outcry since he did not hear "too much yap from the legitimate critics."[40]

The Cardinals roster having finally reached a stage of equilibrium, one St. Louis reporter was still dazed by the number of deals consummated in so short a period of time and opined that perhaps Herzog had gone to the trading well once too often. "I think Herzog should have 'folded 'em,' at least temporarily, when he had all those blue chips stacked in front of him. . . . But you can get too greedy with Lady Luck," and there ensued a waiting game to see if this new cast of characters would deliver the results Herzog expected in 1981.[41]

Come the following season, the retooled Cardinals had the best overall record in the NL East but failed to finish in first place in either half of the strike-split campaign and were shut out of the playoffs. Yet, 1981 brought recognition for Herzog when he was named the United Press International "Manager of the Year"—he also won the award in 1976, while with Kansas City—but the year was tainted by an unfortunate incident involving one of the game's best talents.

In his six years with St. Louis, shortstop Garry Templeton drew raves for his playing ability but also catcalls and criticism for displaying an attitude not in line with a two-time All-Star and Silver Slugger winner. Just 25 years old, he rankled management and fans by loafing at times and complaining about his salary and contract status. In a game on August 26, he struck out but failed to run to first on a dropped third strike. When boos cascaded from the angry crowd, Templeton responded with several obscene gestures and was ejected from the game by the umpire, Bruce Froemming. When Templeton approached the dugout, an infuriated Herzog grabbed him from the top step while teammates separated the two. Templeton was fined and suspended by the team, and underwent a psychiatric analysis before being reinstated. He publicly apologized for his actions.

In the aftermath of the episode, Templeton needed a new home and requested a trade, finding Herzog sympathetic to his plight in the realization that "there was no way the fans of St. Louis were ever going to forgive him."[42] Yet, the Cardinals general manager, fully expecting quality and value in return, was not going let himself be fleeced in a trade either, and when he trained his sights on Ozzie Smith of the San Diego Padres, some tough negotiating was in order to convince the future Hall of Famer to waive his no-trade contract and leave Southern California. Herzog offered a one-year deal with the right to leave St. Louis after the year if he was not satisfied, and Smith agreed to a trade, with Templeton and Sixto Lezcano heading west in exchange for Smith and pitcher Steve Mura.

With his GM cap in place, Herzog astutely recognized the biggest change necessary to retool the Cardinals to maximize their long-range game plan and create the "kind of team I wanted to build to accommodate the ballparks we played in."[43] The capacious dimensions of St. Louis's home park and other multipurpose stadiums of similar design detracted from power-hitting but gave a decided edge to a running game played on Astroturf. Base hits that bounced their way into the power alleys could become triples for batters swift enough to take advantage of finding the gaps. And with the acrobatic Ozzie Smith installed at shortstop, the middle defense would be in excellent hands as well.

It would take Herzog some time to revamp the Cardinals roster, but when he returned to the dugout, there was a greater emphasis on the running game. (See table 7.1.) In 1980, which proved to be Boyer's last as a manager, the team had 49 triples (fourth in the NL) and 117 stolen bases (ninth in the league), but in 1981, Herzog's first full year at the helm, St. Louis legged out 45 triples (first in the NL) and swiped 88 bases (the league's seventh-best total), the latter figures accumulated in the strike-shortened season. Through seasons the Cardinals enjoyed best in the 1980s, they ran well for profit with Vince Coleman, Ozzie Smith, Willie McGee, Terry Pendleton, Tom Herr, and Andy Van Slyke emblematic of the speed game tailored perfectly for Busch Stadium and in road games at similarly configured NL stadiums. In 1984, St. Louis swiped 200 bases for the third year in a row, the first time that had happened since their old in-city rivals, the Browns, had done it from 1914 to 1916.

By the spring of 1982, Herzog had tired of the being a general manager, a direct effect of the "politics of baseball" and the aggravation of dealing with players' agents, so he decided to step away from the front-office side of the business and leave those affairs to Joe McDonald.[44] Complimenting his business partner by emphasizing their closeness, Herzog told the press, "Joe's done all the work. He should get all the credit.

Table 7.1. St. Louis Cardinals Running Game

Year	*Triples*	*League Rank*	*Stolen Bases*	*League Rank*
1980	49	4	117	9
1981*	45	1	88	7
1982†	52	1	200	1
1983	63	1	207	1
1984	44	4	220	1
1985‡	59	1	314	1
1986	48	2	262	1
1987‡	49	2	248	1

*Strike year
†Won World Series
‡Won NL pennant
Source: Baseball-reference.com.

We've always gotten along real well, and in talking about ballplayers in trades, we've always agreed. It'll be like it always was."[45] Nevertheless, they would continue to work closely together, so there is little doubt that Herzog's having a "large say in trades" would impact future personnel moves.[46]

At that moment, the Cardinals' roster was barely recognizable from what it had been two years prior. Bob Forsch, George Hendrick, Keith Hernandez, Tom Herr, Mark Littell, and Ken Oberkfell were the only players who were present on that earlier Opening Day, but the result was a team that contended from wire to wire and prevailed in the NL East, the subsequent league championship series, and the World Series. Another laurel was bestowed on Herzog, the 1982 "Man of the Year" award by *Sporting News*, and the magic he had woven seemed to justify the means by which he attained it. This included a continuation of his policy of not tolerating malingerers, which prompted the June 1983 trade of Hernandez to the Mets—"He traded himself. He wasn't hustling," said Herzog in defense of the deal.[47]

The Cardinals reorganized their front office in late 1984, and supposedly there were to be no changes to general manager Joe McDonald's duties. But on January 3, 1985, McDonald was stripped of his title and recast as a "consultant" until he could find a new job. His firing or resignation—again, the story varied, depending on the source—soon opened the way for Dal Maxvill to take McDonald's place.[48] Herzog reserved judgment on the inexperienced Maxvill, who came to the GM's job with few front-office credentials, but later came to admire him for quickly adapting to the new post.

Trades for power-hitting Jack Clark and front-line starter John Tudor, both of whom "praised Herzog in his general manager's hat for getting them to St. Louis from other clubs," preceded successes that followed in 1985—Herzog earned "Manager of the Year" honors from the Baseball Writers' Association of America—and 1987, when St. Louis advanced to the World Series both years but pulled up short in the seventh game of each tilt.[49] In the first case, Herzog's former team in Kansas City was assisted by a blown call in the bottom of the ninth inning of Game 6—the notorious Don Denkinger ruling that led to the Cardinals' unraveling—and in the second case, the Minnesota Twins took advantage of their four-game, home-field advantage at the raucous Metrodome and outlasted the Cardinals in Game 7.

That 1987 World Series appearance would be Herzog's last high-water mark, and at the age of 58, he gave up managing halfway through St. Louis's 1990 season. *Sports Illustrated* tabbed him the manager of the decade for the 1980s, and after a pause, he landed once more in Anaheim, this time as the Angels' senior vice president for player personnel—and de facto general manager—from September 1991 to January 1994, but there would be no rekindling of the kind of pluck that turned around the fortunes of the Cardinals a decade earlier.

Much space has been devoted here to Whitey Herzog for good reason. Although his time as an actual general manager is short of the tenure of Pat Gillick, John Schuerholz, or many others, the method by which he molded the roster of the St. Louis Cardinals, drawn from his years cutting his teeth with the New York Mets beginning in the mid-1960s, created one of the more dominant teams of the 1980s. "He was a manager, a general manager, a farm director, a player personnel director, a scout, a coach. How many Hall of Fame managers have worn all those hats?" asked relief ace Bruce Sutter, a Cooperstown inductee who saved 127 games during his four years in the employ of Herzog and the Cardinals, and the opening line of Herzog's plaque at the Hall of Fame pays homage to his accomplishments: "*An architect* and respected leader who built and managed teams to six division titles, three pennants, and the 1982 World Series title."[50]

As an innovator, Herzog authored a style of play called "Whitey Ball," which emphasized the elements best capable of playing on the many artificial surfaces in NL ballparks, and the results speak for themselves.

***

Lastly, the achievements of another NL front-office executive contributed greatly to the long-term success of the Los Angeles Dodgers but whose misstep on the eve of a significant commemorative anniversary left his reputation forever tarnished. The legacy of Al Campanis as general manager of one of baseball's most progressive clubs lives on, even as his name has become less enthusiastically attached to the credit he is due for having brought many quality players through the farm system, as well as in trades he made to keep the team competitive.

Born Alessandro Campani in 1916, on the Greek island of Kos, Campanis immigrated to New York as a six-year-old and gained multicultural awareness at an early age, becoming well-versed in Spanish from living in a Puerto Rican neighborhood and learning English as part of his formal education. He grew to enjoy American sports, captained the New York University baseball and football teams, and, in 1940, signed with the Brooklyn Dodgers, for whom he had a checkered minor-league career that spanned the years immediately surrounding World War II.

As a member of Brooklyn's Montreal farm club in 1946, Campanis first encountered Jackie Robinson, recently signed by Branch Rickey. The Dodgers mogul directed Campanis to help Robinson learn the basics of playing second base, and soon Campanis managed Dodgers minor-league clubs until a lucky break led him to a fruitful career change. "The farm director, Branch Rickey Jr., thought he had the makings of a future general manager and brought him to Brooklyn in 1950, as a front office assistant," whereupon "Rickey Sr. sent him to Mexico to use his Spanish in the search for prospects."[51]

Campanis sought young men with natural athletic ability, but he also deemed the mental characteristics of a player almost as important, and the scouts who later reported to him were charged with delivering detailed reports that would help him determine how suitable those players were to the purposes of the Dodgers organization. Because Campanis handled so many chores for Branch Rickey's front office, it was accurately said that he "did everything for the Dodgers except laundry," but by working closely with Fresco Thompson and Buzzie Bavasi, the farm director and general manager, respectively, Campanis honed the skills that enabled him to eventually assume the responsibilities of a GM.[52]

As his career was maturing, Campanis and his scouts unearthed a bevy of talent that became mainstays as the franchise transitioned from Brooklyn to Los Angeles. Through the late 1950s and into the following decade, every position seemed to be covered very capably, from the outfield (Frank Howard, Willie Davis, and Tommy Davis), to the infield (Jim Gilliam, Maury Wills, and Ron Fairly), behind the plate (John Roseboro), and on the mound (Sandy Koufax, Don Drysdale, and Johnny Podres).

Roberto Clemente was discovered by Brooklyn and spent time in their minor-league system, but he was subsequently lost to Pittsburgh; however, other talent reaching the major-league level impressed well enough to earn Rookie of the Year honors: Robinson (1947), pitchers Don Newcombe (1949) and Joe Black (1952), infielder Jim Gilliam (1953), Frank Howard (1960), and infielders Jim Lefebvre (1965) and Ted Sizemore

(1969). The tradition of cultivating outstanding players continued into the 1970s, and although none of these infielders received top rookie laurels, the formidable quartet of Ron Cey (third base), Bill Russell (shortstop), Dave Lopes (second base), and Steve Garvey (first base) became the bedrock for the Dodgers' success into the next decade.

San Diego joined the NL as an expansion team in 1969, and repercussions were felt in Chavez Ravine when Bavasi left the Dodgers to take a job with the Padres, and upon the death of Thompson shortly thereafter—he was intending to fill Bavasi's post—a vacancy was created in the general manager's position. Campanis was at last rewarded when he was named the Dodgers' vice president in charge of player personnel and scouting in early June.

The Dodgers were experiencing a slump in the years following their upset loss at the hands of the Baltimore Orioles in the 1966 World Series, but by 1973, as the vaunted Cey–Russell–Lopes–Garvey infield emerged to join outfielder Bill Buckner and catcher Steve Yeager, Los Angeles reasserted itself by winning the NL pennant in 1974, and dethroning the Cincinnati Reds as NL champions three years later. By 1979, a new string of Rookie of the Year winners began wearing Dodgers Blue: Rick Sutcliffe (1979), Steve Howe (1980), Fernando Valenzuela (1981), and Steve Sax (1982) took the honors, with other notable nonwinners like Greg Brock, Orel Hershiser, Mariano Duncan, and Tim Belcher following later in the 1980s.

In a 1983 interview, Campanis was asked if the team would continue with their ostensibly viable—and successful—strategy of "plugging in players where you need to." His answer revealed the factor that contributed to long-term stability: "When you build a ballclub, you try to build it for a decade."[53] It was exactly this dedication to a futuristic strategy, engendered by Rickey and carried forward by Bavasi and Campanis, that made the Dodgers the model franchise that they were.

Campanis complemented the farm system's production with various trades he made, albeit with varying degrees of success. From 1977 to 1985, he sent away Buckner, Sutcliffe, pitcher Sid Fernandez, and outfielder Candy Maldonado, and received little in return, and Campanis brought in the controversial Dick Allen from the Cardinals in 1971—the moody Allen was popular with many teammates, but his attitude rankled staid members of management, not least of whom was manager Walter Alston—but his trial in Los Angeles lasted only one season. Campanis dealt Allen to the White Sox for southpaw Tommy John, and this trade helped both clubs, as Allen won the AL MVP award in 1972, and John settled in as a member of the Dodgers rotation until mid-July 1974, when he experienced arm pain that ultimately led to the radical tendon-transplant surgery that not only rescued his career, but also became a new standard for repairing damaged elbows.

Other notable transactions involved sending pitcher Doyle Alexander to the Orioles for Frank Robinson (1972), although Robinson did not see eye to eye with Alston and lasted only two years in Los Angeles before he was traded to the Angels for, among others, Andy Messersmith, who finished second in 1974's NL Cy Young Award voting to teammate Mike Marshall, who was acquired from Montreal for Willie Davis in 1974. Outfielder Jim Wynn, who contended for MVP votes that same year, had been imported in a deal for Claude Osteen, and Wynn was later sent to the Atlanta Braves for Dusty Baker (1976). Also that year, Reggie Smith, brought in from St. Louis, joined Baker to solidify the outfield. Campanis sent pitcher Geoff Zahn to the Cubs for pitcher Burt Hooton, who became a reliable starter for nearly a decade beginning in 1975, and when the general manager fleeced the Cleveland Indians in a minor trade a year earlier, he laid the groundwork for future star Pedro Guerrero to gain status as one of the Dodgers' best run-producers in the 1980s. A variety of other players were involved in these transactions, but the bigger names underpinning the trades also had a supporting cast finding its way up from the minors: catcher Mike Scioscia, outfielder Mike Marshall, along with pitchers Bob Welch and Alejandro Peña, to name a few. The diligence exercised by Campanis to adjust the club's personnel and not let the Dodgers rest on their laurels was the team's trademark.

Nor was any trace of discrimination inherent in his modus operandi for signing or trading players. The ethnicity of a player mattered not to Campanis, only the talent that he could bring to the team. So it came as a disturbing shock when, during his appearance on ABC's *Nightline* program of April 6, 1987—this was the evening of Opening Day, as well as a commemoration of the 40th anniversary of Jackie Robinson's groundbreaking debut with Brooklyn—he blurted his infamous remarks about black players lacking "some of the necessities" to assume roles in baseball management.[54]

Summarily dismissed from his job as Dodgers GM following this blunder, one wonders what could have been going through Campanis's mind and how he could have forgotten his earlier work with Jackie Robinson, who was not only a great, pioneering ballplayer but also one who was on the front line of the civil rights movement. "I hope the people in this country can forgive a man who made one mistake," entreated Dodgers manager Tommy Lasorda, but it would be impossible to undo the damage inflicted, and two days after he confounded *Nightline* host Ted Koeppel and a national audience, Al Campanis was out of the job he had held for the past 18 years and removed from the organization with which he had been associated for 47 years.[55]

The rich and deep history of the Dodgers cannot be told without recalling the many names of those who gainfully toiled on the field and in the front office, and this includes the many deeds of Al Campanis. Despite of his poor judgment that one fateful evening, Campanis was a team architect the equal of any of his peers.

***

One decade into the new millennium and years after they stepped away from the game, Pat Gillick, John Schuerholz, and Whitey Herzog were elected to the Baseball Hall of Fame to honor the skill they plied in shaping the teams they served during their lengthy careers. In its own way, such an honor can be thought of as a lifetime achievement award, simply by virtue of the extraordinary length of time required to compile credentials worthy of such recognition. Besmirched as his reputation became, Al Campanis is included here for having been such an integral executive and administrator for the Los Angeles Dodgers.

Some interesting commonalities link this chapter's primary subjects. During the early to mid-1960s, the three eventual Hall of Famers had served in one capacity or another in the up-and-coming Baltimore organization, a crucial time in which the Orioles were developing into a powerhouse girded by the players brought in by Lee MacPhail and Harry Dalton. Shortly after their time in Baltimore and during the earliest years of their respective front-office careers, Gillick (Blue Jays), Schuerholz (Royals), and Herzog (Mets) achieved success with expansion teams, for whom the careful selection of young players and subsequent shepherding of them through the farm system was as vital to the accomplishments of those clubs as it was for the Orioles.

This trio obviously took to heart the lessons they learned in Baltimore, and Gillick especially understood the benefit of bringing in talent from

Latin America, which by the early 1980s had forged a solid track record of producing many quality players for teams besides the Blue Jays. Despite the opprobrium that later befell him, Campanis was with the Dodgers at the moment of baseball's integration and witnessed the immediate impact that minorities had on the game and his own club, in particular. Minority players unquestionably fortified the Los Angeles teams for which Campanis served.

Lastly, Schuerholz, Herzog, and Campanis confronted team rebuilding challenges through the 1980s. In Kansas City, Schuerholz faced the Royals' aftermath of the drug trials and helped to deliver a World Series champion in 1985; Herzog stepped into the Cardinals' breach during the summer of 1980, and two years later St. Louis was on top of the baseball world; and with the heady days of the Koufax–Drysdale tandem now in the past, Campanis wisely drafted a clutch of players that soon molded into the Dodgers' vaunted, long-running infield of the 1970s, to say nothing of the crop of superb rookies that reached Chavez Ravine later in that decade.

These four notables, as well as their contemporaries mentioned earlier, strove to put the best team on the field in pursuit of a World Series championship. The popularity of their respective clubs was in direct proportion to the victories they accumulated—as the saying goes, everyone loves a winner—and the box-office appeal that led to increased revenue streams conspired with new ways to put the game of baseball not only more in the public eye to entice people to come to the ballpark, but also to open their wallets more frequently to purchase products that allowed fans to better identify with their favorite players and teams.

8

MARKETING THE GAME

Several preceding chapters have dealt with the business side of the national pastime, the inner workings that pertain to the infrastructure of Major League Baseball (MLB). Labor, money, the commissionership, franchise formations, and the venues in which the game is played all underpin the operation of the enterprise as a whole. Yet, the game could not rest on the laurels of its being America's preeminent sport and expect that fans would forever willingly part with their discretionary income for the purposes of baseball-related entertainment. Facing increasing competition from football beginning in the late 1960s, baseball had reason to sell itself in ways that would heighten the interest of its longtime supporters and cultivate a fresh, younger generation to carry on the grand tradition of keeping the national pastime foremost in their minds. To this end, marketing baseball to the public also assumed greater importance in every team's business strategy.

Through the 1980s and beyond, the promotion of baseball—and, to be fair, other sports—attracted increasing amounts of attention as cable television networks proliferated throughout the country and delivered more game coverage and related programming to viewers who seemed to be developing an insatiable appetite for such fare. The national pastime's ignorance of salesmanship had been demonstrated through at least the first half of the twentieth century, when baseball was "known for its lack of, or at least modest use of, marketing and promotions," and the game's moguls exhibited a demonstrative sense of hubris because they "believed, essentially, that real men didn't market."[1] But as television and the age of consumerism gained currency in the post–World War II era, it would no longer suffice for baseball teams to simply hang a shingle on the front of the stadium bearing the inscription "Game Tonight."

Coming onto the scene with impeccable timing, Bill Veeck was a "flashpoint of promotions and marketing practices that would become standardized in both minor-league and [major-league] stadiums," his giveaways and special events serving to emphasize the importance of entertainment, if not the playing of the game itself.[2] As teams began to distribute free bats, caps, commemorative items, or other tchotchkes—aside from the staging of such special events as fireworks displays and concerts—these efforts were geared toward increasing attendance at the ballpark, and they formed a winning business strategy throughout the years. Even the complimentary goods underwent an overt change: The cost of those items, formerly borne by the team, were now paid by a business entity, whose own logo or trademark was affixed to the handout. Moreover, "Many products that began as giveaways have become regular team merchandise items without the corporate sponsor label."[3]

In the mid-1980s, the National Association of Professional Baseball Leagues developed a book containing chapters—some written by major-league executives—intended to guide minor-league officials in setting up promotions and delivering a better product and service to their fan base. Peter Bavasi of the Cleveland Indians stated,

> Before you begin to develop your specific strategies and tactics such as dealing with how many and what kinds of promotions you might have and what your new uniforms might look like, or what menu items might change at the concession stands, you'll want to sit down first and decide on a general marketing concept. This will become your guiding principle and will be the conceptual thread that will, or should, run through everything your club does. Every facet of your operation should be tied together with this marketing concept so that you have an orderly and consistent approach and presentation for everything that you do.[4]

To Bavasi's eye, the two most obvious things readily identifiable to fans were the team's colors and logo, and he stressed that although a baseball team offered a unique entertainment option and could insulate itself from outside competition to some degree, club executives still needed to be aware that catering to the public meant cultivating a fan-friendly environment—the better to encourage families and younger customers to come to a clean, safe stadium—and implored teams to share their success stories about what promotions worked well, thereby stimulating creativity among their fellow teams.

A profusion of ideas and gimmicks meant to increase fan interest—and, in some cases, direct participation by game attendees—flourished. Pregame parties, celebrity exhibition games, performance of "The Star-Spangled Banner" by a guest singer, delivery of the first-pitch ball by special courier, on-field Little League activities, and much more added to what was evolving as a carnival-like atmosphere.[5]

Another marketing-industry publication offered a number of ways to increase ticket sales; entertain fans; find, sell, and satisfy corporate sponsors; generate awareness for merchandising opportunities; stage successful events; create in-arena attractions; and increase media sales.[6] Not only were teams eager to satisfy those in the corporate world, but also those same businessmen were anxious to upgrade from company box seats, long a staple for the well-heeled, to more upscale accommodations. "In the late 1980s, a Nabisco executive . . . identified his luxury box access as a tremendous advantage in entertaining key customers," indicating an important sequence in which the team served the need of *its* customer—in this case provision of niceties to a corporate fan—who in turn would serve *his* own need in dealing with his own business clients.[7]

Comfortable seating was not the only amenity to be found in the posh suites: Such culinary delicacies as smoked salmon, beef tenderloin, and guacamole—which could be ordered by patrons in the plusher confines of the Houston Astrodome—were a cut above traditional ballpark offerings, to say nothing of being an additional source of revenue for the team.[8] When the federal government restricted the amount of money that corporations could write off as business expenses, economist Andrew Zimbalist observed, "New limitations on business deductions in the 1986 tax reform do not seem to have deterred noticeably the growth of income from luxury boxes."[9]

At least one team with worries more troublesome than deluxe culinary selections was moved to seek ways to heighten fan interest dimmed by years of lackluster performance on the field. A marketing plan developed for the San Diego Padres in 1983, spoke to the concerted effort mounted by the team to address fans' recent disenchantment, which had been fueled by the players' strike of 1981, the recent loss of stars Dave Winfield (to free agency) and Ozzie Smith (via a trade to St. Louis), and a broad feeling of discontent about everyday economic conditions unrelated to baseball.

In the aftermath of the strike, the Padres created a catchy "Mad Campaign" to instill a spirit meant to channel the anger related to the work stoppage into moving toward positive goals. A comment attributed to local sports reporter Hal Clement—"I'm mad and the Padres are mad and I love it!"—was emblematic of this con brio attitude.[10] But this bravado could endure only for the short term, and the portion of the Padres' 1982 budget earmarked for "our advertising [that] was almost exclusively calculated to influence the desired attitude change" was now reconfigured in 1983, to "support specific major and ongoing promotions. In short, most of the dollars available should be targeted toward opportunities for immediate pay back, a luxury which was not present a year ago."[11]

The plan now focused on four key topics—season tickets, group sales, public relations, and an amalgam of advertising and promotions—that would fortify the team's base for the long haul. San Diego's "public relations director" was expected to "take a strong role in bringing about total coordination of all efforts related to overall marketing of the Padres . . . [and to] ensure coordination of all related tasks carried out by Public Relations, Promotions, Merchandising, and Ticket Sales staffs."[12] Other responsibilities of dealing with the media (press releases, team publications, press box operations) served an important function, and even though San Diego admitted to having a low number of season ticket holders, attendance increased dramatically when manager Dick Williams led the team to a .500 record in 1982, his first season with the Padres.

This reversal in fortune was further enhanced by the "constant behind-the-scenes stroking of the media to maintain a happy, positive feeling toward the Padres," an endeavor that included lunches sponsored by the club for select figures in the press corps; the eagerness of "top people in the organization" to be available to the media; and, not forgetting those purchasing tickets, "some stability on the ballclub enabling fans to identify more closely with the players and the willingness of certain players to become involved within the community."[13] This last point was a source of angst for club officials, who were discouraged by players who were uncooperative or resistant to overtures to make themselves more available to the public. The marketing plan went so far as to recommend that the team use community involvement as a bargaining chip: "During individual player contract negotiations this should be emphasized—and even spelled out in certain cases" to encourage him to be more accessible and visible.[14]

Perceived to lack players of "celebrity status," the Padres selected several regulars and a few pitchers to be promoted as "drawing cards" who would strengthen the bond between the club and its fans.[15] The publicity department was to write up "feature topics" that had more of a human-interest orientation, and these articles could then be distributed to the local media to inform readers, listeners, and viewers about players' hobbies, superstitions, and family activities, or their "success stories" in overcoming such adversities as injuries or other "personal battles."[16]

The Padres were also sensitive to the actions of those not directly employed by the team but who nonetheless contributed to the experience of attending a game, thus the team's interest in hosting a lunch for ushers, parking-lot attendants, and concession-stand workers to "coach them on good behavior toward fans."[17] Not to be overlooked given the Padres' geographic location was the sizable Mexican population in the area, and the ethnic newspapers, magazines, and radio and television outlets that served it were to be drawn into the Padres' sphere as well.

Not wanting to leave any press-related stones unturned, the club sponsored a conference for high school sportswriters and editors, the goal of which was to "communicate and educate the *proper reporting* of Padres baseball to high school journalists, to generate stories in the high school press, and to generate coverage by the San Diego professional media."[18] Although the team got to choose what constituted "proper reporting," the program would still give teenagers an insight to the working world of the media.

Regardless of the age of the press members, they would witness home-game promotions tailored "toward reaching specific demographics" of children (youth baseball days), families (fireworks nights, family bargain nights), or adults (businessman's specials for weekday matinée games), and appearances of the famous San Diego Chicken also featured prominently as an attraction for 10 dates that comprised the "Seasoned Chicken Ticket" program.[19] The Padres were not alone in developing and executing a business plan, and given the economic climate of the age, it was in the best interests of every team to do so.

Putting people in the stands to maximize capacity was a daunting endeavor: Even when traditional doubleheaders were part of the schedule, each club still had to generate enthusiasm for more than 70 home dates, which could be problematic for a poorly performing club. As the era of free agency moved into the 1980s, some teams shifted from a male-oriented promotional focus—female ushers in hot pants were employed in some ballparks—to one that was more family friendly and less reflective of gender stereotyping.

Yet, a multifaceted approach to reaching a broader fan base was instrumental in enabling teams to cast a wider net in the interest of reining in more customers, and technology provided a valuable component in this regard. In Baltimore, where the Orioles barely drew 1 million fans per year during their dynastic heyday from 1969 to 1971, the regime of owner Edward Bennett Williams was marked by an avid willingness to expand efforts to promote the club. The employment of specialized personnel, including those with sales and marketing expertise, allowed the team to exploit previously untapped resources and incorporate them into a revised promotional policy. The Orioles "experimented with a variety of newsletters; installed 'Diamondvision,' a costly, state-of-the-art scoreboard; formed a television production company; introduced a video yearbook; and lined up corporate support for individual promotions."[20]

The generation of cashflow through marketing and merchandising, in particular, was about to take a huge step forward in the 1980s. "Effort should be made to increase public awareness of team logo," the Padres were advised. "In this connection greater opportunities for [the] logo to be displayed should be developed [by] staff wherever and whenever Padres and baseball are involved."[21] An expanded source of revenue was about to enter the coffers of every team through the licensing of merchandise accessible to virtually every fan.

***

Direct marketing of officially licensed major-league merchandise enabled fans to be clad in the jerseys of their favorite club or player, their pates could be adorned with the caps of the teams they followed, and all manner of other apparel and products eventually found ways into the lives of devoted followers. In some instances, items came by way of giveaways at the ballpark, but regardless of the article, these were all intent on enhancing a club's revenue stream while also strengthening the bond between fans and the team and/or the player they liked most. As long as fans had a sense of connection or identification, especially when they were willing to pay for the privilege of sporting a team logo, their feeling of belonging manifested itself for profit, to the delight of product manufacturers and the clubs.

In the wake of the Messersmith decision, the New York Yankees won three consecutive American League pennants and two World Series from 1976 to 1978, and with the team having emerged from its postdynastic doldrums of the late 1960s and early 1970s, their fans quickly became enthusiastic for sporting the colors of a revitalized champion. With Yankees merchandise now a hot commodity, especially after New York's capture of the 1977 Series, there was a natural inclination for the team to want to keep the profits from such sales to themselves. But the Yankees' partnership with Major League Baseball Promotions Corporation (MLBPC) precluded them from attaining this goal.

Founded in the final year of commissioner William Eckert's administration, the MLBPC was established through the collaborative effort of then-attorney Bowie Kuhn and—ironically—Yankees managing general partner Mike Burke, but this entity was a "pale imitation" of its counterpart in the National Football League.[22] Where NFL Properties shared its wealth among all teams, baseball lagged in maximizing its earnings potential until the early 1980s because of the lack of a collective effort among the teams. Less than two months after the Yankees won the World Series in 1977, owner George Steinbrenner saw obvious advantages to retaining more profits from the sale of Yankees merchandise, now on the rise due in no small part to the club's recent success. By freeing the Yankees from their ties to MLBPC, Steinbrenner would be able to monopolize revenue that would otherwise be directed to the promotional corporation.

The Yankees had a valid reason for wanting to remove themselves from the consortium. "Most of the MLBPC revenues have been used to promote baseball [in general]," and MLBPC had paid teams "only token dividends from sales generated from promotional tie-ins and licensing fees."[23] At the 1977 winter meetings, Steinbrenner was talked out of abandoning the group, but he was possessed of a festering resentment that refused to go away. The following November, seven clubs—the Atlanta Braves, Cincinnati Reds, Kansas City Royals, Los Angeles Dodgers, Milwaukee Brewers, Minnesota Twins, and New York Mets—vented to Kuhn because the "Yankees have continued to frustrate the normal conduct of MLBPC's licensing and other promotional activities in 1978 through their refusal and delay in acting upon opportunities generated by MLBPC and its agents on behalf of all Major League Clubs."[24]

Acting as the agent for MLBPC, the Licensing Corporation of America (LCA) had a vested interest baseball's marketing effort: It kept one-third of gross revenues up to $375,000 and 50 percent beyond that amount, and the two parties agreed to work in tandem for purposes of "formulat[ing] an annual 'rate card' of charges" for various categories of licensed products.[25] Yet, LCA emphasized the "continuing involvement and cooperation of *all* Clubs in the two Major Leagues" for maximum financial benefit, and when the Yankees were finally brought to heel—LCA later noted an "oral agreement of December 1978 . . . has been followed by the parties since then, although for various reasons it was never formally executed"—the economic situation began to gain appreciable traction by the early fall of 1981.[26]

Although the Yankees had a valid point regarding the retention of revenue produced by their insignia, Joseph Podesta, the MLBPC president, argued that allowing 26 teams their own latitude would be chaotic. "The needs of such national licensees cannot be filled except by a centralized national program," said Podesta, and "if a centralized program were dismantled, a handful of clubs might retain some significant activity, but licensing by most clubs would diminish significantly."[27] Creeping socialism notwithstanding, this version of revenue sharing was the better alternative.

Meantime, LCA had hardly been an idle bystander once the ink was dry on its agreement with MLBPC. The licensor pledged to continue its efforts to encourage the development of retail floor space dedicated exclusively to baseball products, and evidence of this could be found in the stores of one of the country's largest retailers. J. C. Penney created more than 300 "baseball shops" in its stores, leading directly to the shipment of 300,000 shirts—the "star of the program," noted a baseball promotional kit—and a buyer employed by Hills, a discount department store chain, enthused about the increase in sales of baseball merchandise, which had doubled since 1979.[28] Accommodating gender stereotypes of the age, Hills determined that its "Team shops" were best situated adjacent to existing floor space already stocked with clothing for men and boys. Some other baseball stores, separate from department stores and the like, could be found at or in close proximity to the team's ballpark, for example, the Cincinnati Reds' 580 Gift Shop located at Riverfront Stadium, in addition to its companion Dugout Shop at the Kings Island Amusement Park.

In its quest to promote as effectively as possible, MLBPC material hailed the decade of the 1980s as "promis[ing] to offer the biggest and best marketing opportunity in baseball's hundred-plus years' history," and the ability of an overwhelming number of fans to recognize the logo of their local team (86 percent) and that of MLB (62 percent) was proof of both the public's awareness and the popularity of this "truly American sport."[29] Crucial to maximizing the energy devoted to marketing was MLBPC's revelation that 53 percent of regular and postseason game attendees were women and children, and it was increasingly imperative to sell the sport beyond the once-traditional demographic boundary of an adult male audience—for instance, the one that persisted at Olympic Stadium in Montreal: The Expos' vice president for marketing indicated that the team, whose attendance was 77 percent male, would "focus on women fans and 'make them more sensitive toward our product.'"[30]

Even though Bowie Kuhn had become an embattled commissioner, MLBPC was resting on a solid foundation, and by 1982, the growth in the number of licensed vendors and their wares necessitated the publication of a 48-page catalog so that merchants could quickly reference the burgeoning number of items now on offer assorted into several major categories: apparel, gifts and novelties, linens and housewares, and toys and games. Within these four sections could be found a deluge of products adorned by the logo of one's favorite team: Western-style headwear; shower curtains; automobile floor mats; quilts and comforters; pajamas; disposable lighters; sleeping bags; beverage containers; stickers and decals; iron-on transfers; bracelets and jewelry; key chains; memo pads; rub-on tattoos; wristbands and headbands; and, not least of the lot, the ubiquitous caps, jackets, and T-shirts.

As the 1980s progressed, one business, the New Era hat company, saw its sales of authentic major-league caps quadruple between 1982 (1.4 million units) and 1989 (5.6 million units). Prior to this boom, New Era, in 1978, had been swamped with orders when it took out an advertisement in *Sporting News*; when MLB partnered with New Era in 1986, to create the Diamond Collection brand, the agreement "officially sanctioned the on-field product," and fans could now wear the same cap worn by the players.[31]

The sports marketing industry was thriving to such a degree that in 1989, a new publication, *Team Licensing Business*, was introduced. The magazine's managing editor reported in the inaugural issue that the licensing market for the previous three years enjoyed "enormous, phenomenal growth," and Ralph Irizarry of LCA observed that because the "industry has carved out several niches for consumers," they were now enticed to shop, as demonstrated by the "popularity of authentic products and fashion and upscale merchandise."[32] MLB was paying close attention to buying trends and reacting accordingly: Women purchased 40 percent of licensed products, but they used only half that amount, prompting the desire to "change those statistics by creating new lines of products—especially apparel—with a more feminine flair."[33]

Selling baseball to the public at large was made easier by such players as the Dodgers' Orel Hershiser, whose clean-cut image combined with his on-field accomplishments in 1988 to attract fans and commercial endorsements. The Dodgers ace reaped more than $600,000 in commercial endorsements after his superlative season, while Bo Jackson, an outfielder for the Kansas City Royals who doubled as a running back for the NFL's Los Angeles Raiders, garnered nearly $500,000 in 1989, and had at least one advertising executive salivating over the seemingly "unlimited earnings potential" he saw in the "likeable guy and incredible two-sport athlete."[34] Never bashful about putting himself in front of the public if there was a dollar to be made, Pete Rose set the all-time hits record in late 1985, and "reveled in the attention and hype, orchestrating the chase into a months-long media event" that also became a windfall for him through sales of commemorative merchandise.[35]

As attendance bloomed in the 1980s, the licensing initiative that gained a firm footing under Kuhn had truly taken flight during the tenure of Peter Ueberroth, who "centralized" all the teams' licensing rights under Major League Baseball Properties, an entity that "could drive harder bargains with manufacturers on behalf of all of baseball."[36] Licensed product sales climbed to $200 million in 1987, and two years later had soared to $700 million, and baseball was anticipating sales to reach $1 billion in 1990. Rick White, president of Major League Baseball Properties, credited the reorganization of the licensing structure—the Yankees finally had been brought into line for the betterment of all teams—for the dramatic rise. "Clubs used to do their own thing, and the business was very segmented—without consistency. Licensees didn't feel their interest was being protected because there was no exclusivity," and White predicted that baseball's licensing organization would become even more "sophisticated" moving into the 1990s.[37]

For an extra cost, retail stores could display a neon sign depicting the familiar "Major League Baseball" batter-silhouette logo, ensuring shoppers that the merchandise contained therein was officially licensed and of genuine quality. Naturally protective of its licensing and the agreements signed with authorized vendors, the MLBPC encouraged merchants and licensees to report violators by including a "Trademark Infringement Report Form" in its promotional kit.[38]

The possibility that MLBPC would take legal action was no idle threat. In the summer of 1987, "two investigators working for plaintiff Anheuser-Busch discovered a number of counterfeit and infringing products of various copyrights and trademarks at a company known as Colour-Tex, Inc."[39] Although the items in question were shirts bearing the likeness of Spuds MacKenzie, the brewery's mascot, MLBPC, as the lead plaintiff, was behind the owner of the St. Louis Cardinals in an effort to dissuade other manufacturers from appropriating legally protected material.

Not to be left behind in the scramble for sales was clothing originally featured in such Hollywood-produced baseball films as *Bull Durham*, *The Natural*, *Eight Men Out*, and *Major League*. Whether the apparel related to a minor-league team, a fictitious character, or actual big-league clubs—past or present—there appeared to be no stemming the tide of fans' passion for attire. Indeed, turning back the clock gained new currency: Mitchell & Ness created a line of vintage jerseys, while Roman Company and American Needle and Novelty, Inc., produced selections of retro-style caps, with the target market for these articles being the "older fan—the fan who remembers what baseball was like in the '40s and '50s."[40] Apparel of yesteryear was the foundation of the new Cooperstown Collection, which carried a logo featuring the image of a turn-of-the-century ballplayer and lettering in a stylish, period font.

The number of licensees had mushroomed from 85 in 1982 to 175 seven years later, this growth occurring at the same time Ueberroth established a corporate marketing program that allowed companies the opportunity to sponsor events like giveaways at the ballpark or display signage within the confines of the stadium, often strategically placed so as to be viewable by a television audience. Between 1986 and 1989, MLB grossed more than $45 million from deals with IBM, Coca-Cola, and other corporate giants to underwrite, among many other occasions and services, Philadelphia's Tastykake Lunch Bag Day, Procter & Gamble's "Clean Team" of custodians (who brightened the restrooms at the Oakland Coliseum), the Equitable Financial Old-Timers Game, and the placement of team logos on credit cards. "The Athletics also convinced Lucky's supermarket chain to sign a 10-year deal to build one Little League park per year in needy areas," which helped the game at the grassroots level while at once giving visibility to the food retailer and the baseball team.[41]

While trying at times to tame the enthusiasm for logos—the outsized Louisville Slugger label on Rickey Henderson's bat in the 1989 postseason raised some eyebrows—MLB grew increasingly permeated with advertising and endorsements. A few weeks before Henderson stepped to the plate with his billboard-esque bat, the New York Mets counted no fewer than four corporations that sponsored televised in-game features such as scoreboard updates of other games (Nissan Motors), a review of the day's stock market performance (Dean Witter and American Express), successful execution of a stolen base by a Mets player (again, Nissan), and a nostalgic "Mets Memories" video played on the Shea Stadium scoreboard (The Wiz, a home appliance retailer). The team's director of broadcasting, Mike Ryan, explained that these new ads were "part of a larger advertiser package that goes beyond the usual 30-second spot," and a sponsor had to consider how the club broadcast its game, via local cable outlets or by superstation: A regional restaurant chain with patronage close to the team's home city would receive a better value for locally broadcast advertisements, whereas an automobile manufacturer whose product was available nationwide could benefit from superstation exposure.[42]

For better or worse, depending on whether viewed from the corporate perspective or that of the average fan, advertising was an indelible fixture on baseball's landscape. "Why all the sponsorship clutter?" asked *Sporting News*. "The bottom line is what is best for the customer and what is best for the Mets," replied Ryan. "We're capitalists just like any other team."[43]

***

The connection between fans and the game had been enhanced for decades by the enjoyable hobby of card collecting. For youngsters willing to part with a nickel in the 1960s, they could buy a pack of five trading cards that came with a stick of bubblegum, and the cost of the purchase was easy on a child's budget. For anyone wishing to complete an entire assemblage of more than 600 cards, however, the challenge was to exercise persistence in buying more and more packs that would eventually yield, card by card, the contents of a full set. This rugged, trying journey was part of the fun, and it was renewed annually because each season brought a different style of card design along with new players to collect.

Dating to the 1880s, sports cards—baseball was not alone in this field—produced by cigarette manufacturers, the American Tobacco Company foremost among them, offered a bonus to those purchasing smoking materials. By 1933, Goudey Gum Company's Big League Gum Series marked the introduction of chewing gum to baseball card packs, and in the ensuing years other businesses issued various series of cards. The Topps Chewing Gum Company ultimately prevailed as the sole card producer by 1964.

The value of any particular card could be a subject of great debate. Yet, a general assumption held that a card's worth was in direct proportion to the brightness of a player's star. The hobby was infused with a large degree of naiveté because collecting was done almost exclusively for the simple joy of it, with no expectation of any gain other than personal satisfaction of ownership.

By the early 1970s, several entrepreneurs offered complete sets for sale, obviating the need to buy packs of cards, and their customers were among the estimated 100,000 collectors—including still those youngsters who made purchases at the corner store—who indulged in gathering the reported 250 million cardboard treasures produced by Topps in 1974. The company's vice president and "high priest of baseball cards," Sy Berger, disclosed that perhaps 500 million cards would be issued the following year.[44]

Those inexpensive packs of bubblegum cards had drawn the attention of more than grade-school boys, not a few of whom thrilled to clothes-pinning some of the crisp cardboard pieces to the fender braces of their bicycles to produce a motorcycle-like roar when the wheels were set in motion. As sports-collector shows gained in popularity, baseball memorabilia, especially cards, became the stock in trade at such gatherings. To be sure, bats, balls, jerseys, and team publications like programs and yearbooks, in addition to other paraphernalia and ephemera, could be found, but the preponderance of cards spoke volumes about their availability and popularity.

But the hobby was beginning to take a discernible turn away from the naive aspect of collecting strictly for pleasure. As greater attention was paid to the value of premium cards, no small amount of cachet became attached to pride of ownership of a prized Mickey Mantle card or that of another superstar. Dealers and collectors were increasingly finding common ground to transact business, especially at card shows and conventions that brought them together for such purposes. Eventually, the frequent appearance of a past or current major-league player for autograph-signing sessions at extra cost to attendees added another attraction to the occasion.

But hucksters and quick-buck artists recognized an opportunity, and when cards of certain players became more desirable than others, the economic forces controlling everyday life spread over the collecting hobby as well. "It has been a long-accepted practice for dealers to charge two or three times more for a Mays, Mantle, Kaline, Aaron, or Clemente card, even though they are no rarer than, say, a Moe Thacker or Hector Torres," wrote Bill Madden in *Sporting News*. And the reason for this was simple: "Supply and demand."[45] Creeping into this scene was a heretofore less-obvious facet of this pastime: collecting cards not necessarily for the interest in or love of the game, but simply for the sake of profiteering. Madden feared that this evolution would discourage potential hobbyists who might be "priced out" by greedy dealers before even having a chance to experience what card collecting was supposed to be about. Viewed in retrospect, Madden's statement becomes more poignant in light of the fact that he made it a few years *before* Topps lost its monopolistic grip on card production in 1981.

In an attempt to curb runaway inflation of card prices, one collector from Ohio initiated a project to compute an estimated fair value for scores of cards and collectibles. Upon gathering price information from dealers and collectors throughout the country, Dr. James Beckett compiled the inaugural *Sport Americana Baseball Card Price Guide* in 1979, the first comprehensive volume containing values of all manner of cards. This book served as a preamble to his publication in 1984, of a new monthly magazine, *Beckett Baseball*, which was more time-sensitive to market fluctuation of card prices.

As the collecting hobby gained traction in the 1980s, increasing amounts of attention were being paid to value, and two phenomena entered the scene: the quest for a player's rookie card—or the one best associated with his first appearance on a card—and the general investment value of a card or set of cards. "Buying rookie cards became a way for fans to legally gamble on a player's future," wrote one journalist, and lurking in the minds of many collectors was the thought of owning the next version of the sacred 1952 Topps Mickey Mantle card, the first to be issued by Berger's company.[46] Noting that despite the target market for cards being directed at children between the ages of 7 and 12, a Topps executive commented, "Today's kids are more sophisticated than their fathers and grandfathers. Instead of just buying a pack of cards and taking their chances on who is inside, kids want to find a rookie long shot who they think might become a future star."[47]

If a new player could be quickly identified as a legitimate Hall of Fame candidate and the first issue of his card cost almost the same as a cup of coffee, the return on investment would be many times over the initial price if the player's career did indeed land him in Cooperstown; however, according to the publisher of a hobby trade magazine, there was an ulterior motive to the craze: "Essentially, the entire rookie card phenomenon began as nothing more than dealer hype, a way to sell more new baseball cards than ever before at unprecedented prices."[48] Produced in the mid-1980s, the Topps cards of recent U.S. Olympic baseball players who eventually reached the majors became a point of contention as to whether those constituted rookie cards, and such issues contributed to the fervor of what drew collectors into the hobby.

Even if there was a means of artificial stimulation, the rookie card sensation worked hand in hand with the general allure of cards now "being touted as a legitimate investment alternative to stocks, with reputable financial publications referring to them as 'inflation hedges.'"[49] There was unmistakable, hard evidence to support this claim, and a niche referred to as "nostalgia futures" gained legitimacy. As the 1988 baseball season opened, readers of the *New York Times* learned,

> In what has amounted to an explosion of value, cards bought for mere pennies as part of bubblegum packs just a few years ago have skyrock-

eted in price, with the rookie cards of some superstars now selling for more than $100 and even those of common players commanding prices many times their original cost.[50]

The rising tide of card values seemed to lift all boats during the decade, and even rampant speculation failed to diminish the interest of fans and collectors throughout the 1980s. Ballpark attendance surged during this period, and the swelling popularity of baseball cards seemed a natural extension of the desire to solidify one's affinity for the national pastime. The demand for more and more cards was being satisfied in the aftermath of legal challenges that had been first initiated in 1975, by the Fleer Corporation, against Topps Chewing Gum, Inc., the lone producer of baseball cards at the time, and the Major League Baseball Players Association (MLBPA). At issue was Fleer's complaint that Topps was in violation of antitrust laws:

> An essential ingredient to this enterprise and the keystone of Topps' dominance in this field is *Topps' ownership of exclusive rights to use the names, pictures, signatures, and biographical sketches of most current baseball players for their cards and similar products*. Under a typical contract, a player awards these rights in exchange for a flat fee, and they cover the period of the first five baseball seasons thereafter during which the player is on a major-league roster, with the right in Topps to extend those exclusive rights for an additional two baseball seasons. The contracts are negotiated on an ongoing basis, and their expiration dates are staggered. *This arrangement severely disadvantages the prospective competitor*. Even if it were so remarkably effective as to sign a contract with every ballplayer at the time his agreement with Topps expired, it would not be able to market a substantially complete set of cards for at least a few years.[51]

Decided in July 1980 in favor of Fleer, the suit's verdict opened the way for other producers to manufacture and distribute baseball cards beginning in 1981. The court ordered Topps "permanently enjoined from enforcing or threatening to enforce in any court or in any other manner *the exclusivity clause in its form contract with major-league players*," along with other stipulations that applied to both Topps and the MLBPA.[52] Topps still held firm its association with MLB in conjunction with Licensing Corporation of America—LCA noted its agreement to "deal with Topps . . . in a manner consistent with past relationships between that company and MLBPC recognizing the long-term relationship that has existed between Topps and the baseball community"—but stripped of its monopolistic protection, Topps now found itself in competition with Fleer and another major card producer, Donruss.[53]

The Big Three of baseball cards were joined by a fourth manufacturer in 1988, when Score made its debut, and as hundreds of millions of cards were churned out annually, "precious few investor collectors seemed even to ponder the possibility that [the value of] baseball cards could depreciate."[54] Eventually, 10,000 baseball card shops spread far and wide throughout the country would serve the needs of an estimated 100,000 collectors. The year 1989 gained further attention when yet another producer entered the market, and in this instance, the quality of the card to be created was going to stand apart from any of its predecessors. The addition of this product into an already crowded field was a bold venture on the part of Upper Deck, a card company that promised something radically different.

When Upper Deck incorporated holograms into the high-quality stock on which superbly rendered photographs—in color on both front and back—would be printed, the result was baseball cards with almost otherworldly qualities in both eye appeal and the tactile sense—they felt different when being handled. To enhance the security of the purchasing experience for customers, the cards were bundled in foil packs, which once having been breached to unveil the contents could not be resealed, ensuring that the cards had not been exposed to tampering. The nation's collectors—to say nothing of investors—now had yet another way to spend their money, and although these "didn't have the charm or imagination of a vintage Topps set, the cards had a crisp elegance and simplicity to them."[55]

Gaining instant renown due to the new standards that set their product apart, Upper Deck rode the wave of its popularity into the early years of the 1990s, but in a hobby saturated with the hundreds of millions of cards that had been produced in recent years by five major companies, the bull market was drawing to a close. The chairman of Topps, Arthur Shorin, whose company was not alone in receiving increasing amounts of returned cards unable to be sold, spoke to the new reality: "We see this development as a market contraction rather than a seasonal fluctuation. The speculative frenzy of the last few years is giving way to a hobby reflecting true collector interest."[56]

A shakeout had been due, perhaps overdue, and although the hobby's attractiveness lost some luster—a side benefit was the purging of the shills whose sole concern was a quick profit—the players' strike of 1994 was a "devastating blow to serious fans [and] was particularly fiendish to fans who were also card collectors."[57] The passing of the collecting hysteria, labeled in retrospect by one sportswriter as the "peak of big, dumb baseball card collecting," took more than a few people for a ride, as was the case for those who handed over $300 for a 1989 Fleer card of Billy Ripken—the knob of the bat he was holding in the image contained a block-lettered, obscene nickname—only to find that the card's value had dropped to $15 a few months later.[58] For collectors and self-styled investors, such losses proved to be extremely uncomfortable, but a restoration of sanity was needed to cure this hangover generated by the years-long card party.

Another type of party—or at least a festive gathering with a purpose—was taking shape in the late 1970s and continues in various forms to this day. This was not a product or service created by MLB, but it became a device by which fans could pay especially close attention to actual players who were members of teams fictitiously created by "armchair general managers." For an entrance fee ranging from nominal to extravagant, this new breed of GM could participate in leagues where, as author Peter Golenbock observed, "Baseball is simple. It is played entirely in the mind."[59]

***

Drawing its name from the Manhattan restaurant La Rotisserie Française, where the concept of a new way to follow the game of baseball evolved in the spring of 1980, Rotisserie Baseball was founded by author Dan Okrent, and his notion quickly transformed into what has long been known as fantasy baseball. Participants act as general managers, forming their teams by drafting major leaguers to fill a roster of regular players and pitchers, and the real-life statistics of their club members figure in the number of points that, when accumulated, determine the winning fantasy team, which is rewarded with a cash prize derived from the fees paid by the entrants. These "leagues of the mind," as Golenbock may have put it, could impose their own rules regarding the roster size, number of active players, restrictions on waivers and trades, and so on. More simplistic versions of this game—and based on the author's experience with a "home run pool"—might limit a player's performance simply to how many homers he hit, with no other statistics taken into account.

While the variations of fantasy baseball accrued nothing to major-league coffers, they nonetheless gave reason for their participants to pay attention to box scores with more than just a passing interest. "It has been called the Yuppie aphrodisiac. Once you join a Rotisserie league, nothing else in life takes on as much importance."[60] It was no longer enough for a fantasy participant who may have been, say, a Yankees fan, to get only the score of the Bronx Bombers on any given day because now his or her interest was vested in how well each player on the fantasy roster—now composed of players from *many* teams—performed. In some cases, the quest for information in the pre-internet era turned into a compulsion to secure means to watch out-of-town games, via cable or satellite television, or get the latest scores on ESPN.

Always anxious for any information that would give them an edge—for example, a batter's ability to hit better at home than on the road, how a pitcher fared against right-handed hitters versus lefties—fantasy participants focused more and more on what came to be called sabermetrics, statistics that went far beyond the basic entries of the typical box score. The breakthrough tome of Macmillan's *Baseball Encyclopedia* had, by the early 1980s, been updated roughly every three years since the issuing of the first edition in 1969, but "with the advent of computer technology, the Elias Sports Bureau set out to document the game of baseball as it had never been documented before: by producing a set of statistics that would answer not only the question of 'how many?' but also the questions of 'when?' 'in what context?' and 'with what frequency?'"[61]

Produced annually from 1985 to 1993, *The Elias Baseball Analyst* proclaimed its mission statement on the cover of its first release: "The most complete, detailed analysis of player performance available, from the secret files of the Elias Sports Bureau." Taking the Macmillan data several steps further, Elias produced intriguing essays on all 26 teams that highlighted trends, tics, and foibles that helped or hindered a club or player(s) during the previous season. To wit, a dissection Elias performed on the 1984 Cincinnati Reds, who brought in Pete Rose as player-manager after firing Vern Rapp in the wake of a 51–70 record, is representative of their eye for detail:

> Rose unearthed a player on the Cincinnati bench whom Rapp had ignored: third baseman Wayne Krenchicki, who had been used by Rapp as a pinch-hitter and occasional starter against right-handed pitchers. The most ironic part of Krenchicki's performance for Rose wasn't his .390 batting average but his fielding. Had Rapp looked at Krenchicki at little more closely, he might have found not only a strong bat, but a more than adequate glove.[62]

There followed the hard numbers informing readers of Krenchicki's team-leading 2.24 assists per nine innings for Reds third basemen, better than Nick Esasky (1.91) and Dave Concepcion (1.76). Other sections of the *Baseball Analyst* dedicated to batters and pitchers revealed countless other nuggets and facts—for example, Dan Driessen's uncanny ability to drive in runners on third base with less than two outs (166 out of 250 runners, or 66.4 percent) or pitcher Jack Morris's domination of Carlton Fisk, who had but one hit in 31 at-bats against the ace. Armed with such information, fantasy participants who had Fisk as their regular catcher could use this data to their advantage and sit Fisk out when he was scheduled to face Morris in real life.

And Elias added more fuel to the fire in the debate spawned decades earlier: "Clutch Hitters: They *Do* Exist" was the title of an article in which the authors "define as late-inning pressure situations all appearances in the seventh inning or later, with the batter's team tied or trailing by a margin of three runs or less (or four runs if the bases are loaded)."[63] The best clutch hitter in 1984, according to Elias, was none other than Bill Buckner, who hit a modest .257 with no runners aboard but over twice that, .562, when men were on base.

In 1984, *Sporting News* began printing two annual volumes of box scores, one for each league. The run of these books lasted more than a decade, and they extracted the same information that was part of the weekly's bedrock of baseball coverage. These dual repositories were invaluable to serious fans and researchers in an age before such data became available—and in batter-by-batter detail—on the internet later in the twenty-first century. "Our box scores, in fact, have a reputation for such accuracy that major-league teams *call us* when they are compiling data for use in postseason [press] kits and other publications," the books' editor proudly noted.[64]

Explosions of data and computer use continued to detonate in the 1980s. The Chicago White Sox commissioned an examination of the pitching mechanics of some members of their staff using videos taken during games at Comiskey Park in 1983. Images of the pitchers were then transcribed—after a fashion—into primitive computer stick figures, and the "player's performance profile consists of measurements of various kinematic parameters utilized to quantify the pitching performance," noted Dr. Robert Shapiro, head of the study.[65] "These measurements, based on cinematographic analysis, included information about the timing of the pitch, and measurements taken from the side and from the front views [of the pitcher]." Stride length; angles of the torso, knees, and elbows; release of the ball; and elbow extension at different points of the delivery were scrutinized for two purposes. "This information can then be utilized to identify performance factors or possible injury factors. Secondly, by examining [easily] identifiable positions in the throw, changes within season, between seasons, or after injury can be observed in a pitcher's performance," Shapiro continued. "This type of information should enhance both the coach's and trainer's ability to perform their normal functions," not least of which were proactively discovering the source of possible injuries and development of rehabilitative procedures.

Small computers gained entry into American homes and gradually came to be viewed as another household appliance "no more peculiar than a family possessing a television set in 1950," and the decade of the 1980s "[gave] every sign of being as receptive to technological advance as the 1880s, the last great period of statistical experimentation and innovation in baseball."[66] Aside from the increase in computing power and the growing availability of computers for personal use, the contributions made in 1984 by John Thorn and Pete Palmer in their breakthrough book *The Hidden Game of Baseball* spoke to new ways of looking at traditional statistics, whereby wins by a pitcher and a batter's RBIs were no longer viewed as end-alls for measuring the values previously assigned to them.

Five years later, Thorn and Palmer collaborated with David Reuther to publish *Total Baseball*, which was the "third-generation encyclopedia of the game" that credited the Society for American Baseball Research (SABR) for lending its expertise in formulating a series of new and revised categories of data.[67] This latest tome had the same hardcovered heft as its Macmillan brethren and contained the traditional fare of such offensive data as at-bats, hits, runs batted in, and the like, as well as items referred to as sabermetrics: park factor, runs created, stolen base runs, clutch hitting index, and other new statistics. For pitchers, a park factor was also devised, as were pitching runs, clutch pitching index, wins above team, total pitcher index, and others. The work of Tom Boswell, the *Washington Post* sportswriter whose total average lent an enhanced view to a batter's offensive production, and that of another statistical luminary, Bill James, the inventor of runs created, also could be found in the pages of *Total Baseball*.

For James, in particular, acceptance of the new math by an audience more inquisitive and accepting of his work validated much of what he had been promulgating in his self-published annual *Baseball Abstract*s since the late 1970s. When he transitioned to Ballantine Books in 1982, the publishing company was able to give James a broader range of exposure than he had been able to get on his own, stoking the interest of fans eager to embrace his revisionist views and those of a host of other like-minded sabermetricians whose undertakings were also adding fresh chapters to the game's numerical history or refining the esoteric work of earlier mathematical trailblazers like Branch Rickey, Eldon and Harlan Mills, and Ernie Lanigan.

Despite the bevy of new data that was meant to quantify evermore aspects of the national pastime, conspicuous by its absence from *Total Baseball* was the game-winning RBI (GWRBI), a statistic sanctioned by MLB and introduced in 1980, to attach significance to what was perceived to be the most important run of the game—the one that secured victory. But the effort to employ the GWRBI was laden with a serious fault despite the attempt to emphasize how clutch that RBI was: The batter driving in the go-ahead run in a close game could be thought to have performed more admirably than one who drove in the first (or supposed "winning") run of a contest that became a rout. Yet, the GWRBI made no discernment between the two. To his credit, Keith Hernandez was the all-time leader in this dubious statistic with 129, but the GWRBI became a footnote to history when it was dropped by MLB prior to the 1989 season.

Other statistics, simple and singular in purpose, managed to gain attention through corporate tie-ins. Dating to 1976, Warner-Lambert, the pharmaceutical company famous for its Rolaids antacid tablets, partnered with MLB to create the Rolaids Relief Man Award. Two points were given to a reliever for each win or save he logged, and one point was deducted each time he lost a game. The pitchers with the highest point totals in each league received a trophy whose most prominent feature was a fireman's helmet, symbolic of a reliever's having put out a fire to save a game. This promotion gave the company even more visibility for Rolaids, which also sponsored a tournament on the Professional Bowlers Association schedule.

Not to be left behind, Skoal smokeless tobacco traded on the "pinch" consumption of its product in 1985, and took out a full-page advertisement in *Sporting News* to announce its sponsorship of a contest for a "Pinch Hitter of the Week" and another for the entire season. Already benefiting from prior exposure courtesy of Yankees outfielder Bobby Murcer's country-and-western tune "Skoal Dippin' Man," the tobacconist was leaving the determination of each league's winners to a "special board of editors" charged with evaluating pinch-hitters using a "combination of batting averages, number of hits, and their effect on the outcome of games."[68]

The Rolaids initiative was in place when Peter Ueberroth came to the commissioner's office, and recognizing that baseball could deal from a position of strength as its popularity swelled in the '80s, he decided to raise sponsorship fees from $1 million to $5 million. Gillette, which had handled All-Star Game balloting for many years, balked at the increase and discontinued its relationship, but Warner-Lambert "liked what they had going with the Rolaids Relief Man because the media and fans had caught on to 'How Do You Spell Relief[?]'"[69]

Brand identification of Rolaids through that slogan accomplished an important marketing purpose for Warner-Lambert, just as the major leagues reveled in its new rallying cry coined by baseball's executive director of marketing and broadcasting. Catchphrases in the world of salesmanship and advertising campaigns emanating from offices on Madison Avenue were intended to help corporate clients burnish their public image and sell products and services. The national pastime had its own products to sell, but it mattered little whether associated taglines were generated by an ad agency or created spontaneously within the parochial community of a team's clubhouse or ballpark.

***

Fans' experience at a baseball game was not on sensory overload from the late 1970s to the end of the 1980s in the way that it would be decades later. All the same, the importance of gaining their attention and allowing them to establish an identity with their favorite team could not be underestimated in matters of clubs fostering a sense of belonging to which followers could adhere. During a span of many years the colorful nicknames bestowed on teams—Bronx Bombers, Amazin' Mets, Gashouse Gang, Swingin' A's, Big Red Machine, among others—gave clubs a uniqueness that could not be appropriated by any rivals, and their fans took pleasure in the attendant flattery. Other forms of exclusivity developed into ways for a team to market itself by direct or indirect means.

Recorded in the late summer and early fall of 1978, an album by the rhythm-and-blues group Sister Sledge was released in January 1979, and the title track, "We Are Family," reached the top of *Billboard* magazine's rankings for dance-club songs. The tune's bouncy, disco beat did more than inspire countless numbers of youths to take to the dance floor. While newly acquired Bill Madlock's .328 average in a Pirates uniform was a vital contribution to Pittsburgh's success, the team's adoption of "We Are Family" as a poignant rallying cry provided sustenance for a team possessed of a multiethnic roster. As Pittsburgh persisted in its seasonal journey, the Pirates' trek was accompanied by the up-tempo soundtrack unwittingly provided by Sister Sledge.

The following year, the New York Mets, moribund and smarting from their last-place finish 35 games behind Pittsburgh, tried to harness the star-power of the only player they had worthy of that distinction. By making outfielder/first baseman Lee Mazzilli the centerpiece of its marketing campaign, the new ownership of the Mets acknowledged that a kid who played stickball in nearby Sheepshead Bay was a "valuable property," and the club "planned to paste posters of him in subways as advertisements for the Mets."[70] Although the team ultimately won only four games more than the previous season and moved up one notch in the standings to fifth place, attendance at Shea Stadium in 1980 increased by 403,000 because from May 14 to August 13, the "Mets were as good as any team in the league" and only 7½ games from first place.[71] A swoon in the last six weeks of the season cost the Mets dearly, but the improvement in team performance melded with a focused ad campaign featuring its top player that attracted more fans to Shea.

When a portly 19-year-old from Navojoa, Mexico, arrived in Chavez Ravine in mid-September 1980, the Dodgers caught a glimpse of a future star pitcher whose deeds on the mound would spawn a marketing campaign unto itself. Jumping from Double-A ball to the majors, Fernando Valenzuela was "more than a prospect. He was a novelty. He was fat. He didn't speak any English. He was known to like drinking beer. He looked about 40."[72] The youngest of 12 children from a poor family, Valenzuela was also recognized by Dodgers scouts as a special talent, and in his first 10 appearances in this late-season call-up, he allowed no earned runs in less than 18 innings pitched.

But as he flew from the gate with the Dodgers in 1981, he took the baseball world by storm, winning his first eight starts, five of which were shutouts, and the craze of "Fernandomania" was born. "It wasn't uncommon to see young women waiting for him after a game. He was a big-time celebrity, entering the domain of Cheryl Tiegs and Erik Estrada," and the trappings of his budding stardom included endorsements for soft drinks, breakfast cereal, and baseball equipment.[73]

The girth of Valenzuela's waist and his skyward eye roll as he made his windup on the mound enhanced the mystique of this left-hander from south of the border, and the torrid beginning of his campaign prompted thousands more fans to pass through the turnstiles to watch him pitch compared to other members of the Dodgers rotation. The media flocked to press conferences or otherwise sought out Valenzuela to learn more about him, and what Sister Sledge's tune had become to the Pirates, the Swedish pop group ABBA's hit song "Fernando" became to the home team at Dodger Stadium. Valenzuela took honors as the 1981 National League (NL) Rookie of the Year and Cy Young Award recipient, and he rode the swell of momentum to six straight berths on the league's All-Star Team before his meteoric rise finally dimmed.

To build on the excitement of that year's World Series—the Dodgers swept the last four games to avenge losses to New York in 1977 and 1978—and make fans forget the ugliness of the strike, a brilliant catch-phrase emerged from the mind of Tom Villante, a former Yankees batboy who served admirably as Bowie Kuhn's director of marketing and broadcasting. "Baseball Fever—Catch It!" debuted for the 1982 season and captured the succinct brilliance of a slogan as memorable as any of the best advertising jingles ever coined. Its simple wording could make it applicable to any level of baseball, and souvenir buttons fashioned for major-league teams substituted the generic artwork of a baseball bearing the words "Baseball Fever" with the logo of a specific team to create an "Astros Fever" or "Reds Fever" trinket.

When Roger Craig took the managerial reins of the Giants, by 1987 he was using the term "humm-babe" for general encouragement and morale-boosting chatter so frequently that it grew into a "cult phrase in San Francisco" even though it could have been used in any other baseball town.[74] But in Chicago, specifically on the north side of the city, the Cubs' "Building a New Tradition" campaign of 1982, which hoped to inspire the team to vacate the bottom half of the NL East, where it had finished for most of the previous decade, was replaced the following year with a clever slogan that incorporated its ballpark's absence of artificial lighting: "Come to Wrigley—We'll Surprise the Daylights out of You."[75] Persistence for the Cubs finally paid off in 1984, when they won not only the NL East pennant, but also top recognition by MLBPC for "overall marketing excellence," as well as "generating profitable, well-designed publications."[76] Success again five years later moved the team to create "Boys of Zimmer" T-shirts as a nod to the accomplishment of their second-year manager, Don Zimmer.

In an effort to recast the Orioles from a single-city franchise into one with a broader territorial appeal, Baltimore's Memorial Stadium was marketed as "Birdland" at the behest of owner Edward Bennett Williams, the moniker possibly borrowed from a 1977 song by the same name recorded by the jazz group Weather Report. Whether inspired by music or ornithology, the nickname added freshness to the ballpark's tried and true original name.

The record shows almost universally positive creativity employed by teams in their marketing strategies, but now removed from the familial spirit of the later Willie Stargell era—the future Hall of Famer retired in 1982—the Pirates embarked twice on dubious promotional efforts. Turning an ad campaign for New York state tourism on its head, Pittsburgh took aim at its cross-state rival by twisting "I Love New York" into "I don't love Philadelphia" and using it on a series of billboards in advance of the Bucs' 1984 home opener. As Opening Day drew closer, alterations would rephrase the wording to "I don't love the Phillies" and once more to "I don't love the Phillies. Come to Opening Day." An illustrative heart with a slash through its center and the correspondingly timed appearances of the slogans were the Pirates' way of "just having some fun with it," said the team's marketing director, "with no malice intended."[77] But a scribe took the organization to task for a similar display four years later:

> The Pirates have one of baseball's most exciting clubs. That's why their marketing people should be ashamed of themselves for that cheap

> "Hate New York" advertising they used to try to sell tickets for the Mets' first visit to Pittsburgh. The Bucs entered the series in second place and on a winning streak. And if that wasn't enough promotion . . . then why didn't the Pirates promote their young club instead of using a tired old gimmick[?] It's just another case of being riddled with marketing people who think the game is just another product. Winning is the best promotion going, and that's what should have been promoted by the overzealous Pittsburgh flacks.[78]

Even in an age before political correctness was affixed to most public discourse, the decision to use a hate theme against the Mets may have been fallout from the New Yorkers' penchant in recent years to show too much swagger as they laid waste to opponents during their march to the 1986 World Series.

By whatever means fans were attracted to the ballpark, they arrived through the 1980s in growing numbers. The multitudes were entertained by such character mascots as the wildly popular San Diego Chicken, Phillie Phanatic, Montreal's Youppi!, and even the Yankees' short-lived "Dandy." They greeted fans and pulled pranks at their respective venues, although Mr. Met, a denizen at Shea Stadium since its opening in 1964, was shelved 15 years later. All the while, teams added a burgeoning amount of special "days" and "nights" to their home schedules. The latter included the infamous "Disco Demolition Night" at Comiskey Park, which became overrun by an unruly mob between games of a scheduled doubleheader on July 12, 1979, and although such disturbances were extremely rare, the playing of recorded, modern music on evermore powerful sound systems was overtaking the performance of the live organ music that had long been an entertainment staple at most stadiums.

There is no small amount of irony that the closing theme song of the television highlight show *This Week in Baseball*, introduced in 1977 and hosted by former Yankees announcer Mel Allen, was a stirring orchestral tune called "Gathering Crowds," written by English composer John Scott. Crowds did indeed gather, at the ballpark and in front of the television set, to watch and enjoy the national pastime as never before. Promotion of the game to induce the general public to put it foremost in their mind—and hopefully use discretionary income to buy its products and tickets—had taken giant strides since the days when Branch Rickey's "concept of marketing was to put a talented and interesting team on the field and let fans flock to it."[79] Fans lacking the deep corporate pockets necessary to purchase full-season tickets found teams offering partial plans available for fewer games but at a more affordable price, and teams were willing to sell ducats in advance either way because it was, literally, all money in the bank.

The attitudes of teams had changed so radically 40 years after Rickey's dismissive comments that they ignored the creation of sound business strategies at their own peril. No better proof of this can be found than the case with Charlie Finley's Oakland Athletics in the late 1970s, by which time most of his star players had fled via free agency, and a "survey financed by the Oakland Coliseum reveal[ed] that the East Bay baseball fan barely knows who the A's players are anymore."[80]

Running counter to Finley's blind eye was the entrepreneurial spirit of the San Diego Padres' Steve Garvey, who took the initiative to found the Garvey Marketing Group and, by 1985, was offering "public relations, marketing, and financial services to professional athletes."[81] Although Garvey's company was tailored to the needs of individuals rather than teams, his vision nonetheless indicated awareness of the advantages of marketing at a personal level and the benefits to be reaped from engaging such services.

***

As more money permeated baseball's post-Messersmith landscape, ways for the national pastime to give back to fans and the community in general also gained visibility. Players and teams were never lacking for causes to which they could donate their time, if not actual funding. The list of charitable endeavors could fill many pages, but a representative sampling is worth noting: Reggie Jackson's antidrug public-service announcement; the Seattle Mariners' Celebrity Golf Tournament and Auction to benefit the Cystic Fibrosis Foundation; the involvement of many star players on the California Angels who stumped for cystic fibrosis, diabetes, and pediatric cancer; Minnesota Twins owner Carl Pohlad, "who purchased the ballclub in 1984 [and] ushered in an unprecedented era of community service, as did such stars as Kent Hrbek, Kirby Puckett, Dave Winfield, and Manager Tom Kelly"; and the decades-long commitment of the Boston Red Sox to the Jimmy Fund and the Dana-Farber Cancer Institute.[82]

Charity extended to the box office, even if a club's profit margin suffered a bit, and a team's sensitivity to those fans with lesser or more modest financial means encouraged the offering of discounted tickets as a lure to come to a game. As spring training commenced in 1983, the same Oakland team whose previous owner gave the back of his hand to its devotees was now offering "half-price entry to the disabled, the elderly, active military personnel, and children 14 years old or younger."[83]

Connecting with fans through reduced-price admission was a sound business tactic, but for die-hards willing to shell out large sums of money, beginning in the mid-1980s there was a unique opportunity to gain what might be considered the apotheosis of access to MLB, albeit void of currently active players. When a restaurateur suggested to former Cubs catcher Randy Hundley that he create a baseball camp for adults, the innocent suggestion blossomed into the niche market of fantasy camps where men—and later women—older than the age of 35 spent a full week in a spring training milieu partaking of drills, batting practice, and squad games against fellow campers, under the watchful eye of former players recruited for the occasion. "The concept has been widely imitated" by other clubs, but the trailblazing Hundley can take credit for making reality out of a fan's dream to actually take the field with past players of their favorite team.[84]

Other old-timers were brought together by Jim Morley, a real-estate mogul who founded the Senior Professional Baseball Association in 1989. The Florida-based league was patterned after the Senior Professional Golfers Association Tour and featured an array of recently retired major leaguers, not least of whom were Rollie Fingers and Fergie Jenkins, but the circuit failed to grab the public's attention, and it folded after just two seasons.

Enjoying a longer run than the senior league, although failing to gain permanent traction, was baseball at the Summer Olympic Games, which at least put the sport in a broad, international spotlight. Sporadic attempts dating to 1912, were made to play baseball as a demonstration sport, and dormant since 1964, it was revived in 1984, as a tournament rather than a medal event. Although the U.S. team lost to Japan in the championship, its roster was laden with many collegiate players set to move to the major leagues, including Will Clark, Mark McGwire, Billy Swift, Oddibe McDowell, Barry Larkin, Shane Mack, and Chris Gwynn. In 1988, the United States avenged its loss by defeating Japan, with Jim Abbott pitching the Americans to the tournament victory.

The success in the pair of tournaments helped to secure baseball as an official Olympic sport from 1992 into the early twenty-first century, and the notables of the 1988 squad—Abbott, Charles Nagy, Andy Benes, Robin Ventura, Mickey Morandini, and Tino Martinez would see significant playing time in the majors—bolstered the stature of the amateur game and helped several big-league teams promote themselves as now employing former Olympic stars.

***

Old-line baseball ownership that eschewed marketing in the early to mid-twentieth century unwittingly slipped into a stagnant business model in which its teams presented an unadorned product that promoted and sold itself to the buying public with little more than whatever excitement the team generated by virtue of its performance on the diamond. Always conscious of how much money was being spent, especially on player salaries, club moguls failed to understand the axiom that one had to spend money to make money. But when post–World War II consumerism spurred vast economic growth and the medium of television opened new methods of advertising, corporate marketing in American business took on another dimension of sophistication to reach more and more people.

It took time for baseball to catch up, but when the game broadened its fan base and exposure through several phases of expansion in the 1960s and 1970s, the challenge to the popularity of the national pastime posed by professional football was met. The renaissance of the Yankees championship teams beginning in 1976 reestablished baseball as the king of sports in the country's biggest market and among its vast fandom.

As baseball's popularity rose through the 1980s, an unmistakable symbiosis took hold as attendance soared and marketing efforts conflated with the growing number of licensees whose wares were made available to consumers. Teams like the Padres took action to examine every aspect of how to better position the club for promotional purposes, an approach that was a far cry from the sclerotic, hands-off approach of previous generations of management. The attitude of "business first" was further solidified under Peter Ueberroth, himself a successful entrepreneur, albeit his being one of the more dispassionate commissioners to hold the position when the issue was pure love of the game. The fan experience at the ballpark was evolving with the introduction of mascots and other modern entertainments, and an awareness that females had to be made as welcome as their male counterparts served to bolster attendance while also contributing to a more family-friendly environment.

Fan interest spread via other channels—for instance, card collecting and participation in nascent fantasy leagues—and all the while sales of merchandise climbed because devotees of the game enjoyed not only showing the colors of their favorite team, but also wearing the same paraphernalia as the players. By the end of the decade, the game's prosperity had never been better, with more people than ever before—appropriately attired, of course—watching baseball, and marketing strategists continued to seek other ways to build on this wave of enthusiasm and success.

Baseball fever was contagious to the delight of all.

9

SOCIETAL ISSUES

Most of the latter part of the 1970s proved to be an unsettling time as the nation tried to steady itself following an embargo of foreign oil entering the United States, an economic recession, the country's withdrawal from an unpopular war, and a political crisis that forced a presidential resignation. One historian chronicled a series of "laments" infecting the broad scope of American society: the persistence of "self-indulgence and consumption," a loss of the "sense of civic-mindedness," and the "spread of disrespect for authority."[1] Still retaining its status as a superpower, the United States was nonetheless smarting from the black eyes resulting from these assorted calamities, and the administrations of the next two presidents, whose terms were also roiled by several crises, did little to assuage the country's angst.

Running concurrent to these events, baseball was undergoing its own transition into a post–reserve clause era after 1976. The economics of the game were about to transmogrify; an emboldened Major League Baseball Players Association evinced less and less reluctance to butt heads with team ownership; and players, now becoming increasingly well-monied, could be rightfully accused of taking self-indulgence to a new level. Baseball was also subject to the forces of an evolving national scene that through the 1980s continued to wrestle with issues of race and gender, the reshaping of attitudes in a climate of the game's growing prosperity, and a better awareness of handicapped citizens.

***

To this day in the United States, there is a continuing racial divide that, despite the strides taken toward equality during a span of many decades, refuses to be erased from America's civic, cultural, and ethnically diverse landscape. Yet, as black baseball players followed Jackie Robinson's path to the major leagues in 1947 and beyond, the number of roster spots taken by minorities escalated appreciably in the ensuing decades. National League (NL) teams especially acted more quickly than their counterparts in the American League (AL) to sign African American talent, and expanded scouting in Latin America for players also became a beneficial endeavor for many clubs.

By the mid-1960s, the number of black players in Major League Baseball (MLB) peaked at 18 percent, and their dominant trait was an ability to achieve beyond the standard set by their white counterparts. Released in 1983, a study by a Harvard graduate student determined that standout blacks found welcome company with white players, but the situation was different for those whose ability fell short of a Willie Mays or a Hank Aaron. According to one press release, "Talented blacks are treated well, but mediocre blacks are discriminated against. You just don't see blacks in the majors unless the player is a star."[2] The study confirmed the rising number of black athletes moving away from baseball and into the ranks of professional football and basketball, and it also speculated that "white nonprofessional [baseball] coaches' prejudice may help explain the lack of black players," an indication that discrimination at the high school or college levels might be diverting blacks away from the diamond.[3]

Like other major sports, baseball offered little in the way of employment when a black player's career was over, and the report concluded that blacks were "underrepresented in positions of responsibility both on and off the field," and a "shortage of black scouts . . . and an increasing emphasis on college drafting create barriers for blacks entering professional baseball, and provide the most convincing evidence of the source of the black player shortage."[4]

Frustration was evident in the voice of Lou Brock of the St. Louis Cardinals. Brock told a beat writer in the summer of 1979, "There are very few places in this game for a black guy when he retires. . . . He's not moved into the front office. He's not moved into a managerial position. He's not made a scout, no matter what he's accomplished, no matter what he knows."[5] Three months later, Commissioner Bowie Kuhn was informed by his marketing director that the Jackie Robinson Foundation had proposed the creation of "sports management workshops" in conjunction with universities and MLB to help "minority youths (primarily blacks and Spanish)" learn the craft of serving in front offices and working in public relations.[6]

Monte Irvin, the former Negro League and New York Giants standout then working in Kuhn's office, received a letter from the baseball coach at Southern University asking for direction in helping to establish a "Black College Baseball Association that could benefit our programs."[7] As the year drew to a close, pressure came to bear directly on the commissioner, who received a mailgram from the president of the Southern Christian Leadership Conference (SCLC) asking for a meeting to "discuss matters relative to racial bias in Major League Baseball."[8] SCLC president Reverend Joseph Lowery had announced that his group was going to investigate the lack of "equal opportunity for black involvement in every level of operations in both baseball and [professional] football."[9] Several weeks before Lowery contacted Kuhn, a story had leaked to the media in which the director of the National Football League Players Association, Ed Garvey, had accused NFL commissioner Pete Rozelle of being "responsible for a consistent pattern of racism" in the league.[10]

Briefly on his heels, Kuhn recovered quickly to inform Lowery that he disagreed with his assessment of any bias in baseball, and in a draft memo to the minister he "suggest[ed] that the purpose of a meeting is more for publicity than for a constructive discussion of matters pertaining to our game."[11] Kuhn was irked because he had been called by a reporter from the *Atlanta Constitution* with questions about Lowery's accusation *before* the mailgram arrived, but Kuhn's reply appeared not to have reached the intended recipient. "Several weeks ago we wired you concerning racism in baseball, requesting a meeting," responded Lowery in a mid-February 1980 follow-up. "You have ignored our requests [*sic*] for some unexplainable reason. Is it plain discourtesy or racism?"[12]

This time, Kuhn instructed that a conference call be arranged between Lowery and Bud Selig and Peter O'Malley, two club owners who were cochairing a committee on minority hiring in baseball, to discuss the matter. Yet, nearly a week later, attempts by Kuhn's office for such a call had not been answered by the SCLC, and the matter apparently passed with no further action by either party.

Kuhn told *Sporting News* in the summer of 1980 that most AL and NL skippers apprenticed in managerial roles for minor-league teams, "but not many of today's big-league players want to go down to the minors to manage."[13] Following a visit to that year's College World Series, Kuhn had been lobbied by the athletic director of Creighton University to consider the school's recently resigned baseball coach, Jerry Bartee, for some type of employment, hopefully at the major-league level. "He is a bright young man with a fine future," was one endorsement of the former coach, adding, "In the right spot in professional baseball, he could be a great asset."[14] Kuhn passed the recommendation to Selig and O'Malley, but Bartee's career path led him to the school system in Omaha, Nebraska, where he became a high school principal.

On the eve of the 1981 season, Kuhn's office was apprised of the status of front-office and managerial personnel, with attention focused on blacks. At that time, a mere eight former major leaguers—four of whom were black—who had been retired since 1970, could be found working in a front office, and only two of them held positions with serious responsibility: Hank Aaron as Atlanta's director of player development and Tommy Harper of the Red Sox, who was Boston's first-base coach, the rest working in sales or community relations, or serving as consultants or assistants. Only 9 of 31 men "who had significant careers as major-league players [and] now in front offices" were black, and the low overall percentages were ascribed to high salaries paid to players during their career, as well as "outside offers that are too attractive" to entice them into front-office jobs. This situation was "true of all players, not just blacks," and the memo to Kuhn further excused the general lack of involvement by player alumni because "better-trained executive talent is coming along [whose] talent many times exceeds that of players because they have geared themselves for such careers."[15]

One former player who pioneered the minority breakthrough into the managerial ranks was Frank Robinson, who became baseball's first black manager in 1975. The hiring of Robinson by the Cleveland Indians "suggest[ed] that race no longer remained a divisive issue in major-league clubhouses by the mid-1970s," and although Robinson suffered the same fate as most managers—fired in June 1977, he soon joined the coaching staff of the California Angels—a full year lapsed before baseball's second black manager, Larry Doby of the Chicago White Sox, took the helm of a major-league club.[16]

Robinson's composite record with the Indians was just under .500, neither bad nor great considering the amalgam of youth and veterans on the roster, and to say nothing of the scrutiny to which he was subjected as the first black manager. Short of being able to deliver a pennant to Cleveland, which was an unrealistic expectation in itself, Robinson was consigned to failure, but he remained connected to the game in coaching and front-office positions, and was given other managerial opportunities in the next three decades.

While Robinson's modicum of success with the Indians was far from discouraging, "major-league executives remained hesitant to offer leadership positions to African Americans due to a fear of disapproval from players and fans, and to a distrust of placing authority into the hands of blacks."[17] In similar fashion, by late 1980 teams in the National Football League were just as leery of sanctioning black participation in managerial ranks: Almost half of the organization's 1,260 players were black, but none were head coaches, and less than 5 percent of assistant coaches (10 of 225 positions) were black.[18]

Working to Robinson's advantage was his lengthy tenure in a major-league uniform and his well-earned reputation as one of the most dominant players of the 1960s, so he was hardly an unknown quantity. By apprenticing in Winter League baseball, he had acquired valuable training, and an apt description held that during the course of his managerial career—16 seasons, the last of which he served at the age of 70—Robinson "transitioned from being a 'black manager' to a manager who happened to be black."[19]

Maury Wills, fleet afoot as a base-stealing shortstop for several teams in the NL, was named manager of the Seattle Mariners late in the 1980 season, but he had shunned the advice of former Dodgers executive Buzzie Bavasi to acquire managing experience in the minor leagues before committing to a job in the majors, and the results showed. Completely out of his depth, Wills was fired just four weeks into the 1981 campaign. While Robinson reemerged with the Giants and Orioles in the 1980s, the only other black manager in that decade was Cito Gaston, who began his stint with the Toronto Blue Jays in 1989 and soon guided them to World Series titles in 1992 and 1993.

In the spring of 1980, and at last seeing a need for an "intensified effort in minority hiring," the commissioner's office sought the assistance of a consultant with a forte in that area. But when a vice president with the firm, Ronald Walker of Korn/Ferry International, was given the scenarios of how baseball could generally increase the numbers of minority

Figure 9.1. Another Robinson breaks a different color barrier: In April 1975, Frank Robinson became baseball's first black manager when he took the helm of the Cleveland Indians. Serving as a player-manager his first two seasons, Robinson eventually managed four teams in 16 years, but he did not enjoy the same level of success in this role that he did as a player. National Baseball Hall of Fame and Museum

employees, as well as find a candidate fluent in Spanish to handle a job related to Latin American affairs, he "suggest[ed] that his emphasis would be on manpower resources *outside of baseball*."[20] Walker envisioned searching for candidates at colleges offering a program in sports administration, but curiously he shunned recommending anyone who already had experience with baseball, at either the minor- or major-league levels.

Little progress for minority hiring in management was made during the remainder of Bowie Kuhn's term, and when Peter Ueberroth assumed the commissioner's seat, the trend continued in part because he was preoccupied with the game's drug problems and labor issues. But in the spring of 1985, Hank Aaron held a lengthy conversation with the commissioner "about blacks in management and coaching, and [Ueberroth] promised to work diligently on it."[21] A few months later, the commissioner was requested by noted Negro League historian John Holway to draw inspiration from former commissioner Happy Chandler, who "has spoken out eloquently, in Cooperstown and elsewhere, in favor of racial equality in the Veterans Committee election process."[22]

By 1986, Holway observed, seven consecutive years had passed without a former Negro League player having been inducted into the Hall of Fame, and the best candidate, Ray Dandridge, had for several years fallen one vote short of being elected by the Veterans Committee. Holway advanced several proposals that would give deserving black veterans better consideration: altering the composition of the 18-member committee from 15 whites and 3 blacks to 9 of each race to correct the obvious imbalance; setting a quota that would allow 2 white *and* 2 black candidates to be elected rather than only 2 in total; or reestablishing the disbanded Negro League committee to examine the worthiness of past players. "The Hall of Fame election policy is the last bit of blatant racism left in baseball," Holway argued.[23]

In early March 1987, the Veterans Committee, without changing the demographic composition of its membership, mustered the 14 votes necessary to sanction Dandridge's entrance to Cooperstown, but the balloting was shrouded in mystery. "Unlike the Baseball Writers' Association of America, which reveals its entire vote each January, the Veterans Committee never releases the breakdown of its voting," reported *Sporting News*.[24] The honor was a worthy milestone for Dandridge, whose cause was promoted by committee member Roy Campanella's claim that he was the "Brooks Robinson of the Negro Leagues," but another eight years would pass before the next Negro Leaguer, Leon Day, would join Dandridge in the Hall of Fame.

Using his position of prominence to lobby on behalf of minorities during the 1986 winter meetings, Peter Ueberroth addressed the annual gathering and expressed a desire to commemorate the 40th anniversary of Jackie Robinson's integration of the national pastime. As the commissioner rhetorically asked those in attendance, "Are we providing enough opportunities for minorities, particularly blacks, in baseball?" with the answer obviously in the negative, one reporter could not help but see the exact problem of which the commissioner spoke: "One look across the room told the story. Other than Hank Aaron, the Atlanta Braves vice president in charge of player personnel, there was not a black executive in sight."[25]

As introspective questions about minority hiring were mulled over in front offices and plans in the coming baseball season to honor Robinson were drawn up, a firestorm erupted on the evening of April 6, 1987. Appearing as a guest on the ABC News program *Nightline* was Al Campanis, the Los Angeles Dodgers executive who had served with the team dating to its years in Brooklyn. Campanis was no stranger to some of the franchise's most stirring moments, not least of them Robinson's seminal debut, but when queried by host Ted Koppel about the dearth of minorities employed in baseball management, Campanis astounded viewers by declaring, "They may not have some of the necessities to be, let's say, a field manager or, perhaps, a general manager," and then, digging deeper the hole into which he had blundered, he followed this misstep with his determination that blacks were not good swimmers "because they don't have the buoyancy."[26] This last remark evoked the unpleasant memory of Twins owner Calvin Griffith's statement in September 1978, in which he criticized blacks for not attending baseball games but preferring to "fill up a rassling ring and put up such a chant it'll scare you to death."[27]

Close associates of Campanis excused his egregious error or otherwise apologized for the remarks as being out of character, but no amount of damage control rendered on his behalf could spare him the forced resignation from an organization he had served for more than four decades. Acknowledging that a culture of bias was part of the game, Frank Robinson said that Campanis had "let out what we'd known all along. That attitude had been something we had been trying to tell people about, that these things were going on, that these thoughts existed."[28] Campanis's own apologies and his progressive record of bringing many black and Latino players to the major leagues still could not redeem him.

After a lengthy meeting with Peter Ueberroth—the same kind of chat that did *not* take place with Bowie Kuhn—a minister regarded the commissioner's being "sensitive to the situation," and he anticipated an "opportunity through Mr. Campanis." He added, "Sometimes God brings good out of evil."[29] The speaker was the Reverend Joseph Lowery, who seven years earlier had made little headway in gaining the attention of Ueberroth's predecessor.

A chain of vacancies led to the naming of one high-profile executive. Ueberroth's departure in April 1989, allowed Bart Giamatti to become commissioner, while creating the need for a new NL president. As this changing of the guard was in progress, Bill White, a slick-fielding African American first baseman who was a five-time NL All-Star, contemplated relinquishing his job as a broadcaster for the New York Yankees—he was, in fact, baseball's first black broadcaster—a position he had held for nearly two decades, to seek employment in the world of business. But his plans took an unexpected turn when a search committee of NL owners contacted him late in 1988, regarding the imminent opening in the league president's office.

White was contacted by Peter O'Malley of the Dodgers, who was earnestly attempting to gauge his interest in the position. Leery that O'Malley was acting only for the sake of appearances, White rejected the offer out of hand, but a follow-up call by O'Malley piqued White's interest, and he agreed to an interview with the committee. Impressed by what they learned in the discussion, including the divorced White's candid admission that he was in a relationship with a white divorcée, the committee interviewed at least one other black candidate, former NL Most Valuable Player (MVP) Joe Morgan. Weeks went by with no word as to an offer, but at last O'Malley informed White that the NL presidency "was mine—if I would take it."[30]

This bit of reticence stemmed from White's understanding that he would be transitioning from a broadcast job that allowed for some leisure time away from the ballpark to an executive's full-time position that would place far greater demands on him. Thoughtful contemplation led him to accept the job because "throughout my life, a challenge has been something that is hard for me to resist."[31] White commenced his duties on April 1, 1989, when Giamatti officially moved into the commissioner's office. Five months later, former pitcher Joe Black was hired by Giamatti's successor, Fay Vincent, as a part-time consultant to assist players with personal problems, and the recently retired Don Baylor became an assistant to Milwaukee general manager Harry Dalton.

There was another segment of the population whose attachment to the game of baseball was almost exclusively in an indirect manner, as gender stereotypes continued to prevail even beyond several waves of feminism that occurred in earlier portions of the twentieth century. The role of women remained at the outer fringes of the national pastime, but by the 1970s, their lot was slowly undergoing changes that signaled increasing participation in the traditionally male-dominant realm of baseball.

***

The twentieth century witnessed a transformation in the role of women as they struggled against chauvinism and for equal rights. The vital part played by women during the intrepid days of World War II's "Rosie the Riveter" was soon relegated to history—established as a wartime entertainment, the All-American Girls Professional Baseball League later followed suit—as the country transitioned into the postwar era, with men and women returning to their assumed places in public and private realms.

"Between 1900 and the 1960s, women's presence and skill in a masculine domain had become integral to the process of making and managing gender in American society," and one of the biggest voices in the latter part of this time frame was that of Betty Friedan, whose book *The Feminine Mystique*, published in 1963, "struck a nerve by sketching the outlines of a world assigned to women to decorative and supportive roles in a rampantly materialistic consumer culture."[32] Friedan's opus served as a cornerstone for reform that was consistent with other movements of the twentieth century's most turbulent decade.

As more stakes were driven into the ground by proponents of the women's liberation movement, contemporaneous advertisements for Virginia Slims cigarettes, the first such product created specifically for women, declared, "You've come a long way, baby," a sentiment that gained increasing traction when Billie Jean King defeated Bobby Riggs in a "Battle of the Sexes" tennis match held in September 1973. In an editorial heading that borrowed from the cigarette ad, *Sporting News* noted the appearance of two "girl reporters" who spoke with players—appropriately swathed with postshower towels to preserve modesty—in the dressing room at the conclusion of the 1975 National Hockey League All-Star Game. Robin Herman, a 23-year-old correspondent for the *New York Times*, broke new ground when she joined radio reporter Marcelle St. Cyr at the Montreal Forum in becoming the first women to enter this male bastion.

Two years later, the Chicago White Sox hired Mary Shane as a play-by-play announcer, another first in the world of baseball. Trying her hand at sportscasting for a Milwaukee radio station in 1975, the following year Shane had the opportunity to speak with White Sox broadcaster Harry Caray, who was impressed to the point of asking her to call some game action. Shane later accepted an offer to join the White Sox radio team for 20 games during the 1977 season.

Drawing immediate notice was the fact that Shane would be working for the team owned by renowned maverick Bill Veeck, leading to the obvious conclusion that her hiring was just one more ploy executed by the publicity-seeking mogul. Shane was cognizant of the pressure she would be facing, and that "one of the burdens of being a pioneer was that she could not joke around" in the course of her duties.[33] But team officials found her to be out of her element and an object of "male resentment," and she was terminated before the conclusion of the season. Yet, she later broke new ground as a reporter covering the Boston Celtics of the National Basketball Association.

The significance of Shane's contribution cannot be overlooked because of the challenges she faced as a woman given a traditionally exclusive male role. Working mostly in the press box and away from the clubhouse ameliorated the degree of hostility and abuse Shane encountered, but that provided little comfort for other female reporters soon to follow her. Among them, and in the fashion of Robin Herman, were Jane Leavy, who covered the Orioles for the *Washington Post* from 1978 to 1983 and went on to author several critically acclaimed baseball biographies, and Melissa Ludtke, a reporter for *Sports Illustrated.*

Herman's work at the Montreal Forum did not go unnoticed by baseball's hierarchy. As Opening Day in 1975 drew near, Bowie Kuhn advised the 24 major-league front offices that a "unified stand" had to be taken against the incursion of female reporters into their teams' clubhouses.[34] Those whose privacy stood to be violated the most by women in such facilities—the players—were not consulted about the issue by the commissioner's office, but this question was likely ignored lest a contradictory finding skewer Kuhn's edict—which, in fact, happened in at least one instance.

In the summer of 1976, few New York Yankees players voiced objection to women entering their clubhouse, but when the commissioner's office learned the results of this informal poll, it struck fear into the powers that be. Unable to countenance the potential of the Yankees clubhouse being the first domino to fall and thereby opening a floodgate of women into other teams' facilities, Yankees management overruled the approval of the players. Kuhn stepped into the fray again during the 1977 World Series when Ludtke, credentialed to ply her trade, was denied access to the clubhouses of both the Yankees and Los Angeles Dodgers, despite her being allowed access to the Yankees manager's office during the recent American League Championship Series.

Kuhn, a lawyer who should have known better regarding issues of fair labor practices, declared that the players' right to privacy held priority over allowing a female member of the press to do her job, justifying the barring of Ludtke "solely on the basis of her sex."[35] AL president Lee MacPhail toed the party line established by the commissioner, but Ludtke's fellow writers working the Series believed that she was entitled to the same access that they were allowed. Another scribe, in particular, was having none of it because she, too, was denied entry to baseball clubhouses. "Bowie Kuhn may have gone too far," was the lead of an early November 1977 column by Stephanie Salter in the *San Francisco Examiner*. Salter further detailed some of the humiliating experiences endured by Ludtke.[36]

Salter's commentary in a second article called out Kuhn for casting about to find excuses for enforcing his ban, including being "afraid the athletes' children will be subject to ridicule by the presence of a woman in their fathers' clubhouse" and "fear that a woman will 'excite' the players to the point . . . that they cannot perform their on-field duties."[37] Slights and insults small and large by players only exacerbated the disconsolation felt by Salter, Ludtke, and other women reporters. Endless waiting for postgame quotes only to be told that there was no time for an interview, the hurling of sexual epithets, overt reinforcement of gender stereotypes ("You're trying to do a woman's job in a man's world"), and questions about retention of virginity were accompanied by a truly ironic gem: Salter "explained to a black ballplayer that his vote to bar me from the clubhouse was discrimination and watched him smile [as he] said, 'You bet it is.'"[38]

With legal action against baseball brewing—Time, Inc., was the parent company of *Sports Illustrated*, which was a plaintiff, along with Ludtke, in a lawsuit against Kuhn, MacPhail, the Yankees, New York mayor Abe Beame, and two other city officials—the commissioner's office was keeping an eye on events and devising how best to address the growing controversy. Taking issue with the stories written by Salter, Kuhn's public relations director told Kuhn and his counsel, "Many of the facts in the first of two articles and some in the second are totally erroneous," and, "It may not fit our purposes to answer Ms. Salter, but it seems to me that there may come a time in conversations with *Sports Illustrated* attorneys that we could urge that the dissemination of facts be more accurate if they are circulated at all."[39] Rushing to the commissioner's defense was the director of publicity for the San Francisco Giants, who informed Bob Wirz, his opposite number in Kuhn's office, "Stephanie knows the Giants players took a vote as to whether or not she should be admitted into the locker room. The majority said 'no.' That was not mentioned in the articles."[40]

Kuhn released a statement denouncing the lawsuit, claiming, "Our position has been that if [*Sports Illustrated*] could satisfy that we violated any law, we would change our position," while also arguing that although "general statutes [prohibit] discrimination in places of *public accommodation*, the personal dressing quarters of players cannot reasonably be regarded as a place of public accommodation."[41] In fact, it was this point that worked in favor of women reporters as the litigation played out.

The recent renovation of Yankee Stadium, which was completed in time for the 1976 season, came at a cost to the city of New York of about $50 million, with the team leasing the facility from the city. Thus, being city-owned rather than team-owned, the stadium was a public building from which the public could not be excluded. Also, the argument about privacy protection ran counter to the Fourteenth Amendment guaranteeing equal and due process, a point that became especially salient in a championship team's clubhouse. A judgment of the court, which found in favor of Ludtke in September 1978, was as follows:

> At least during World Series games, male members of the news media with television cameras have been allowed to enter the Yankee locker

> room immediately after the games and broadcast live from that location. In this connection, only a backdrop behind the player standing in front of the camera is provided to shield other players from the "roving eye" of the camera. These locker room encounters are viewed by mass audiences, which include many women and children. This practice, coupled with defendants' practice of refusing to allow accredited women sports reporters to enter the locker room, shows that the latter is "substantially related" only to maintaining the locker room as an all-male preserve.[42]

Kuhn lamented the outcome, realizing that any future lawsuits brought individually against other teams would yield the same results. Now dragged into a phase of progressivism, he stodgily conceded, "We had fought on an issue of principle and lost. Like it or not, we now had to accommodate to the new realities."[43] On the day of the ruling, the Mets' Jerry Koosman was asked by a correspondent from CBS Radio if he would wear a towel as he headed for his postgame shower. Answering the question with one of his own, the pitcher wondered, "Where do you get undressed to put a towel on?"[44]

Preparations the following spring to address the new realities included Kuhn notifying teams that the "previous guidelines issued by this office respecting female media personnel are hereby withdrawn."[45] Although Kuhn himself would no longer set policy for all of baseball—this was now up to the individual clubs—he determined that most teams would adhere to a protocol in which *all* members of the press would be allowed access or *no* members would be allowed.

Eighteen clubs favored "nondiscriminatory" practices, while eight others had to be coaxed into adopting them, and the Baltimore Orioles were likely among the latter group. "I think they ought to have two things," said manager Earl Weaver sardonically. "The women should have a letter from their parents and a letter from [team public relations director] Bob Brown."[46] Compliance was at last reached, and the Ludtke case was settled. Yet, open-door policies for women did not instantly translate into welcoming acceptance by clubhouse denizens. As Kuhn told baseball's Executive Council, "The problem had been an awkward one, and . . . a painful period of adjustment was now necessary."[47]

Where Weaver was mocking in his view of women reporters, others could be blatantly hostile. During his second tour with the Mets in 1981, slugger Dave Kingman "shouted foul remarks at any woman who entered the clubhouse," and a few years later while with the Oakland Athletics he developed a keen dislike for Susan Fornoff of the *Sacramento Bee*, to whom he sent a live rat in a pink carton while she was in the press box.[48] "If you know me, you know I'm a practical jokester," responded Kingman, but his alibi was unconvincing since he had previously spoken "public innuendoes about Fornoff's sexual habits [and smashed] his baseball bat on a table she [was] leaning against."[49]

Other incidents followed: a bilingual tirade by Toronto's George Bell against WFAN's Suzyn Waldman and verbal abuse in the form of a questionable chant directed at Melody Simmons by several Oriole players. "I looked up the word in the *Dictionary of Slang*. It doesn't mean 'broad,'" Simmons determined.[50] In his first stint as manager of the California Angels, Gene Mauch refused to shake hands with Lisa Saxon of the *Los Angeles Daily News*, who had attempted to introduce herself as the new beat writer covering the team. She had a modicum of better luck in dealing with Mauch's successor, as John McNamara counseled her—brusquely at times—on how a reporter should ask a difficult question. In 1985, Saxon also experienced a more cordial reaction during her reacquaintance with Mauch, who upon his return to the Angels dugout duly acknowledged her professionalism: "I just want you to know that I respect the hell out of you. You are the best writer on this beat."[51]

Respect for women in the media was often a commodity in short supply, and another episode of player versus female reporter drew Commissioner Peter Ueberroth into the picture within days of him assuming office. With the New York Yankees in the midst of a 1980s swoon during which they were absent from the postseason playoffs, one of the team's regional beat writers was reassigned by her newspaper to cover the 1984 National League Championship Series (NLCS) between the San Diego Padres and Chicago Cubs. Claire Smith, employed by the *Hartford Courant*, found herself set upon by several members of the Padres after Game 3 at Wrigley Field.

After being showered with verbal abuse and subsequently removed from the visitors' clubhouse by a Padres employee—this outrage committed despite an edict from the league that allowed access to any credentialed member of the press—Smith was accommodated by Padres first baseman Steve Garvey, who granted her an interview in the corridor. "As soon as Garvey heard about the problem, he left the clubhouse and told me to calm down," she said a week after the incident. "He told me he would stay as long as I wanted, and I was able to get my job done."[52] Meeting Peter Ueberroth shortly thereafter, Smith was advised by the commissioner to let him know of any further trouble, and in the spring of 1985, he issued a memorandum to each team clearly indicating that the "clubhouses must be 'open and all accredited members of the media will be given the same access.'"[53]

Smith accomplished more than her work for that fateful day in Chicago: She moved on to write for the *New York Times*—from 1978 to 1980, the sports department there had been under the purview of Le Anne Schreiber, the only woman to serve as editor—and her hometown *Philadelphia Inquirer*. In 2017, Smith became the first woman to earn the coveted J. G. Taylor Spink Award, immortalizing her in the writers' wing of the Baseball Hall of Fame. In like fashion, Christie Blatchford, an award-winning reporter based in Toronto, gained membership in the Canadian News Hall of Fame in 2019, her reputation for hard-edged journalism having outlasted the rigors of her time in the Blue Jays clubhouse.

Figure 9.2. Through her perseverance in the sometimes hostile environment of a major-league clubhouse, Claire Smith plied her craft as a reporter for several major newspapers and later as a news editor for ESPN. She became the first woman to be honored as the recipient of the J. G. Taylor Spink Award. National Baseball Hall of Fame and Museum

Yet, these high honors are rare, and the toll taken on women reporters could be daunting. After Lisa Saxon found her concentration wandering by the late 1980s, she was diagnosed with "combat fatigue," a result that was far beyond the bounds of what any member of the sporting press should have to endure as an occupational hazard.[54] The circumstances of young women reporters in a clubhouse populated by players in varying states of undress—to say nothing of their temperament—also created a new ethical conundrum: Could such comingling open the way to potential romantic or sexual relationships? This possibility was an offshoot of another dilemma concerning what limits existed concerning the issue of socialization between players and the press. "How should [female reporters] handle the long-standing tradition of sportswriters' informal post-game drinks with players, coaches, and managers? . . . How much fraternizing was permissible with the players on your beat?"[55]

Many years after she moved on from her days as a beat reporter, Claire Smith reflected on the passing of former coach and manager Jim Frey, who served as a coach under Mets manager George Bamberger in 1982. Smith noted that the pair came from a "generation of uniformed guys who grew up crusty and never grew out of it. With Jimmy, locker room talk flowed easily—until the first wave of women started to cover the game." She then described a way to defuse any awkwardness:

> Bamberger and Jimmy were constantly chastising each other if the curse words they were otherwise choking back slipped out in my presence. One day, as they chirped at each other as they grappled with the new normal, I shared with them an adage umpires often used: "As long as what you're saying does not contain the word 'you,' then no offense taken. This is your home. I'm just visiting and am not here to change the way you speak!" Bambi, Jimmy, and I laughed. From that point on, [we] were extremely comfortable while pursuing our professions in each other's company. Could they make sailors blush? You bet. Were they also old-school gents trying to get it right? Absolutely. I will always be grateful for that.[56]

At least those working in the media could fall back on the legal concept of freedom of the press as a means to justify one's employment; however, working on the field in the capacity of an umpire, whose mere presence almost guaranteed that verbal abuse was part of the milieu, was a different matter. The first woman to take the field as a paid arbiter was a

South Dakotan named Amanda Clement, who umpired from 1904 to 1911 in Upper Midwest semipro games, but the first steps toward that occupation in the modern era were taken by Bernice Gera, a lover of baseball who longed for a job in a major-league front office in the mid-1960s. When her queries were ignored by every team, she replied to an advertisement in *Sporting News* to apply for classes at an accredited umpiring school in Florida.

Using the alias "Bernie Gera" to sidestep the obvious gender implication of her real first name, she was accepted to the program but summarily dismissed upon the revelation of her true identity. Undeterred, Gera moved on to an umpiring program that accepted her, and she finally earned an assignment in the New York–Penn League. Gera debuted on June 24, 1972, an occasion greeted with a high degree of fanfare that quickly deflated when she reversed herself on a call in the opening game of a doubleheader and incurred the wrath of the manager whose team was now on the wrong side of her decision. Gera immediately fled the ballpark—and professional baseball—after this one game, and several years would pass before another woman, Christine Wren, attempted to join the umpiring fraternity.

Wren accomplished more than Gera by dint of perseverance, umpiring for several years at the Class A level but finally conceding to the rigors of traveling on her own and the physical punishment inflicted on her body during games, to say nothing of the insults and taunts that came with the territory. Efforts by Julie Zeller Ware (Little League umpiring school), Perry Barber (Japanese baseball and the Cape Cod League), and Theresa Cox (Double-A Southern League) led them to success at different levels of the game during the 1980s. There was another woman who excelled at umpiring school, as well as the minor-league level, and Pam Postema impressed as being the most likely candidate to break the glass ceiling leading to the major leagues.

Athletically inclined and described as a "personable brunette," Postema apprenticed in the Gulf Coast Rookie League and the Florida State League for three years, finally earning a promotion to the Double-A Texas League in 1981.[57] Levelheaded when it came to her craft, Postema nonetheless gave as good as she got when disputes arose, and she was not bashful in returning salty language initiated by managers or players. Neither did she hold back when the occasion warranted an ejection, although some felt that she was too quick to exercise her thumb. An "unrepentant"

Postema explained, "If they're hassling me from the bench, I pick out a face I know and dump him."[58]

Continuing through the 1980s in the Pacific Coast League and handling other assignments in Puerto Rican and Colombian winter leagues, by 1987 Postema had impressed to such a degree that she was chosen to work home plate at the annual Hall of Fame game held as part of induction weekend in Cooperstown. While the contest was merely an exhibition affair, pressure was brought to bear on her with baseball's top brass in attendance, Commissioner Ueberroth and both league presidents, Bobby Brown of the AL and Bart Giamatti of the NL. By the following season, Postema had plateaued at the highest minor-league rank, and with nothing left to prove in the minors, her situation begged the question of if and when she would be called up for big-league duty.

Thought to be a finalist for one of two umpiring positions in the NL, Postema served her 12th and what turned out to be her final year as an arbiter. In November 1989, she was released, along with seven other Triple-A colleagues, who, after three consecutive years at that level, were deemed unfit for promotion to the major leagues.

Pam Postema's fate was not entirely preordained, but the long odds she faced and the finality of her struggle reflected the gender bias permeating baseball. Undaunted while chasing the dream of attaining a coveted position of responsibility working in the game, Postema, like the women reporters of the same era, persevered and, if nothing else, reinforced the notion that the world did not always belong to men, as overarching as that status may have seemed. Yet, as painful as Postema's experience became in falling short of a major-league job, nothing can diminish her many accomplishments: Serving as a Triple-A crew chief; the high-profile exhibition games she umpired; and the accolades she won from a host of major-league managers, among them pennant-winners Chuck Tanner and Roger Craig, offer definitive proof that her time on the diamond was hardly fruitless.

The Orioles provided fertile ground for a woman who applied her visionary eye to the architectural project she was to undertake in the construction of a replacement for the team's aged Memorial Stadium. Hailing from Jackson, Mississippi, Janet Marie Smith earned her bachelor's degree in architecture from Mississippi State University in 1981, and three years later she added a master's degree in urban planning from the City College of New York to her academic credentials. Smith's voca-

Figure 9.3. Despite achieving a rank as one of the best umpires in the Pacific Coast League, Pam Postema was unable to break the glass ceiling to land a job in the major leagues. National Baseball Hall of Fame and Museum

tion was no accident, as she followed the same path taken by her father, Thomas Henry Smith, himself an architect who assisted in founding the program from which his daughter would earn her undergraduate degree.

While in Baltimore during the Orioles' woeful 1988 season, the baseball-loving Smith visited Memorial Stadium for the simple pleasure of going to a game, and it was there that she learned of the team's plans to move to a new stadium near the city's Inner Harbor. "It took me a few days, but I suddenly realized that was the project I had been looking for. If the Orioles were going to move downtown, I felt like it would be a great way to use what I had studied—architecture and urban planning," she told her hometown newspaper years later.[59] Persistent in her attempts to contact Orioles president Larry Lucchino, Smith at last succeeded, and in 1989, she landed a position as architectural consultant for a project that was not for the faint of heart.

Smith was charged with adhering to Lucchino's desire to create an old-style ballpark—use of the term "stadium" was greatly discouraged—that would incorporate modern amenities to make the fan experience of attending a game more pleasurable. Such an incongruous melding was achieved through her efforts, not least of which included a contentious battle to repurpose the former Baltimore & Ohio Railroad warehouse building. Her ability to look beyond the impulse others had to raze the landmark structure was emblematic of the deft hand she applied in steering the project to the stunning finale that became Oriole Park at Camden Yards, which opened in 1992. "Smith became the Johnny Appleseed of Lucchino's vision," wrote architectural critic Paul Goldberger as a tribute to her "tenacity and sharp eye for detail," which influenced other ballpark projects on which she worked well into the twenty-first century.[60]

Jobs held by women that relate to the national pastime—and indeed other sports as well—continued to expand throughout the years. An observation by the writer Jean Hastings Ardell provides a fitting summation of the issue: "What does it mean that women are now involved in so many aspects of the game? For one, it reflects the ideal that all Americans deserve a fair chance to compete."[61] A person's qualifications should always transcend any and all demographic traits, and recognition of this situates society in a better place. "Laws were being rewritten to reduce discrimination," wrote one historian, "*attitudes in the workplace were slowly changing*, [and] women were staking their claim to independent thought and action."[62]

To be sure, the reshaping of attitudes was sine qua non to overcoming the stereotypes that had long separated the sexes, but the slow evolution of moods and behavior toward the acceptance of women in new roles was accompanied by a demeanor of some players that signaled a willingness to express a more rebellious or flamboyant side of their personalities.

***

No suggestion can be made that combativeness, demonstrations of arrogance, or showmanship on the part of players suddenly arose when true free agency became a reality after the 1976 season. For several seasons, ace reliever Al Hrabosky had already employed a menacing persona on the mound—this accompanied his physical appearance, which was highlighted by his Fu Manchu mustache—in becoming an integral member of the St. Louis Cardinal bullpen. His actions were diametrically opposed to the benign antics of Detroit's Mark Fidrych, who brought his own brand of entertainment to the ballpark for his starting assignments; even their nicknames, "the Mad Hungarian" for the former and "the Bird" for the latter, were quite telling.

In general terms, baseball's pastoral qualities have always been balanced by a rough-and-tumble element, sometimes on the very same play, as when a middle infielder gracefully turns a double-play pivot but is immediately involved in a collision with a hulking baserunner. The charging of the mound by a hit batsman—or one nearly hit—to quickly settle the score with an offending pitcher has featured frequently for many decades, and, of course, abuse heaped on umpires by those afield, in the dugout, or in the stands has been a ballpark staple since time immemorial. On rarer occasions, fighting in the stands, undertaken by groups of fans with competing interests in the teams at play, also posed a problem. As the national pastime moved into the modern era with a complement of 26 teams, trouble was brewing that was discerned by the commissioner.

"The vast majority of baseball patrons are well behaved, orderly fans who attend the games to experience the excellent play and root for their favorites," noted an internal memo from the office of Bowie Kuhn at the close of 1977.

> There are, however, a small minority of individuals who attend games occasionally to commit violence under the cloak of anonymity which the crowd provides. They are not unique to baseball, or even to sports,

> and they can be found anywhere large numbers of people gather for a common purpose.[63]

At that moment, the focus was on people in the stands rather than those on the diamond, but this would evolve in the coming years.

A comprehensive plan to deal with crowd control was unanimously embraced by all teams and included six major points: Stadiums were to be staffed by security personnel whose numbers were to be adequate to the purpose "but few enough to avoid the appearance of an armed camp"; strict policies to prosecute those breaking laws should be carried out; adequate communications systems within the stadium were to enable rapid responses to trouble; coordination with local law enforcement agencies would augment on-site security; "use of public address announcements and press reports to encourage favorable deportment in the stands" was important to delivering timely information; and means were to be implemented to analyze each crowd to find commonalities likely to trigger an unwanted episode—for example, the appearance of a controversial player or expected tension brought on by a tight pennant race or other important games.[64] Some precautionary measures—plain-clothes security mingling among the crowd and use of closed-circuit television monitoring to find those hurling objects onto the field—as well as quick action to keep minor incidents from getting out of hand, were credited with easing the level of unpleasantries.

Beyond the control of security personnel and baseball administrators, however, were forces impacting the public at large, whose standards of behavior were not what they had been in an earlier era. As tolerance of foul language abated, allowing it to seep into mainstream mores of verbal expression, it was inevitable that epithets and obscenities would be heard at games. Regardless of the behavioral issue, baseball officials "are aware that the social problems outside the stadium are bound to find their way into the ballpark, and we are trying to meet this challenge. *Certainly the lowering of moral standards, the erosion of attitudes and respect, and the disintegration of social barriers have had their effect on all forms of human activity.*"[65]

Yet, for all the concern in the commissioner's office about fan behavior, altercations on the field among uniformed personnel and umpires did not bode well either. "The year [1977] has been punctuated by unseemly displays of belligerence, previously not thought of in connection with the game," editor Joe Marcin told readers of *Sporting News*.[66] A litany of misfortunes brought unflattering publicity, with the Pittsburgh Pirates involved in a disproportionate number of them: Umpire Bruce Froemming was sent reeling after colliding with Coach Al Monchak, who had unintentionally bumped into the ump while trying to restrain an outraged Al Oliver from attacking him; Oliver's teammate, Frank Taveras, was suspended for hurling his bat at Joe Hoerner after being hit by a pitch; Mike Schmidt of the Phillies suffered a minor finger fracture in a scuffle with Bucs pitcher Bruce Kison; and catcher Ed Ott put his collegiate wrestling experience to use by body-slamming the Mets' Felix Millan when the second baseman stuck the ball in Ott's face following a rolling slide on a force play.

Hitters digging in at the plate, especially those crowding it to reach outside pitches, were staking their claim to what they believed rightfully belonged to them. Reggie Smith of the Dodgers refused to back down when he felt he was being targeted while in the batter's box. "If that pitcher is throwing at me, I want him to know I'm going to do something about it," warned the outfielder, who had already had a pair of run-ins that year.[67] Smith and Cesar Cedeño also were each willing to go into the stands to confront hecklers, which both did in 1981.

Bob Fishel, a former Yankees executive now serving as an assistant to AL president Lee MacPhail, alleged, "There are still fights on the field, but no more than in other eras of baseball. Fan rowdyism is the only area that would seem to have increased."[68] Yet, he offered no proof to substantiate his claim despite disturbances in the stands being a valid cause for concern. At the time Fishel made his comments, the baseball world was more than a year away from the disastrous "Disco Demolition Night" hosted by the White Sox at Comiskey Park, an event that continues to live in infamy. The dubious promotion originally carried the innocuous tag of "Teen Night" and was orchestrated by Bill Veeck's son Mike. Fans averse to the disco music craze of the mid- to late 1970s were admitted for 98 cents if they brought a disco record to the ballpark, with all donated records to be assembled in a crate and blown up between games of a doubleheader on July 12, 1979. Local radio host Steve Dahl served as the emcee of the explosion, but when teeming young fans stormed the stadium and subsequently the playing field, even entreaties by Bill Veeck himself could not restore order as the "smell of marijuana wafted through the grandstand."[69]

However, drawing scrutiny were exactly the incidents between players about which Fishel was dismissive. Kuhn was concerned about a possible increase in the number of batters being hit by pitches, and although a distinction needs to be drawn between a pitch that gets away from a pitcher and one thrown—or perceived to be thrown—deliberately, any batter believing he was intentionally hit or knocked down was a potential candidate to visit the mound.

Still, a control artist like Ferguson Jenkins, who walked roughly two batters per nine innings pitched, quickly raised suspicion for brushing men away from the plate, especially those who were able to tag Jenkins for a home run. These were hardly instances of pitches merely slipping, and *Sports Illustrated* believed that a "mad-as-hell tension" was fueling the foul mood that seemed to infect so many players.[70]

Making clear that he would have none of it was Reggie Jackson, who in the spring of 1980 put "headhunters" on notice. The Yankees slugger was reacting to a number of recent pitches by the Twins' Jerry Koosman that had sent him sprawling, and on the eve of a rematch the following week, Reggie issued a warning through the print media. "You have to pick the right time," he said of when he might find it necessary to charge the mound. "But anything I do in reference to retaliation is all spontaneous. And if Koosman keeps throwing at my head, I'm gonna have to fight him someday."[71]

Kuhn reiterated the comparative statistics and the distortion thought to be caused by television, but he also confessed that baseball was a "game which is contested between highly intense and competitive players, and violence cannot be entirely prevented."[72] Not mentioned was the possibility that batters were taking umbrage at being targeted by pitchers whose hit by pitches could cause serious enough injuries to impact a player's future, which was also to say his performance not only on the field, but also at the negotiating table where a high-stakes contract could be at risk.

But the preponderance of incidents were rooted in hit batters that could instigate horrific brawls—the notorious August 1984 fight between the San Diego Padres and Atlanta Braves led to 17 ejections—or cause serious injuries, for instance, the 24-stitch gash suffered by the Cubs' Andre Dawson in July 1987, when he was hit in the face by an Eric Show pitch—again, the Padres were involved—leading to another melee. Upset by the scale of Dawson's injury and the resulting fracas, NL president Bart Giamatti announced, "Any act that, in my opinion, is intended to cause severe physical harm to an opposing player—as for instance by throwing intentionally at a batter's head, fighting on the field, or sliding with a rolling block—will henceforth result in the most severe penalties, including suspension."[73] Although the Jack Hamilton pitch that struck Tony Conigliaro 20 years before Dawson's injury was acknowledged to be unintentional, no one needed a reminder of the catastrophic damage that could be caused by a pitch to the face.

Fracases instigated by beanballs and other pitches were only part of the story of disturbances on the field. Suspensions were handed out for umpire-bumping incidents—managers Dave Bristol and Dallas Green, along with infielders Carney Lansford of the Angels and Oakland's Wayne Gross, to name a few—and no attempt can be made to present highly driven athletes as choir boys. The animus of Ted Williams toward the press, the combativeness of Leo Durocher, and many other examples throughout the years indicate that players and managers in a more modern era were, if anything, simply carrying on an inglorious tradition of the game. But a stinging incident of August 1981, gave reason for pause and highlighted an emboldened change in player attitudes.

St. Louis shortstop Garry Templeton, a 25-year-old bona fide talent who seemed destined for the Hall of Fame, had endured a rocky relationship with the Cardinals front office concerning salary issues, and a fuss about his selection to the 1979 All-Star Team—his statement "If I ain't startin', I ain't departin'" originated in an interview Templeton had with broadcaster Jack Buck, from whom he took the line—raised eyebrows.[74] Shortly after the 1981 players strike was settled, Templeton fanned in a home game against the Giants, but he failed to run to first base on the dropped third strike. Facing a chorus of boos as he returned to the dugout, Templeton reacted by giving the crowd two obscene gestures, and he was physically pulled off the field by manager Whitey Herzog, who was livid with his shortstop. "If the other players hadn't come between us, I guess we'd have had a pretty good fight right then and there. I'd never been so mad at a player," Herzog recalled, and he defended the subsequent trade that sent Templeton to San Diego because "there was no way the fans of St. Louis were ever going to forgive him."[75]

Templeton was suspended by the Cardinals and agreed to psychiatric treatment before ultimately being dealt to the Padres, but his predicament prompted some members of baseball management to detect a diminishing general respect for authority that seemed to be girded by long-term contracts. Referring to the beginning of the era of free agency, Baltimore pitching coach Ray Miller said, "Until the last five years, no player would have dreamed of doing what Templeton did. It's only the security of a long-term guaranteed contract that could delude a player into thinking he could insult the fans who pay his salary."[76]

Indeed, Templeton was in the second year of a six-year, $4 million deal, and his demeanor embodied an altered work ethic now tainted by the comfort of a huge amount of money. For Herzog's part, he continued as the Cardinals manager, but despite the success he enjoyed—one World Series title and two other NL pennants helped him earn his place in the Hall of Fame—he had seen enough by the halfway point of the 1990 season. "The changing attitude of the players really got to him, in addition to the indifferent attitude he faced in his own front office," noted St. Louis coach and manager Red Schoendienst of the frustration that at last took its toll on Herzog.[77]

Overt displays of defiance against managers had featured in the recent past, not least of which were two disreputable incidents. In the spring of 1977, Texas Rangers manager Frank Lucchesi was attacked by infielder Lenny Randle, who appeared to be in jeopardy of losing his job to a highly touted rookie, Bump Wills. Randle had taken exception to a comment attributed to Lucchesi—"I'm sick and tired of punks making $80,000 a year moaning and groaning about their situation," the dollar figure referring to Randle's salary—and the manager later confessed to the Texas front office that "'punks' was an unfortunate choice of words."[78] Engaging the manager initially in what seemed to be ordinary, on-field conversation prior to an exhibition game, Randle suddenly struck Lucchesi with a flurry of punches and inflicted substantial damage, including a concussion and triple fracture of Lucchesi's cheek bone that required surgery.

A second furor erupted during a nationally televised game at Fenway Park in June 1977, when a near-brawl took place in the visitors' dugout. Reggie Jackson was pulled from right field in the middle of the sixth inning and confronted Yankees skipper Billy Martin when he arrived at the bench. Martin thought Reggie to be loafing on a base hit by Jim Rice, which the Boston designated hitter hustled into a double, infuriating the manager. Affirming his authority, Martin felt no guilt about showing up Reggie since he believed his outfielder had shown *him* up by casually chasing down Rice's hit. Martin and Reggie were separated before punches could be thrown, but the set-to, which was seen nationally on NBC's *Game of the Week*, did nothing to quell the unstable atmosphere of the Yankees clubhouse.

Where Lucchesi and Martin drew the line—or at least tried to—in handling their players, Vern Rapp of the St. Louis Cardinals found himself subjected to "sheer insubordination" by reliever Al Hrabosky, who made no secret of his disdain for the manager's directive to remove facial hair and follow the club's dress code.[79] Another handful for various managers since his debut in 1964, former AL MVP Dick Allen landed with the Oakland Athletics in 1977, the first season that followed the departure of the team's core of best players to free agency. Correctly described by his biographer as an individualist, Allen's predilection for living life on his terms was frequently interpreted by authority figures as indiscipline. As his playing time diminished with the Athletics, he was "under the impression that . . . he was free to come and go as he pleased," which fitted well with teammates who "were traipsing around the vast foul territory at the Oakland Alameda Coliseum and conversing with fans while the game was taking place; other players retreated to the clubhouse during the game to listen to the radio and drink beer."[80]

Had the time line of his career been a bit different, Allen may have found comfort playing for Davey Johnson, who brought a different mindset to Shea Stadium when he was named manager of the Mets in 1984. Johnson's permissive attitude toward his players fitted well with the times, as a shift in that decade's popular culture saw an increasing degree of solipsism infecting youth and young adults. An affluent portion of the latter group became known as "yuppies," whose wealth and confidence in their ability to improve their lot led to a craving for consumer goods previously unattainable, as well as products connoting status and prestige. No small degree of condescension attended this lust for materialism in many forms: luxury automobiles, preppy wardrobes and designer clothes, home entertainment systems, and even Perrier bottled water. The use of cocaine, as pointed out previously, also grew as status symbol.

Johnson stepped into a major-league milieu stained by drug scandals, with worse to follow that would directly impact his charges. Yet, by employing the vast trove of young talent at his disposal, Johnson crafted a lineup envied by the competition, and the World Series championship the Mets captured in 1986 was a culmination of the previous two years' effort to escape the moribund era since the team's last appearance in the

Figure 9.4. His scowl and Fu Manchu mustache gave Al Hrabosky the intimidating persona he wanted to convey while on the mound. Unafraid of the batters he faced, neither was the "Mad Hungarian" daunted by the dress code of the St. Louis Cardinals, which prohibited facial hair. Hrabosky defied one of his managers through "sheer insubordination" by not following the club's policy. National Baseball Hall of Fame and Museum

playoffs in 1973. In the course of reaching the pinnacle of the game's achievements, however, the Mets made more than their share of enemies as they developed a braggadocio that corresponded to the degree of success they enjoyed on the field. Keith Hernandez admitted that the Mets "emerge[d] as the tough and arrogant baseball team everyone loved to hate," and "four pretty nasty bench-clearing brawls" did little to win them admiration.[81]

When the players caused much damage to the interior of the airplane carrying them back to New York after the NLCS in Houston—the celebration obviously got way out of hand—United Airlines sent the team a bill in the expectation of recouping the cost of repairs. The front office passed the bill along to Johnson, and the manager was outraged—not at the ill behavior of his players, but rather at the front office for having the gall to expect either him or his players to provide reimbursement. Feeling entitled to do as they pleased earned the Mets the bull's-eyes they wore on their backs and made them the most despised team in the NL, if not all of baseball. Winning only one more divisional pennant in 1988, the Mets disappointed few of their rivals as they collapsed under the weight of the self-indulgence that was entirely of their own making. Athletic stardom, big-money contracts, a championship ring, and a sex-drugs-and-rock-and-roll mentality undermined a club that was staffed to create a dynasty capable of stretching into the 1990s.

Other uncouth comportment caused disdain in the most public of places. In a letter to Bowie Kuhn alerting him to undignified behavior by uniformed personnel during a standard pregame ritual, a fan from New Jersey protested what he viewed as a lack of patriotic respect.

> When our national anthem is played or sung at our baseball games, the TV shows the game at its worst. The players, managers, and others not only do not stand at attention, they grin, they shift positions, they talk—but worse, they chew—gum, snuff, or tobacco . . . [and] they spit. . . . Their conduct is not only disgusting. It tells our youth who are watching their "heros" [*sic*] that the national anthem is merely something that has to be done before the game can start.[82]

Casting off the stoicism of such 1960s heroes as Mickey Mantle, Bob Gibson, and Al Kaline—these future Hall of Famers had retired before the Messersmith decision was announced—the newer generation of ballplayers was less reserved, enjoyed time before the cameras, and felt unrestrained in showing emotions between the foul lines. This new freedom was personified by Rickey Henderson, Dennis Eckersley, Reggie Jackson, and Gary Carter, each of whom also found their place in Cooperstown.

Players' flamboyance and demonstrative attitudes echoed the "baseball fever" inherent in the game's swelling popularity beyond 1977. The cultlike status enjoyed by the men on the field was infused with degrees of machismo large and small on display in almost every game: fleet-of-foot outfielders chasing down fly balls; speedy runners dashing on the basepaths; sluggers swinging mightily in an attempt to clout a tape-measure home run; workhorse pitchers hurling inning after grueling inning; and even the umpires employing the stamina required to man their positions, which afforded no opportunity to sit in the dugout for a between-inning break. In some cases, however, this virile façade was only a cloak for a distinct minority of baseball personnel whose sexual orientation remained closely guarded, and revelation of their homosexuality in a less enlightened age held a peril of its own at a time when AIDS had recently emerged as a new and unsettling health crisis.

***

Sharing the details of his closeted life in a 1990 autobiography, umpire Dave Pallone described his journey as an arbiter playing out against a backdrop of his conflicted heterosexual feelings and the discovery of his true self as a gay man. The circumstances of his vocation were complicated when he was brought to the NL as a replacement umpire in 1979, when unionized officials went on strike. Ostracized by almost all of the regular umpires when the dispute was settled, Pallone was burdened by the "scab" label rather than any fallout related to his sexual orientation, which was not yet known to the public.

Excelling in his chosen profession, Pallone was named to work the 1983 All-Star Game and the 1987 NLCS, and he persevered despite his lover having died in an automobile accident, but by 1986, rumors began to surface about his being in the company of other men. "The real problem wasn't *being* gay," Pallone later admitted, "it was the fear of people *finding out* I was gay. . . . This horrifying fear of exposure is the Achilles' heel of every hidden life."[83] Having developed a close working relationship with fellow umpire Paul Runge, Pallone came out to his wife when she asked him directly about his sexuality, and she in turn told Runge. In the meantime, in 1988 Pallone had his infamous run-in with Reds manager Pete Rose, and then his name had been tied to an upstate New York sex ring involving young boys. Knowing he was innocent, Pallone fought the charges: "Christ, I *gotta* clear my name. Nothing else matters," he declared.[84]

At the time that Pallone was learning his craft in the minor leagues, Glenn Burke had arrived with the Los Angeles Dodgers in 1976, seeing spot duty in center field and pinch-running on a few occasions. After spending the following April and May at Triple-A Albuquerque, Burke was recalled and spent the rest of the year playing under new manager Tommy Lasorda. Burke's role did not change significantly, but he saw more playing time and appeared in seven postseason contests.

Already set with their established Cey–Russell–Lopes–Garvey infield and an outfield fronted by veterans Dusty Baker, Rick Monday, and Reggie Smith, the Dodgers were primed to continue holding Cincinnati's "Big Red Machine" at bay. Lasorda had a deep bench at his disposal, which included Burke, but the organization had an image to maintain, and Burke contended that owner Walter O'Malley directed general manager Al Campanis to persuade the outfielder to strongly consider a heterosexual marriage. Catering to large crowds showing up at Chavez Ravine was foremost in the minds of management as well. Said Burke "They knew I was gay and were worried about how the average father would feel about taking his son to a baseball game to see some fag shagging fly balls in center field."[85]

By 1978, and now in his third year serving as, for all practical purposes, a defensive replacement, he was traded to Oakland in mid-May. Despite trying to keep his sexual orientation under wraps, Burke was "very uneasy" to have been sent packing but admitted, "I probably should have seen the trade coming. Lasorda knew I was tight with his gay son Spunky [Tom Jr.]."[86]

Burke said he did not gain a full realization about his homosexuality until he was 23 years old. He claimed that the number of gay baseball players was consistent with the general ratio of gays in society and alleged that two MVPs from the 1970s were "well known in the gay community."[87] Unlike Pallone, who became a pariah among his peers due to a labor issue, Burke was embraced by his teammates and the staff of the Dodgers, not least including a playful camaraderie with Lasorda. But Burke's interaction with the manager began to curdle, in no small part

Figure 9.5. Playing in an era when gay athletes remained closeted, Glenn Burke lived an uncomfortable "double life" in an attempt to keep his sexual orientation private. National Baseball Hall of Fame and Museum

due to a suspected relationship between Burke and Lasorda's son—"I've never responded to that suspicion. That's my business," Burke later wrote—and when Spunky passed away due to complications from AIDS in 1991, Lasorda attributed his death to cancer or pneumonia, depending on the source, rather than honestly confront his son's sexuality.[88]

In 1979, Burke, having been at a remove from Los Angeles and that city's high-profile glamor scene, was beginning to feel more comfortable in his new personal surroundings when a story in the local press informed readers that a ballplayer had been spotted in the gay section of San Francisco. This news was disturbing to Burke, who only sought to maintain a degree of privacy away from the ballpark.

Citing the inevitability of being discovered to be gay, Burke voluntarily retired to give himself a measure of relief about the "double life" he led, but he had a change of heart as spring training of 1980 approached.[89] With a pinched nerve now healed during the winter, Burke anticipated a return to the game and was further encouraged by the naming of Billy Martin as the new Oakland manager. Burke presumed Martin would run the team with his customary iron fist and instill a winning spirit into a lackluster team, but Burke's enthusiasm was pierced when he learned that the new skipper let it be known to some other players that "no faggot's going to ever play on my ballclub."[90]

After being optioned to the minors at Ogden and facing an issue that landed him on the team's suspended list, Burke faded away from baseball, and although his sexual orientation had been known for some time, it was publicly affirmed through a 1982 *Inside Sports* magazine feature. Still in fine athletic trim, Burke played in a San Francisco–based gay softball league and ran sprints at gay athletic events, but his life was ruined by a descent into cocaine use, homelessness, and contraction of AIDS, the latter contributing to his death in 1995 at the age of 42. Tribute was later paid to baseball's first openly gay player when Burke was inducted into the National Gay and Lesbian Sports Hall of Fame in 2013, and Baseball Reliquary's "Shrine of the Eternals" two years later.

The plight of Dave Pallone and Glenn Burke brought to light the difficulty of gay men who are fully qualified to hold a particular job yet whose sexual orientation runs counter to the standard defined by society. In the realm of athletics, such a standard assumes there to be no trace of homosexuality to upset the traditional image of males and the roles held by them. As gays and lesbians acquired a greater sense of freedom and escaped the stigma long attached to their preferences, another segment of the population was raising awareness to break down barriers that prevented those with handicaps from fully integrating into their communities.

***

The health of finely honed athletes like MLB players is presumed to be excellent, from both the physical and mental aspects of their well-being. Yet, frailties of the human condition do not put them all on a level playing field. As detailed in Rick Swaine's compendium of more than two dozen baseball players afflicted with all manner of impairments, disorders, or extreme injuries, this select group succeeded in reaching the major leagues through dint of their efforts in surmounting overwhelming challenges.

The rigors faced by the athletically inclined were daunting, but moving into the 1980s, several players proved more than capable of overcoming obstacles that would have thwarted even those free of such constraints. In the early years of that decade, the Minnesota Twins were revamping their lineup with a cavalcade of young players who would turn an also-ran team into a solid contender in the AL West. As Gary Gaetti, Kent Hrbek, Frank Viola, and Tom Brunansky found their way into regular duty—and shortly before Kirby Puckett's arrival—another promising outfielder made a favorable impression with his stellar season in Class A ball in 1981. Jim Eisenreich was viewed as an undersized player, but his robust offensive production earned him a trip to the Twins' spring training camp the following season as a nonroster invitee. Again proving that his fine year in Wisconsin Rapids was not a fluke, he made the major-league roster and remarkably staked his claim to the job as center fielder on Opening Day.

Quickly growing comfortable as a Twins rookie did not jibe with a neurological disorder that had plagued Eisenreich since his youth. Described in early press accounts as afflicted by "stage fright," he would exhibit involuntary facial tics and jerking movements.[91] Treatments in the form of hypnosis and medication had limited success: although in better control of his actions, Eisenreich found that the prescriptions hampered his playing ability.

A frustrating pattern took shape for the next few years as Eisenreich alternately played and retired from baseball—taking the field when feeling up to the task but retreating as his health prevented him from performing well. At times he was tripped up by refusing assignment to a farm team to work his way back to Minnesota or accepting a demotion but then not following his treatment protocol. Realizing the extent of Eisenreich's natural playing talent, the Twins remained steadfast in their hope that he could conquer his issue, but ultimately his 1986 retirement ended his days with the team. In 1987, he was acquired by Kansas City, where he was reunited with Billy Gardner, his old Twins manager, who was now with the Royals. Having at last been correctly diagnosed with and treated for Tourette's syndrome, Eisenreich flourished in his new home, where he gained increasing amounts of playing time after paying some dues in the minor leagues for two seasons. For a decade beginning in 1989, he played in at least 105 games per season and was a member of two World Series teams, including the champion 1997 Florida Marlins.

Another instance of a player failing to let a handicap derail his wish to achieve on the diamond was demonstrated by Jim Abbott, who debuted with the Angels in 1989, after succeeding in several youth and high school sports before moving on to the University of Michigan. Born without a right hand, Abbott excelled as a pitcher, adopting a smooth method of donning and removing his fielder's glove as needed, and he was a threat at the plate as well, hitting over .400 during his senior year of high school. As a Wolverine, he gained increasing amounts of recognition as a superb hurler, capturing significant honors, including a Most Courageous Athlete Award from the Philadelphia Sportswriters Association, Big Ten Conference Player of the Year, and the Golden Spikes Award as the nation's best amateur baseball player.

So well regarded had Abbott become that he was named to the U.S. Pan American team, for whom he pitched a three-hit win against Cuba, and also the 1988 U.S. Olympic squad, pitching in the gold-medal-winning contest to beat Japan. Skipping his final year of eligibility at Michigan, Abbott entered the amateur draft and was selected by the California Angels in the first round, and to much fanfare and attention by the media, he not only earned a spot on the team in 1989, but also immediately became the fifth man in the rotation, breaking even with a 12–12 record and 3.92 ERA in 29 starts. It was a season of on-the-job training for a youngster whose place on the roster was criticized by some as being more for public relations purposes. Yet, there was substance to Abbott's deeds to warrant his not being sent to the minor leagues for an apprenticeship.

In his third year with the Angels, he placed third in voting for the AL Cy Young Award, and after a trade to the New York Yankees, he fash-

Figure 9.6. Born without a right hand, Jim Abbott leaped from college baseball to the California Angels starting rotation in 1989. He won 87 games in the course of 10 seasons with four major-league teams, and the challenge he overcame gave inspiration to those with physical handicaps. National Baseball Hall of Fame and Museum

ioned a no-hitter in 1993. While his career path beyond his high-water mark of 18 wins in 1991 had markings more in line with those of a journeyman, Abbott led by example and "[gave] renewed hope to thousands with disabilities. He once estimated that he had at least one scheduled meeting with a disabled child during every road series of his career."[92]

Lastly, one player taken by the New York Mets in the 1986 amateur draft deserves notice, as his story is a reprise of the earlier role of the deaf-mute outfielder William "Dummy" Hoy from the nineteenth century. Curtis Pride was born deaf, the impairment resulting from his mother having contracted German measles while she was pregnant. Both a gifted student and athlete, Pride alternated time in the classroom and on the diamond in dual pursuits of a degree and a baseball career, his ability to read lips from an early age proving instrumental to each endeavor. After a six-year stint in the Mets farm system, he signed with the Montreal Expos in 1993 and spent portions of 11 seasons with six teams, serving primarily as a pinch-hitter and extra outfielder.

Like Jim Eisenreich and Jim Abbott, Curtis Pride also received the Tony Conigliaro Award, this trio of determined ballplayers defying the obstacles placed before them due to innate conditions of which they had no control. Firmly in their command, however, was an indomitable spirit that allowed them to overcome their handicaps and employ their athleticism to the utmost of their ability. Their stories cannot help but inspire others and further alleviate any stigma related to circumstances that would otherwise have held them back from reaching for their dreams.

***

The broad landscape of American society includes contours shaped by culture and politics, as well as elements of everyday life and their accompanying foibles. Not immune from this scene is the national pastime, which has been affected for more than a century by ongoing controversies of race, women's struggle for equal rights, evolving attitudes among many segments of the population, and, in more recent times, an increased sensitivity for those who are handicapped.

In the period from the late 1970s through the end of the following decade, baseball was overlaid by these events and circumstances, all part and parcel of the new developments and changes in the country, if not the world at large. The factors related to this dynamic continuum comprise but a narrow band of baseball's rich history. Yet, they capture the essence of the age. They also constituted another stepping-stone as the game coursed through the modern era.

AFTERWORD

The topics presented in the preceding chapters gave their own texture and contours to baseball during the baker's dozen's worth of years that comprise the onset of the free-agency era. Other periods of the game's long history have been colored by their own respective quirks, traits, trials, and tribulations, but of more immediacy within the entirety of these pages are the major themes readily identifiable with the late 1970s and the decade that followed. That baseball's popularity in this period continued to flourish is a testimony to its durability in withstanding the severe turbulence it encountered while making that upward journey.

As the national pastime weathered the challenges of labor unrest and the eternal struggle with regard to salaries and revenue, proving that the game was not going to be ruined by exorbitant player paychecks, baseball entered a new phase of maturity in the latter part of the twentieth century. The fever gripping so many fans seemed to run on a parallel track with a restoration of America's confidence in the 1980s. Changing attitudes, hubris, and self-indulgence, all of which were found in the country's society at large, came with their own consequences to infect the national pastime. Yet, these characteristics burnished this age with its own uniqueness. At the beginning of that decade, few saw the coming demise of multipurpose stadiums, and only a like number may have recognized the pernicious steroid issue in a rudimentary form. These are areas offering fodder for deeper examinations to be written about baseball's history in the 1990s and beyond.

Shedding degrees of innocence with each passing generation, baseball in this latest stage of modernity surmounted difficulties, reaped rewards, and dispelled any notion that it was falling out of favor with the American public. Fans were in a forgiving mood following the disruption of the 1981 schedule by a mid-season strike, and they resumed flocking to stadiums once labor peace was restored. The cocaine scandal that broke shortly thereafter became another link in a chain of misfortunes to taint the game, but enthusiasm demonstrated by the game's devotees showed the degree of resilience inherent in baseball.

By the end of the 1980s, the triumph of small-market teams put the lie to the theory that success belonged only to the big-city clubs or those with deep pockets. Fans in New York, Philadelphia, and Los Angeles celebrated World Series wins, but they toasted champions in Baltimore and Oakland, too. Faithful followers in the greater Midwest were rewarded when St. Louis, Detroit, Kansas City, and Minnesota delivered the Commissioner's Trophy to their towns. And although it became evident that no dynasties were in the making, hope sprang eternal that there was legitimate reason for optimism for many fans throughout the United States and Canada at the dawn of a new season because maybe this would be *the* year for their team.

Through it all, baseball's marketing efforts put ever-increasing amounts of merchandise in the hands of fans who turned into shoppers anxious to show their team spirit by donning a new cap and T-shirt or otherwise putting to good use some product bearing the logo of their favorite club. And while all of this was taking place, the influences of society continued to run concurrently to impact the game through equality issues related to race, gender, and handicapped awareness emblematic of a new focus on cultural diversity.

From 1977 through 1989, baseball enjoyed a most healthy growth spurt that enabled it to not only survive, but also thrive. As the national pastime exhibited strength to withstand an assortment of body blows—most of these were self-inflicted, it should be noted—its adaptation to the pressures and effects of modern times enabled and facilitated a transition into the latest portion of the twentieth century, not least of which included the realization of expansion efforts that failed to bear fruit in the 1980s but would ultimately bring the game to still more people in the decade that followed.

This heady period was comprised of halcyon days particular to its own circumstances, and several decades later it is the subject of nostalgic discussions similar to those that were evoked by a different generation of fans recollecting how baseball was in the 1950s or 1960s. Contemporaneous days become the "good old days" in a later era, and time moves on to make its own new memories in the process.

NOTES

PREFACE

1. Joe Marcin, Larry Wigge, Carl Clark, and Larry Vickery, eds., *Official Baseball Guide for 1978* (St. Louis, MO: Sporting News, 1978), 309.

1. THE FIGHT OVER LABOR

1. "Let the Buyer Beware," *Sporting News*, July 16, 1977, 15.
2. Murray Chass, "Jackson Signs Yankee Contract for Five Years and $2.9 Million," *New York Times*, November 30, 1976, 47.
3. Bill Veeck, quoted in Ken Denlinger, "Falling Angels," *Washington Post*, July 6, 1977.
4. Paul Dickson, *Bill Veeck: Baseball's Greatest Maverick* (New York: Walker & Company, 2012), 303.
5. Dickson, *Bill Veeck*, 303.
6. Abdul Jabil, quoted in Jack Lang, "Bostock, Seven Others Await Re-Entry Bonanza," *Sporting News*, November 19, 1977, 46.
7. Calvin Griffith, quoted in Rod Carew, with Ira Berkow, *Carew* (New York: Simon & Schuster, 1979), 227.
8. Calvin Griffith, quoted in Bob Fowler, "Calvin Sinks to Knees, Riddled by Twindom," *Sporting News*, October 21, 1978, 23.
9. John Helyar, *Lords of the Realm: The Real History of Baseball* (New York: Ballantine, 1994), 308.
10. Bowie Kuhn, quoted in Dan Levitt, "Figuring Out Free Agency," in Steve Weingarten and Bill Nowlin, eds., *Baseball's Business: The Winter Meetings,*

Volume 2, 1958—2016 (Phoenix, AZ: Society for American Baseball Research, 2017), 122.

11. Al Rosen, quoted in Jerome Holtzman, "More Than 40 Million Caught 'Baseball Fever,'" in Joe Marcin, Larry Wigge, Carl Clark, Craig Carter, and Larry Vickery, eds., *Official Baseball Guide for 1979* (St. Louis, MO: Sporting News, 1979), 310.

12. Associated Press story, June 17, 1981.

13. Marvin Miller, quoted in Jerome Holtzman, "More Than 40 Million Caught 'Baseball Fever,'" in Joe Marcin, Larry Wigge, Carl Clark, Craig Carter, and Larry Vickery, eds., *Official Baseball Guide for 1979* (St. Louis, MO: Sporting News, 1979), 311.

14. George Steinbrenner, quoted in Jerome Holtzman, "More Than 40 Million Caught 'Baseball Fever,'" in Joe Marcin, Larry Wigge, Carl Clark, Craig Carter, and Larry Vickery, eds., *Official Baseball Guide for 1979* (St. Louis, MO: Sporting News, 1979), 312.

15. Richie Phillips, quoted in Clifford Kachline, "Ump Walkout, Yanks' Troubles Dominated," in Larry Wigge, Carl Clark, Craig Carter, and Joe Marcin, eds., *Official Baseball Guide for 1980* (St. Louis, MO: Sporting News, 1980), 300–301.

16. "San Francisco–New York Box Score," *Sporting News*, May 12, 1979, 21.

17. Furman Bisher, "Where's the Loyalty to Umps?" *Sporting News*, May 5, 1979, 9.

18. Bowie Kuhn, *Hardball: The Education of a Baseball Commissioner* (New York: Times Books, 1987), 206.

19. Minutes of the major-league Executive Council meeting, June 28, 1979, Papers of Bowie K. Kuhn, BAMSS100, National Baseball Hall of Fame Library, National Baseball Hall of Fame, Cooperstown, New York, Series I, Subseries 2, Box 4, Folder 10, Financial Committee, 1978–1982.

20. Memo, John E. Fetzer to Bowie Kuhn, May 17, 1979, Papers of Bowie K. Kuhn, BAMSS100, National Baseball Hall of Fame Library, National Baseball Hall of Fame, Cooperstown, New York, Series IV, Subseries 3, Box 15, Folder 19, Memo: Big Spending. Emphasis added.

21. Memo, C. Raymond Grebey to Chief Executive Officers, August 26, 1981, Papers of Bowie K. Kuhn, BAMSS100, National Baseball Hall of Fame Library, National Baseball Hall of Fame, Cooperstown, New York, Series I, Subseries 2, Box 4, Folder 10, Financial Committee.

22. Kuhn, *Hardball*, 333.

23. Marvin Miller, *A Whole Different Ball Game: The Sport and Business of Baseball* (New York: Birch Lane Press, 1991), 285.

24. Miller, *A Whole Different Ball Game*, 290.

25. Strike advertisement, Major League Executive Council Meeting, March 24, 1980, Papers of Bowie K. Kuhn, BAMSS100, National Baseball Hall of Fame Library, National Baseball Hall of Fame, Cooperstown, New York, Series I, Subseries 1, Box 2, Folder 3, Executive Council Meetings, 1980–1981.

26. Player quotes memo, Major League Executive Council Meeting, n.d., Papers of Bowie K. Kuhn, BAMSS100, National Baseball Hall of Fame Library, National Baseball Hall of Fame, Cooperstown, New York, Series I, Subseries 1, Box 2, Folder 3, Executive Council Meetings, 1980–1981.

27. Murray Chass, "A Breather for Baseball," *Sporting News*, June 7, 1980, 9.

28. Murray Chass, "Plan for Compensation Study Is Basis of Pact," *Sporting News*, June 7, 1980, 9. Emphasis added.

29. Dave Distel, "Winfield Has Padres Checking Dollars and Sense," *Los Angeles Times*, March 1, 1980, 1.

30. Associated Press story, July 12, 1980.

31. Clifford Kachline, "Labor Strife, Big Salaries Topped '80 News," in Larry Wigge, Carl Clark, Craig Carter, and Joe Marcin, eds., *Official Baseball Guide for 1981* (St. Louis, MO: Sporting News, 1981), 310. The website baseball-reference.com shows gaps in the years Winfield was under contract to the Yankees, but his package would seem to approach $20 million. Why a salary this high warranted a cost-of-living benefit as part of the package was not explained.

32. Ken Picking, "A 'Shocking' Pact for Claudell," *Sporting News*, November 29, 1980, 48.

33. "Major League Flashes," *Sporting News*, September 6, 1980, 32.

34. Bake McBride, quoted in Hal Bodley, "Bake's Knees Ache, But His Bat Smokes," *Sporting News*, August 16, 1980, 21.

35. "Kuhn Remarks at Seminar," August 13, 1980, Papers of Bowie K. Kuhn, BAMSS100, National Baseball Hall of Fame Library, National Baseball Hall of Fame, Cooperstown, New York, Series I, Subseries 2, Box 4, Folder 10, Financial Committee.

36. Marvin Miller, quoted in Ralph Ray, "A Strike? Players Must Act Fast," *Sporting News*, March 7, 1981, 13.

37. Clifford Kachline, "Baseball Takes Lumps, Survives Stormy, Strike-Plagued Season," in Larry Wigge, Carl Clark, Dave Sloan, Craig Carter, and Barry Siegel, eds., *Official Baseball Guide for 1982* (St. Louis, MO: Sporting News, 1982), 5.

38. Kachline, "Baseball Takes Lumps," 5.

39. Ray Grebey, quoted in Kachline, "Baseball Takes Lumps," 6.

40. Murray Chass, "Owners Reject Player-Pool Plan," *Sporting News*, June 20, 1981, 13. Emphasis added. See also *Silverman v. Major League Baseball Player Relations Committee, Inc.*, 516 F. Supp. 588, 589 (S.D.N.Y. 1981).

41. Minutes, June 10, 1981, Executive Council Meeting, Papers of Bowie K. Kuhn, BAMSS100, National Baseball Hall of Fame Library, National Baseball Hall of Fame, Cooperstown, New York, Series I, Subseries 1, Box 2, Folder 3, Financial Committee. Kuhn's marginalia—"Judge Werker 6/10/81"—provides the only clue to the origin of this single-page document.

42. Kuhn, *Hardball*, 343.

43. Ed Farmer, quoted in Ralph Ray, "Players Pay Up to Get Home," *Sporting News*, June 27, 1981, 3.

44. Miller, *A Whole Different Ball Game*, 302, 303.

45. Letters to "Voice of the Fan," *Sporting News*, June 13–20, 1981, 6.

46. Milton Richman, UPI column, June 18, 1981.

47. Joe Marcin, "TSN Readers Speak Out on Strike," *Sporting News*, July 18, 1981, 24.

48. Kachline, "Baseball Takes Lumps," 7.

49. Ray Grebey, "Answers to Your Questions," 1981 booklet, Papers of Bowie K. Kuhn, BAMSS100, National Baseball Hall of Fame Library, National Baseball Hall of Fame, Cooperstown, New York, Series II, Subseries 2, Box 3, Folder 8.

50. Randy Galloway, "Season Over, Chiles Thinks," *Sporting News*, August 1, 1981, 31.

51. Kachline, "Baseball Takes Lumps," 8.

52. Miller, *A Whole Different Ball Game*, 312.

53. Larry Wigge, "Deprived Fans Go Star Crazy," in Larry Wigge, Carl Clark, Dave Sloan, Craig Carter, and Barry Siegel, eds., *Official Baseball Guide for 1982* (St. Louis, MO: Sporting News, 1982), 207.

54. Kuhn, *Hardball*, 361.

55. Helyar, *Lords of the Realm*, 307.

56. John Maes, "Voice of the Fan," *Sporting News*, August 22, 1981, 6.

57. Helyar, *Lords of the Realm*, 343.

58. Miller, *A Whole Different Ball Game*, 325.

59. Clifford Kachline, "Drug Problem Throws Cloud over Bright Baseball Picture," in Joe Hoppel, ed., *Official Baseball Guide for 1984* (St. Louis, MO: Sporting News, 1984), 16.

60. Kachline, "Drug Problem Throws Cloud over Bright Baseball Picture," 16.

61. Clifford Kachline, "Selection of Commissioner Highlights Year in Baseball," in Dave Sloan, ed., *Official Baseball Guide for 1985* (St. Louis, MO: Sporting News, 1985), 7.

62. Helyar, *Lords of the Realm*, 348.

63. Miller, *A Whole Different Ball Game*, 388.

64. "Our Opinion," *Sporting News*, August 12, 1985, 7.

65. Murray Chass, "Peace Be with Baseball," *Sporting News*, August 19, 1985, 3.

66. Chass, "Peace Be with Baseball," 3.

67. Miller, *A Whole Different Ball Game*, 335.

68. Clifford Kachline, "Big Individual Performances Highlight Exciting '86 Season," in Dave Sloan, ed., *Official Baseball Guide for 1987* (St. Louis, MO: Sporting News, 1987), 9.

69. Peter Ueberroth, quoted in Helyar, *Lords of the Realm*, 355.

70. Ed Edmonds and Frank G. Houdek, *Baseball Meets the Law: A Chronology of Decisions, Statutes, and Other Legal Events* (Jefferson, NC: McFarland, 2017), 138.

71. Edmonds and Houdek, *Baseball Meets the Law*, 143.

2. MONEY, MONEY, MONEY

1. Buster Olney, *The Last Night of the Yankee Dynasty: The Game, the Team, and the Cost of Greatness* (New York: Ecco, 2004), 27.

2. baseball-reference.com. (accessed May 21, 2019).

3. Meeting minutes, December 9, 1980, Papers of Bowie K. Kuhn, BAMSS100, National Baseball Hall of Fame Library, National Baseball Hall of Fame, Cooperstown, New York, Series I, Subseries 1, Box 2, Folder 2, Executive Council Meetings.

4. Meeting minutes, June 3, 1982, Papers of Bowie K. Kuhn, BAMSS100, National Baseball Hall of Fame Library, National Baseball Hall of Fame, Cooperstown, New York, Series I, Subseries 1, Box 2, Folder 5, Executive Council Meetings.

5. James Edward Miller, *The Baseball Business: Pursuing Pennants and Profits in Baltimore* (Chapel Hill: University of North Carolina Press, 1990), 275.

6. Tom Villante, "Revenue Sharing, Telecommunications," November 19, 1980, Papers of Bowie K. Kuhn, BAMSS100, National Baseball Hall of Fame Library, National Baseball Hall of Fame, Cooperstown, New York, Series I, Subseries 1, Box 2, Folder 2, Executive Council Meetings.

7. Tom Villante, "Revenue Sharing, Telecommunications," November 19, 1980, Papers of Bowie K. Kuhn, BAMSS100, National Baseball Hall of Fame Library, National Baseball Hall of Fame, Cooperstown, New York, Series I, Subseries 1, Box 2, Folder 2, Executive Council Meetings.

8. Memo, "Negotiating Climate," October 12, 1982, Papers of Bowie K. Kuhn, BAMSS100, National Baseball Hall of Fame Library, National Baseball Hall of Fame, Cooperstown, New York, Series IV, Subseries 2, Box 7, Folder 3,

Contract Negotiations—NBC and ABC, 1983. Emphasis added; Villante, "Revenue Sharing, Telecommunications."

9. Villante, "Revenue Sharing, Telecommunications."

10. William Y. Giles to Bowie Kuhn, January 19, 1981, Papers of Bowie K. Kuhn, BAMSS100, National Baseball Hall of Fame Library, National Baseball Hall of Fame, Cooperstown, New York, Series IV, Subseries 2, Box 9, Folder 18, TV and Radio.

11. Bowie Kuhn, Eddie Einhorn, and Bill Giles, "Local Pay TV," May 10, 1983, Papers of Bowie K. Kuhn, BAMSS100, National Baseball Hall of Fame Library, National Baseball Hall of Fame, Cooperstown, New York, Series I, Subseries 1, Box 3, Folder 3, Executive Council Meeting—NYC.

12. William Y. Giles to Bowie Kuhn, March 4, 1981, Papers of Bowie K. Kuhn, BAMSS100, National Baseball Hall of Fame Library, National Baseball Hall of Fame, Cooperstown, New York, Series IV, Subseries 2, Box 9, Folder 18, TV and Radio.

13. Meeting minutes, February 16–17, 1982, Papers of Bowie K. Kuhn, BAMSS100, National Baseball Hall of Fame Library, National Baseball Hall of Fame, Cooperstown, New York, Series I, Subseries 1, Box 2, Folder 5, Executive Council Meetings. Emphasis added.

14. Meeting minutes, May 10, 1982, Papers of Bowie K. Kuhn, BAMSS100, National Baseball Hall of Fame Library, National Baseball Hall of Fame, Cooperstown, New York, Series I, Subseries 1, Box 2, Folder 5, Executive Council Meetings.

15. Statement of R. E. Turner III, April 28, 1982, Papers of Bowie K. Kuhn, BAMSS100, National Baseball Hall of Fame Library, National Baseball Hall of Fame, Cooperstown, New York, Series I, Subseries 1, Box 2, Folder 10, Executive Council Meeting—NYC.

16. Meeting minutes, February 16–17, 1982, Papers of Bowie K. Kuhn. Emphasis added.

17. Meeting minutes, February 16–17, 1982, Papers of Bowie K. Kuhn.

18. Ed Edmonds and Frank G. Houdek, *Baseball Meets the Law: A Chronology of Decisions, Statutes, and Other Legal Events* (Jefferson, NC: McFarland, 2017), 136.

19. "Analysis of Claims Made by Players Association Re: Major League Baseball Broadcasting Revenues," April 21, 1982, Papers of Bowie K. Kuhn, BAMSS100, National Baseball Hall of Fame Library, National Baseball Hall of Fame, Cooperstown, New York, Series III, Subseries 3, Box 5, Folder 4, Major League Meeting—Chicago.

20. Edmonds and Houdek, *Baseball Meets the Law*, 136.

21. Clifford Kachline, "Big Individual Performances Highlight Exciting '86 Season," in Dave Sloan, ed., *Official Baseball Guide for 1987* (St. Louis, MO: Sporting News, 1987), 11.

22. Ballard Smith, "Revenue Sharing Report," n.d., Papers of Bowie K. Kuhn, BAMSS100, National Baseball Hall of Fame Library, National Baseball Hall of Fame, Cooperstown, New York, Series I, Subseries 2, Box 6, Folder 2, Revenue Sharing Committee Meeting. Although this report is not dated, the folder containing it is dated April 27, 1982.

23. Smith, "Revenue Sharing Report."

24. Smith, "Revenue Sharing Report."

25. Smith, "Revenue Sharing Report."

26. Smith, "Revenue Sharing Report."

27. James E. Walter, "Revenue from the Sale of Radio and T.V. Broadcasting Rights: 1976–1982," n.d., Papers of Bowie K. Kuhn, BAMSS100, National Baseball Hall of Fame Library, National Baseball Hall of Fame, Cooperstown, New York, Series I, Subseries 2, Box 6, Folder 2, Revenue Sharing Committee Meeting.

28. Ed Durso to Bowie Kuhn, May 5, 1982, Papers of Bowie K. Kuhn, BAMSS100, National Baseball Hall of Fame Library, National Baseball Hall of Fame, Cooperstown, New York, Series I, Subseries 1, Box 2, Folder 10, Executive Council Meeting.

29. Lea Winfrey, "Just How Sick Is the NBC-TV Network?" *Philadelphia Inquirer*, January 30, 1983.

30. Dick Brescia to Bowie Kuhn, August 26, 1983, Papers of Bowie K. Kuhn, BAMSS100, National Baseball Hall of Fame Library, National Baseball Hall of Fame, Cooperstown, New York, Series IV, Subseries 2, Box 11, Folder 3, TV and Radio; Meeting minutes, May 24, 1984, Papers of Bowie K. Kuhn, BAMSS100, National Baseball Hall of Fame Library, National Baseball Hall of Fame, Cooperstown, New York, Series III, Subseries 2, Box 2, Folder 7, Special Joint Meeting—Chicago.

31. Sandra Salmans, "Hollywood Takes on HBO," *New York Times*, February 3, 1983; Meeting minutes, January 26, 1983, Papers of Bowie K. Kuhn, BAMSS100, National Baseball Hall of Fame Library, National Baseball Hall of Fame, Cooperstown, New York, Series I, Subseries 1, Box 2, Folder 7, Executive Council Meetings.

32. Jane Leavy, "Baseball Making Plans for Pay-Cable TV Network," *Washington Post*, April 13, 1983.

33. "TV Deal Might Save Kuhn," *USA Today*, March 9, 1983, 2C.

34. Turner quoted in Associated Press story, April 19,1983.

35. Press release, April 22, 1983, Papers of Bowie K. Kuhn, BAMSS100, National Baseball Hall of Fame Library, National Baseball Hall of Fame, Cooperstown, New York, Series IV, Subseries 2, Box 9, Folder 16, TV and Radio.

36. Bill Giles to Bowie Kuhn, May 30, 1984, Papers of Bowie K. Kuhn, BAMSS100, National Baseball Hall of Fame Library, National Baseball Hall of Fame, Cooperstown, New York, Series IV, Subseries 2, Box 9, Folder 5, Memo—A Pay Channel.

37. Peter Gammons, "A.L. Beat," *Sporting News*, May 13, 1985, 23.

38. Peter Gammons, "A.L. Beat," *Sporting News*, August 26, 1985, 42.

39. "A Tough Off-Season Agenda," *Sporting News*, November 4, 1985, 8; Moss Klein, "A. L. Beat," *Sporting News*, April 17, 1989, 14.

40. Fay Vincent, quoted in Dave Nightingale, "Vincent: Baseball Obligated to Continue as Public Service," *Sporting News*, February 12, 1990, 9.

41. Chuck Adams to Bowie Kuhn, August 26, 1982, Papers of Bowie K. Kuhn, BAMSS100, National Baseball Hall of Fame Library, National Baseball Hall of Fame, Cooperstown, New York, Series VI, Subseries 3, Box 15, Folder 11, Financial Information/*Newsweek* Interview.

42. Dave Nightingale, "Heading Toward a Black Hole?" *Sporting News*, December 31, 1990, 28.

43. Nightingale, "Heading Toward a Black Hole?" 29.

44. Kenneth Winter and Michael J. Haupert, "MLB Leaks Financial Statements: A Factual Analysis," in William M. Simons, ed., *The Cooperstown Symposium on Baseball and American Culture, 2011–2012* (Jefferson, NC: McFarland, 2013), 100.

45. Meeting minutes, March 6, 1980, Papers of Bowie K. Kuhn, BAMSS100, National Baseball Hall of Fame Library, National Baseball Hall of Fame, Cooperstown, New York, Series I, Subseries 1, Box 2, Folder 2, Executive Council Meetings.

46. "1980 Financial Information Questionnaire," Papers of Bowie K. Kuhn, BAMSS100, National Baseball Hall of Fame Library, National Baseball Hall of Fame, Cooperstown, New York, Series I, Subseries 2, Box 4, Folder 10, Financial Committee.

47. Meeting minutes, September 8, 1980, Papers of Bowie K. Kuhn, BAMSS100, National Baseball Hall of Fame Library, National Baseball Hall of Fame, Cooperstown, New York, Series I, Subseries 1, Box 2, Folder 2, Executive Council Meetings.

48. Meeting minutes, September 8, 1980. Emphasis added.

49. George Steinbrenner to Leland S. MacPhail, September 16, 1980, Papers of Bowie K. Kuhn, BAMSS100, National Baseball Hall of Fame Library, National Baseball Hall of Fame, Cooperstown, New York, Series I, Subseries 2, Box 4, Folder 10, Financial Committee.

50. "Report of Finance Committee," June 14, 1982, Papers of Bowie K. Kuhn, BAMSS100, National Baseball Hall of Fame Library, National Baseball Hall of Fame, Cooperstown, New York, Series I, Subseries 1, Box 2, Folder 11, Executive Council Meeting.

51. Executive Council notes, Exhibit A, June 14, 1982, Papers of Bowie K. Kuhn, BAMSS100, National Baseball Hall of Fame Library, National Baseball Hall of Fame, Cooperstown, New York, Series I, Subseries 1, Box 2, Folder 11, Executive Council Meeting.

52. Bowie Kuhn, Charles S. Feeney, and Leland S. MacPhail to major-league clubs, January 6, 1983, Papers of Bowie K. Kuhn, BAMSS100, National Baseball Hall of Fame Library, National Baseball Hall of Fame, Cooperstown, New York, Series I, Subseries 1, Box 3, Folder 1, Executive Council Meeting.

53. Ernst & Whinney to Bowie Kuhn, August 13, 1984, Papers of Bowie K. Kuhn, BAMSS100, National Baseball Hall of Fame Library, National Baseball Hall of Fame, Cooperstown, New York, Series VI, Subseries 7, Box 25, Folder 6, Audited Financial Statements for MLB.

54. MLB consolidated condensed income statement exhibit C-2, December 8, 1981, Papers of Bowie K. Kuhn, BAMSS100, National Baseball Hall of Fame Library, National Baseball Hall of Fame, Cooperstown, New York, Series I, Subseries 1, Box 2, Folder 5, Executive Council Meeting; "Combined Summary of Operations," n.d., Papers of Bowie K. Kuhn, BAMSS100, National Baseball Hall of Fame Library, National Baseball Hall of Fame, Cooperstown, New York, Series VI, Subseries 7, Box 25, Folder 5, Audited Financial Statements for MLB.

55. "Schedule IV," 1983 season, Papers of Bowie K. Kuhn, BAMSS100, National Baseball Hall of Fame Library, National Baseball Hall of Fame, Cooperstown, New York, Series VI, Subseries 7, Box 25, Folder 6, Audited Financial Statements for MLB.

56. "Combined Summary of Operations," n.d., Papers of Bowie K. Kuhn, BAMSS100, National Baseball Hall of Fame Library, National Baseball Hall of Fame, Cooperstown, New York, Series I, Subseries 2, Box 4, Folder 10, Financial Committee; Series VI, Subseries 7, Box 25, Folders 5, 6, Audited Financial Statements.

57. "Combined Summary of Operations," n.d., Papers of Bowie K. Kuhn, BAMSS100, National Baseball Hall of Fame Library, National Baseball Hall of Fame, Cooperstown, New York, Series I, Subseries 2, Box 4, Folder 10, Financial Committee; Series VI, Subseries 7, Box 25, Folders 5, 6, Audited Financial Statements.

58. Bowie Kuhn, quoted in Clifford Kachline, "Labor Strife, Big Salaries Topped '80 News," in Larry Wigge, Carl Clark, Craig Carter, and Joe Marcin, eds., *Official Baseball Guide for 1981* (St. Louis, MO: Sporting News, 1981), 297.

59. Kachline, "Labor Strife, Big Salaries Topped '80 News," 311.

60. Dusty Baker, quoted in Kachline, "Labor Strife, Big Salaries Topped '80 News," 311.

61. Kachline, "Labor Strife, Big Salaries Topped '80 News," 312–13.

3. A TALE OF THREE COMMISSIONERS

1. Bowie Kuhn, quoted in Clifford Kachline, "Baseball Takes Lumps, Survives Stormy, Strike-Plagued Season," in Larry Wigge, Carl Clark, Dave Sloan, Craig Carter, and Barry Siegel, eds., *Official Baseball Guide for 1982* (St. Louis, MO: Sporting News, 1982), 24.

2. Jerome Holtzman, "Owners Telling Kuhn to Cut Back Powers If He Wants to Stay," *Chicago Tribune*, October 18, 1981, Section 4, 2.

3. Bowie Kuhn, *Hardball: The Education of a Baseball Commissioner* (New York: Times Books, 1987), 9.

4. Kuhn, *Hardball*, 9.

5. Kuhn, *Hardball*, 366.

6. Kuhn, *Hardball*, 11.

7. E. J. Bavasi to Bud Selig, December 14, 1982, Papers of Bowie K. Kuhn, BAMSS100, National Baseball Hall of Fame Library, National Baseball Hall of Fame, Cooperstown, New York, Series VI, Subseries 1, Box 4, Folder 5, Kuhn Departure from Office.

8. L. S. MacPhail to Dan Galbreath, June 15, 1983, Papers of Bowie K. Kuhn, BAMSS100, National Baseball Hall of Fame Library, National Baseball Hall of Fame, Cooperstown, New York, Series VI, Subseries 1, Box 8, Folder 5, BKK Personal Notebooks.

9. Kuhn, *Hardball*, 416.

10. Kuhn, *Hardball*, 426.

11. Murray Chass, "Kuhn Reportedly to Stay in Post until Sept. 30," *New York Times*, March 3, 1984, 19.

12. Bill Conlin, "N.L. Beat," *Sporting News*, February 20, 1984, 36.

13. Dick Young, "Young Ideas," *Sporting News*, August 27, 1984, 7.

14. "Kuhn's Legacy Recognized," *Baltimore Morning Sun*, July 11, 1984, 1E

15. Associated Press release, September 1984, Papers of Bowie K. Kuhn, BAMSS100, National Baseball Hall of Fame Library, National Baseball Hall of Fame, Cooperstown, New York, Series VI, Subseries 1, Box 4, Folder 14, Information Department.

16. Murray Chass, "Bowie Kuhn: He Gave Baseball a Corporate Image," *Inside Sports*, November 1984.

17. Jerry Reinsdorf, quoted in Dave Nightingale, "Concessions Strengthen Ueberroth Post," *Sporting News*, March 12, 1984, 53.

18. "Our Opinion," *Sporting News*, March 19, 1984, 6.

19. Broadcast excerpt transcript, Radio TV Reports, Inc., September 1, 1984, Papers of Bowie K. Kuhn, BAMSS100, National Baseball Hall of Fame Library, National Baseball Hall of Fame, Cooperstown, New York, Series VI, Subseries 1, Box 8, Folder 5, BKK Personal Notebooks.

20. Ed Durso to Bowie Kuhn, August 31, 1984, Papers of Bowie K. Kuhn, BAMSS100, National Baseball Hall of Fame Library, National Baseball Hall of Fame, Cooperstown, New York, Series III, Subseries 3, Box 7, Folder 1, Meeting Agendas.

21. Bowie Kuhn to Peter Ueberroth, August 31, 1984, Papers of Bowie K. Kuhn, BAMSS100, National Baseball Hall of Fame Library, National Baseball Hall of Fame, Cooperstown, New York, Series III, Subseries 3, Box 7, Folder 1, Meeting Agendas.

22. Roy J. Harris Jr., "Summer Olympics Operated at Surplus Totaling $150 Million," *Wall Street Journal*, September 12, 1984.

23. Steve Hershey, "Ueberroth Gets Baptism by Fire," *USA Today*, October 2, 1984.

24. Peter Ueberroth, quoted in George Vecsey, "The Grace of Steve Garvey," *New York Times*, October 10, 1984, B13.

25. Peter Ueberroth, quoted in Dave Nightingale, "Peter V. Ueberroth," *Sporting News*, June 25, 1984, 40.

26. Leonard Koppett, "Ueberroth Faces Different Kind of Authority in His New Post," *Sporting News*, August 27, 1984, 9.

27. Tom Bradley, quoted in Bella Stumbo, "Ueberroth: 'Ruthless and Shy,'" *Los Angeles Times*, June 24, 1984.

28. Koppett, "Ueberroth Faces Different Kind of Authority in His New Post," 9.

29. Peter Ueberroth, quoted in Larry King, "Ueberroth: Game Can't Rest on Laurels," *Sporting News*, December 10, 1984, 12.

30. Ross E. Davies, "1984—Superstationary," in Steve Weingarten and Bill Nowlin, eds., *Baseball's Business: The Winter Meetings, Volume 2, 1958–2016* (Phoenix, AZ: Society for American Baseball Research, 2017), 171.

31. Mark Heisler, "New Commissioner Just Might Take Two and Then Hit to Right," *Los Angeles Times*, September 20, 1984.

32. Robert Ajemian, "Master of The Games," *Time*, January 7, 1985, 36.

33. George Steinbrenner, quoted in Julie Ward, "Ueberroth Strikes Again," *USA Today*, March 19, 1985, 1C, 2C.

34. Maury Allen, "Kenesaw Would Have Loved Ubie," *New York Post*, August 9, 1985, 101.

35. Hal Lancaster, "Despite the Adulation, Baseball's Ueberroth Is Facing Tough Game," *Wall Street Journal*, October 18, 1985, 1.

36. Kuhn, *Hardball*, 329.

37. John Helyar, *Lords of the Realm: The Real History of Baseball* (New York: Ballantine, 1994), 336.

38. Phil Pepe, "Ubie, Aaron Gaffes Mar Awards Dinner," *New York Daily News*, January 29, 1987.

39. John Nelson, "Ueberroth Meets with Rev. Jackson," *Albany (NY) Times Union*, April 21, 1987, D2.

40. Peter Ueberroth, quoted in Dave Nightingale, "'Iron Fist' Going Back in the Glove," *Sporting News*, January 5, 1987, 54.

41. Joe Gergen, "Airport Metal Detectors in On-Deck Circles?" *Sporting News*, August 24, 1978, 10.

42. Helyar, *Lords of the Realm*, 341.

43. Helyar, *Lords of the Realm*, 341, 343.

44. Dave Nightingale, "Ueberroth a One-Term Commissioner," *Sporting News*, December 21, 1987, 44.

45. Memo to major-league owners, June 7, 1988, Papers of Bowie K. Kuhn, BAMSS100, National Baseball Hall of Fame Library, National Baseball Hall of Fame, Cooperstown, New York, Series VIII, Box 5, Folder 33, Peter Ueberroth.

46. Peter Ueberroth, quoted in Dave Nightingale, "Ueberroth's Farewell Warning," *Sporting News*, January 2, 1989, 61.

47. Memo to major-league owners.

48. Ronald Blum, "Ueberroth Won't Serve Second Term," *Albany (NY) Times Union*, June 8, 1988, D1.

49. Mark Whicker, "What Did Ueberroth Do for Game?" *Albany (NY) Times Union*, December 7, 1988.

50. Ed Edmonds and Frank G. Houdek, *Baseball Meets the Law: A Chronology of Decisions, Statutes, and Other Legal Events* (Jefferson, NC: McFarland, 2017), 142–43.

51. Helyar, *Lords of the Realm*, 363.

52. Phil Mushnick, "Equal Time," *New York Post*, October 7, 1988, 114.

53. George Steinbrenner, quoted in "Boss: Ubie bailed out on MLB," *New York Post*, June 29, 1989.

54. Bob Verdi, "Did Ueberroth Pass a Torch or a Live Grenade?" *Sporting News*, May 8, 1989, 5.

55. Robert P. Moncreiff, *Bart Giamatti: A Profile* (New Haven, CT: Yale University Press, 2007), 8–9.

56. Moncreiff, *Bart Giamatti*, 14.

57. Bart Giamatti, quoted in Moncreiff, *Bart Giamatti*, 70.

58. Moncreiff, *Bart Giamatti*, 75.

59. Dave Nightingale, "Trades May Steal Show at Nashville," *Sporting News*, December 5, 1983, 44.

60. Untitled article, *New Haven Register*, September 28, 1984, 1, A. Bartlett Giamatti Folder, National Baseball Hall of Fame Library, National Baseball Hall of Fame, Cooperstown, New York.

61. Moncreiff, *Bart Giamatti*, 136.

62. Moncreiff, *Bart Giamatti*, 139.

63. John Thorn, ed., *The Armchair Book of Baseball II* (New York: Charles Scribner's Sons, 1987), ix. Emphasis added.

64. Giamatti quoted in Hal Bodley, "New NL President Avoiding Party Line," *USA Today*, June 13, 1986, 8C.

65. Peter Pascarelli, "Sure, Rose Was Wrong, But He Wasn't Alone," *Sporting News*, May 16, 1988, 24.

66. Pete Rose, quoted in Hal McCoy, "Rose: 30-Day Penalty Overkill," *Sporting News*, May 16, 1988, 49.

67. "Our Opinion," *Sporting News*, September 19, 1988, 4.

68. A. Bartlett Giamatti, "The Story of Baseball: You Can Go Home Again," *New York Times*, April 2, 1989, S10.

69. Clifford Kachline, "The Unusual and Unexpected Became the Norm in Tragic '89," in Dave Sloan, ed., *Official Baseball Guide for 1990* (St. Louis, MO: Sporting News, 1990), 11.

70. Associated Press release, September 1, 1989, A. Bartlett Giamatti Folder, National Baseball Hall of Fame Library, National Baseball Hall of Fame, Cooperstown, New York.

71. Jerry Izenberg, "Baseball Fans Lost a Friend," *New York Post*, September 3, 1989, 74.

72. "A Torch Passed between Friends," *Washington Post*, September 3, 1989.

73. David Bohmer, e-mail to author, June 25, 2019.

74. Bohmer, e-mail to author, June 25, 2019.

75. David Bohmer, e-mail to author, July 20, 2019.

76. Kuhn, *Hardball*, 440.

4. THE PERVASION OF DRUGS

1. "Texas League Notes," *Sporting News*, September 8, 1948, 28.

2. "Quotes" column, *Sporting News*, December 20, 1950, 23; Roscoe McGowen, "Jackie a Tennyson Brook? He's Ready for Another Run," *Sporting News*, April 6, 1955, 10.

3. *Avant Garde* advertisement, *Sporting News*, October 28, 1967, 11. Only 14 issues would be published from January 1968 through July 1971.

4. "Caught on the Fly," *Sporting News*, February 14, 1970, 46.

5. Jim Bouton, *Ball Four*, 20th anniversary ed., edited by Leonard Schecter (New York: Wiley, 1990), 157.

6. Bob DiPietro, "Players Pledge Support of Kuhn's Antidrug Drive," *Sporting News*, March 20, 1971, 54.

7. Paul Gardner, "Drug Usage in Sports—A Delicate Problem," *Sporting News*, December 11, 1971, 39.

8. Bowie Kuhn, *Hardball: The Education of a Baseball Commissioner* (New York: Times Books, 1987), 304.

9. Bob Addie, *Sporting News*, February 6, 1971, 14.

10. Matt Mitchell, "Rozelle's Dope Crackdown Blasted by Garvey," *Sporting News*, May 18, 1974, 53.

11. Matt Schudel, "Bob Welch, Cy Young-Winning Pitcher Who Overcame Struggles with Alcohol, Dies at 57," *Washington Post*, June 10, 2014, https://www.washingtonpost.com/sports/bob-welch-cy-young-winning-pitcher-who-overcame-struggles-with-alcohol-dies-at-57/2014/06/10/ba9f92a6-f0d2-11e3-9ebc-2ee6f81ed217_story.html (accessed July 30, 2019).

12. Executive Council meeting minutes, December 9, 1980, Papers of Bowie K. Kuhn, BAMSS100, National Baseball Hall of Fame Library, National Baseball Hall of Fame, Cooperstown, New York, Series I, Subseries 1, Box 2, Folder 2, Executive Council Meeting Minutes.

13. Nathan Michael Corzine, *Team Chemistry: The History of Drugs and Alcohol in Major League Baseball* (Urbana: University of Illinois Press, 2016), 98.

14. Henry Fitzgibbon to Bowie Kuhn, October 22, 1979, Papers of Bowie K. Kuhn, BAMSS100, National Baseball Hall of Fame Library, National Baseball Hall of Fame, Cooperstown, New York, Series III, Subseries 1, Box 1, Folder 2, General Managers Meetings.

15. Henry Fitzgibbon to Bowie Kuhn.

16. Joe Falls, "What Gal Golfers Need Most Is Female Arnie," *Sporting News*, July 9, 1977, 40.

17. Darrell Porter, with William Littlefield, *Snap Me Perfect! The Darrell Porter Story* (Nashville, TN: Thomas Nelson Publishers, 1984), 101.

18. Porter, *Snap Me Perfect!*, 169.

19. Porter, *Snap Me Perfect!*, 185.

20. Glenn Sparks, "Darrell Porter," in Bill Nowlin, ed., *Kansas City Royals: A Royal Tradition* (Phoenix, AZ: Society for American Baseball Research, 2019), 109.

21. Hal Bodley, "Phils 'Scandal' Fizzles Out," *Sporting News*, August 16, 1980, 10.

22. Dick Kaegel, "Little Misuse of Drugs Seen," *Sporting News*, August 16, 1980, 10.

23. See page 39 of the August 23, 1982, issue of *Sporting News* for a typical example.

24. Chris Cobbs, "Increasing Drug Use Is a Big NBA Concern," *Sporting News*, September 6, 1980, 26.

25. Kuhn, *Hardball*, 305.

26. "Judge Wipes Fergie's Record Clean," *Sporting News*, January 3, 1981, 53.

27. Kuhn, *Hardball*, 306.

28. Dave Nightingale, "Recovery at the Meadows Means Treating More Than the Symptoms," *Sporting News*, November 21, 1981, 14.

29. President's Antidrug Program note, n.d., Papers of Bowie K. Kuhn, BAMSS100, National Baseball Hall of Fame Library, National Baseball Hall of Fame, Cooperstown, New York, Series VI, Subseries 1, Box 11, Folder 5, Staff Meeting Notes.

30. "Baseball Cocaine Woes Huge, Says Clinic Chief," *Sporting News*, September 6, 1982, 65.

31. Marvin Miller, *A Whole Different Ball Game: The Sport and Business of Baseball* (New York: Birch Lane Press, 1991), 389.

32. Jim Reeves, "Sample Boots One Talking on Drugs," *Sporting News*, June 13, 1983, 26. Emphasis added.

33. Dave Nightingale, "Sam McDowell Makes His Pitch," *Sporting News*, March 7, 1983, 15.

34. Tommy Lasorda, quoted in Gordon Verrell, "Howe Treated; Landreaux, Too," *Sporting News*, January 31, 1983, 38.

35. Steve Howe, quoted in Verrell, "Howe Treated; Landreaux, Too," 38.

36. Bowie Kuhn to all major-league clubs' chief executive officers et al., July 1, 1983, Papers of Bowie K. Kuhn, BAMSS100, National Baseball Hall of Fame Library, National Baseball Hall of Fame, Cooperstown, New York, Series I, Subseries 1, Box 3, Folder 5, Executive Council Meeting.

37. John Candelaria, quoted in Stan Isle, "Caught on the Fly," *Sporting News*, August 22, 1983, 13.

38. Bowie Kuhn to all major-league players, July 1, 1983, Papers of Bowie K. Kuhn, BAMSS100, National Baseball Hall of Fame Library, National Baseball Hall of Fame, Cooperstown, New York, Series I, Subseries 1, Box 3, Folder 5, Executive Council Meeting.

39. Ed Durso to Bowie Kuhn, September 9, 1983, Papers of Bowie K. Kuhn, BAMSS100, National Baseball Hall of Fame Library, National Baseball Hall of Fame, Cooperstown, New York, Series I, Subseries 1, Box 3, Folder 7, Executive Council Meeting. Emphasis added.

40. Bowie Kuhn notes, n.d., Papers of Bowie K. Kuhn, BAMSS100, National Baseball Hall of Fame Library, National Baseball Hall of Fame, Cooperstown, New York, Series I, Subseries 1, Box 3, Folder 7, Executive Council Meeting. These notes in Kuhn's writing were likely from September 9, 1983.

41. Peter Gammons, "A.L. Beat," *Sporting News*, December 5, 1983, 40.

42. Peter Gammons, "A.L. Beat," *Sporting News*, August 22, 1983, 23.

43. Kuhn, *Hardball*, 315.

44. Corzine, *Team Chemistry*, 105.

45. Bowie Kuhn, "Decision in the Matter of Vida Blue," July 13, 1984, Papers of Bowie K. Kuhn, BAMSS100, National Baseball Hall of Fame Library, National Baseball Hall of Fame, Cooperstown, New York, Series VI, Subseries 1, Box 8, Folder 5, BKK Personal Notebooks.

46. Richard I. Bloch, "Decision No. 61, Grievance of Vida Blue," July 13, 1984, Papers of Bowie K. Kuhn, BAMSS100, National Baseball Hall of Fame Library, National Baseball Hall of Fame, Cooperstown, New York, Series VI, Subseries 1, Box 8, Folder 5, BKK Personal Notebooks.

47. Anne Morgan, *Prescription for Success: The Life and Values of Ewing Marion Kauffman* (Kansas City, KS: Andrews and McMeel, 1995), 278.

48. Bob Wirz, press release, July 26, 1984, Papers of Bowie K. Kuhn, BAMSS100, National Baseball Hall of Fame Library, National Baseball Hall of Fame, Cooperstown, New York, Series VI, Subseries 1, Box 8, Folder 5, BKK Personal Notebooks.

49. Ed Durso to Bowie Kuhn and Sandy Hadden, January 12, 1984, Papers of Bowie K. Kuhn, BAMSS100, National Baseball Hall of Fame, National Baseball Hall of Fame Library, Cooperstown, New York, Series I, Subseries 1, Box 3, Folder 9, Executive Council Meeting.

50. Whitey Herzog and Kevin Horrigan, *White Rat: A Life in Baseball* (New York: Harper & Row, 1987), 148–49.

51. Herzog and Horrigan, *White Rat*, 149.

52. Herzog and Horrigan, *White Rat*, 151.

53. Ralph Ray, "Moffett's Remarks Stir Up a Ruckus," *Sporting News*, March 5, 1984, 58.

54. Milton Richman, "Baseball Should Be Rid of Drug Users," n.d. References in the article to Bowie Kuhn indicate that it is likely from sometime in 1984.

55. Response to Morgan, Lewis & Bockius memorandum, April 12, 1984, Papers of Bowie K. Kuhn, BAMSS100, National Baseball Hall of Fame Library, National Baseball Hall of Fame, Cooperstown, New York, Series I, Subseries 1, Box 3, Folder 10, Executive Council Meeting.

56. Al Rosen, quoted in Dave Nightingale, "Baseball's Drug Policy: Still Piecemeal," *Sporting News*, April 9, 1984, 31.

57. August A. Busch Jr. and Fred L. Kuhlmann to Leland S. MacPhail Jr., April 6, 1984, Papers of Bowie K. Kuhn, BAMSS100, National Baseball Hall of Fame Library, National Baseball Hall of Fame, Cooperstown, New York, Series I, Subseries 1, Box 3, Folder 10, Executive Council Meeting.

58. Major-league Joint Meeting minutes, June 21, 1984, Papers of Bowie K. Kuhn, BAMSS100, National Baseball Hall of Fame Library, National Baseball Hall of Fame, Cooperstown, New York, Series III, Subseries 2, Box 2, Folder 6, Joint Meetings.

59. "Owners Balk at New Drug Program," *Sporting News*, June 4, 1984, 52.

60. Gene Autry to Eddie Chiles, June 13, 1984, Papers of Bowie K. Kuhn, BAMSS100, National Baseball Hall of Fame Library, National Baseball Hall of Fame, Cooperstown, New York, Series VI, Subseries 1, Box 8, Folder 5, BKK Personal Notebooks.

61. Bob Wirz, press release, June 21, 1984, Papers of Bowie K. Kuhn, BAMSS100, National Baseball Hall of Fame Library, National Baseball Hall of Fame, Cooperstown, New York, Series I, Subseries 1, Box 3, Folder 12, Executive Council Meeting.

62. Murray Chass, "Players Nix Mandatory Drug-Testing Program," *Sporting News*, May 20, 1985, 19.

63. Richie Phillips, quoted in Chass, "Players Nix Mandatory Drug-Testing Program," 19.

64. Peter Ueberroth, quoted in Murray Chass, "Players Alone in Drug Testing Rejection," *Sporting News*, May 27, 1985, 37.

65. Dan Donovan and Toni Locy, "Users Unnamed in Drug Indictments," *Sporting News*, June 10, 1985, 35.

66. Murray Chass, "Drug Indictments Match Home Dates," *New York Times*, June 6, 1985, D21.

67. Adam Renfroe Jr., quoted in Chass, "Drug Indictments Match Home Dates," D21.

68. Murray Chass and Michael Goodwin, "Baseball and Cocaine: A Deepening Problem," *New York Times*, August 19, 1985, A1.

69. Dick Kaegel, "Little Misuse of Drugs Seen," *Sporting News*, August 16, 1980, 10. Emphasis added.

70. "Mets' Hernandez Admits 'Massive' Use of Cocaine," *Los Angeles Times*, September 6, 1985.

71. Rusty Staub and Phil Pepe, *Few and Chosen: Defining Mets Greatness across the Eras* (Chicago: Triumph, 2009), 19. Emphasis in original.

72. "Who Deserves Apology?" *Sporting News*, September 23, 1985, 8.

73. Marvin Miller, quoted in Ross Newhan, "Marvin Miller Urges Players to Fight Tests: Ex-Union Head Fears Loss of Solidarity over Drugs," *Los Angeles Times*, March 8, 1986.

74. Clifford Kachline, "Big Individual Performances Highlight Exciting '86 Season," in Dave Sloan, ed., *Official Baseball Guide for 1987* (St. Louis, MO: Sporting News, 1987), 7–8.

75. Donald Fehr, quoted in "Drug Testing Decision a Victory for Players," *Sporting News*, August 11, 1986, 16. Emphasis added.

76. "Drug Abuse in the Workplace: Hearing before the Select Committee on Narcotics Abuse and Control, House of Representatives, 99th Congress, Second Session, May 7, 1986," *National Criminal Justice Reference Service*, https://www.ncjrs.gov/pdffiles1/Digitization/106276NCJRS.pdf (accessed August 15, 2019).

77. Lonnie Smith, quoted in Mark Di Ionno and Bob Klapisch, "Drug-Enfarcement," *New York Post*, July 29, 1987, 70.

78. Peter Ueberroth, quoted in Bob Nightingale, "Lonnie Won't Escape Test," *Sporting News*, August 10, 1987, 26.

79. "Destructive Use of Drugs," *Sporting News*, March 11, 1972, 12; Harold Connolly, quoted in Richard O. Davies, *Sports in American Life: A History*, 2nd ed. (West Sussex, UK: Wiley-Blackwell, 2012), 347.

80. Dave Dorr, "Steroids Called Best Friend for Olympians," *Sporting News*, July 3, 1976, 47.

81. Craig Neff, "Caracas: A Scandal and a Warning," *Sports Illustrated*, September 5, 1983.

82. "Do Coaches Really Care?" *Sporting News*, January 28, 1985, 7.

83. Corzine, *Team Chemistry*, 141.

84. Jeffrey Dunn, "Jose Canseco," *Society for American Baseball Research*, https://sabr.org/bioproj/person/37e0251c (accessed August 26, 2019).

85. Associated Press, "A Timeline of Steroids in Baseball," *Denver Post*, December 13, 2007, https://www.denverpost.com/2007/12/13/a-timeline-of-steroids-in-baseball/ (accessed August, 26, 2019).

86. Corzine, *Team Chemistry*, 141.

87. "H.R. 5210—Anti-Drug Abuse Act of 1988, 100th Congress (1987–1988)," *Congress.gov*, https://www.congress.gov/bill/100th-congress/house-bill/05210 (accessed August 26, 2019). Emphasis added.

88. Art Spander, "'Better Living through Chemistry' a Fallacy," *Sporting News*, October 10, 1988, 15.

89. Elliott J. Gorn and Warren Goldstein, *A Brief History of American Sports* (Urbana: University of Illinois Press, 2004), 246, 248.

5. TAKE ME OUT TO THE (NEWER) BALLPARK

1. "Ground Rules," *On Deck, 1987 Seattle Mariners Official Program*, 26.

2. "Welcome to the Kingdome," *On Deck, 1987 Seattle Mariners Official Program*, 66.

3. Bob Condotta, "Ten Years after the Kingdome Tiles Fell," *Seattle Times*, July 19, 2004.

4. William Borders, "Montreal's Olympic Market: The World," *New York Times*, January 14, 1967, 37.

5. Rory Costello, "Olympic Stadium (Montreal)," *Society for American Baseball Research*, August 15, 2013, https://sabr.org/bioproj/park/477659 (accessed September 27, 2019). Costello's essay, which provided much information for this section, garnered the 2014 McFarland–SABR Baseball Research Award.

6. Ian MacDonald, "Bronfman Blast Delays Expo Stadium Contract," *Sporting News*, January 15, 1977, 41.

7. Ian MacDonald, "Expos Give Perez a Lesson in Warm Welcome," *Sporting News*, May 7, 1977, 9.

8. "Roger Landry," *1980 Le magazine Expos*, volume 1.

9. Stew Thornley, "Metropolitan Stadium (MN)," *Society for American Baseball Research*, January 8, 2012, https://sabr.org/bioproj/park/d3635696 (accessed September 28, 2019).

10. Stew Thornley, "Metrodome (Minneapolis)," *Society for American Baseball Research*, https://sabr.org/bioproj/park/b6255f4d (accessed September 28, 2019).

11. Mike Trombley, e-mail to author, September 26, 2019.

12. Roy Hartsfield, quoted in Paul Patton, "Those First Day Blue Jays," *1989 Toronto Blue Jays Scorebook*, 61.

13. Don Denkinger, quoted in Neil MacCarl, "Pitching Is Sharp in Jays' Getaway," *Sporting News*, May 14, 1984, 23.

14. Paul Goldberger, *Ballpark: Baseball in the American City* (New York: Alfred A. Knopf, 2019), 194.

15. Dave Nightingale, "Revealing the Warts," *Sporting News*, June 5, 1989, 10.

16. Wayne Terwilliger, quoted in Bob McCoy, "Keeping Score," *Sporting News*, September 18, 1989, 10.

17. Kim Lockhart, "First Game, Open Mouths," *1989 Toronto Blue Jays Scorebook*, 99, 100, 104.

18. James Thompson, quoted in Bob McCoy, "Keeping Score," *Sporting News*, August 14, 1989, 8.

19. Dave van Dyck, "Losing Streak Ruins Comiskey's Birthday," *Sporting News*, July 15, 1985, 25.

20. Peter Gammons, "A.L. Beat," *Sporting News*, February 10, 1986, 39.

21. Kevin Sweeney, "Voice of the Fan," *Sporting News*, August 11, 1986, 6.

22. Alan Grelman, quoted in Dave van Dyck, "State Bails Out Sox," *Sporting News*, December 22, 1986, 46.

23. Philip H. Bess, "Preface," in Philip J. Lowry, *Green Cathedrals* (Cooperstown, NY: Society for American Baseball Research, 1986), 15. Emphasis in original.

24. Carrie Muskat, "Memories in the Making," *1992 Chicago White Sox Yearbook*, 49.

25. Charles C. Euchner, "The Making of Baltimore's Camden Yards," in Steven A. Riess, ed., *Major Problems in American Sports History* (Boston: Wadsworth, 1997), 429.

26. Euchner, "The Making of Baltimore's Camden Yards," 429–30.

27. "About Maryland Stadium Authority," https://www.mdstad.com (accessed October 7, 2019). Emphasis added; Euchner, "The Making of Baltimore's Camden Yards," 432.

28. James Edward Miller, *The Baseball Business: Pursuing Pennants and Profits in Baltimore* (Chapel Hill: University of North Carolina Press, 1990).

29. *1991 Baltimore Orioles Media Guide*, 105.

30. *1992 Baltimore Orioles Media Guide*, 28.

31. Janet Marie Smith, "Back to the Future: Building a Ballpark, Not a Stadium," in William M. Simons, ed., *The Cooperstown Symposium on Baseball and American Culture, 2013–2014* (Jefferson, NC: McFarland, 2015), 55–56.

32. David Ashton, quoted in James Dodson, "Attention to Detail: The Camden Yards Story," *1993 All-Star Game Program* (Baltimore), 25.

33. Smith, "Back to the Future," 57.

34. Timothy Jurkovac, "Celebrating Nostalgia: Legalizing Extortion and Subsidizing Greed: The Hegemony of the Retro Ballpark," in William M. Simons, ed., *The Cooperstown Symposium on Baseball and American Culture, 2011–2012* (Jefferson, NC: McFarland, 2013), 137.

35. Goldberger, *Ballpark*, 317, 320.

36. Michael Friedman, "The Social Construction of Baseball Stadiums as Cathedrals of Consumption," in William M. Simons, ed., *The Cooperstown Symposium on Baseball and American Culture, 2015–2016* (Jefferson, NC: McFarland, 2017), 155–56.

37. Goldberger, *Ballpark*, 235.

6. EXPANSION, RUMORS OF EXPANSION, AND OWNERSHIP CHANGES

1. Commissioner's office memo to Long-Range Planning Committee, November 4, 1983, Papers of Bowie K. Kuhn, BAMSS100, National Baseball Hall

of Fame Library, National Baseball Hall of Fame, Cooperstown, New York, Series VI, Subseries 1, Box 4, Folder 10, Expansion—1983. The draft of "Major League Expansion Criteria," dated September 15, 1967, was included with the memo.

2. Commissioner's office memo to Long-Range Planning Committee.

3. Fran Zimniuch, *Baseball's New Frontier: A History of Expansion, 1961–1998* (Lincoln: University of Nebraska Press, 2013), 118.

4. L. S. MacPhail to AL general managers, August 27, 1976, Papers of Bowie K. Kuhn, BAMSS100, National Baseball Hall of Fame Library, National Baseball Hall of Fame, Cooperstown, New York, Series II, Subseries 3, Box 9, Folder 8, NLRB Subpoena and Hearing—1976–1981 Expansion Draft.

5. Gregory H. Wolf, "1975: The Threat of Free Agency and the Return of the Master Showman," in Steve Weingarten and Bill Nowlin, eds., *Baseball's Business: The Winter Meetings, Volume 2, 1958–2016* (Phoenix, AZ: Society for American Baseball Research, 2017), 99.

6. Frank P. Jozsa Jr., *Major League Baseball Expansions and Relocations: A History, 1876–2008* (Jefferson, NC: McFarland, 2009), 35.

7. Art Spander, "Giants' Fate Simmers on Back Burner," *Sporting News*, January 31, 1976, 33.

8. Ed Prell, "Majors Split on Expansion: Kuhn's Hot Potato," *Sporting News*, January 31, 1976, 33; Hy Zimmerman, "Seattle Lukewarm to Offer of Expansion Club," *Sporting News*, January 31, 1976, 34.

9. Larry Millson, "The Business of the Blue Jays," in Eric Zweig, ed., *Toronto Blue Jays Official 25th Anniversary Commemorative Book* (Toronto: Dan Diamond and Associates, 2001), 186.

10. James Edward Miller, *The Baseball Business: Pursuing Pennants and Profits in Baltimore* (Chapel Hill: University of North Carolina Press, 1990), 179.

11. Prell, "Majors Split on Expansion," 33; Zimmerman, "Seattle Lukewarm to Offer of Expansion Club," 34.

12. "Decision Re: Major League Expansion Plans," April 16, 1976, Papers of Bowie K. Kuhn, BAMSS100, National Baseball Hall of Fame Library, National Baseball Hall of Fame, Cooperstown, New York, Series VI, Subseries 2, Box 13, Folder 6, Toronto/Washington Decision Re: Expansion Plans, 1976. Emphasis added.

13. "Decision Re: Major League Expansion Plans."

14. Bowie Kuhn, *Hardball: The Education of a Baseball Commissioner* (New York: Times Books, 1987), 194.

15. A. L. Butterfield, "Voice of the Fan," *Sporting News*, September 18, 1976, 4; Gary Lyndaker, "Voice of the Fan," *Sporting News*, February 21, 1976, 4.

16. Jerome Holtzman, "Players, Lawyers Gained; Attendance Up," in Joe Marcin, Larry Wigge, Carl Clark, and Larry Vickery, eds., *Official Baseball Guide for 1978* (St. Louis, MO: Sporting News, 1978), 315.

17. Meeting minutes, June 6, 1978, Papers of Bowie K. Kuhn, BAMSS100, National Baseball Hall of Fame Library, National Baseball Hall of Fame, Cooperstown, New York, Series I, Subseries 1, Box 2, Folder 1, Executive Council Meetings.

18. Holtzman, "Players, Lawyers Gained; Attendance Up," 315.

19. Bill Veeck, quoted in Paul Dickson, *Bill Veeck: Baseball's Greatest Maverick* (New York: Walker & Company, 2012), 320.

20. Dickson, *Bill Veeck*, 323.

21. Clifford Kachline, "Labor Strife, Big Salaries Topped '80 News," in Larry Wigge, Carl Clark, Craig Carter, and Joe Marcin, eds., *Official Baseball Guide for 1981* (St. Louis, MO: Sporting News, 1981), 318.

22. Randy Galloway, "Corbett's Wings Clipped on Sundberg Pact," *Sporting News*, February 23, 1980, 38.

23. Hal Bodley, "Ownership Goal Reality to Giles," *Sporting News*, November 14, 1981, 50.

24. Bodley, "Ownership Goal Reality to Giles," 50.

25. Kevin Hennessy, "Calvin Griffith," *Society for American Baseball Research*, April 17, 2014, https://sabr.org/bioproj/person/5c118751 (accessed November 5, 2019).

26. Dick Young, "Young Ideas," *Sporting News*, October 24, 1983, 6.

27. Tom Gage, "Fetzer Sells Tigers for $43 Million," *Sporting News*, October 24, 1983, 28.

28. Anne Morgan, *Prescription for Success: The Life and Values of Ewing Marion Kauffman* (Kansas City, KS: Andrews and McMeel, 1995), 268.

29. Morgan, *Prescription for Success*, 294.

30. Morgan, *Prescription for Success*, 304.

31. Earl Lawson, "Schott Purchases Control of Reds," *Sporting News*, January 7, 1985, 36.

32. Marge Schott, quoted in Stan Isle, "Boycott in Bloom," *Sporting News*, July 29, 1985, 10.

33. Warren Corbett, "Marge Schott," *Society for American Baseball Research*, January 8, 2012, https://sabr.org/bioproj/person/09e49f1e (accessed November 16, 2019).

34. John J. Goldman and Elizabeth Mehren, "Sermons on the Mound: Baseball Commissioner Peter Ueberroth Preaches about a Clean-Cut, Drug-Free, Financially Sound National Pastime. And He Means Business," *Los Angeles Times*, July 13, 1986.

35. Bowie Kuhn personal notes, March 9, 1983, Papers of Bowie K. Kuhn, BAMSS100, National Baseball Hall of Fame Library, National Baseball Hall of Fame, Cooperstown, New York, Series I, Subseries 1, Box 3, Folder 7, Tab 7, Executive Council Meetings.

36. "Preliminary Long-Range Issues," Pacific Select Corp memo, November 2, 1983, Papers of Bowie K. Kuhn, BAMSS100, National Baseball Hall of Fame Library, National Baseball Hall of Fame, Cooperstown, New York, Series VI, Subseries 1, Box 4, Folder 10, 1983/Expansion.

37. Chub Feeney expansion notes, July 20, 1984, Papers of Bowie K. Kuhn, BAMSS100, National Baseball Hall of Fame Library, National Baseball Hall of Fame, Cooperstown, New York, Series VI, Subseries 1, Box 4, Folder 11, Pros and Cons of Expansion.

38. Bill Conlin, "Ueberroth's Repeat Message Falls Flat," *Sporting News*, December 17, 1984, 45.

39. Norm Clarke, "Ueberroth: Expansion Is Closer," *Kansas City Star*, February 23, 1987.

40. Bob Whelan, "1987—Changing Times—Collusion III," in Steve Weingarten and Bill Nowlin, eds., *Baseball's Business: The Winter Meetings, Volume 2, 1958–2016* (Phoenix, AZ: Society for American Baseball Research, 2017), 193.

41. J. C. Bradbury, *The Baseball Economist: The Real Game Exposed* (New York: Dutton, 2007), 73.

7. FRONT-OFFICE ARCHITECTS

1. Lee Lowenfish, *Branch Rickey: Baseball's Ferocious Gentleman* (Lincoln: University of Nebraska Press, 2007), 286.

2. John Kieran, quoted in Mark L. Armour and Daniel R. Levitt, *In Pursuit of Pennants: Baseball Operations from Deadball to Moneyball* (Lincoln: University of Nebraska Press, 2015), 58.

3. Gabe Paul, quoted in Jennie Paul, with Jody Lynn Smith, *The Yankee Princess: Why Dad and I Were in a League of Our Own* (Columbia, MD: Silloway Press, 2011), 185.

4. Pat Gillick, quoted in Marty Tschetter, "Molded by Scouting," *Memories and Dreams* 33, no. 4 (Summer 2011): 13.

5. Pat Gillick, quoted in Frank Fitzpatrick, "The Education of Pat Gillick," *Philadelphia Inquirer*, July 22, 2011, C5.

6. Pat Gillick Hall of Fame induction speech, July 24, 2011, Lawrence Patrick David Gillick Folder, National Baseball Hall of Fame Library, National Baseball Hall of Fame, Cooperstown, New York.

7. Pat Gillick, quoted in Fran Zimniuch, *Baseball's New Frontier: A History of Expansion, 1961–1998* (Lincoln: University of Nebraska Press, 2013), 155.

8. Pat Gillick, quoted in Wayne Parrish, "Gillick and Beeston," in Eric Zweig, ed., *Toronto Blue Jays Official 25th Anniversary Commemorative Book* (Toronto: Dan Diamond and Associates, 2001), 184.

9. Todd Zolecki, "Gillick's Mission," *Philadelphia Inquirer*, November 3, 2005.

10. Stephen Brunt, "Epy's Academy," in Zweig, *Toronto Blue Jays Official 25th Anniversary Commemorative Book*, 175.

11. Stephen Brunt, "Epy's Academy," in Eric Zweig, ed., *Toronto Blue Jays Official 25th Anniversary Commemorative Book* (Toronto: Dan Diamond and Associates, 2001), 175.

12. Parrish, "Gillick and Beeston," 183.

13. Pat Gillick press conference transcript, December 6, 2010, asapsports.com, Lawrence Patrick David Gillick folder, National Baseball Hall of Fame Library, National Baseball Hall of Fame, Cooperstown, New York.

14. John Schuerholz Hall of Fame induction speech, July 30, 2017, asapsports.com, John Schuerholz folder, National Baseball Hall of Fame Library, National Baseball Hall of Fame, Cooperstown, New York.

15. John Schuerholz Hall of Fame induction speech.

16. John Schuerholz Hall of Fame induction speech.

17. Mike McKenzie, "Schuerholz New G.M. of Royals," *Sporting News*, October 24, 1981, 32.

18. Mike Fish, "TSN Executive of the Year, John Schuerholz," *Sporting News*, December 16, 1985, 45.

19. Daniel R. Levitt and Mark Armour, "John Schuerholz," *Society for American Baseball Research*, September 20, 2018, https://sabr.org/node/44114 (accessed December 31, 2019).

20. John Schuerholz, quoted in Carroll Rogers Walton, "The Architect," *Memories and Dreams* 39, no. 1 (Spring 2017): 20.

21. John Schuerholz Hall of Fame induction speech; Walton, "The Architect," 20.

22. John Schuerholz, quoted in "My Business Is Baseball," *The Squire* (Johnson County/Kansas City), March 20, 1986, 11–12.

23. Whitey Herzog, quoted in Robert L. Burnes, "Mold of Successful Manager," *St. Louis Globe-Democrat*, October 5, 1982, 1.

24. Dan O'Neill, "Whitey Herzog: The Pride of New Athens," *St. Louis Post-Dispatch*, July 18, 2010.

25. Whitey Herzog media information sheet, Whitey Herzog Folder, National Baseball Hall of Fame Library, National Baseball Hall of Fame, Cooperstown, New York.

26. Joe McGuff, "A's Shake Up Staff, Hire Coach Herzog," *Sporting News*, November 28, 1964, 20.

27. Barney Kremenko, "Mets Pick Herzog to Handle Key Job as a Super Sleuth," *Sporting News*, November 12, 1966, 42.

28. Whitey Herzog and Kevin Horrigan, *White Rat: A Life in Baseball* (New York: Harper & Row, 1987), 79.

29. Kansas City Royals news release, July 30, 1975, Whitey Herzog Folder, National Baseball Hall of Fame Library, National Baseball Hall of Fame, Cooperstown, New York.

30. Herzog and Horrigan, *White Rat*, 86.

31. Bill Nowlin, "Ted Williams," in Steve West and Bill Nowlin, eds, *The Team That Couldn't Hit: The 1972 Texas Rangers* (Phoenix, AZ: Society for American Baseball Research, 2019), 233.

32. Herzog and Horrigan, *White Rat*, 96.

33. Herzog and Horrigan, *White Rat*, 100.

34. Gary Ronberg, "Herzog's Firing Burns Up Fans," *Boston Globe*, October 14, 1979, 50.

35. Herzog and Horrigan, *White Rat*, 117.

36. Doug Feldman, *Whitey Herzog Builds a Winner: The St. Louis Cardinals, 1979–1982* (Jefferson, NC: McFarland, 2018), 116.

37. Whitey Herzog, quoted in Rick Hummel, "Herzog Finds New Manager: Himself," *Sporting News*, November 8, 1980, 52.

38. Herzog and Horrigan, *White Rat*, 121.

39. Ted Simmons, quoted in Will Grimsley, "St. Louis Cards Dealt New Deck," *News-Herald* (Panama City, FL), March 16, 1981, 2B.

40. Whitey Herzog, quoted in Grimsley, "St. Louis Cards Dealt New Deck," 2B.

41. Rich Koster, "Herzog Should Have Quit While Step Ahead," *St. Louis Globe-Democrat*, December 13, 1980.

42. Herzog and Horrigan, *White Rat*, 136.

43. Herzog and Horrigan, *White Rat*, 121.

44. Feldman, *Whitey Herzog Builds a Winner*, 120.

45. Whitey Herzog, quoted in Rick Hummel, "Herzog Gives GM Position to McDonald," *St. Louis Post-Dispatch*, April 4, 1982, 1.

46. Rick Hummel, "Man of Year Herzog: His Own Man," *Sporting News*, January 3, 1983, 3.

47. Mark Everson, "Keith, Whitey Trade Cross Words," *New York Post*, June 27, 1984.

48. Rick Hummel, "McDonald Is Out as Cards' G.M.," *Sporting News*, January 14, 1985, 49.

49. Rick Hummel, "Homecoming for Herzog," *St. Louis Post-Dispatch*, August 3, 2010.

50. Whitey Herzog feature, *Memories and Dreams* 41, no. 5 (Fall 2019): 26. Emphasis added.

51. Warren Corbett, "Al Campanis," *Society for American Baseball Research*, https://sabr.org/bioproj/person/2f3e0527 (accessed January 6, 2020).

52. Corbett, "Al Campanis."

53. Terry Johnson, "A Conversation with Al Campanis," *Dodger Blue*, October 30, 1983, 7.

54. Al Campanis, quoted in "Al Campanis Is Dead at 81; Ignited Baseball over Race," *New York Times*, June 22, 1998.

55. Tommy Lasorda, quoted in Steve Dilbeck, "Lasorda: Forgive One Mistake," *USA Today*, April 9, 1987, 5C.

8. MARKETING THE GAME

1. Mathew J. Bartkowiak and Yuya Kiuchi, *Packaging Baseball: How Marketing Embellishes the Cultural Experience* (Jefferson, NC: McFarland, 2012), 28–29.

2. Bartkowiak and Kiuchi, *Packaging Baseball*, 29.

3. Robert F. Lewis II, *Smart Ball: Marketing the Myth and Managing the Reality of Major League Baseball* (Jackson: University Press of Mississippi, 2010), 45.

4. Peter Bavasi, "Baseball Marketing: The Big Picture Concept," in *Promotions and Operations Handbook* (St. Petersburg, FL: National Association of Professional Baseball Leagues, 1985).

5. Stedman Graham, Joe Jeff Goldblatt, and Lisa Delpy, *The Ultimate Guide to Sport Event Management and Marketing* (New York: McGraw-Hill, 1995).

6. Alan Friedman, ed., *500 Great Sports Promotion Ideas* (Chicago: Team Marketing Report, 1994).

7. Phil Schaaf, *Sports Marketing: It's Not Just a Game Anymore* (Amherst, NY: Prometheus, 1995), 16.

8. Andrew Zimbalist, *Baseball and Billions: A Probing Look Inside the Big Business of Our National Pastime* (New York: Basic Books, 1992), 55.

9. Zimbalist, *Baseball and Billions*, 55–56.

10. "1983 San Diego Padres Marketing Plan," 77, BL 77.2015.41, MFF583, National Baseball Hall of Fame Library, National Baseball Hall of Fame, Cooperstown, New York.

11. "1983 San Diego Padres Marketing Plan," 21.

12. "1983 San Diego Padres Marketing Plan," 32.

13. "1983 San Diego Padres Marketing Plan," 40.

14. "1983 San Diego Padres Marketing Plan," 45.

15. "1983 San Diego Padres Marketing Plan," 44.

16. "1983 San Diego Padres Marketing Plan," 61–62.

17. "1983 San Diego Padres Marketing Plan," 44.

18. "1983 San Diego Padres Marketing Plan," 74. Emphasis added.

19. "1983 San Diego Padres Marketing Plan," 81, 86.

20. James Edward Miller, *The Baseball Business: Pursuing Pennants and Profits in Baltimore* (Chapel Hill: University of North Carolina Press, 1990), 269.

21. "1983 San Diego Padres Marketing Plan," 91.

22. John Helyar, *Lords of the Realm: The Real History of Baseball* (New York: Ballantine, 1994), 336.

23. "Yankee Promo Unit Back in the Fold," *Advertising Age*, December 19, 1977.

24. Clark C. Griffith and William Y. Giles to Bowie Kuhn, November 8, 1978, Papers of Bowie K. Kuhn, BAMSS100, National Baseball Hall of Fame Library, National Baseball Hall of Fame, Cooperstown, New York, Series IV, Subseries 1, Box 4, Folder 9, Steinbrenner v. MLB Promotion Corp. The coauthor of this memo was the son of Twins owner Calvin Griffith.

25. Joseph P. Grant to Joseph L. Podesta, September 23, 1981, Papers of Bowie K. Kuhn, BAMSS100, National Baseball Hall of Fame Library, National Baseball Hall of Fame, Cooperstown, New York, Series IV, Subseries 1, Box 4, Folder 9, Steinbrenner v. MLB Promotion Corp.

26. Joseph P. Grant to Joseph L. Podesta. Emphasis in original.

27. Joseph L. Podesta to major-league club chief executives, March 29, 1982, Papers of Bowie K. Kuhn, BAMSS100, National Baseball Hall of Fame Library, National Baseball Hall of Fame, Cooperstown, New York, Series IV, Subseries 1, Box 4, Folder 9, Steinbrenner v. MLB Promotion Corp.

28. "Major League Baseball Licensed Merchandise Sets Retail Record," Major League Baseball/LCA Promotional Kit, Papers of Bowie K. Kuhn, BAMSS100, National Baseball Hall of Fame Library, National Baseball Hall of Fame, Cooperstown, New York, Series VI, Subseries 3, Box 15, Folder 21, Major League Baseball Promotion Corp Manual 1981.

29. "Major League Baseball: A Licensing Opportunity," Major League Baseball/LCA Promotional Kit, Papers of Bowie K. Kuhn, BAMSS100, National Baseball Hall of Fame Library, National Baseball Hall of Fame, Cooperstown, New York, Series VI, Subseries 3, Box 15, Folder 21, Major League Baseball Promotion Corp Manual 1981.

30. Stan Isle, "Rusty Has Spread His Hits Around," *Sporting News*, January 24, 1983, 7.

31. James Lilliefors, *Ball Cap Nation: A Journey through the World of America's National Hat* (Covington, KY: Clerisy Press, 2009), 52.

32. Tracey Benson, "Team Licensing: A State of the Market Report," *Team Licensing Business*, February 1989, 13.

33. Benson, "Team Licensing," 14.

34. "Orel Commitments," *Sporting News*, December 4, 1989, 60; Richard Rosenblatt, "Selling of Bo Moves into New Dimension," *Sporting News*, July 31, 1989, 50.

35. Clifford Kachline, "'85 On-Field Accomplishments Overshadow Baseball's Woes," in Dave Sloan, ed., *Official Baseball Guide for 1986* (St. Louis, MO: Sporting News, 1986), 4.

36. Helyar, *Lords of the Realm*, 379.

37. Rick White, quoted in Tracey Benson, "Major League Baseball Steps Up to the Plate," *Team Licensing Business*, May 1989, 17.

38. "Trademark Infringement Report Form," Major League Baseball/LCA Promotional Kit, Papers of Bowie K. Kuhn, BAMSS100, National Baseball Hall of Fame Library, National Baseball Hall of Fame, Cooperstown, New York, Series VI, Subseries 3, Box 15, Folder 21, Major League Baseball Promotion Corp Manual 1981.

39. *Major League Baseball Promotion v. Colour-Tex*, 729 F. Supp. 1035 (D.N.J. 1990), *JUSTIA*, https://law.justia.com/cases/federal/district-courts/FSupp/729/1035/1492895/ (accessed February 14, 2020).

40. "Marketing the Past," *Team Licensing Business*, September 1989, 49.

41. Glen Macnow, "Ueberroth's Legacy: Sponsorship Bonanza," *Sporting News*, June 26, 1989, 53.

42. Steve Viuker, "Now Wait Just a Sponsored Minute!" *Sporting News*, September 18, 1989, 60.

43. Mike Ryan, quoted in Viuker, "Now Wait Just a Sponsored Minute!" 60.

44. Bill Fleischman, "Baseball Cards: Real Trophies to Collectors," *Sporting News*, June 28, 1975, 29.

45. Bill Madden, "The Sports Collector," *Sporting News*, January 8, 1977, 44.

46. Dave Jamieson, *Mint Condition: How Baseball Cards Became an American Obsession* (New York: Atlantic Monthly, 2010), 155.

47. Katherine Munhall, "What a Card! The Popularity of Baseball Cards and Other Collectibles Is No Joke," *Team Licensing Business*, May 1989, 29.

48. Bob Lemke, quoted in David Moriah, "Premiere Prints," *Memories and Dreams* volume 41, no. 6 (Winter 2019): 30.

49. Jamieson, *Mint Condition*, 155, 156.

50. Robert Mcg. Thomas Jr., "Investors Hope a Rich Future Is in the Cards," *New York Times*, April 10, 1988, H1.

51. *Fleer Corp. v. Topps Chewing Gum, Inc.*, 415 F. Supp. 176 (E.D. Pa. 1976), *Court Listener*, https://www.courtlistener.com/opinion/2248705/fleer-corp-v-topps-chewing-gum-inc/ (accessed February 16, 2020). Emphasis added.

52. *Fleer Corp. v. Topps Chewing Gum, Inc.*, Civ. A. No. 75-1803, June 30, 1980, *Casetext*, https://casetext.com/case/fleer-corp-v-topps-chewing-gum-inc-4#p497 (accessed February 16, 2020). Emphasis added.

53. Joseph P. Grant to Joseph L. Podesta.

54. Jamieson, *Mint Condition*, 156–57.

55. Jamieson, *Mint Condition*, 165.

56. Arthur Shorin, quoted in Pete Williams, *Card Sharks: How Upper Deck Turned a Child's Hobby into a High-Stakes, Billion-Dollar Business* (New York: Macmillan, 1995), 247.

57. Richard Runnion, "Effect of Baseball Strike Is in the Cards, Too," *Chicago Tribune*, June 18, 1995.

58. Grant Brisbee, "The Bill Ripken F*** Face Card, 30 Years Later," *SBNation*, January 25, 2019, https://www.sbnation.com/mlb/2019/1/25/18174412/bill-ripken-card-1989-fleer-frick-face-look-google-wont-index-this-if-the-url-has-the-actual-swear (accessed January 28, 2019).

59. Peter Golenbock, *How to Win at Rotisserie Baseball: The Strategic Guide to America's New National (Armchair) Pastime* (New York: Vintage, 1987), 4.

60. Golenbock, *How to Win at Rotisserie Baseball*, 4.

61. Seymour Siwoff, Steve Hirdt, and Peter Hirdt, *The 1985 Elias Baseball Analyst* (New York: Collier, 1985), 3.

62. Siwoff, Hirdt, and Hirdt, *The 1985 Elias Baseball Analyst*, 109.

63. Siwoff, Hirdt, and Hirdt, *The 1985 Elias Baseball Analyst*, 353.

64. Craig Carter and Larry Wigge, eds., *National League 1984 Box Score Book* (St. Louis, MO: Sporting News, 1984), 3. Emphasis in original.

65. Robert Shapiro and James Boscardin, "Pitching Mechanics and Performance of Members of the Chicago White Sox: Preliminary Report (1983)," 7–8, MFF669, National Baseball Hall of Fame Library, National Baseball Hall of Fame, Cooperstown, New York.

66. John Thorn and Pete Palmer, with David Reuther, *The Hidden Game of Baseball: A Revolutionary Approach to Baseball and Its Statistics* (Garden City, NY: Doubleday, 1984), 37, 38.

67. John Thorn and Pete Palmer, with David Reuther, *Total Baseball* (New York: Warner Books, 1989), 686.

68. Skoal advertisement, *Sporting News*, April 8, 1985, 31.

69. Bob Wirz, *The Passion of Baseball: A Journey to the Commissioner's Office of Major League Baseball* (Autryville, NC: Ravenswood, 2016), 225.

70. Pat Calabria, "Just the Kid Next Door," *Sporting News*, August 16, 1980, 3.

71. Jack Lang, "Torre's Kids Learned Late-Season Lesson," in Larry Wigge, Carl Clark, Craig Carter, and Joe Marcin, eds., *Official Baseball Guide for 1981* (St. Louis, MO: Sporting News, 1981), 36.

72. Mark Heisler, "He Came, He Pitched, He Conquered," *Sporting News 1982 Baseball Yearbook*, 6.

73. Jeff Katz, *Split Season: Fernandomania, the Bronx Zoo, and the Strike That Saved Baseball* (New York: St. Martin's, 2015), 81.

74. Paul Dickson, *The Dickson Baseball Dictionary* (New York: Facts on File, 1989), 215.

75. Stan Isle, "Rusty Has Spread His Hits Around," *Sporting News*, January 24, 1983, 7.

76. Stan Isle, "Caught on the Fly," *Sporting News*, November 19, 1984, 57.

77. Jack Schrom, quoted in Stan Isle, "Caught on the Fly," *Sporting News*, March 5, 1984, 21.

78. Peter Pascarelli, "N.L. Beat," *Sporting News*, July 11, 1988, 29.

79. Andy McCue, *Mover and Shaker: Walter O'Malley, the Dodgers, and Baseball's Westward Expansion* (Lincoln: University of Nebraska Press, 2014), 75.

80. Tom Weir, "Survey Paints Bleak Picture for A's," *Sporting News*, January 20, 1979, 45.

81. Phil Collier, "Garvey Is a Dynamo On and Off Field," *Sporting News*, April 29, 1985, 24.

82. *1999 Minnesota Twins Community Report*, 2–3.

83. Kit Stier, "Community Effort in A's Marketing," *Sporting News*, February 21, 1983, 40.

84. Skip Myslenski and Linda Kay, "The Men of Summer, Back in 1982 . . .," *Chicago Tribune*, December 23, 1985.

9. SOCIETAL ISSUES

1. James T. Patterson, *Restless Giant: The United States from Watergate to Bush v. Gore* (New York: Oxford University Press, 2005), 70, 71.

2. Press release, "Discrimination Found in Major League Baseball," n.d., Papers of Bowie K. Kuhn, BAMSS100, National Baseball Hall of Fame Library, National Baseball Hall of Fame, Cooperstown, New York, Series VI, Subseries 4, Box 19, Folder 7, Racial Discrimination in MLB. This document is likely from mid-September 1983.

3. Lenny Mendonca, "Racial Discrimination in Major League Baseball," Harvard University, senior honors thesis, March 23, 1983, 77, Papers of Bowie K. Kuhn, BAMSS100, National Baseball Hall of Fame Library, National Base-

ball Hall of Fame, Cooperstown, New York, Series VI, Subseries 4, Box 19, Folder 7, Racial Discrimination in MLB.

4. Mendonca, "Racial Discrimination in Major League Baseball."

5. Lou Brock, quoted in Rick Hummel, "For Blacks in Baseball, Where Is the Glory?" *Atlanta Constitution*, August 16, 1979, D1.

6. Tom Villante to Bowie Kuhn, November 16, 1979, Papers of Bowie K. Kuhn, BAMSS100, National Baseball Hall of Fame Library, National Baseball Hall of Fame, Cooperstown, New York, Series I, Subseries 2, Box 5, Folder 5, Peter O'Malley and Bud Selig Committee.

7. Leroy Boyd to Monte Irvin, December 11, 1979, Papers of Bowie K. Kuhn, BAMSS100, National Baseball Hall of Fame Library, National Baseball Hall of Fame, Cooperstown, New York, Series I, Subseries 2, Box 5, Folder 5, Peter O'Malley and Bud Selig Committee.

8. Reverend Joseph E. Lowery to Bowie Kuhn, December 17, 1979, Papers of Bowie K. Kuhn, BAMSS100, National Baseball Hall of Fame Library, National Baseball Hall of Fame, Cooperstown, New York, Series I, Subseries 2, Box 5, Folder 5, Peter O'Malley and Bud Selig Committee.

9. Reverend Joseph E. Lowery, quoted in Associated Press article, December 17, 1979, Papers of Bowie K. Kuhn, BAMSS100, National Baseball Hall of Fame Library, National Baseball Hall of Fame, Cooperstown, New York, Series I, Subseries 2, Box 5, Folder 5, Peter O'Malley and Bud Selig Committee.

10. "Garvey Accuses NFL, Rozelle of Racism," *Los Angeles Herald Examiner*, November 16, 1979, D3.

11. Bowie Kuhn to Joseph Lowery, December 18, 1979, Papers of Bowie K. Kuhn, BAMSS100, National Baseball Hall of Fame Library, National Baseball Hall of Fame, Cooperstown, New York, Series I, Subseries 2, Box 5, Folder 5, Peter O'Malley and Bud Selig Committee.

12. Joseph E. Lowery to Bowie Kuhn, February 21, 1980, Papers of Bowie K. Kuhn, BAMSS100, National Baseball Hall of Fame Library, National Baseball Hall of Fame, Cooperstown, New York, Series I, Subseries 2, Box 5, Folder 5, Peter O'Malley and Bud Selig Committee.

13. Bowie Kuhn, quoted in Ralph Ray, "Kuhn Fields the Questions," *Sporting News*, August 16, 1980, 34.

14. Dan Offenburg to Bowie Kuhn, June 20, 1980, Papers of Bowie K. Kuhn, BAMSS100, National Baseball Hall of Fame Library, National Baseball Hall of Fame, Cooperstown, New York, Series I, Subseries 2, Box 5, Folder 5, Peter O'Malley and Bud Selig Committee.

15. "Blacks in Baseball," April 1, 1981, Papers of Bowie K. Kuhn, BAMSS100, National Baseball Hall of Fame Library, National Baseball Hall of Fame, Cooperstown, New York, Series VI, Subseries 3, Box 15, Folder 4, Blacks in Baseball.

16. Brian J. Richards, "Half-Broken Barriers: Frank Robinson, Major League Baseball, and American Race Relations in the 1970s," State University of New York College at Oneonta, master's thesis, 2007, i.

17. Richards, "Half-Broken Barriers," 2.

18. "Study Chides NFL on Few Black Aides," *New York Times*, October 28, 1980, A37.

19. Richards, "Half-Broken Barriers," 71.

20. Alexander Hadden to Bowie Kuhn, May 7, 1980, Papers of Bowie K. Kuhn, BAMSS100, National Baseball Hall of Fame Library, National Baseball Hall of Fame, Cooperstown, New York, Series I, Subseries 2, Box 5, Folder 5, Peter O'Malley and Bud Selig Committee. Emphasis added.

21. Hank Aaron, quoted in Stan Isle, "Caught on the Fly," *Sporting News*, June 3, 1985, 30.

22. John B. Holway to Peter V. Ueberroth, August 12, 1985, Papers of Jules Tygiel, BAMSS34, National Baseball Hall of Fame Library, National Baseball Hall of Fame, Cooperstown, New York, Box 2, Folder 11.

23. John Holway, "Bringing Balance to Hall of Fame," *New York Times*, August 3, 1986, 5-2.

24. Jack Lang, "Dandridge Is a Surprise Selection," *Sporting News*, March 16, 1987, 23.

25. Bob Hertzel, "Ueberroth Aims to Open Executive Doors for Minorities," *Pittsburgh Press*, December 9, 1986.

26. Steve Springer, "The *Nightline* That Rocked Baseball," *Los Angeles Times*, April 6, 1997, C1.

27. Calvin Griffith, quoted in Rod Carew, with Ira Berkow, *Carew* (New York: Simon & Schuster, 1979), 234.

28. Frank Robinson, quoted in Bill White, with Gordon Dillow, *Uppity: My Untold Story about the Games People Play* (New York: Grand Central Publishing, 2011), 185.

29. Reverend Joseph Lowery, quoted in "Ueberroth 'Sensitive' to Minorities," *USA Today*, April 22, 1987.

30. White, *Uppity*, 189.

31. White, *Uppity*, 190.

32. Susan Cahn, "Women Competing/Gender Contested, 1930s–1950s," in Steven A. Riess, ed., *Major Problems in American Sports History* (Boston: Wadsworth, 1997), 368; James T. Patterson, *Grand Expectations: The United States, 1945–1974* (New York: Oxford University Press, 1996), 361.

33. Peter Morris, "Mary Shane," *Society for American Baseball Research*, January 8, 2012, https://sabr.org/bioproj/person/6d1d92c8 (accessed April 1, 2020).

34. Dan Levitt, "Facts from the Ludtke v. Kuhn Case (1978)," in Steve Weingarden and Bill Nowlin, eds., *Baseball's Business: The Winter Meetings, Volume 2, 1958–2016* (Phoenix, AZ: Society for American Baseball Research, 2017), 130.

35. Levitt, "Facts from the Ludtke v. Kuhn Case (1978)," 131.

36. Stephanie Salter, "Kuhn Challenges Women and Time," *San Francisco Examiner*, November 7, 1977, 51.

37. Stephanie Salter, "Women Writers Discriminated Against? You Bet!" *San Francisco Examiner*, November 8, 1977.

38. Salter, "Women Writers Discriminated Against?"

39. Bob Wirz to Bowie Kuhn and Sandy Hadden, November 15, 1977, Papers of Bowie K. Kuhn, BAMSS100, National Baseball Hall of Fame Library, National Baseball Hall of Fame, Cooperstown, New York, Series VIII, Box 3, Folder 6, Melissa Ludtke.

40. Stu Smith to Bob Wirz, n.d., Papers of Bowie K. Kuhn, BAMSS100, National Baseball Hall of Fame Library, National Baseball Hall of Fame, Cooperstown, New York, Series VIII, Box 3, Folder 6, Melissa Ludtke.

41. "Commissioner's Statement Regarding Ludtke (*Sports Illustrated*) Lawsuit," December 30, 1977, Papers of Bowie K. Kuhn, BAMSS100, National Baseball Hall of Fame Library, National Baseball Hall of Fame, Cooperstown, New York, Series VIII, Box 3, Folder 6, Melissa Ludtke. Emphasis added.

42. *Ludtke v. Kuhn*, 461 F. Supp. 86 (S.D.N.Y. 1978), *JUSTIA*, https://law.justia.com/cases/federal/district-courts/FSupp/461/86/2266331/ (accessed April 4, 2020).

43. Bowie Kuhn, *Hardball: The Education of a Baseball Commissioner* (New York: Times Books, 1987), 300.

44. Jerry Koosman interview transcript, September 25, 1978, Papers of Bowie K. Kuhn, BAMSS100, National Baseball Hall of Fame Library, National Baseball Hall of Fame, Cooperstown, New York, Series VIII, Box 3, Folder 6, Melissa Ludtke.

45. Bowie Kuhn to all major-league clubs, "Access of Female Reporters to Club Facilities," March 9, 1979, Papers of Bowie K. Kuhn, BAMSS100, National Baseball Hall of Fame Library, National Baseball Hall of Fame, Cooperstown, New York, Series VIII, Box 3, Folder 6, Melissa Ludtke.

46. Earl Weaver, quoted in "Kuhn Changes Policy for Women in Media," *Sporting News*, March 31, 1979, 55.

47. Executive Council meeting minutes, July 7, 1979, Papers of Bowie K. Kuhn, BAMSS100, National Baseball Hall of Fame Library, National Baseball Hall of Fame, Cooperstown, New York, Series I, Subseries 1, Box 2, Folder 1, Executive Council.

48. Jack Lang and Peter Simon, *The New York Mets: Twenty-five Years of Baseball Magic* (New York: Henry Holt and Company, 1986), 181.

49. Tony Kornhiser, "Kingman's Rat: Just How Funny," *Washington Post*, June 27, 1986.

50. Melody Simmons, quoted in Ira Berkow, "Barfield Is More Than a Ballplayer," *New York Times*, July 20, 1989, B-9.

51. Gene Mauch, quoted in Rebecca Sheir, "'We Just Wanna Be a Part of It': The Women Who Fought to Cover MLB," *WBUR*, September 1, 2017, https://www.wbur.org/onlyagame/2017/09/01/women-baseball-writers-saxon-ludtke-claire-smith (accessed July 30, 2019).

52. Claire Smith, quoted in George Vecsey, "Sports of the Times: The Grace of Steve Garvey," *New York Times*, October 10, 1984, B-13.

53. Sally Tippett Rains, "An End to Open Locker Room Dilemma?" *Sporting News*, April 8, 1985, 44.

54. Sheir, "'We Just Wanna Be a Part of It.'"

55. Jean Hastings Ardell, *Breaking into Baseball: Women and the National Pastime* (Carbondale: Southern Illinois University Press, 2005), 206.

56. Claire Smith Facebook posting, April 15, 2020.

57. Stan Isle, "Caught on the Fly," *Sporting News*, January 3, 1981, 53.

58. Pam Postema, quoted in Hastings Ardell, *Breaking into Baseball*, 153.

59. Janet Marie Smith, quoted in Billy Watkins, "Jackson's Smith: A True Baseball Hero," *Clarion Ledger*, November 7, 2015.

60. Paul Goldberger, *Ballpark: Baseball in the American City* (New York: Alfred A. Knopf, 2019), 220.

61. Hastings Ardell, *Breaking into Baseball*, 219.

62. Peter Doggett, *There's a Riot Going On: Revolutionaries, Rock Stars, and the Rise and Fall of the '60s* (New York: Canongate, 2007), 492. Emphasis added.

63. "Crowd Control—Baseball," December 29, 1977, Papers of Bowie K. Kuhn, BAMSS100, National Baseball Hall of Fame Library, National Baseball Hall of Fame, Cooperstown, New York, Series VI, Subseries 3, Box 16, Folder 9, Violence.

64. "Crowd Control—Baseball."

65. "Crowd Control—Baseball." Emphasis added.

66. Joe Marcin, "Baseball Joining a Trend to Sports Violence," *Sporting News*, September 10, 1977, 25.

67. Reggie Smith, quoted in Marcin, "Baseball Joining a Trend to Sports Violence," 36.

68. Bob Fishel to Bob Wirz, January 3, 1978, Papers of Bowie K. Kuhn, BAMSS100, National Baseball Hall of Fame Library, National Baseball Hall of

Fame, Cooperstown, New York, Series VI, Subseries 3, Box 16, Folder 9, Violence.

69. Paul Dickson, *Bill Veeck: Baseball's Greatest Maverick* (New York: Walker & Company, 2012), 314.

70. Steve Wulf, "They're Up in Arms over Beanballs," *Sports Illustrated*, July 14, 1980, 27.

71. Reggie Jackson, quoted in Mike Marley, "Reggie: The Human Target," *New York Post*, May 9, 1980.

72. Bowie Kuhn to Rep. Harold C. Hollenbeck, July 3, 1980, Papers of Bowie K. Kuhn, BAMSS100, National Baseball Hall of Fame Library, National Baseball Hall of Fame, Cooperstown, New York, Series VI, Subseries 3, Box 16, Folder 9, Violence.

73. Bart Giamatti, quoted in Dave van Dyck, "Apology Fails to Mollify Dawson," *Sporting News*, July 20, 1987, 27.

74. Nick Waddell, "Garry Templeton," in Tom Larwin and Bill Nowlin, eds., *San Diego Padres: The First Half-Century* (Phoenix, AZ: Society for American Baseball Research, 2019), 130.

75. Whitey Herzog and Kevin Horrigan, *White Rat: A Life in Baseball* (New York: Harper & Row, 1987), 136.

76. Ray Miller, quoted in Thomas Boswell, "The Changing Code of Conduct in Baseball," *Washington Post*, August 30, 1981.

77. Red Schoendienst, quoted in Doug Feldman, *Whitey Herzog Builds a Winner: The St. Louis Cardinals, 1979–1982* (Jefferson, NC: McFarland, 2018), 238.

78. Frank Lucchesi, quoted in Randy Galloway, "Randle Frustration Explodes in Fistic Fury," *Sporting News*, April 16, 1977, 20.

79. Neal Russo, "Truce Arranged, Cards Remove Hrabosky's Ban," *Sporting News*, June 4, 1977, 30.

80. Mitchell Nathanson, *God Almighty Hisself: The Life and Legacy of Dick Allen* (Philadelphia: University of Pennsylvania Press, 2016), 325, 323.

81. Keith Hernandez and Mike Bryan, *If at First* (New York: Penguin, 1987), 438.

82. Harold F. Gee to Bowie Kuhn, June 25, 1983, Papers of Bowie K. Kuhn, BAMSS100, National Baseball Hall of Fame Library, National Baseball Hall of Fame, Cooperstown, New York, Series VI, Subseries 1, Box 11, Folder 5, Staff Meeting Notes.

83. Dave Pallone, with Alan Steinberg, *Behind the Mask: My Double Life in Baseball* (New York: Viking, 1990), 266–67. Emphasis in original.

84. Pallone, *Behind the Mask*, 310. Emphasis in original.

85. Glenn Burke, with Erik Sherman, *Out at Home: The True Story of Glenn Burke, Baseball's First Openly Gay Player* (New York: Berkley Books, 1995), 9.

86. Burke, *Out at Home*, 9.

87. Burke, *Out at Home*, 10.

88. Burke, *Out at Home*, 24.

89. Burke, *Out at Home*, 66.

90. Billy Martin, quoted in Burke, *Out at Home*, 68.

91. Patrick Reusse, "Twins Rookie Battles a Nervous Disorder," *Sporting News*, May 17, 1982, 32.

92. Rick Swaine, *Beating the Breaks: Major League Ballplayers Who Overcame Disabilities* (Jefferson, NC: McFarland, 2004), 18.

BIBLIOGRAPHY

BOOKS

Armour, Mark L., and Daniel R. Levitt. *In Pursuit of Pennants: Baseball Operations from Deadball to Moneyball*. Lincoln: University of Nebraska Press, 2015.

Bartkowiak, Mathew J., and Yuya Kiuchi. *Packaging Baseball: How Marketing Embellishes the Cultural Experience*. Jefferson, NC: McFarland, 2012.

Beckett, James. *The Official 1996 Price Guide to Baseball Cards*. New York: House of Collectibles, 1995.

Bouton, Jim. *Ball Four*, 20th anniversary ed. Edited by Leonard Schecter. New York: Wiley, 1990.

Bradbury, J. C. *The Baseball Economist: The Real Game Exposed*. New York: Dutton, 2007.

Brown, Bob, ed. *The House of Magic, 1922–1991: 70 Years of Thrills and Excitement on 33rd Street*. Baltimore, MD: The Orioles, Inc., 1991.

Burke, Glenn, with Erik Sherman. *Out at Home: The True Story of Glenn Burke, Baseball's First Openly Gay Player*. New York: Berkley Books, 1995.

Carew, Rod, with Ira Berkow. *Carew*. New York: Simon & Schuster, 1979.

Carter, Craig, ed. *Official Baseball Guide for 1992*. St. Louis, MO: Sporting News, 1992.

Carter, Craig, and Larry Wigge, eds. *National League 1984 Box Score Book*. St. Louis, MO: Sporting News, 1984.

Corzine, Nathan Michael. *Team Chemistry: The History of Drugs and Alcohol in Major League Baseball*. Urbana: University of Illinois Press, 2016.

Dahl, Steve, Dave Hoekstra, and Paul Natkin. *Disco Demolition: The Night Disco Died*. Chicago: Curbside Splendor, 2016.

Darling, Ron, and Daniel Paisner. *The Complete Game: Reflections on Baseball, Pitching, and Life on the Mound*. New York: Alfred A. Knopf, 2009.

Davies, Richard O. *Sports in American Life: A History*, 2nd ed. West Sussex, UK: Wiley-Blackwell, 2012.

Dickson, Paul. *Bill Veeck: Baseball's Greatest Maverick*. New York: Walker & Company, 2012.

———. *The Dickson Baseball Dictionary*. New York: Facts on File, 1989.

Doggett, Peter. *There's a Riot Going On: Revolutionaries, Rock Stars, and the Rise and Fall of the '60s*. New York: Canongate, 2007.

Edmonds, Ed, and Frank G. Houdek. *Baseball Meets the Law: A Chronology of Decisions, Statutes, and Other Legal Events*. Jefferson, NC: McFarland, 2017.

Feldman, Doug. *Whitey Herzog Builds a Winner: The St. Louis Cardinals, 1979–1982*. Jefferson, NC: McFarland, 2018.

Friedman, Alan, ed. *500 Great Sports Promotion Ideas*. Chicago: Team Marketing Report, 1994.

Gillette, Gary, and Pete Palmer, eds. *The ESPN Baseball Encyclopedia*, 4th ed. New York: Sterling, 2007.

Goldberger, Paul. *Ballpark: Baseball in the American City*. New York: Alfred A. Knopf, 2019.

Golenbock, Peter. *How to Win at Rotisserie Baseball: The Strategic Guide to America's New National (Armchair) Pastime*. New York: Vintage, 1987.

Gorn, Elliott J., and Warren Goldstein. *A Brief History of American Sports*. Urbana: University of Illinois Press, 2004.

Graham, Stedman, Joe Jeff Goldblatt, and Lisa Delpy. *The Ultimate Guide to Sport Event Management and Marketing*. New York: McGraw-Hill, 1995.

Hastings Ardell, Jean. *Breaking into Baseball: Women and the National Pastime*. Carbondale: Southern Illinois University Press, 2005.

Helyar, John. *Lords of the Realm: The Real History of Baseball*. New York: Ballantine, 1994.

Hernandez, Keith, and Mike Bryan. *If at First*. New York: Penguin, 1987.

Herzog, Whitey, and Kevin Horrigan. *White Rat: A Life in Baseball*. New York: Harper & Row, 1987.

Hoppel, Joe, ed. *Official Baseball Guide for 1984*. St. Louis, MO: Sporting News, 1984.

Jamieson, Dave. *Mint Condition: How Baseball Cards Became an American Obsession*. New York: Atlantic Monthly, 2010.

Jozsa, Frank P., Jr. *Major League Baseball Expansions and Relocations: A History, 1876–2008*. Jefferson, NC: McFarland, 2009.

Kates, Maxwell, and Bill Nowlin, eds. *Time for Expansion Baseball*. Phoenix, AZ: Society for American Baseball Research, 2018.

Katz, Jeff. *Split Season: Fernandomania, the Bronx Zoo, and the Strike That Saved Baseball*. New York: St. Martin's, 2015.

Krell, David, ed. *The New York Mets in Popular Culture: Critical Essays*. Jefferson, NC: McFarland, 2020.

———, ed. *The New York Yankees in Popular Culture: Critical Essays*. Jefferson, NC: McFarland, 2019.

Kuhn, Bowie. *Hardball: The Education of a Baseball Commissioner*. New York: Times Books, 1987.

Lang, Jack, and Peter Simon. *The New York Mets: Twenty-five Years of Baseball Magic*. New York: Henry Holt and Company, 1986.

Larwin, Tom, and Bill Nowlin, eds. *San Diego Padres: The First Half-Century*. Phoenix, AZ: Society for American Baseball Research, 2019.

Leavy, Jane. *The Last Boy: Mickey Mantle and the End of America's Childhood*. New York: HarperCollins, 2010.

Lewis, Robert F., II. *Smart Ball: Marketing the Myth and Managing the Reality of Major League Baseball*. Jackson: University Press of Mississippi, 2010.

Lilliefors, James. *Ball Cap Nation: A Journey through the World of America's National Hat*. Covington, KY: Clerisy Press, 2009.

Lowenfish, Lee. *Branch Rickey: Baseball's Ferocious Gentleman*. Lincoln: University of Nebraska Press, 2007.

———. *The Imperfect Diamond: A History of Baseball's Labor Wars*. Lincoln: University of Nebraska Press, 1980.

Lowry, Philip J. *Green Cathedrals*. Cooperstown, NY: Society for American Baseball Research, 1986.

Marcin, Joe, Larry Wigge, Carl Clark, and Larry Vickery, eds. *Official Baseball Guide for 1978*. St. Louis, MO: Sporting News, 1978.

———, eds. *Official Baseball Guide for 1979*. St. Louis, MO: Sporting News, 1979.

McCue, Andy. *Mover and Shaker: Walter O'Malley, the Dodgers, and Baseball's Westward Expansion*. Lincoln: University of Nebraska Press, 2014.

Miller, James Edward. *The Baseball Business: Pursuing Pennants and Profits in Baltimore*. Chapel Hill: University of North Carolina Press, 1990.

Miller, Marvin. *A Whole Different Ball Game: The Sport and Business of Baseball*. New York: Birch Lane Press, 1991.

Moncreiff, Robert P. *Bart Giamatti: A Profile*. New Haven, CT: Yale University Press, 2007.

Morgan, Anne. *Prescription for Success: The Life and Values of Ewing Marion Kauffman*. Kansas City, KS: Andrews and McMeel, 1995.

Mullins, Bill. *Becoming Big League: Seattle, the Pilots, and Stadium Politics*. Seattle: University of Washington Press, 2013.

Nathanson, Mitchell. *God Almighty Hisself: The Life and Legacy of Dick Allen*. Philadelphia: University of Pennsylvania Press, 2016.

Nowlin, Bill. *Tom Yawkey: Patriarch of the Red Sox*. Lincoln: University of Nebraska Press, 2018.

———, ed. *Kansas City Royals: A Royal Tradition*. Phoenix, AZ: Society for American Baseball Research, 2019.

Olney, Buster. *The Last Night of the Yankee Dynasty: The Game, the Team, and the Cost of Greatness*. New York: Ecco, 2004.

Pallone, Dave, with Alan Steinberg. *Behind the Mask: My Double Life in Baseball*. New York: Viking, 1990.

Patterson, James T. *Grand Expectations: The United States, 1945–1974*. New York: Oxford University Press, 1996.

———. *Restless Giant: The United States from Watergate to Bush v. Gore*. New York: Oxford University Press, 2005.

Paul, Jennie, with Jody Lynn Smith. *The Yankee Princess: Why Dad and I Were in a League of Our Own*. Columbia, MD: Silloway Press, 2011.

Pessah, Jon. *The Game: Inside the Secret World of Major League Baseball's Power Brokers*. New York: Little, Brown and Company, 2015.

Porter, Darrell, with William Littlefield. *Snap Me Perfect!: The Darrell Porter Story*. Nashville, TN: Thomas Nelson Publishers, 1984.

Promotions and Operations Handbook. St. Petersburg, FL: National Association of Professional Baseball Leagues, 1985.

Riess, Steven A., ed. *Major Problems in American Sports History*. Boston: Wadsworth, 1997.

Rosen, Ruth. *The World Split Open: How the Modern Women's Movement Changed America*. New York: Penguin, 2000.

Schaaf, Phil. *Sports Marketing: It's Not Just a Game Anymore*. Amherst, NY: Prometheus, 1995.

Simons, William M., ed. *The Cooperstown Symposium on Baseball and American Culture, 2009–2010*. Jefferson, NC: McFarland, 2010.

———, ed. *The Cooperstown Symposium on Baseball and American Culture, 2011–2012*. Jefferson, NC: McFarland, 2013.

———, ed. *The Cooperstown Symposium on Baseball and American Culture, 2013–2014*. Jefferson, NC: McFarland, 2015.

———, ed. *The Cooperstown Symposium on Baseball and American Culture, 2015–2016*. Jefferson, NC: McFarland, 2017.

Siwoff, Seymour, Steve Hirdt, and Peter Hirdt. *The 1985 Elias Baseball Analyst*. New York: Collier Books, 1985.

Sloan, Dave, ed. *Official Baseball Guide for 1985*. St. Louis, MO: Sporting News, 1985.

———, ed. *Official Baseball Guide for 1986*. St. Louis, MO: Sporting News, 1986.

———, ed. *Official Baseball Guide for 1987*. St. Louis, MO: Sporting News, 1987.

———, ed. *Official Baseball Guide for 1988*. St. Louis, MO: Sporting News, 1988.

———, ed. *Official Baseball Guide for 1989*. St. Louis, MO: Sporting News, 1989.

———, ed. *Official Baseball Guide for 1990*. St. Louis, MO: Sporting News, 1990.

Snyder, Brad. *A Well-Paid Slave: Curt Flood's Fight for Free Agency in Professional Sports*. New York: Plume, 2007.

Staub, Rusty, and Phil Pepe. *Few and Chosen: Defining Mets Greatness across the Eras*. Chicago: Triumph, 2009.

Swaine, Rick. *Beating the Breaks: Major League Ballplayers Who Overcame Disabilities*. Jefferson, NC: McFarland, 2004.

Thorn, John, ed. *The Armchair Book of Baseball II*. New York: Charles Scribner's Sons, 1987.
Thorn, John, and Pete Palmer, with David Reuther. *The Hidden Game of Baseball: A Revolutionary Approach to Baseball and Its Statistics*. Garden City, NY: Doubleday, 1984.
———. *Total Baseball*. New York: Warner Books, 1989.
Trager, James. *The New York Chronology*. New York: HarperResource, 2003.
Vecsey, George. *Joy in Mudville: Being a Complete Account of the Unparalleled History of the New York Mets from Their Most Perturbed Beginnings to Their Amazing Rise to Glory and Renown*. New York: McCall, 1970.
Weingarten, Steve, and Bill Nowlin, eds. *Baseball's Business: The Winter Meetings, Volume 2, 1958–2016*. Phoenix, AZ: Society for American Baseball Research, 2017.
West, Steve, and Bill Nowlin, eds. *The Team That Couldn't Hit: The 1972 Texas Rangers*. Phoenix, AZ: Society for American Baseball Research, 2019.
White, Bill, with Gordon Dillow. *Uppity: My Untold Story about the Games People Play*. New York: Grand Central Publishing, 2011.
Wigge, Larry, ed. *Official Baseball Guide for 1983*. St. Louis, MO: Sporting News, 1983.
Wigge, Larry, Carl Clark, Craig Carter, and Joe Marcin, eds. *Official Baseball Guide for 1980*. St. Louis, MO: Sporting News, 1980.
———, eds. *Official Baseball Guide for 1981*. St. Louis, MO: Sporting News, 1981.
Wigge, Larry, Carl Clark, Dave Sloan, Craig Carter, and Barry Siegel, eds. *Official Baseball Guide for 1982*. St. Louis, MO: Sporting News, 1982.
Williams, Pete. *Card Sharks: How Upper Deck Turned a Child's Hobby into a High-Stakes, Billion-Dollar Business*. New York: Macmillan, 1995.
Wirz, Bob. *The Passion of Baseball: A Journey to the Commissioner's Office of Major League Baseball*. Autryville, NC: Ravenswood, 2016.
Zachter, Mort. *Gil Hodges: A Hall of Fame Life*. Lincoln: University of Nebraska Press, 2015.
Zimbalist, Andrew. *Baseball and Billions: A Probing Look Inside the Big Business of Our National Pastime*. New York: Basic Books, 1992.
Zimniuch, Fran. *Baseball's New Frontier: A History of Expansion, 1961–1998*. Lincoln: University of Nebraska Press, 2013.
Zweig, Eric, ed. *Toronto Blue Jays Official 25th Anniversary Commemorative Book*. Toronto: Dan Diamond and Associates, 2001.

SPECIAL COLLECTIONS

A. Bartlett Giamatti Folder. National Baseball Hall of Fame Library, National Baseball Hall of Fame, Cooperstown, New York.
Lawrence Patrick David Gillick Folder. National Baseball Hall of Fame Library, National Baseball Hall of Fame, Cooperstown, New York.
Papers of Bowie K. Kuhn. National Baseball Hall of Fame Library, National Baseball Hall of Fame, Cooperstown, New York.
Papers of Jules Tygiel. National Baseball Hall of Fame Library, National Baseball Hall of Fame, Cooperstown, New York.
Robert Shapiro, Ph.D., and James Boscardin, M.D. "Pitching Mechanics and Performance of Members of the Chicago White Sox: Preliminary Report," MFF669, National Baseball Hall of Fame, Cooperstown, New York.
Whitey Herzog Folder. National Baseball Hall of Fame Library, National Baseball Hall of Fame, Cooperstown, New York.

UNPUBLISHED WORKS

Mendonca, Lenny. "Racial Discrimination in Major League Baseball." Harvard University, senior honors thesis, March 23, 1983.

Richards, Brian J. "Half-Broken Barriers: Frank Robinson, Major League Baseball, and American Race Relations in the 1970s." State University of New York College at Oneonta, master's thesis, 2007.

PUBLICATIONS

1984 Olympic Baseball Scorecard Magazine

Advertising Age

Albany (NY) Times Union

Atlanta Constitution

Atlantic

Baltimore Morning Sun

Baltimore Sun

Boston Globe

Boston Herald American

Chicago Tribune

Clarion Ledger (Jackson, Mississippi)

Denver Post

Inside Sports

Journal of Legislation

Kansas City Star

Los Angeles Herald-Examiner

Los Angeles Times

Memories and Dreams

New Haven Register

New York Daily News

New York Post

New York Times

New Yorker

News-Herald (Panama City, Florida)

Oneonta Daily Star (Oneonta, New York)

Orange Coast Magazine

Philadelphia Inquirer

Pittsburgh Press

San Francisco Examiner

Seattle Times
Sporting News
Sporting News 1982 Baseball Yearbook
Sports Inc.
Sports Illustrated
Sports Marketing Journal
Squire (Johnson County/Kansas City)
St. Louis Globe-Democrat
St. Louis Post-Dispatch
Team Licensing Business
Time
USA Today
Wall Street Journal
Washington Post

BASEBALL TEAM PUBLICATIONS

1993 All-Star Game Program (Baltimore)
1991 Baltimore Orioles Media Guide
1992 Baltimore Orioles Media Guide
1989 Baltimore Orioles Program (September)
1992 Baltimore Orioles Program (June)
1993 Baltimore Orioles Program, first edition
1987 California Angels Media Guide
1992 California Angels Media Guide
1992 Chicago White Sox Program, volume 1, edition 2
1992 Chicago White Sox Yearbook
1980 Le magazine Expos, volume 1
1999 Minnesota Twins Community Report
1984 Minnesota Twins Program
1991 Minnesota Twins Yearbook
1980 Montreal Expos Magazine, volume 12, number 4
1991 Montreal Expos Magazine, volume 5, number 2
1998 Seattle Mariners Community Report
1990 Seattle Mariners Magazine, volume 2, issue 1
1987 Seattle Mariners Official Program
1989 Toronto Blue Jays Scorebook

1989 Toronto Blue Jays Yearbook
Dodger Blue

WEBSITES

asapsports.com
ballparksofbaseball.com
baseball-almanac.com
baseball-reference.com
baseballhall.org
beckett.com
casetext.com
congress.gov
courtlistener.com
en.wikipedia.com
encyclopedia.com
espn.com
flashbak.com
forbes.com
globalsportmatters.com
houston.astros.mlb.com
law.justia.com
m.mlb.com
mdstad.com
mlb.com
mlb.mlb.com
money.cnn.com
my.clevelandclinic.org
ncjrs.gov
newgeography.com
nps.gov
nydailynews.com
omaha.com
parcolympique.qc.ca
roadsidephotos.sabr.org
sabr.org
sabrbaseballcards.blog

sbnation.com
scholarship.law.nd.edu
seminoles.com
si.com
stltoday.com
theatlantic.com
theglobeandmail.com
theguardian.com
thepostgame.com
thesportsnotebook.com
toronto.com
torontosun.com
uni-watch.com
upi.com
wbur.org
wgntv.com
whitesoxinteractive.com
youtube.com

INDEX

ABOUT THE AUTHOR

Paul Hensler received his master's degree in history from Trinity College in Hartford, Connecticut, and has been a member of the Society for American Baseball Research (SABR) for more than 30 years. The author of three previous books, he has contributed to numerous SABR publications, as well as articles and book reviews for *NINE: A Journal of Baseball History and Culture*. Hensler has presented at the SABR national convention (2012 and 2017), the *NINE* Spring Training Conference (2018 and 2020), and many times at the Cooperstown Symposium on Baseball and American Culture. Lifelong residents of Connecticut, he and his wife live in the town of Ellington.